An Amazon was used as an emblem for the New World, following the practice of representing the three parts of the Old World (Asia, Africa, Europe) with female figures, by Cesare Ripa. *From the 1630 edition of* Iconologia, *published at Padua. Photograph and permission by the Huntington Library.*

THE ISLAND OF
CALIFORNIA
A History of the Myth

by
DORA BEALE POLK

University of Nebraska Press
Lincoln and London

⊖ The paper in this book meets the minimum requirements of American
National Standard for Information Sciences—Permanence of Paper for Printed
Library Materials, ANSI Z39.48-1984.

First Bison Books printing: 1995
Most recent printing indicated by the last digit below:
10   9   8   7   6   5   4   3   2   1

Library of Congress Cataloging-in-Publication Data
Polk, Dora.
The island of California: a history of the myth / by Dora Beale Polk.
p.   cm.
Originally published: Spokane, Wash.: Arthur H. Clark Co., 1991, in series:
Spain in the West.
Includes bibliographical references (p.   ) and index.
ISBN 0-8032-8741-0 (alk. paper)
1. California—Discovery and exploration.   2. Baja California (Mexico)—Dis-
covery and exploration.   3. Geographical myths.   I. Title.
F864.P67   1996
979.4'01—dc20
95-603   CIP

Dedication
To the Beales and the Polks

CONTENTS

Illustrations

Acknowledgments

For various kind offices, thanks are due: Dr. Hazard Adams, Dr. Kenneth J. Ames, Dr. Karl W. E. Anatol, Mr. Roy V. Boswell, Dr. Boris Catz, Mr. Peter K. Clark, Mr. Robert A. Clark, Dr. Beverly J. Delong-Tonelli, Mrs. Edna Freeman & Ms. Rita Beale, Mrs. Carol Georges, Dr. Nicholas P. Hardemann, Mr. Francis Herbert, Mr. Colin Ireland, Mr. Terry Kay, Mrs. Jeane Kernodle, Dr. Joseph H. Krause, Dr. Roland Mathias, Dr. Charles E. May, Dr. Audrey Peterson, Dr. John Pohlmann, Ms. Loraine Rutt, Dr. Marlene M. Schulz-Walent, Mr. R. F. Vincent, Dr. Helen Wallis, Dr. David A. Williams, Mrs. Rosemarie Williamson, Mrs. Cynthia Woods.

A special debt is owed to Vera Hickman for prompting the idea for this book, and for providing assistance and encouragement.

Help has been generously given by, and gratefully received from, many libraries, including California State University Libraries at Long Beach and Fullerton, the Research Library of the University of California at Los Angeles, the British Library, the Royal Geographic Society Library, the Huntington Library, the Bancroft Library, the Library of Congress, and the National Maritime Museum at Greenwich.

Especially appreciated was the award by California State University at Long Beach of a sabbatical leave and assigned time for research and writing.

Without Olga E. Beale and Margaret Jones Beale Stockwell the work would not have been possible.

Introduction

California excites interest, envy, and longing throughout the world. It is a beacon for innumerable refugees, immigrants and tourists from all quarters of the globe, seeking freedom, excitement, or improved economic opportunities.

California is often compared to a loadstone, or a magnet, or the moon drawing the tides. On occasion, California is fancifully described as an enchantress—Circe, or one of the Sirens or the Lorelei. Every utopian name imaginable has been applied at some time—Atlantis, Arcadia, Avalon, the Garden of Eden, El Dorado, the Elysian Fields, the Garden of the Golden Apples, the Happy Valley, the Isle of the Blest, the Land of Milk and Honey, the Land of Prester John, Mecca, the New Jerusalem, the Pleasure Dome of Kublai Khan, the Promised Land, the Terrestrial Paradise, and Treasure Island.

These exotic names may sound like fancy metaphors to people who think the romantic appeal of California is found in the make-believe world of Disneyland, the glamor of Hollywood, the fun-and-sun cult, and the glitter of a highly sophisticated modern state. But many of the above descriptions are far from being mere journalistic hyperbole. They are vestiges of dreams seriously associated with California. These dreams date back to a time long before the lust for gold and the hunger for land attracted newer kinds of dreamers into the state in the middle of the nineteenth century. In fact, they were part of the intellectual and emotional freight brought by Columbus and other explorers to the New World. To examine the bearing of those fifteenth-century ideas on California's discovery is one way for the state to celebrate the Quincentenary.

This book deals with certain of those ancient, commonly-held, dreams. The focus is on particular myths of ideal islands, especially on one thought to be rich in gold, pearls, precious gems, and obliging women. These myths are traced back to the grains around which successive layers of expectation and desire took form. Brought westward by the Spanish conquistadores, they significantly influenced the discovery and exploration of California.

In the minds of some explorers, those island myths became fixed ideas. Out of them grew the obsession that California was an island. This notion persisted on and off through two centuries following California's discovery. How the misconception evolved, how it kept recurring, and how it was finally put to rest, is what this book is all about.

Anybody who has felt the irresistible pull of California will feel some affinity with this fascinating tradition. Though the dream didn't—couldn't—literally come true, California remains symbolically an enchanted isle.

A Note on Origin and Format of the Work

This book grew out of a larger interest in man's emerging consciousness and the history of ideas. Its subject matter is an extended example of the thesis that myths start as notions or speculations waiting to be tested, only to become entrenched and resistant to the onslaughts of empirical and rational disproofs. Such a study inevitably involves some discussion of the ways people learn and think.

The book owes something to many disciplines besides the study of myth: to literature, psychology, geography, cartography, and history. Being interdisciplinary, it relies on the primary scholarship of others in the different fields combined. The many creditors in divers fields are recorded in the footnotes and bibliography at the end of the book. For those who abominate such machinery, brief references to sources are furnished in the text.

Particular debt is owed to Hubert Howe Bancroft and Henry Raup Wagner. Both scholars appreciated the significant interaction of myth and empiricism in California's history. Their work is valued for a sweeping vision of the explorers' preconceptions and suppositions as well as of events. They were each as much interested in the facts of fictions as in facts in the historian's sense. As Bancroft saw his mission: "Conjecture is to be recorded no less than the known, theory preceding and overshadowing knowledge." More than that, he felt obliged "to note the rumors on which theories were made to rest."[1]

Bancroft and Wagner developed valuable insights into the island myth of California.[2] Both historians described two major manifestations of that myth over time. Bancroft believed the two were related, though the evidence was not available to him to support his hunch. Wagner threw even more light on the manifestations of the myth, but warned against connecting them. More recently, geographer John Leighly's instructive essay treats the two emanations, but does not specifically bridge them.[3]

Coincidence seems an implausible explanation for the recurrence of a myth in the same context. This is especially so when the recurrence happens in the span of a single lifetime. Myths often lie dormant until changed circumstances stimulate new growth. Awareness of the characteristic persistence and continuity of myth prompted another look at the subject of the dream island of California.

Old ground was re-covered. Included in the review were various early narratives and histories; such original documents as have been published in collections, especially translations; works of numerous researchers of the last and present centuries; and many old maps.

From this review came the conclusion that the separate emanations of the California island myth are connected to each other. More than that, they are links in a long chain of tradition about fabulous islands. Special attention was paid to the forging and coupling of the links in the California segment. As Bancroft and Wagner conjectured, the second manifestation of the island myth of California seems to have been initiated by Drake's entry into the South Sea.

The book was written with the general reader in mind. Chronological narration was selected as the simplest vehicle. That age-old method of story-telling suited the subject matter: the fictions of myth and the adventures of exploration. This evolutional method also lends itself to tracing strands of myth through repeated collisions with reality. In this progressive unfolding of belief and event, the device of foretelling is used to alert readers to what will bear on later developments. Where facts are scarce, the narrative is suspended to essay some speculative and inferential arguments. Much search and research remains to be done. This work will serve as just another tentative contribution to a continuing investigation and debate.

This approach called for letting the records speak for themselves as far as possible. An eloquent rationale for this technique has been made by A.L. Rowse, in his preface to *The Expansion of Elizabethan England*:

> Even those who are most doubtful of the process of historical transmission must perceive the advantage of quoting largely from original sources: these are the very words of the actors, their emotions and thoughts that they are expressing or disguising, the very rhythms of their inner natures that all words betray. Then, too, their words are so fresh, so shining and full of life, where ours are worn down, defaced or deadened by use. I make no apology for quoting so much.[4]

A similar principle informed that classic model in the history of ideas, Arthur O. Lovejoy's *The Great Chain of Being:*

> Citations of illustrative passages . . . will, I dare say, seem to some readers too abundant. But in my own reading of works of this character I have often been exasperated by finding *précis* or paraphrases where I desiderated the actual language of the authors whose ideas were under consideration; and my rule has therefore been to give the words of relevant texts as fully as was consistent with reasonable brevity. On the other hand, no attempt has been made to include the whole mass of possible illustrations; the volume makes no pretension to be even approximately, a *corpus* of the texts in which the central and the related ideas dealt with occur.[5]

Readers who have suffered the frustration of getting a summary when the situation cries out for the exact text will welcome this policy. Readers who find quotations tedious—especially quotations showing incremental changes in repeated myths—will know how to skim or skip.

The collection of supporting passages may be useful as a source book. For that reason most quotations, even very short ones, are set off from the context—except for fragments integrated into sentences. Quotations are drawn from the very texts that brought the story to light during the haphazard meandering of personal reading. Older works and translations that had stimulated interest were not forsaken without good cause. The reading and writing process rather resembled the casual transmission of myth itself. Indeed, as historian William H. McNeill reminds us, we are all writing our own myths: "One historian's truth becomes another's myth even at the moment of utterance."[6] A baroque and existential method of research would seem to stand as good a chance as any of getting at the truth—poetic, if not historical.

Part One

Chapter I

Fifteenth-Century Mariners Inherit Medieval Myths

The story of the dream island of California doesn't begin with the Spanish discovery of California some four and a half centuries ago. It begins much further back than that. The ingredients of the dream were already ancient when Europe reawakened to the possibility of a global earth at the end of the Middle Ages.

Bizarre as some of those dream ingredients were, they were revitalized alongside what we now regard as more scientific notions in the period marked by the revival of classical learning. They formed an integral part of the intellectual cargo of the mariners who set sail to westward in the last decade of the fifteenth century. A close look at that cargo of old dreams and "new" ideas will start us on the road to understanding the California island dream.

What exactly was stowed in the mariners' heads when they embarked on their historic quest? We know they didn't have the slightest suspicion of the existence of the lands that came to be called the New World. Their chief hope was that they would reach the mystery-shrouded regions called "Ind" or "the Indies." These names designated far more than the India and East Indies we know today. The vast, vague area bordered such rumored realms as Cathay, Mangi, Tartary, and the great unknown ocean to their east. The Asian landmass was then thought of as a much larger area than it turned out to be.

Up to that time, those regions had been approached only by traveling east from Europe. But if the world really was a sphere, and Asia bent around it toward Europe, then Asia should be equally accessible by sailing west. The "Sea of Darkness" was assumed to stretch continuously west from Europe to those rich, exotic shores. The breadth of that ocean was believed to be very much narrower than it ultimately proved.

The mariners' minds were not entirely a blank about those distant unknown regions. Their imaginations were stuffed with various expectations. These came from the common stock of tales transmitted by the culture from generation to generation. This body of received material, called the dreamstock for short, formed the basis of personal aspirations of the mariners.

Our interest in the dreamstock will be primarily with promised places, many of which turned out to be imaginary in the course of events. The shorthand term "dream destinations" provides a useful, neutral way to describe these mythical places. Components of these dream destinations embedded in the dreamstock would one day combine into the island dream of California.

Where and how did the dreamstock originate? We can only guess at this, for it is the very stuff of emerging consciousness. It came into being long before man grew analytical or self-aware enough to take note of his own mental evolution. Perhaps the process of creating legend went somehow like this. From earliest times, sketchy reports by side-tracked travelers or sailors blown off course would have spread from ear to mouth and mouth to ear. As is the way with rumor, these tidbits would have been embellished and distorted into all sorts of outlandish tales about what might lie beyond the then-known world. Gossip being what it is, speculations of the more cautious, tentative sort would certainly have lost out to more wild and passionate fancies. Exciting stories get retold and thus are more likely to endure.

The most subjective and unfounded of these forms are what are most often called "myths." But the word "myth" also has a positive connotation. It can mean the imaginative "explanations" that human beings improvise when they wonder about, or try to make sense out of, such matters as the nature of their universe and their place in it. When people don't have, or can't get, the facts, these myths or "explanations" have the standing of hunches or hypotheses waiting to be tested.

This process is not always understood or esteemed. Fifteenth-century sailors have often been derided as naive for swallowing the inherited myths and legends whole. Yet surely those mariners weren't any more credulous than people today who speculate about possible forms of life in other galaxies—a necessary part of the scientific process. One man's gullibility is another man's open-mindedness. Only by trying out the various claims, however improbable or implausible, against actual experience, could the explorers hope to differentiate the imaginary from the real.

This went not only for received opinions of monsters and marvels, but for the newer or revived theories of the round earth, which might provide the means to get to them. Theorizing is an imaginative act. A theory becomes "scientific" only if it happens to test out. In the history of consciousness, fictions are built as bridges for discovering facts. Myth and science march hand in hand.

Hypothesizing involves risks—risks of ridicule, risks of trial, risks of failure. Columbus no doubt enjoyed having the last laugh on the courts of Portugal and England, who found the views of the explorer too amusingly preposterous to be taken seriously.

When a myth or a theory proves not to hold water, the rational mind will throw it out or modify it as the case may be. This is what happened repeatedly in the period of intense exploration and discovery of the New World. However, some personalities stick doggedly to their beliefs, even to the point of denying, misinterpreting, or ignoring, countervailing facts as they come in. Some go so far as to fly in the face of all contrary evidence, so great is their emotional need to cling to a dream or a position. They are the people who give myth a bad name. When such irrationality occurs, myth deserves to be ranked with delusion, illusion, superstition and fallacy.

We all know enthusiasts who refuse to acknowledge evidence, or who will not admit to a flaw in their reasoning. And the fifteenth to eighteenth centuries had their own share of stubborn romanticizers, nuts and zealots, driven to hang on to some fiction or another at all odds. We will meet some of these in the unfolding story of the California island dream. But for the moment, we ought not to let this deviant form of mythicizing cloud our eyes to the valuable part played by myth in expanding human knowledge. This venerable use of the human imagination assists us in solving problems and mysteries. It moves us to action, and advances our understanding of the self and its contexts. Myths are our own bootstraps by which we pull ourselves up.

The dreamstock was contained in many kinds of literature ranging from Homer's epics to the far-fetched romances of the Middle Ages. Myths and legends cropped up in various philosophies, scriptures, histories and treatises running from Plato to the Christian fathers. An influential compilation of literary sources was made by Cardinal Pierre d'Ailly about 1410. Columbus himself was an avid reader of that work, called *Ymago Mundi*, Image of the World, published in 1480.

Other rich and compendious sources of dream materials were works of the later medieval period that had the appearance of what we would today call travel books. These carried not only classical and Christian legends, but matter from the ancient histories and myths of the East. For the sake of brevity, we shall call these works the "oriental travelogues," though they have long since been judged to be more fantasy than fact.

Among these works was the famous *Letter of Prester John*. This purported to be an account of experiences of a Christian priest turned Oriental potentate. This mythic character represented both a success story for westerners and a friendly liaison between West and East. The extraordinary document circulated widely throughout Europe, first in Latin, later in the vernaculars, in many versions, from the twelfth to fifteenth centuries.

Other famous accounts carrying eastern dream-destination material were Marco Polo's *Book*, written about 1298, and the *Travels of Sir John Mandeville*, written about 1357. These also had wide circulation, copied from their originals, or translated into various languages, in the centuries following their creation.

The narrators of these works are presumably assumed personae. Scholars have long debated the authorship of *Mandeville's Travels*. The narrator is no more likely to have been a globe-trotting knight of the title's name than a certain Frenchman who had barely stirred out of his own country.

The device of a fictional narrator befitted the telling of fantastic tales "borrowed" from a wealth of sources. It also served as a convenient cover for imparting unorthodox material and opinion. But fifteenth-century mariners gave the old works full faith and credit as journalistic, literal, reportage. Every word was taken at face value. Thus the ancient myths recounted in these works took on a testimonial validity, especially when wish-images and exciting stories were repeated from work to work. We now know writers copied from each other; then, the repetitions would have sounded like corroborations by independent witnesses.

The travel writers often had something to say about the sphericity of the world—a principle known to the ancients but largely forgotten in the Dark Ages. Perhaps mentions of the roundness of the earth led fifteenth-century mariners to regard those medieval writers as wise before their time. In statements like the following, Mandeville must have been perceived as anticipating the "new" thinking well over a century before Columbus began to press his suit:

Men may well perceive that the land and the sea be of round shape . . . Men may environ all the earth of all the world, as well underneath as above, and return again to their country . . . For wit ye well, that we and they that dwell under us be feet against feet . . . And they have there the day when we have the night.[1]

Such a view would have won credence for whatever else Mandeville had to say—including far-fetched stories of monsters and marvels on the far side of the world.

Pierre d'Ailly also, in *Ymago Mundi,* asserted that "the world is of spherical or round shape." At the same time, he could say that the far side was inhabited by "evil spirits, demons, and wicked and noxious beasts."[2] This coupling of what we now deem superstition with fact seems odd to us, until we remember that scientific thought was just awakening. Many churchmen had resisted the notion of a round world because the thought of ordinary honest people living "feet against feet" struck them as senseless and abhorrent. Then someone pointed out that the "antipodes" made a fine abode for demons. What more appropriate way for them to live their malign, unnatural lives than upside-down on the underside? In this manner, the notion of a round world came by degrees to sound less and less objectionable to unsophisticated diehards.

Now at the end of the fifteenth century, the sphericity of the earth had become the more acceptable idea, and it was the monster stories that gained credibility by being yoked with it. When it came to believing in the monsters, common sense was the best persuader, anyway. If nature made dwarfs and two-headed infants in one's own parish, any kind of creature was possible. An omnipotent God could do anything and everything, and probably did. Moreover, one-eyed men or giants were no less conceivable to fifteenth-century sailors than science-fiction creatures are to us today. The relationship between imagination, reason and fact in both instances is the same. Similarly, dragons, unicorns and griffins were just as worthy of being entertained as possibilities as weird beasts like camels, elephants, and hippopotami.

Of course, sensational material about monsters was no attraction to the mariners. Such monsters would rank as perils when they sailed to the far side of the world. It wasn't curiosity that drove them so much as the urge for gain. Every monster story was balanced by a marvel to excite their greed.

All the oriental travelogues carried tales of vast realms governed by rich potentates dripping with precious gems and living in sumptuous gold palaces like Solomon's. Such a potentate was Prester John, whose lands "be under us," reported Mandeville, "in the low part of the earth toward the east."[3] So by crossing the ocean to the west, mightn't one quickly arrive at this treasure house, and at least establish a profitable trade? Likewise, such a westward journey must lead to the rich, lush, eastern realm of Kublai Khan described so vividly by Marco Polo.

But those fabulous continental realms were not the only dream destinations motivating mariners to sign on for the voyages. The dreamstock told of many islands to be found en route. Some of these legendary islands had their mythical locations in the dark, vast, western ocean we now call the Atlantic. Among the places supposed to lie beyond the Pillars of Hercules—the Straits of Gibraltar—were places like Hi Brasil, the Fortunate or Happy Isles, Antilia, St. Brandon's Isle, and the lost, dragon-guarded, pearl-rich island-continent of Atlantis. By following the sun's path, one might, like Hercules, arrive at the Garden of the Golden Apples in the Isles of the Blest, watched over by a fearsome dragon, and adorned by a bevy of nymphs called the Hesperides. And those who knew the Arthurian romances perhaps wondered about the other Isle of Apples—Avalon—with its community of mysterious queens. Ideal islands and enchanted gardens, often reputed to be populated with extraordinary women, abounded in those westering dreams. A quest for these Atlantic islands was stepped up by Portuguese sailors and West-of-England-men in the decades preceding Columbus's voyage. Indeed, these probes had begun with the discovery, or rediscovery and settlement, of such islands as the Cape Verdes and Azores, which became important way stations.[4]

In addition to the dream destinations associated with the western sea, the Atlantic Ocean, there were island realms that tradition located beyond the then-known world, farthest east from Europe. These should now be readily reached by sailing west around a spherical world. Such islands included not only those already known, as some of the East Indies, but many still of legendary status. So, for example, as Columbus himself noted, the fabled Ophir and Tarsis of the Bible waited to be found.[5] Gold and gems comparable to those that graced Solomon's temple would reward those who took the risks of seeking them.

Nor were named islands the whole of it. The oriental travelogues carried accounts of great numbers of unexplored or unidentified islands lying in the Indian Ocean and the great Oriental Ocean, as the vast reaches to the south and east of Asia were called. Belief in these islands has not been sufficiently stressed in many modern works dealing with the westward explorations. Such accounts often leave the impression that the quest was for spice islands only in the limited sense of what we now call the Moluccas and East Indies. Because of this confusion, the more general dream of myriads of rich islands situated off Cathay and Ind has been understated. Yet the story of the dream island of California cannot adequately be unfolded until we grasp the crucial part that these dream islands played in the imaginations of the mariners. The psychology of the explorers *before* events and reality impinged to modify their perspective is here our main concern.

Mandeville gives accounts of "many great divers isles and large" in Prester John's domain. Besides those he treats in detail, others are reported:

> Many other isles there be in the Land of Prester John, and many great marvels, that were too long all to tell.[6]

Nor were these the only wonderful islands on the far side of the earth. Further east again from Prester John's kingdom, which meant closer still to Europe if the world was a sphere and you sailed westward around it, lay "the isles beyond Ind, where be more than 5000 isles." Many of these must be as endowed with amazing treasures as other realms Mandeville described elsewhere, where rich gold lay on the surface of the earth in large nuggets washed up by the rain, or mined and refined by ants. A limitless supply of ready-cut diamonds was assured by the fact that there were male and female stones that could "engender commonly and bring forth small children, that multiply and grow all year." Like the diamond, the pearl also "congealeth and waxeth great of the dew of heaven." These riches could be harvested in full confidence that they would all grow back again next season, "some of the greatness of a bean, and some as great as a hazel nut."

The best news was that these treasures weren't valued by the primitive inhabitants of the islands. Uncivilized kings wearing necklaces of many hundreds of pearls "know not the virtue" or worth of them because they "set no price on riches." All of this suggested that even if the great territorial expanses were already taken by your Prester Johns and Kublai Khans, it wouldn't be too difficult to become a potentate oneself of one of the many precious island realms. There was opportunity for everyone.

For actually, Mandeville's figure of 5000 islands was a conservative one, as he himself amends:

> In Ind and about Ind be more than 5000 isles and great that men dwell in, without those that be uninhabitable, and without other small isles.[7]

Marco Polo's estimate was even greater:

You must understand that in speaking of the Indian Islands we have described only the most noble provinces and kingdoms among them; for no man on earth could give you a true account of the whole of the Islands of India . . . It is a fact that in this Sea of India there are 12,700 Islands, inhabited and uninhabited, according to the charts and documents of experienced mariners who navigate that Indian Sea.[8]

The same figure is given in the Aragonese version of Marco Polo's *Book*, the version most likely to have been known by the questing mariners:

En estas partes d'India ya xii mil dcc yslas entre grandes et chicas que son habitadas.[9]

And still these were not all. In speaking of the "Ocean Sea"—the part called the "Eastern Sea of Chin"—in which lay the Island of Zipangu (Japan), Polo stated:

According to what is said by the experienced pilots and mariners of those parts, there be 7459 Islands in the waters frequented by the said mariners . . . The riches of those islands is something wonderful, whether in gold or precious stones, or in all manner of spicery.[10]

The number is also rendered 7,448, as shown in the chart Sir Henry Yule made of Polo's claims,[11] and on the Münster map (Plates 31a, b). And the Aragonese version gives yet another number: "vii mil cccxl yslas."[12]

Henry R. Wagner recognized Polo as the most likely immediate source of the mariners' belief when, in his study of conquistadores at the threshold of California, he observed in passing: "I cannot account for the wide-spread belief of the time that islands were numerous . . . and rich otherwise than by assuming that it emanated from Marco Polo's book."[13]

In fact, belief in a myriad of isles dotting the great mysterious Indian Sea and greater Oriental Ocean must have been pervasive and powerful in the medieval period. Many sources give testimony of them, building on Ptolemy's own island claims. In his translation of Marco Polo's *Book*, Yule cites other authorities than Polo for the huge numbers of islands in the Indian Ocean:

An approximation to 12,000 as a round number seems to have been habitually used in reference to the Indian Islands; John of Montecorvino says they are many more than 12,000; Jordanus had heard that there were 10,000 *inhabited.*[14]

It is well known that islands excite the imagination of the maturing individual—witness the host of children's fictions with such settings. Ontogeny here clearly recapitulates phylogeny; the island image emerges as a significant symbol in evolving consciousness. The island is a controllable, perfectible world in miniature. Through the ages it has been used to represent the ideal in every form—material, emotional and spiritual.

Leonardo Olschki has provided an absorbing study of what he calls *romanticismo insulare* in his *Storia Letteraria delle Scoperte Geografiche.*[15] This "insular romanticism" or "romance of islands" was intimately related in medieval literature to the mystical, the fabulous, the fantastic, and the marvelous. All kinds of fictions—utopian and adventure stories, fables, romances, poems of chivalry, and moral and philosophic tales—were set in ideal islands. These idyllic, mysterious, Arcadian microcosms were often situated in the middle of vast oceans. Olschki summarizes this propensity:

> A general tendency of geography and romance prevailing in those days was to locate in an insular landscape the scene of adventures and the place of wonders and marvels. The development of this insular romanticism follows in uninterrupted succession from the romance of the "Table Ronde" until the Spanish Amadís, the scene of which is an archipelago of more or less phantastic islands.[16]

Islands of the Arthurian cycle, such as Avalon, were set in the western ocean, off the Cornish, Welsh, Breton, and Irish seaboards. Settings of later fictions were influenced by the oriental travel tales.

Olschki's reference above to the "Spanish Amadís" is to an Iberian romance called *Amadís de Gaula,* published in Spain in the early sixteenth century from a much older source. With its setting of "an archipelago of more or less phantastic islands," it had a special relationship to Columbus's discoveries. It was to have an even greater significance in California's story, as will be unfolded in Chapter X.

Another strand in this medieval preoccupation with islands was—in Luis Weckmann's words—"the uncontested doctrine that all islands belong to the Holy See, a curious medieval theory whose ultimate basis lay in the 'Donation of Constantine.' "[17] That fourth-century emperor was supposed to have given dominion over Italy and the Occident to the Bishop of Rome—though the eighth-century document spelling this out is now deemed a forgery. Tacitly included in this gift were islands in the western ocean. In 1091, Pope Urban II expanded this claim to include *all* islands. After all, hadn't islands always been havens for monastic communities and religious groups? The alms called "Peter's Pence" was really an insular tax empowered by this authority.

The "Omni-Insular Doctrine" was, of course, predicated on the medieval world view. The whole inhabited and habitable world was called the *oikoumene* (or *oecumene* as preserved in "ecumenical"). It was perceived as a single landmass. The three continents of Asia, Africa, and Europe came together at the center of the earth—all maps being centered on Jerusalem. Together the continents formed one huge island floating on the primordial waters. Known and unknown islands in the encircling Oceanus were all subject to the Holy See (*see* Plate 1).

This world view coupled with the rage for islands, would influence perceptions in the Age of Exploration. The Old World went on being viewed as a single great island, while the New World was seen as a vast oceanic area sprinkled with a host of mysterious and marvelous islands, no other dry land being possible. This profound distinction between the geographical nature of the Old and New Worlds explains why the "Americas" were characterized as insular for several decades following the discoveries. It also explains why, as their size "increased," some explorers kept insisting they were part of Asia.[18]

The medieval craze for islands was inevitably reflected in many fifteenth- and sixteenth-century documents authorizing westward exploration. In giving permission to Columbus to sail west on their behalf, Ferdinand and Isabella appointed him Admiral for the voyage and Viceroy and Governor "in all those islands and mainlands which by his labour and industry shall be discovered or acquired in the said Ocean." The expression "islands and mainlands" is repeated several times in the Capitulations.[19] Explorers for Portugal and England got similar instructions. In 1497, Henry VII gave John Cabot leave to "find, discover and investigate whatsoever islands, countries, regions, or provinces . . . which before this time were unknown."[20] So Cabot's discovery of "the New Isle"—as the "New Found Land" was first described—and Columbus's discovery of the islands of the "Indies" would simply have confirmed what was expected.[21]

As the explorations progressed, the "Omni-Insular Doctrine" would come to play a crucial part in the assignment of temporal power over newly-discovered and contested islands. In 1493, under authority of this doctrine, the Spanish-born Pope Alexander VI would "draw" a north-south line to divide the Atlantic islands between Spain and Portugal. Spain got the western hog's share, as confirmed by the Treaty of Tordesillas.

PLATE 1. A circlet of islands is depicted in the great Oceanus surrounding the known world in this *mappa mundi* from a late thirteenth-century Latin psalter. The Terrestrial Paradise is at the top, which is east. It contains the faces of Adam and Eve, and discharges the great treasure-laden rivers. A row of monsters is ranged along the "underside." (Discussion on pages 28-29, 34.) *Photograph and permission by the British Library (ADD.MSS. 28681, f. 9).*

What do medieval maps tell us, both about this intense interest in islands and about the claims in the oriental travelogues of a multitude of islands lying in the great Oriental Ocean? Not many maps were made before the sixteenth century, and those that have survived are fewer still. Moreover, before the European revival of the work of Ptolemy, those that represented the world were little more than primitive pictorializations called *mappae mundi*. One of these is prefixed to a Latin psalter written and illuminated in England in about the third quarter of the thirteenth century (*see* Plate 1). Its circular shape doesn't represent a globe so much as a disk—as the *orbis terrarum*, the circle of the earth, was conceived to be. The *oikoumene*, the habitable earth, is depicted as a continuous mass, a huge island—which, in effect, it was—floating flat upon the waters. Of greatest interest to our present study are the numerous, mostly unnamed islands in the surrounding ocean circling the edge. These must have had the sense of mystery and otherness that other planets have for us today.[22]

The famous Catalan Atlas of 1375—now in the Bibliothèque Nationale, Paris—is largely derived from the narratives of Polo. It supports the notion of many islands in an oriental ocean. Multi-colored and gilded islands festoon that eastern sea, their jeweled look conveying an impression of great riches there. The Fra Mauro map, circa 1459, preserved in Venice, also depicts an open ocean south and east of Asia, with a chaplet of islands.

Of more interest to us are maps made just prior to the explorations. Indicative of the preoccupation with islands and papal dominion over them is the work of Henricus Martellus Germanus. In the 1480s, living in Italy, he penned an *Insularium Illustratum*, an illustrated account of islands in the Mediterranean and adjoining seas. The manuscript in the British Library contains a map of the world. This follows the Ptolemaic map to the usual cutoff point on the Asian landmass; but it extends it beyond that point, depicting a great oriental ocean beyond Asia's eastern coast. This ocean teems with islands.[23] Another map by Martellus, the unique painted wall map in the Yale Library, shows many more islands still, including Cipangu (Japan) and Java Major and Minor, in this great ocean. This map is dated 1489–90 (*see* Plate 2). Francesco Rosselli of Florence engraved a copperplate of Martellus' map in 1493, though the islands are fewer than in the original.[24]

Martellus was probably influenced by Paolo dal Pozzo Toscanelli's rectangular map, a copy of which was sent to the King of Portugal in 1474. Another copy was supposedly sent to Columbus in 1481. Neither is now extant. We can only make some rough guesses at what it may have contained (*see* sketch map, Plate 3). The guesses are based on a letter purported to have accompanied the map to the King of Portugal:

> To show the said route on a map . . . I send it to His Majesty made and drawn by my hand; whereon is given all the extremity of the west, starting from Ireland southwards to the end of Guinea [Africa] with all the islands that are on this route, opposite which, due west, is the beginning of the Indies with the islands and places . . . rich in all manner of spice, and of jewels, and of precious stones; and be not amazed if I call west [the place] where the spice grows, for it is commonly said that it grows in the east, yet

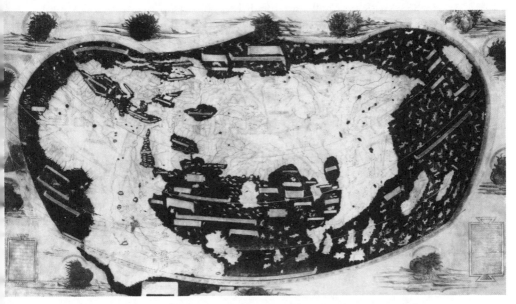

PLATE 2.   The great Oriental Ocean is full of Polo's and Mandeville's myriad islands in this painted wall map by Henricus Martellus Germanus, 1489-90   (above). This ocean was added to the revived map of Ptolemy (below) by converting the land at the end of that map into a terminal peninsula of Asia. (Discussion also on pages 53 ff., 60.) *Photograph and permission for Martellus's map by the Beinecke Rare Book and Manuscript Library, Yale University. Ptolemy's map is from* Claudii Ptolemaei Geographia, *ed. C. F. A. Nobbe (Leipzig, 1843-5).*

whoso steers west will always find the said parts in the west, and whoso goes east overland will find the same parts in the east.[25]

Also akin to the Toscanelli map, as to the Martellus map, was the famous globe of Martin Behaim of Nuremburg, made in 1491–92. Like the maps, the globe follows the Ptolemaic map for the Asian mainland, but extends beyond the landmass, continuing on around the globe as the island-studded eastern ocean from the later medieval tradition. The Behaim globe expresses clearly the merging of the two traditions of western islands, out in the Atlantic, and eastern islands in an oriental ocean. This is captured in a sketch of the ocean hemisphere of the globe (Plate 3). The sketch map also shows why those mariners dared to set sail across that awesome ocean to the west. The distance to the mainland of Cathay and Ind was estimated at a quarter or less of the distance that it actually was. Without such an underestimate, and without the possibility of island-hopping as promised by the myths, this great enterprise might never have been tackled at that time.[26]

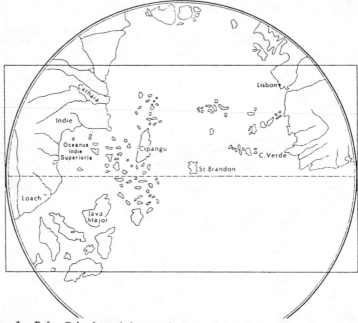

PLATE 3.   Before Columbus sailed, many islands were believed to lie in the unknown ocean west of Europe and east of Cathay and Ind, as shown on this simplified hemisphere sketch map of the Nürnberg globe made by Martin Behaim in 1492. A rectangle has been superimposed to suggest Toscanelli's lost map. (Discussion on pages 30, 43.) *Facsimile gores appear in* E. G. Ravenstein, Martin Behaim, His Life and His Globe (*London, 1908*).

Chapter II

The Mariners' Dream Destinations
Include Island Paradises

Among the promised many-thousand isles of Ind were several that particularly excited the imaginations of the mariners. These specific dream destinations would play an important part in the development of the California island myth. However far-fetched they may seem to us now, they had the full weight of many centuries of authority behind them.

The ultimate ideal haven on earth was the Garden of Eden, the Terrestrial Paradise. Today, even among orthodox Christians, this is taken allegorically. But at the time of the great discoveries, it was still believed to be an actual, literal, locale, capable of precise location if men ever dared to travel to the remote, mysterious corners of the earth.

From its brief mention in the *Letter of Prester John,* we perceive that the desire to reach this ideal locale was as much material as spiritual. It was reputed to be a place of the most extraordinary wealth. This is inferred from the rich detritus of the rivers that flowed from it:

Between us and the Saracens there flows a river called Ydonis which comes from the terrestrial paradise and is full of precious stones.[1]

So where could this treasure house be found? "The first place in the East is Paradise," said the sixth-and-seventh-century encyclopedist, Isadore of Seville. No, far out in the Western Ocean said the refractory Celts. Indeed St. Brendan had sailed westward in a curragh and reached a flower-decked, fruit-laden "Land of Promise"—more like a pre-Christian Otherworld than a Christian Eden. Still, if you viewed the world as spherical, didn't East and West amount to the same thing?[2]

The oriental travel writers and late medieval commentators continued to worry the question of the whereabouts of Paradise, as in this account from Mandeville:

And beyond the land and the isles and the deserts of Prester John's lordship, in going straight toward the east . . . there is the dark region . . . And that desert and place of darkness endure from this side unto Terrestrial Paradise, where Adam, our first father, and Eve were put, that dwelled there but little while: and that is towards the East at the beginning of the earth.[3]

Mandeville doesn't take up the tricky problem of how a round earth can have a starting point. But at least his description suggests that the earthly paradise must be the first place to be reached by those sailing from the west. Not that one could expect to visit it directly; no one could get there "except by the special grace of God." Nevertheless, one could reap the benefits of being near Paradise, and taste the joys of the sweet, treasure-laden waters that flowed from it, as Pierre d'Ailly tells it in his *Ymago Mundi*:

> There is a fountain in the Terrestrial Paradise which waters the Garden of Delights and which flows out by four rivers . . . the Phison, which is to say the Ganges, the Gihon, which is none other than the Nile, the Tigris and the Euphrates . . . The Terrestrial Paradise, according to Isidore, Joseph Damascene, Bede, Strabo, and the masters of Histories, is a pleasant place, situated in certain regions of the East, at a long distance by land and by sea from our inhabited world; it is so elevated that it touches the Lunary Sphere, and the water of the Deluge did not reach there. It is not necessary to understand by that truth that the Terrestrial Paradise attained the Circle of the Moon; it is an hyperbolic expression here meaning simply that its altitude relative to the level of the low earth is incomparable.[4]

The Terrestrial Paradise was usually depicted on the *mappae mundi* described in Chapter I. In the example (Plate 1), east is at the top, and in this elevated position we see Adam and Eve in a walled garden from which the great rivers flow. Even when the revival of Ptolemy produced what to us today is a more recognizable map, some of the Christian material continued to be incorporated. The so-called "Paris Map" (Plate 4) still has the look of a *mappae mundi*, except that the east is now where we expect to find it, to the right, and the map looks more "modern" in its general appearance. Yet the Terrestrial Paradise is still located in the far east. It is an almost circular island highlighted by a diamonded girdle of mountains in a circling archipelago.[5]

It was generally believed that the waters flowing from the Terrestrial Paradise created the fabulous islands in both the Indian Sea and the great Oriental Ocean of the Indies, though there is no clear notion of how this works. Here is Mandeville's confused account:

> All the country of Ind is divided into isles by the great rivers that come from Paradise, that part all the land into many parts. And also in the sea he hath full many isles.[6]

D'Ailly contends further that the tributaries of the four great rivers that flow from Paradise likewise "form an infinity of islands." The abundant flow of its own waters was what made the Terrestrial Paradise itself an island. It was also envisaged that the sweet waters of the rivers must run underground to rise at their presumed sources in the middle of the continents.

The mariners doubtless did not trouble their heads with these

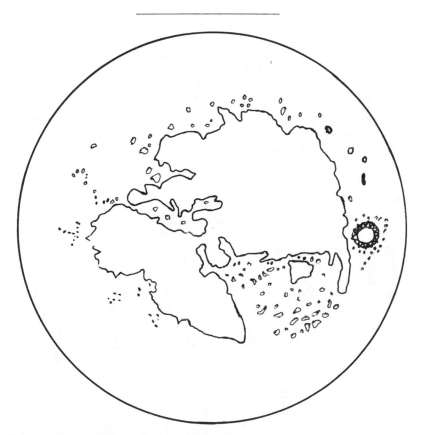

PLATE 4.   The single, huge island of the habitable world is surrounded by many small islands in a map dubbed the Paris Map, made shortly before Columbus sailed, and rendered here in outline. Though bearing some resemblance to the medieval *mappae mundi*, east is now to the right. Farthest east is the Terrestrial Paradise. The original is in the Bibliothèque Nationale.

refinements. It was enough for them to know that the rivers of Paradise carried sands of gold and precious gems to the myriad islands that they hoped to find.

Even if one was too sinful to aspire to reaching the Terrestrial Paradise itself, there was a kind of substitute Eden that one might reasonably hope to come across instead. This was the island to which Adam and Eve were exiled after being driven from the Garden. Here is how Mandeville described that second-best dream destination:

> In that isle is a great mountain. And in mid place of the mount is a great lake in a full fair plain: and there is great plenty of water. And they of the country say that Adam and Eve wept upon that mount an 100 year, when they were driven out of paradise, and that water, they say, is of their tears; for so much water they wept, that they made the aforesaid lake. And in the bottom of that lake men find many precious stones and great pearls.

As distinct from the Garden of Delights in Paradise, a Garden of Earthly Delights was also to be found among the rich far eastern islands approachable by sailing west. If one had a taste for sensuous pleasures and were prone to lechery, one could dream of happening upon such an island, complete with comforts, wealth and maidens, as certain eastern potentates enjoyed:

> Beside the Isle of Pentexoire, that is the land of Prester John, is a great isle, long and broad, that men call Mistorak . . . There was dwelling there, sometime, a rich man . . . full of tricks and of subtle deceits. And he had a full fair castle . . . And within those walls he had the fairest garden that any man might behold . . . And he had also, in that place, the fairest damsels that might be found, under the age of 15 years, and the fairest young striplings that men might get, of that same age.

In Marco Polo's account, the lord of the corrupt garden "kept at his court a number of youths of the country," who dallied with the damsels in sumptuous pavilions and palaces "flowing freely with wine and milk and honey and waters."[7] But such ecstatic privileges had frightful costs, as Friar Odoric's description details. When the lord had need of an assassin—the term derives from the Arabic for hashish addict—he would drug one of the young men and remove him from his garden. Then, "through the youth's great lust to get back into his paradise," the lord could manipulate him to do his killing.[8]

Superstitious fear and an obligation to do the Church's bidding no doubt dampened the mariners' interest in this alluring but risky dream. More to their taste would be a dream island where sensual and sexual pleasures could be had without adverse consequences—some island paradise where sex was free, unencumbered by responsibility. Amazingly enough, there *was* such an island in the pagan dreamstock—no doubt a fantasy of adventurers through the ages. This perfect dream destination was the island fastness of the Amazons.

As the story unfolds, this myth of the Amazons will be seen to play an important part in the explorations toward, and the discovery of, California. We need to know a bit about them. Who exactly were they?

A vast amount has been written in the history of literature describing these extraordinary women. Many modern studies have helped collect the record.[9] A few common features will suffice as background for our present story.

The origin of the Amazon legend is obscure. It is not known whether it had any basis in history. Probably less fact than fiction, the Amazons are among the oldest mythological characters to come down to us. In ancient Greek literature, they were said to be a nation of women who took after their mother, the nymph Harmonia, in grace and beauty, and after their father, Ares, in warlike disposition. In their independent isolation at the edge of the known world, they were a great fascination and challenge to the kind of men who loved danger and courted it for its own sake. Women who had small need of men represented the ultimate challenge to such heroes as Theseus (who is reputed to have carried off their queen) and Jason and his men seeking the Golden Fleece—with whom fifteenth-century mariners were eager to identify.

The tradition of a Realm of Women is also found in ancient oriental mythology. There, apparently, three such realms were featured; one "among the south-western Barbarians," one "south of the Onion Range" or in the Western Sea, and one "that seems not to belong to mankind."[10] This latter is associated with a legendary country far to the east of Japan and Korea, across the Great Ocean, a country called Fou-sang. A Chinese account of such a realm reveals that at the end of the fifth century a Buddhist priest was blown off course toward that land. It had many marvels and strange societies:

> To the north-west, there exists a kingdom of women, who take serpents for husbands. These reptiles are otherwise inoffensive. They live in holes, while their wives or concubines live in houses and palaces, and exercise all the responsibilities of state.[11]

This account goes on to claim that the women of this gynarchy are born of birds who "produce human beings:"

The males born of these birds do not live. The daughters only are raised with care by their fathers . . . From the time that they begin to walk, they become mistresses of themselves. They are all of a remarkable beauty and very hospitable, but they die before they are thirty.

Accounts of marvels such as giant trees, lakes of tar, and burning mountains invite identification of Fou-sang with California.[12] It can be reasonably argued that it was there the Japan Current and the prevailing westerlies would most likely have carried a lost craft. If this is right, the association of the Amazon legend with California would then have occurred a thousand years before the Spanish were to carry it from the opposite direction, a curious coincidence. It is even more fascinating to consider that these two instances might be two ends of the same myth, girdling the earth to meet in this remote location. For though these occurrences may seem to be totally independent of each other, separated as they are by a great gulf of time, space, and culture, they may ultimately have derived from a common source. The legend could have been carried from the Orient to the Mediterranean, or vice versa, by pilgrims and traders between the two regions. It might then have been carried in opposite directions to the farthest reaches east and west, to meet again in the place we now call California.

In Europe the legend of the Amazons was repeated and elaborated through the Middle Ages, and their supposed location is even placed on some early maps. One of the jeweled islands clustered on the Catalan map of 1375 is a Realm of Women. Almost every oriental travel writer had something to say about an extraordinary community of women. Each retelling must have seemed to reinforce the Amazons' authenticity. If the original Letter of Prester John did not treat the legend, it was soon added to the many versions and translations in the course of the Letter's widespread circulation.[13] Any text the mariners knew would have contained something like this account:

> In another region of the wilderness we have a country that extends for forty-two days' journey and it is called the Great Feminie . . . In that land there are three queens and many other ladies who hold their land from them. And when these three queens wish to wage war, each of them leads with her one hundred thousand armed women, not counting those who drive the carts, horses, and elephants with the supplies of food. And know that they fight bravely like men. No male can stay with them over nine days, during which he can carouse and amuse himself and make them conceive. But he should not overstay, for in such a case he will die.[14]

Prester John's Great Feminie is an island by virtue of its being encircled by a river flowing from the Terrestrial Paradise, carrying gold and precious gems. This fourfold association of (a) islands, (b) riches, (c) the Terrestrial Paradise, and (d) the Amazons, would have perhaps formed a union in the mariners' imaginations, so that to call up one feature of the foursome was to call up all.

Mandeville's "lond of Amazoyne" or "lond of Femynye"—or "Maidelond," as one fourteenth-century English translation calls it[15]— is described like this:

> This land of Amazonia is an isle, all environed with the sea save in 2 places, where be 2 entries. And beyond that water dwell the men that be their paramours and their lovers, where they go to solace them when they will.[16]

These women, who "will not suffer any men amongst them to be their sovereigns," call their own shots in governing, fighting and raising their female young. Boy children are sent to their fathers or else slain.

Marco Polo's *Book* carries this variation of the legend:

> . . . You will find the two Islands, Male and Female, lying about 30 miles distant from one another . . . In the Island however which is called Male, dwell the men alone, without their wives or any other women. Every year when the month of March arrives the men all set out for the other Island, and tarry there for three months. They return to their own Island, and pursue their husbandry and trade for the other nine months . . . As for the children which their wives bear to them, if they be girls they abide with their mother; but if they be boys the mothers bring them up till they are fourteen, and then send them to their fathers.[17]

Like these examples, most other versions of the Amazon legend combined the exciting ingredients of a rich island haven with a company of vigorous, self-sufficient women who solicited male attention on a casual, sporadic basis. Far from expecting payment or commitment in return, they gave generous presents of gold and gems when they dispatched their consorts from their kingdom. A ready-made dream of such bounties and benefits without responsibilities must surely have had very great appeal for those adventurous voyagers.

That the mariners knew these myths is doubted by the sceptics on the grounds that so few works were then in Spanish. True, most works were in Latin. The vernacular languages were only just beginning to get established in the cultural mainstream. But both Catalan and Aragonese versions of Polo's Book had existed since early in the fourteenth century.

Here is part of the preceding quotation from the extant Aragonese manuscript that was once in Juan Fernández de Heredia's famous library:

> Aquestas dos islas, la una es de las fembras et la otra de los honbres [sic]; en aquella de los hombres no sta nenguna fembra, ni en la de las fembras nengun hombre; mas quant viene março, abril et mayo, los hombres passan en la isla de las fembras et aqui stan aquestos tres meses en grant solaz con ellas, et apres sende tornan los hombres en lur ysla.[18]

But, say those scoffers whose books still linger in the libraries, many seamen couldn't read, or didn't have access to these manuscripts. They did, however, have access to the popular literature of ballads and romances, originally sung by minstrels. There are, for example, two surviving versions of El Libro de Alexandre, the Book of Alexander the Great, perhaps representing separate oral sources. This thirteenth-century romantic epic is based on the Macedonian king's exploits, but a good deal of legendary material of all kinds is interwoven with the history. The visit of an Amazonian-style queen to Alexander runs on for many stanzas. The beginning of this episode in the two versions tells that " A rich queen, lady of the land said to be a feminine one, came there to the King," attended by three hundred mounted virgins.[19] This beautiful lady came for the sole purpose of conceiving a female heir to the throne by a sire of so distinguished an imperial lineage. This titillating tale must surely have ranked high in popularity.

Moreover, even if ordinary seamen couldn't read Latin, many of their officers could. It was the custom throughout Europe for the better-off families to give their sons a classical education. Works had always circulated freely among those educated in the international languages. The invention of the printing press facilitated this process. Also, with the implications of the round-earth theory causing such excitement, ambitious adventurers had all the more incentive for reading. They combed the texts for secrets that might earn them their first thousand ducats. We may be sure that these tales spread to illiterate members of the crew on the wharves and at the scuttlebutt.

The popularity of dream-destination material among Iberian mariners can be deduced from an increase in translations and publications in Spanish and Portuguese in the first decades of the sixteenth century. An existing and continuing interest is apparent from the way oriental travel tales were recycled in this period. Strangely enough, the voyages of exploration eastward or westward whetted rather than curbed the appetite for dream myths. The old stories were often adapted to meet

contemporary tastes. Gómez de Santisteban, pretending to write factu-
ally about the travels of a prince in his *Book of the Infante Dom Pedro*,
jazzed up his episode of a visit to the Amazon gynecocracy by describing
it in courtly terms:

> Afterward we went to the Amazons . . . and paid our respects to the
> queen. Among them there is a queen and countesses and duchesses and
> princesses and lady-knights and lady-squires and lady-footsoldiers . . .
> The city mothers said: "What manner of temptation moved you to enter
> our lands and our province?" and asked whether we had entered to do
> some multiplying [pro prole generanda] . . . We said "God forbid that we
> should ever be here for that action," but rather that it was our desire to go
> to Prester John of the Indies . . . Dom Pedro instructed Garci Ramirez to
> tell the Queen . . . that he was so poor he could not go on to the Indies if
> she did not aid him. Then the Queen said: "We decree that twenty marks
> in gold bullion be given to the poor traveling companion and vassal of the
> Lion King of Hispania."[20]

The old stories were recirculated too, in voluminous Spanish romances brought out by publisher Jacobo Cromberger and others. The most
famous of these romances, the *Amadís de Gaula*, figures prominently in
the story of the dream island of California, and will be discussed in
Chapter X.

In this period of flux, here at the interface between myth and reality,
the market for fantasy was as strong as the market for letters and journals
of real experiences from the New World. Both were published side by
side; both were consumed with the same voracious curiosity. Belief in
the myriad islands and in the specific dream destinations among those
islands remained powerful throughout the voyages of Columbus and his
successors. Such myths would ultimately be carried alive and kicking
across the threshold of California.

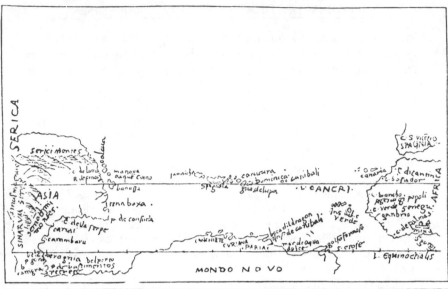

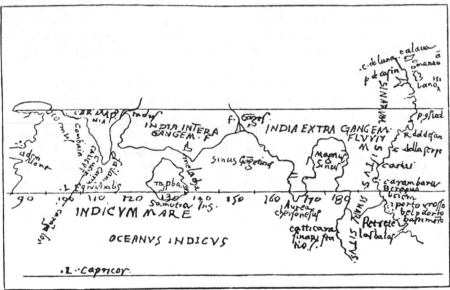

PLATE 5.   Columbus's "isles of Ind" and his belief that Central America was Asia's terminal
peninsula are shown on these sketch maps attributed to Bartolomeo Columbus, circa 1506.
An opening at Beragua and Belporto suggests a waterway to Cattigara, the Sinus Magnus,
the Aurea Chersonesus, and the Indian Ocean. (Discussion on pages 44, 53-4, 64, 67.)
*From facsimiles of sketches in the margin of a letter preserved in the National Library of Florence,
in F. R. von Wieser,* Die Karte des Bartolomeo Colombo *(Innsbruck, 1893). Photograph by
the Huntington Library.*

Chapter III

COLUMBUS CARRIES THE MYTHS TO HIS ISLAND DISCOVERIES

Columbus himself demonstrates the way the great medieval dream myths were carried west. Luis Weckmann cites Columbus's records in support of the view that "the Middle Ages found their last expression in the Spanish New World." Weckmann observes:

> Columbus, the first link between the Old World and the New, stands in a clearer light, perhaps, if we envisage him not so much as the first of the modern explorers but as the last of the great medieval travelers.[1]

Whatever the skeptics say, Columbus read about the dream myths discussed in the previous chapters, and believed what he read. Although said to be only a middling scholar, he certainly had a working knowledge of several languages—at least Latin, Genoese Italian, Castilian Spanish and some Portuguese.

And he also had the books. Part of his library is preserved in the Biblioteca Colombina in Seville founded by his son Ferdinand. Latin annotations in the margins, written in his own hand, make it clear that he thoroughly digested and accepted such works as Pierre d'Ailly's *Ymago Mundi* and Marco Polo's *Book*.

This is what he wrote next to d'Ailly's comments on the Terrestrial Paradise, quoted on page 34 above:

> Fons est in paradiso
> Paradisus est locus
> amenissimus in oriente[2]

These statements translate into "A fountainhead is in paradise," and "Paradise is the most pleasant place in the Orient." The jottings imply an unquestioning acceptance.

Columbus's belief in the lore of islands was purportedly reinforced by Toscanelli's maps and letters. There the goal of the great westering experiment was again expressed in traditional medieval terms—the rich islands and provinces of Ind. Columbus is said to have set great store by these letters. They stimulated his reading of the old cosmographies and travelogues.

Proof that Columbus's expectations were rooted in these medieval sources is provided by his first letter following his discovery.[3] Here he describes his discovery as "all the islands of India." India is used in the larger sense of the Greater Indies, discussed earlier. Columbus's term, "Las Indias," went on being applied to that specific group of islands long after it was clear that he was nowhere near Asia. His mistaken belief is perpetuated to this day in the name "West Indies," and in the designation of native Americans as "Indians." Yet his conclusion was a reasonable inference. He had been directed to look for islands, he expected islands, and islands were what he found. These facts and fallacies are depicted in Bartolomeo Columbus's sketchmaps on Plate 5.

After that, it was reasonable to expect everything else to turn out as he had read or heard. Matching up realities to myths, Columbus praised the climate of the islands, their landscape, flora and fauna, in utopian terms. Before he could have done much checking, he declared the islands would yield "many spices and great mines of gold and of other metals." He stated plainly that he had reached "the end of the Orient," and that "over there" the continental realm of the Great Khan must lie.

His geographical ideas now being "proven," it was likely he would soon meet up with monsters. This is implied in statements in his letter that he had not yet "found monsters nor had report of any, except in an island which is the second at the entrance to the Indies." He also reports "two provinces where I have not been" where "the people are born with tails," and an island where "people have no hair." We recognize these as yarns straight out of Polo and Mandeville. But Columbus must have felt the myths confirmed as truths when he came upon the worst kind of monsters, the "very ferocious" Caribales (or Canibales) "who eat human flesh."

Columbus's belief in the myths also led him to report, still in his first letter, on a strange custom between the cannibals and Amazon-like women:

> These are those who have intercourse with the women of Matremomie, which is the first island met on the way from Spain to the Indies, in which there is not one man. These women use no feminine exercises, but bows and arrows of cane . . . and they arm and cover themselves with plates of copper, of which they have plenty.

Drawing his letter to a close, Columbus compliments himself on his achievement. He has contradicted "those who judged it more a fable than that there was anything in it." "It" must surely include not only the hypothesis that the world was round, but claims about fabulous places and beings mentioned in literature throughout the ages.

Throughout all the other records of Columbus's voyages that have come down to us there is abundant evidence that he continued to believe in fabulous islands and monster myths until his last breath. And through the rich tapestry of these records can be traced repeated patterns of dream-destination myths that would ultimately feature in the California island dream.

In the journal of the first voyage, reference to the island of the Amazons is made in several entries:

> January 6: In the area to the South, there is another large island in which there is a much greater quantity of gold than in this one, in such an amount that they collected pieces larger than beans, and in the Island of Española they collected from the mines pieces of gold like grains of wheat. He said that that island is called *Yamaye*. Also . . . the Admiral found out that there, to the east, there was an island where there were only women, and this he said he knew from many persons . . .

> January 9: The day before, when the Admiral was going to the River of Gold, he said he saw three sirens that stood high out of the sea but they weren't as beautiful as some would have them, since their faces looked somehow like those of a man . . .

> January 13: Of the island of Matinino, the Indian said it was entirely populated by women without men, and that there was a lot of *tuob*, that is, gold or copper, and that it is farther to the east of *Carib* . . .

> January 15: He was determined to go to the island of Matinino, of which it is said it is entirely populated by women without men . . .

> January 16: The Indians told him that by going that way he would find the island of *Matinino*, which is said to be populated by women without men, which the admiral greatly wanted to obtain . . . but he says for certain that these women were there, and that at a certain time of the year men came to them from said *Island of Carib*, which he says was 10 or 12 leagues from them, and if they gave birth to a male, they sent him to the island of the men, and if to a girl, they kept her with them.[4]

The island Matinino (which seems never to be spelled the same way twice) may be seen on the endpapers' map.

Further experience did not weaken the myth. Columbus' second expedition came upon still another island believed to be inhabited by Amazons, namely Guadaloupe:

The lady cacique whom they captured said that this island was inhabited by women only . . . The men from another island . . . used to come at a certain season of the year to sport with the women and lie with them. The same was true of the women of another island called Matrimino of which she told all those yarns that one reads about the Amazons.[5]

The lady chieftain and her daughter were taken on board for transport back to Spain as a curiosity.

The question of whether Columbus had indeed found the Amazons—or even whether there were Amazons to be found—was hotly debated in the next several decades. In the First Decade of *De Orbe Novo*, Peter Martyr gives the Amazon account as fact reported by Columbus's men:

Straight ahead to the north appeared a large island . . . called Madanina . . . inhabited exclusively by women . . . It appeared that the cannibals went at certain epochs of the year to visit these women, as in ancient history the Thracians crossed to the island of Lesbos inhabited by Amazons . . . It is claimed that these women know of vast caverns where they conceal themselves if any man tries to visit them at another than the established time . . . The north wind renders this island unapproachable, and it can only be reached when the wind is in the south-west.[6]

In his Third Decade, Martyr calls the Amazon report "an exploded belief" arising from the "masculine courage" shown by the island women in battle. In the Fourth Decade, Martyr reiterates this view: "I think this story is a fable." By the Seventh Decade, however, Martyr begins to defer to more influential authorities:

Information concerning the island of Matanino, which I have said was inhabited by women resembling Amazons, but concerning which I only repeated what was told me, is still doubtful. Alfonso Argoglio, secretary to the Emperor in Castile . . . affirms that the story is authentic.

And a little later Martyr writes:

It appears that one must . . . believe what has been told concerning those islands inhabited only by women.

Amazonia wasn't the only dream destination Columbus thought he had discovered. On his first voyage he argued that the islands had to be "at the end of the Orient" because that was where the Terrestrial Paradise was located, and he knew he was in the vicinity of the Terrestrial Paradise, "a most temperate place," because he had "sailed that winter without anchoring and always had fair weather."[7] This location of the Terrestrial Paradise at the end of the Orient—the farthest point that could be reached, but never was, when travel from Europe was only eastward—is consistent with the excerpt from Mandeville quoted on pages 33–34 above.

On his third voyage Columbus discovered the northern coast of South America. Bartolomé de las Casas offers this account of Columbus's deductions:

> Not finding islands now proves to him that the land whence he came is a great continent, and that there is the Terrestrial Paradise; "for all men say," says he "that that is at the end of the Orient, and that it is," says he.

Columbus's "Letter to the Sovereigns" of October 18, 1498, spelled out his convictions about the Terrestrial Paradise. His conclusion rested on a bizarre argument. He contended that the world was not spherical, but pear-shaped, protruding in one spot "like a woman's teat on a round ball." As he approached the land of Gracia, as he called the Paria Peninsula, the people became whiter and more handsome, and the weather grew milder, because it was "the highest land in the world and the closest to the sky." Here, presumably, he located his protuberance, the place of Paradise.

He goes on in the letter to discuss various authorities on the Terrestrial Paradise, revealing his deep knowledge of the dreamstock:

> Holy Scripture testifies that Our Lord created the Terrestrial Paradise and planted in it the tree of life, and that a fountain sprang up there from which flow the four principal rivers of the world . . . I do not find and have never found any Latin or Greek work which definitely locates the Terrestrial Paradise in this world, nor have I seen it securely placed on any world map on the basis of proof.

He is ready now to resolve the age-old mystery of the location of Eden. It is bound to be in the vicinity of the Gulf of Paria, filled by the sweet waters of the Orinoco River:

> I return to my discussion of the land of Gracia and the river and lake I found there, so large that it may better be called sea than lake . . . I say that if this river does not originate in the Terrestrial Paradise, it comes and flows from a land of infinite size to the south, of which we have no knowledge as yet. But I am completely persuaded in my own mind that the Terrestrial Paradise is in the place I have described, and I rely upon the arguments and authorities cited above.

The different myths were inextricably interwoven in the minds of fifteenth-century explorers. Once Columbus had put forward his theory that the Terrestrial Paradise was located on what we know today as the continent of South America, there would be those who would immediately make associations with the Amazons.

In his study of the Amazons in the New World, Irving A. Leonard maintains that Columbus himself "was certain that still others of this race [the Amazons] could be reached on the continental mainland by passing through cannibal country."[8] Leonard cites claims of explorers penetrating the Orinoco basin from the coast of Venezuela.[9] Here, in the hinterland of Columbus's experiences in the Gulf of Paria is where one would expect the myth to grow. The sixteenth-century historian Oviedo gives us an account of the supposed discovery of such women in that area:

> Going into Tierra Firme, Governor Jeronimo Dortal and the Spaniards discovered, in many parts, villages where the women are queens or chieftains and absolute mistresses, and they, and not their husbands— although they have them—order and govern, and one especially, called Orocomay, whom the people for more than thirty leagues around her village obey . . . She is served only by women, and no men live in her village or in her circle, except those whom she calls to order them to do something, or to send them to war.[10]

Oviedo repeats this passage in the chapter where he deals with the history of exploration of the region of Meta, Paria and the Orinoco.

Another report, cited by Leonard, came from campaigns in the valley of Bogotá from 1536 to 1539, as the interior was penetrated more and more:

> We got news of a tribe of women who live by themselves . . . within three or four days journey . . . that were very rich in gold.[11]

When an even greater river than the Orinoco was found to the south, it was predictable that the locus of the Amazons should be shifted to that vast, mysterious region. It was almost to be expected that Francisco Orellana would think he had located these women on the river that now bears their name. Nor did the pursuit end there. Amazons were next reported in Paraguay, then on the Rio de la Plata. At the end of the sixteenth century the South American branch of the myth was as vital as ever. When Sir Walter Raleigh came to the continent to claim Guiana for England in 1595, he took note of the native gold trade and the proximity of the Amazons, whose "chiefest strength and retracts are in the Island situate on the South side of the entrance . . . of the mouth of said river."[12]

But this chase has taken us many thousand miles in the wrong direction, and a century too far ahead of the main story. Let us return to Columbus. What made him think that he was close to the Terrestrial Paradise?

He was apparently persuaded of this by his encounter with the great force of the Orinoco in the Gulf of Paria. After the limpid waters of the islands, this was an alarming and extraordinary experience. Here is his account of his perilous navigation through the Boca de la Sierpe—the Mouth of the Serpent:

> There came a current from the south as strong as a mighty flood, with such great noise and din that it terrified all hands, so that they despaired of escaping, and the ocean water which confronted it coming from the opposite direction, caused the sea to rise, making a great and lofty tidal wave which tossed the ship on top of the bore, a thing which none had ever heard or seen.[13]

"Even today," he concludes, "I feel that fear within me, lest the ship be swamped."

Through another channel named the Boca del Dragon (see Plate 5, top) he had a similar experience:

> He found a great contest between the fresh water seeking an exit to the sea and the salt water of the sea seeking an entrance into the gulf; and it was so furious and violent that it raised a great tidal bore with a very high crest, and with this the two waters raised from east to west a noise and a thundering, very great and terrifying.

But why should this awesome phenomenon have caused him to deduce that he was near to the Terrestrial Paradise? The myths led him to this view. An essential ingredient of dream destinations was that they were hard of access. The way to them was fraught with obstacles inspiring awe and terror. So Pierre d'Ailly wrote of the great barrier keeping men from Paradise:

> It is said that the fall of those waters make such a noise that the inhabitants of those islands are born deaf.[14]

And here is Mandeville's description of the approach to the Terrestrial Paradise:

> For the water runneth so rudely and so sharply, because that is cometh down so outrageously from the high places above, that it runneth in waves so great, that no ship may row or sail against it. And the water roareth so, and maketh so huge noise and so great tempest, that no man may hear

another in the ship, though he cried with all the strength that he could in the highest voice that he might. Many great lords have assayed with great will, many times, to pass by those rivers towards paradise, with full great companies. But they might not speed in their voyage. And many died for weariness of rowing against those strong waves. And many of them became blind, and many deaf, for the noise of the water. And some were perished and lost within the waves. So that no mortal may approach to that place, without special grace of God.[15]

In the legend of the Amazons, too, inaccessibility of their realm is a stock feature. In the various classical versions, Amazonia is relegated either to some extremely mountainous, rocky wilderness, or to an isolated island, as in the *Letter of Prester John*, where the Great Feminie is "encircled by a river . . . so wide that nobody can cross it except in big boats or ships."[16] This situation is echoed in Mandeville's description of "an isle closed all about with water," which can only be entered at two possible places.[17] Putting all the obstacles together, one gets a composite picture: Amazonia is an almost impenetrable fortress on a rockbound, tempest-lashed island of towering mountains. It is full of hidden caverns, guarded by ferocious, monstrous beasts or bestial men like cannibals, and is located somewhere just beyond the periphery of the known world. Peter Martyr's description of Columbus's Amazons (*see* page 46) captures most of the traditional ingredients.

It is easy to understand why this feature of formidable barriers is common to dream destination stories. Human psychology has always coupled aspiration with struggle. What is valued is hard to achieve, and what is hard to achieve is valued. Thus, in myth and legend generally, ideal objectives usually resist attainment. None of the dream destinations discussed above was expected to be won without great ordeal that tested the mettle of the quester.

As we trace the dream that became California along the various stages toward its realization, we shall be looking for both the archetypal dream destinations and the mythic barriers that made the ideal so difficult to attain.

Chapter IV

VESPUCCI'S NEW CONTINENT
IRONICALLY BOOSTS ISLAND THEORIES

In contrast to Columbus, Amerigo Vespucci paid only diplomatic lip service to the myth of the Terrestrial Paradise. This is how he puts it in an account of his voyage of 1499 addressed to Lorenzo de Pier Francesco de' Medici:

> The trees, too, were so beautiful, and smelt so sweetly, that we almost imagined ourselves in a terrestrial paradise.[1]

The sense of "almost imagined" is repeated in another passage:

> In the fields flourish so many sweet flowers and herbs, and the fruits are so delicious in their fragrance, that I fancied myself near the terrestrial paradise.

Without stretching out his neck, Vespucci has undermined the myth by rendering it metaphoric, or hypothetical, as here:

> If there is a terrestrial paradise in the world, it cannot be far from this region. The country . . . facing the south has such a temperate climate, that in winter they have no cold, and in summer they are not troubled with heat.

This position is consistent with the frame of mind of one who says of himself:

> I am one of those, who like St. Thomas, are slow to believe.

This difference between the literal and metaphorical valuation of the myth of the Terrestrial Paradise defines the difference between Columbus and Vespucci in their way of looking at the world.[2] Yet, in making the comparison, we have no cause to depreciate either. Vespucci may hew more closely to the twentieth-century model of the empiricist. But the momentous adventure of the westward exploration needed a leader with a mix of credulity and missionary zeal as well as practicality. Left to a Vespucci, a primary voyage might never have gotten off the ground. As it was, the visionary forerunner served as the strop on which later, freer, thinkers could hone their reasoning.

Perhaps the contrast between Columbus's unquestioning faith and Vespucci's skepticism stemmed, in part, from a difference in the authorities they read. For Columbus, what his varied sources said matched his experience. So, on May 14, 1494, when sailing through what he called "the Queen's Garden" off Cuba's southern coast, Columbus was reminded of Mandeville's assertions:

> Next day, at sunrise, they looked from the top of the mainmast and saw the sea full of islands to all the four winds, and all green and full of trees, the loveliest sight that eyes have seen. And the admiral wished to go to the south and to leave these islands on the right hand, but, remembering that he had read that all the sea is so entirely filled with islands, and that John Mandeville says that in the Indies there are more than five thousand islands, he resolved to go forward . . . And the farther he went, the more islands they discovered, and on one day he caused to be noted a hundred and sixty-four islands.[3]

By contrast, Amerigo's experience in 1497 was quite at odds with accounts that *he* had read. He was obviously not acquainted with Polo and Mandeville, or any of the works Columbus studied:

> Steering our course through the great Western Ocean, [we] spent eighteen months in our expedition, discovering much land, and a great number of islands, the largest part of which were inhabited. As these are not spoken of by ancient writers, I presume they were ignorant of them.[4]

Apparently his sources had been mainly literary:

> If I am not mistaken, I well remember to have read in one of their books which I possessed, that this ocean was considered unpeopled; and our poet Dante also held this opinion, judging by the twenty-sixth canto of L'Inferno, where he sings the fate of Ulysses.

For the record, Dante's Canto 26 reads, in translation:

> "Oh, brothers," I began, "who to the west
> Through periods without number now have reached
> To this the short remaining watch, that yet
> Our senses have to wake, refuse not proof
> Of the unpeopled world, following the track
> Of Phoebus."

The obvious clash between personal and received opinion left Vespucci in no doubt what to believe. For him, experience was "worth more than theory." Trusting his own sense and senses more than authority, he pledges to relate only what he has "personally seen," or "heard of from men of credibility," doing so with "much care," and "without any romantic addition to the truth."[5] This manifesto of a rational and empirical methodology was delivered at a time when Columbus held to his prejudices and delusions with irrational obstinacy. No doubt the contrast of a common-sense approach helped win Vespucci the renown which resulted in the southern continent being named for him—to Columbus's great detriment.

Yet, ironically, Vespucci would turn out to be no less a perpetuator of medieval myths than was Columbus. This will be shown by tracing the geographic conceptions of both through the first decade of the discoveries. There was no sudden enlightenment of the existence of a new world of massive continents, as sometimes seems the case from textbook versions. A lot of conflict and confusion characterized the collision of the myriad-island myths with the explorers' real-life experiences. The struggle to define the New World's geography would impact sharply on California's discovery, as will be shown in later chapters.

Let us review the geographical "findings" of Columbus first. As already seen, it was bad luck that Columbus, by nature an enthusiast rather than an objective inquirer, should have had experiences that matched the myths. After "confirming" the existence of Polo's and Mandeville's island-studded Oceanus, Columbus never doubted that Cathay and Mangi were close at hand.

Meeting up with Cuba on his first voyage, Columbus jumped to the conclusion he had reached the Asian mainland.[6] On his second voyage this delusion deepened. He "reasoned" that the tip of Cuba was the point near Zaitun on Polo's Asian province of Mangi. "Therefore" the peninsula containing Cattigara must lie southwestward. This was a compounding of imagination on imagination, for that peninsula had been molded by late fifteenth-century mapmakers (see Martellus' map, Plate 2) out of the land which formed the eastern end of the revived map of Ptolemy. The modification had been made to accommodate Polo's Oriental Ocean beyond the extremity of Asia. Sometimes this imaginary terminal peninsula on the post-Ptolemy maps was confused—even by Columbus himself, and by Peter Martyr—with the Golden Peninsula (Aurea Chersonesus), the present-day Malaya. It was, however, a gratuitous addition stretching Asia to a greater breadth than it would later prove to be. Between the Golden Peninsula and the imaginary one of Cattigara, mapmakers concocted the so-called Sinus Magnus, the Great Bay of the Mare Indicum, the Indian Ocean, to fill the imagined space (see Ptolemy's map, Plate 2).

On his last voyage, Columbus was still looking for that terminal peninsula, still believing Cuba part of mainland Asia.[7] Sailing southwest from Cuba, he thought he was shortcutting from one point to another on the continuous continental Asian coastline. His course and search were actually along the coast of present-day Honduras and south to what he named Veragua or Baragua. Told by the natives of a sea at nine days overland to the west, Columbus surely interpreted this as the Sinus Magnus.[8] All this is shown on the sketch maps on Plate 5.

Columbus had apparently found enough islands to satisfy his understanding of the Polo-Martellus-Behaim claims. Only islands situated between the tropics were of any interest anyway. It was commonly supposed that the hot sun was needed to generate gold and precious gems. Beyond the cape of Cattigara the multitude of rich islands of the Indian Ocean beckoned, besides the promises of the huge Asian continent.

Columbus's fixation on Asia led to the misconception that he was ignorant of having discovered a New World. Yet he had himself spoken in 1498 of "these lands which are an Other World," and even declared in his apocalyptic voice:

> God made me the messenger of the new heaven and the new earth . . . and He showed me the spot where to find it.[9]

Moreover, as Las Casas noted (*see* page 47), Columbus knew he had discovered more than islands in the great ocean. In despatches of his third voyage Columbus states his deduction that the copious waters of the Orinoco must flow from a "tierra infinita:"

> This river proceeds from a land of infinite size to the south, of which we have no knowledge as yet . . . I have come to believe that this is a mighty continent which was hitherto unknown.

Though neither these despatches nor Las Casas' account were published until recent times, Vespucci would certainly have heard that view. In fact, Peter Martyr had broadcast to his contemporaries, quite early on, that Columbus had "discovered this unknown land, and . . . found indications of a hitherto unknown continent."[10] But instead of opening to experience, Columbus stuck to his fixed idea of a narrow ocean between Europe and Ind, claiming as late as 1503:

> The world is but small; the dry part of it is six parts, the seventh only is covered by water . . . I saw that the world is not so large as the common crowd says it is.[11]

The "common crowd" had been getting its opinions to a large extent from Peter Martyr's published letters. It is to these letters we must look for the rising challenge to Columbian views—often credited to Vespucci.

Peter Martyr's well-trained and acutely critical mind carefully evaluated all the news of the explorations. Lacking first-hand experience, he at first could only repeat Columbus's belief that "these islands do belong . . . to India" in the sense that they must be "those whereof mention is made among cosmographers as lying outside [or beyond] the eastern Ocean and adjacent to India."[12] But he accepted such a view only reluctantly because "the size of the globe suggests otherwise." And by November 1493 he was beginning to doubt the globe so small, and the extent of ocean so narrow, as Columbus's claim of reaching Asia would make them.

With such reservations, it is no surprise to find him recording between 1493 and 1494 such phrases as "the hidden half of the globe," "the half part . . . of the earth," and wrapping up this concept in the phrase *ab occidente hemisperii antipodum*—the antipodes in the Western Hemisphere. It took but a small step to the concept of a "new world." He first uses the term *de orbe novo*—which became the title of his famous collection of letters in published form—in a letter of May, 1494:

> When treating of this country one must speak of a new world, so distant is it and so devoid of civilisation and religion.

Again on October 20, 1494, he writes:

> Day by day more and more marvellous things are reported from the new world *(ab orbe novo)*.

Before the end of the century, many among the "common crowd" shared Peter Martyr's perceptions. The theory went this way. The Old World stretched eastward from Spain to Asia's extremities. It must be that the New World—the "hidden half of the globe" now being revealed—would equal it in breadth. This antipodean hemisphere formed a counterpoise to the *oikoumene*, being opposite to it in nature. Whereas the Old World was composed predominantly of the single landmass of the three joined continents, the New World must, as long believed, be predominantly oceanic. Any dry land in the aqueous part of the "terraqueous globe" could only be islands. This theory began, however, to be sorely tested with the confirmation of a southern landmass of continental proportions as the century turned.

Since Peter Martyr proclaimed his perception of the "New World" several years before Vespucci first set sail, it is clear that Vespucci could not have earned the credit given him for this concept. In fact, Vespucci subscribed to, and was acting on, Columbus's views as late as 1499. Sailing westward in that year from landfall on present-day French

Guiana, Vespucci confirmed what Columbus had recognized in 1498—
that the coast was continental in extent:

> After having sailed about four hundred leagues continually along the
> coast, we concluded that this land was a continent.[13]

Vespucci shared Columbus's view that this continent must somehow be
part of Asia:

> This continent . . . might be bounded by the eastern parts of Asia, this
> being the commencement of the western part of the continent.

Further on in the same narrative, he again calls it "a very large
country of Asia."

More than this, in 1499, Vespucci searched, as had Columbus, to find
a waterway leading to the Indian Ocean. Although he gives no clear
account of where he was looking in the area, there is no doubt he sought
the tip of Asia's terminal peninsula:

> It was my intention to see whether I could sail around a point of land,
> which Ptolemy calls the Cape of Cattegara (which is near the Great Bay).
> In my opinion it was not far from it, according to the degrees of latitude
> and longitude.

The "Great Bay" is a translation for the Sinus Magnus, that imaginary
arm of the Indian Ocean between Aurea Chersonesus and the equally
imaginary Cattigara peninsula (see Plates 2 and 5).

In the next year or so, other explorers coursed the newly discovered
mainland coast. By 1500, its continuity between the Gulf of Paria and
Cape San Roque—the eastern angle of Brazil—must have been taken
as proved.[14] Then comes Vespucci on his third, most famous voyage,
making landfall near that cape.

Vespucci's extant accounts do not link his continental experience of
1499 with that of 1501. His reticence may be accounted for in terms of
diplomatic tact. His first experience was under the flag of Spain; the
second in the service of the Portuguese to check out Pedro Alvares
Cabral's touching at the "Island of the True Cross," and other earlier
sightings of Brazil. If it turned out to be one huge continent it would be
split by the Tordesillas line between the two Iberian powers, so the
situation was politically tricky. The lack of technical ability to determine longitude may have prompted the use of the equator as the
dividing line. Vespucci seems to use this method to suggest his two
experiences might involve two separate continents:

This continent commences at eight degrees south of the equinoctial line.[15]

By contrast, the "other" continental coast he had reported in 1499 was located five degrees and more *above* the equator (*see* Plate 6).

This distinction of a fertile continent *south* of the equator was *the* exciting news of 1501, for reasons expressed by Vespucci as follows:

> The ancients thought there was nothing south of the equinoctial line but an immense sea, and some poor and barren islands . . . The things which have been lately ascertained by us, transcend all their ideas . . . The present navigation has controverted their opinions . . . Beyond the equinoctial line, I found countries more fertile and more thickly inhabited than I have ever found . . . in Asia, Africa, and Europe.

Implicit in this passage is the fundamental change of view occurring to Vespucci during this third voyage. Whereas in 1499 he had viewed the continental coast as part of Asia, in 1501 he differentiates his new continent from the ancient tripartite *oikoumene*. It is, he proclaims unequivocally, "a fourth part of the world," a fourth continent.

In 1501 no man had more overall understanding than Vespucci of this huge new continent. He coasted many hundreds of leagues of it southwestward:

> We sailed so far along the coast that we passed . . . beyond the winter tropic, towards the Antarctic Pole, which was here elevated fifty degrees above the horizon.

For this achievement, it was not unreasonable for Vespucci's contemporaries to name the southern continent after him. It was the subsequent spreading of the name to the whole of the New World that denied Columbus his true deserts (*see* Plate 7).

When Bartolomé de Las Casas reinstated Columbus as the prime discoverer, he did so by "joining up" his piecemeal discoveries of the mainland. He had to show that "the whole was one continuous land" even from Veragua, where Columbus had hoped to find a strait:

> All the land that . . . any others discovered of the region called the main was all one coast, and continuous with what the Admiral discovered. Others . . . say it is all one coast from Paria . . . As he was the first discoverer of those Indies, so he was also of the whole of our mainland, and to him is due the credit.[16]

In the half century that elapsed until this reinstatement, a battle of wits raged over the definition of the New World. In effect the struggle was the classic one between *a priori* and *a posteriori* modes of thinking. Columbus had made up his mind before the fact. He carried his model with him, always trying to fit reality to it, always reasoning deductively from the general preconception to the particulars, ignoring the discrepancies. Vespucci—the Vespucci revealed in 1501, at least—operated closer to the other mode. Like Peter Martyr, he was more disposed to reason inductively from facts acquired empirically, to stay open to experience, and stand ready to modify tentative conclusions as new facts came in. The process of coming to understand the nature of the New World was rather like doing a jigsaw puzzle without the help of a picture on the box. With pieces already come to hand, a master image had to be posited, then tested and adapted as new discoveries were made. The art of this method was working with a provisional, fluid, ever-changing hypothesis until the last piece was put in place. The process is comparable to the technique of imaging employed in space probes of today. It involves the balanced interplay of analytic and holistic functions of what are now judged as left and right brain activities respectively.

After 1501, the huge southern continent had to be included in the master picture. One would have expected the medieval myriad-island myths to lose their force. But that wasn't quite how it went. Vespucci seems to have conceptualized the new continent as surrounded by water when only parts of the northern and eastern coastlines had been sailed. We have seen that both Columbus and Vespucci had viewed it as disconnected from the Asian mainland by a waterway around or through Veragua or south of Paria. It remained only to prove that ocean lay to south and west of the new continent, to make of it a massive island.

At this juncture, with no hard evidence to point the way, Vespucci must have reached his hypothesis from some kind of prepossession— perhaps suggested by Peter Martyr's concept of the antipodean oceanic hemisphere. The mythos of the islands was still deep in the collective consciousness. It was only luck that Vespucci's preconception of a southern waterway came true. That strait *might* have proved as intractable as the northern strait turned out to be.

Vespucci apparently was trying to find the termination of the land when he sailed south-southwest along the coast in 1501, perhaps even going as far as Patagonia.[17] A few years later, from 1506 to 1508, we learn of his involvement in getting expeditions together to continue his quest for land's end, perhaps on the analogy of the Portuguese having rounded the Cape of Good Hope. Although such plans did not mature, their momentum culminated in Magellan's expedition a decade or so later.

In fact, Vespucci was acknowledged as a pioneer in the quest for a southern strait by Magellan himself. This is suggested by the following comment in Lopez de Gómara's *Historia de las Indias*:

> It would be greatly to his [Magellan's] shame to return . . . without sighting the strait he sought, or the end of the land. It could be done since . . . Americo Vespucci had been near this place.[18]

Magellan was presumably motivated by the same impulse as Vespucci: a hope or hunch that this previously unknown hunk of land, big enough to call a continent, was, nevertheless, islanded.

Bearing out that this indeed was Vespucci's view is a comment by the famous globe-maker Johann Schöner. In a tract of 1533 refuting Vespucci's interpretation of the fourth part of the world, Schöner asserts:

> Americus Vespuccius . . . thought that the said part . . . was an island which he caused to be called after his own name.[19]

The most compelling evidence of Vespucci's belief in the island nature of the new continent is to be found in the very tract where the name of Amerigo is conferred. This is the famous *Cosmographiae Introductio* by Martin Waldseemüller, published at St. Dié in 1507. In the translation made from the Latin by Joseph Fischer and F.R. von Wieser, we have this famous passage:

> Now, these parts of the earth have been more extensively explored and a fourth part has been discovered by Amerigo Vespucci (as will be set forth in what follows). Inasmuch as both Europe and Asia received their names from women, I see no reason why any one should justly object to calling this part Amerige, i. e., the land of Amerigo, or America, after Amerigo, its discoverer, a man of great ability. Its position and the customs of its inhabitants may be clearly understood from the four voyages of Amerigo, which are subjoined.[20]

But for the purposes of this study, the paragraph which immediately follows this much-quoted statement is of far greater significance. Since Waldseemüller relies heavily on Vespucci's ideas, the passage is important for showing how Vespucci's definitions fitted into the island myths, perpetuating them:

> Thus the earth is now known to be divided into four parts. The first three parts are continents, while the fourth is an island, inasmuch as it is found to be surrounded on all sides by the ocean. Although there is only one

ocean, just as there is only one earth, yet being marked by many seas and filled with numberless islands, it takes various names.

This view is figured forth on the map accompanying the tract (Plate 6). The map is famous for being the first to bear the name "America" on the southern part of the southern continent. On the right hand side of the map Waldseemüller depicts many small islands off the coast of Asia. They resemble the mass of islands of Henricus Martellus (Plate 2). On the left, the western side, the new mainland is peculiarly split south of Paria into two large islands among many smaller ones. Of these two, the northern island is the embryo of Central and North America, with an open ocean to the north. The huge southern continent's southern extremity is conveniently covered by the margin and a decision deferred. In the small inset map, Waldseemüller hedged his bets by joining the two large islands into one, in case no central westward waterway was found.

George E. Nunn thought that Waldseemüller's map was a way of expressing the two opposing conceptions of east-west distances.[21] The right-hand ocean seems to represent the extra distance posited by the anti-Columbians. However this may be, the effect of Waldseemüller's map was to suggest that the New World was separated from Asia by another segment of ocean as wide as the Occidental Ocean between Lisbon and the Caribbean. This map was executed several years before Balboa got wind of his "other ocean" from the Comogre Indians near Darien.

Waldseemüller's rendering-after-Vespucci actually amounted to a natural development of the Toscanelli-Martellus-Behaim vision. To thinkers like Vespucci, the fact that, in an expanded ocean, some of those islands had turned out to be very much larger than originally thought, didn't invalidate the whole concept. Ironically, then, Vespucci's diagnosis of continents appears to have left the island-studded Oceanus concept quite intact. Vespucci's main difference with Columbus in 1501 was his belief that they were still among the islands with a considerable distance yet to go to reach the Asian mainland. And there were many more of those "numberless" islands yet to find.

Indeed, the island mythology was so deeply ingrained, the diehards did not take readily to continental theories. They never stopped trying to "break up" discoveries too large for the concept "island." One could never be sure—so their argument went—what lay behind the indentations in a coastline that might appear contintental in extent. This continuing rage for islands helped fuel a frantic search for straits through-

PLATE 6.   Two huge islands lie beyond the "West Indies" on Martin Waldseemüller's map of 1507, the northern one labeled "Paria" for Columbus's mainland discovery, the southern one "America" after Vespucci. The western hemisphere is here conceived as a single immense ocean crowded with large and small islands, including the Polo-Martellus-Behaim islands on the east (right) side of the map. (Discussion also on page 84.) *From a facsimile made by J. Fisher and F. R. von Wieser of the sole surviving copy discovered at Schloss Wolfegg. Photograph by the Library of Congress.*

out the sixteenth century. The numerous quests for, and claims of, straits across the New World will be shown to have great bearing on the island dream of California.[22]

For these "insularists," as we shall call these believers in a New World composed of islands, rumors of an "other ocean" or "second sea" could have come as no surprise. They would not have seen it as "other" or "second" at all. As Martin Waldseemüller had contended, there was "only one ocean," with the different areas of seas and gulfs and sinuses taking "various names." The Ocean of the Greater Indies was continuous with the Western Ocean—the Atlantic. This was compatible with the medieval idea of a single, encircling Oceanus, a vast stretch of water punctuated by islands—some now seen as larger than suggested by the literature, and as yet not completely circuited.

Yet in the way it challenged Columbus's view, Waldseemüller's map had the air of innovation. To us today, in its coming closer to the extent of ocean between the New World and Asia, it seems to prefigure the next phase of exploration. Nunn warns us, however, against inferring that there was already actual knowledge of the true state of things. Even by 1520, when Peter Apian popularized the map still further (see Plate 10), reality had still scarcely begun to tally with the theory.

In the early sixteenth century, a number of globes were made depicting the nature of the New World as a huge ocean containing a complex of islands isolated from the Old World.[23] The so-called Lennox globe in the New York Public Library is dated circa 1510. It seems, however, to antedate the Waldseemüller map in concepts, since little of the landmass we now call North America is shown. The huge "island" lying mostly south of the equator is not yet called "America," but rather, "Mundus Novus." The southern tip is drawn with a solid line, however, as though it had already been "doubled." The whole west coast is dotted as unproved.

The Green (or Quirini) globe of 1513–1515 in the Bibliothèque Nationale (see Plate 7) continues Waldseemüller's conception. As M. Gabriel Marcel points out, it resembles the globes of Johann Schöner dated 1515. This Paris Green globe is famous for spreading the name America beyond the southern continent. E.L. Stevenson observes:

> A very important and interesting feature of the globe is the appearance of the name "America" no less than four times in the New World: twice in what we now call North America and twice in South America. It is, indeed, the oldest known cartographical monument on which the name America is given both to the north and south continental areas.

PLATE 7. A multi-islanded configuration of the New World in a single huge ocean is shown on a globe in the Bibliothèque Nationale dubbed the Paris Green or Quirini Globe. Dated 1513, it follows Waldseemüller's conception. The name "America" is now applied not only to the southern island-continent, but to islands embryonic of Central and North America. (Discussion also on pages 74, 134.) *From a photograph in M. Gabriel Marcel, Reproductions de Cartes & de Globes Relatifs à la Découverte de l'Amérique (Paris: Ernest Leroux, Editeur, 1893). Photograph courtesy of the University of California at Los Angeles.*

A legend gives Columbus credit for discovering the West Indies, but to Vespucci goes the honor for the other parts. Besides the huge southern continent, Central America (clearly labeled America) is represented as an island, as is the nucleus of North America.

Magellan said he had seen a chart by Martin of Bohemia showing a waterway around the tip of South America. All the above are Behaim globes in the sense they perpetuate the "insularist" vision.

The question of whether the New World was a complex of islands separate from Asia was not resolved once and for all by the post-Vespucci reappraisal. Columbus's view persisted in the minds of many mapmakers. Between 1506 and 1508, concurrent with Waldseemüller's tract and map, Contarini, Ruysch and Rosselli were incorporating parts of the North American discoveries into the continent of Asia.[24] Their maps followed the model set by Juan de la Cosa in 1500, and bear certain resemblances to the Bartolomeo Columbus sketch maps (Plate 5).

Francesco Rosselli's oval planisphere of 1507–1508 (see Plate 8) demonstrates this Columbian view. The area of Labrador, discovered by the Cabots for England is integrated into the Asian continent. The ocean forms an inverted S-curve from the North Atlantic into the Caribbean, turning southward to wash Asia's terminal peninsula, then flowing into the Mare Indicum (the Indian Ocean) and the southern seas. In contrast to Waldseemüller's map, there is no place for a North Pacific to emerge in due time and circumstance. This oceanic configuration, rather than Waldseemüller's, is likely to have influenced Balboa's imaging.

Although Rosselli shows Cuba as an island, he labels his Asiatic coastline with names given by Columbus to Central America when he thought he was coasting Asia. We can make out the names Beragua and Belpuerto.

In the next few decades, as the size of the northern landmass "grew," many mapmakers connected North America to Mangi and Cathay by various devices. Some of these "continentalists"—as such cartographers shall be called to distinguish them from the "insularists"—depicted North America as identical with Asia, or contiguous to other Asian provinces (see Plates 12, 13, & 25a). Some differentiated it from Asia, while joining it by a land bridge. When South America was proved to be attached to Central America, it, too, became an appendage of Asia in the judgment of the continentalists. In their vision of the new discoveries, all mainlands were joined to form a new globe-wide concept of the oikoumene (see Plate 14).

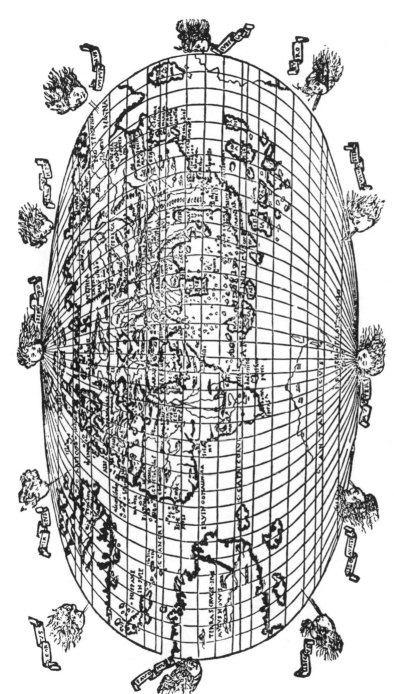

PLATE 8.   The innumerable islands of the Indian Ocean are given focal emphasis on Francesco Rosselli's oval planisphere of 1507-08. The joining of the North American discoveries to Asia leaves no space for Martellus's Oceanus Orientalis or its profusion of islands, though his post-Ptolemaic terminal peninsula of Asia is retained. This "continentalist" conceptualization, and the names "Beragua" and "Belporto" on the "Cattigara peninsula," tie this to the Columbian model. It would influence Balboa to interpret his "other ocean" as the South Sea. (Discussion also on page 67.) *From a facsimile of the map in Bartolommeo da li Sonetti's Isolario Photograph by the Huntington Library.*

Johann Schöner turned from the insularist persuasion to the continentalist. His "Geographical Tract" of 1533 is where he attributes to Vespucci the belief that South America was an island. But, says Schöner, Vespucci was wrong. What Vespucci discovered was really Indiae-Superioris—the Upper Indies:

> Americus Vespuccius, sailing along the coasts of Upper India, from Spain to the west, thought that the said part which is connected with Upper India, was an island which he caused to be called after his own name. But now other hydrographers of more recent date have found that that land and others beyond constitute a continent, which is Asia, and so they reached as far as the Molucca Islands in Upper India.[25]

The new land, said Schöner, was not, after all, the "fourth part" of the world as Vespucci claimed:

> Thanks to the very recent navigations . . . by Magellan . . . it has been ascertained that the said country was the continent of Upper India, which is a part of Asia.

The debate between "continentalists" and "insularists" raged throughout the century as each group struggled to fit its different dreams into the tight shoe of reality. Both groups would contribute, each in its own way, to the concept of the dream island of California.

Chapter V

BALBOA'S SOUTH SEA
PROMISES A MYRIAD OF ISLANDS

Before California could be discovered, certain other major events had to occur. What we now call the Pacific Ocean first had to be reached, and its shoreline probed in various directions.

Everybody knows the story. It begins with Vasco Nuñez de Balboa learning from the "Indians" around Darien of the existence of "the second sea" across what was not yet apprehended as an isthmus. We have seen that Columbus had already received similar news.[1] But he had fitted it into his preconceived model, and assumed it was the Sinus Magnus, arm of the Indian Ocean. He had tried his best to find and sail around the "Cape of Cattegara" to enter it.

What was Balboa's conceptualization of this other ocean? If he had seen Waldseemüller's map, he might have viewed it as the area of the great Oriental Ocean off Ciamba and Loach (or Locach), provinces of the Asian mainland. But Nunn thinks that Balboa followed the Columbian model, as represented on maps by Bartolomeo Columbus and Rosselli (Plates 5 & 8).[2] On that premise, Balboa would then have viewed the promised ocean as the Sinus Magnus.

Balboa's contribution was to shortcut the approach to the second ocean, whatever it might turn out to be. It was the best part of a decade since Columbus's last search for the chimeric waterway. Though the quest for a strait was ongoing (and would continue well into the next decade), frustration took its toll. From Balboa's perspective, it was imperative to push overland, and at least establish what was on the other side.

But whatever Balboa surmised about the "identity" of that ocean, we may be sure he thought himself on the verge of discovering rich islands. The Polo estimate was of more than twelve thousand islands in the Mare Indicus. What treasure-island dreams Balboa must have dreamed!

Balboa's hopes must have been fanned to euphoria by native accounts of gold on the shores of the "other ocean." The old stories in the medieval travelogues were proving out, even to the ignorance of the natives about the value of the wealth lying at their fingertips. This was apparent in the disdain shown by the son of the chief of the Comogre Indians when he told Balboa:

> If your hunger for gold be so insatiable . . . I will show you a region flowing with gold, where you may satisfy your ravening appetites . . .
>
> And when you are passing over these mountains (pointing with his finger toward the south mountains) you shall see another sea, where they sail with ships as big as yours (meaning the caravels) using both sails and oars as you do, although the men be as naked as we are. All the way that the water runs from the mountains and all that side lying toward the South, brings forth gold abundantly.[3]

If we have any doubt that Balboa still nursed the common dreams, we have only to reread his famous letter to King Ferdinand:

> January 20, 1513 . . . Your Most Royal Majesty must command that . . . about five hundred men or more come from the island of Española, so that . . . I can . . . invade the interior of the country and pass to the other sea of the region of the south . . . I, my Lord, have been quite near those mountains, within a day's journey . . . The Indians say that the other sea is three day's journey from there; . . . they state that along all the rivers of the other coast there is gold in great amount and in very large grains; . . . I believe that *in that sea are many islands where are many huge pearls in large quantity* [italics added] . . . If Your Most Royal Highness would be kind enough to give and send me men . . . the land will be coursed, and the secrets of it, and of the other sea of the south side, will be known.[4]

Balboa's own version of the historic sighting of the "austral sea" has not come to light. But the following well-known account by Oviedo is based on first-hand testimonies. It conveys the excitement of Balboa and his men at this new stimulant of the old stock of dreams:

> On a Tuesday, the twenty-fifth of September of the year one thousand and five hundred and thirteen, at ten o'clock in the morning, Captain Vasco Nuñez, going ahead of all those he was leading up a bare high hill, saw the South Sea from its summit . . .
>
> And immediately he turned toward the soldiers, happily raising his eyes and hands to Heaven . . .
>
> And he commanded that all those who accompanied him should kneel down with him and give thanks to God, and should pray very devoutly that He permit them to discover and see the great secrets and riches which lay in that sea and coast.[5]

Peter Martyr gives us this account of the next historic moment, after Balboa left the heights of Quarequa:

[They] made the descent from the mountain ridge to the shores of the much-desired ocean in four days. Great was their joy; and in the presence of the natives they took possession, in the name of the King of Castile, of all that sea and the countries bordering on it.[6]

Their joy arose not only from their having reached the coast of gold, and the pearl islands of the Gulf of San Miguel, but from the confidence that "all that sea" now claimed for Spain contained the coveted myriad isles of Ind.

The very name *Mar del Sur*, "South Sea," contributed to the high state of excitement which accompanied the discovery. It suggested that here could be found all the stuff of dreams. But why was the new ocean given such a name? What exactly could Balboa have meant when he called it "the other sea of the region of the south," *la otra mar de la parte de medio dia*, in his letter of January, 1513? As has been often pointed out, there was a local sense in which the other ocean lay roughly southward (*see* Plate 9). The isthmus trends from east to west, water lying north and south. And it was southward that Balboa gazed from the Cumbre de Quarequa when he first set eyes on it. Maps of the period label the Caribbean side "Mar del Norte," and the south side "Mar del Sur," but not for purely local reasons. The northern part of the Atlantic had long been dubbed the North Sea.

A more likely reason for the name of South Sea is that Balboa thought he was gazing on the Oceanus Meridies or Meridionales. This view is consistent with Nunn's contention that Balboa followed the Columbian model. Balboa's choice of *medio dia* to mean "south" in the above quotation supports this argument. It derives from the Latin *meridies*, a variant of *medidies*, meaning, literally, "midday." This Oceanus Meridies was the Southern Ocean sailed by the Portuguese when they rounded the Cape of Good Hope into the Mare Indicum Meridionale—the South Indies Sea. It was the ocean of the southern antipodes, full of the rich spice and jewel-laden islands of the east described by medieval travelers. Under the Columbian model, with North American discoveries integrated into Asia, there was little room for an Oceanus Orientalis (that would become a North Pacific in due course).

Balboa's formal proclamation of December 1514 fixed the name as the *Tierra Nueva a la parte del Mar del Sur*. The King reinforced this in his letter of August, 1514:

This is just to let you know how gratifying it was to see your letters and to learn from them the things that you have discovered in those regions of the New Land of the *Mar del Sur* and of the Gulf of San Miguel, for which I give many thanks to Our Lord.[7]

Further enhancing the symbolic value of the name was the South Sea's reputation for being benign, pacific, in its nature. The prospect of an easy time in harvesting the promised riches must have doubly excited Balboa when he heard the report of the Comogre Indians:

> They tell me that the other sea is very good to navigate in canoes because it is continually gentle, that it never grows rough like the sea on this side according to what the Indians say.

We witness, here, perhaps, the germ of the South Sea's future, permanent name.

But in the meantime, what can Balboa have made of the contrary winds and storms in the Gulf of San Miguel, as described here by Peter Martyr:

> Chiapes [a local chieftain] did his best to discourage this expedition, advising Balboa not to risk it in the gulf at this time of year, as during those three months it was so stormy that navigation became impossible . . . The Spaniards had scarcely reached the open ocean when they were assailed by such violent storm that they did not know where to steer or to take refuge.[8]

Did Balboa and his men superstitiously construe this setback as an obligatory obstacle—the necessary ordeal for the attainment of an ideal quest? Did the fearful roaring noise that filled the islands suggest the archetypal terrors of the ocean at the approach to Paradise?

Whatever they may have felt, their adverse experiences were not enough to suppress the benign associations of the "peaceful sea." These were perpetuated when Magellan conferred official standing on the name Pacific. The name would become especially useful for those able to differentiate that vast new extent of ocean from the real South Sea.

Yet even after that event, many would go on calling it the South Sea, for the power of that name quickly shifted from its literal to its symbolic values as the promises of rivers of gold and islands of pearls were realized. True to the old legends, the Indians casually dumped their pearls in baskets, and picked up nuggets or grains of gold in the *barrancas* or gullies after heavy rain. Balboa was showered with these precious gifts. And the names "Isla de Perlas" and "Isla Rica" testify to what he found in his exploration of the gulf.

A quick harvest of large pearls certainly kept the dream of the myriad

isles of Ind alive. The historian Oviedo has this to say about pearl fishing
in the newly-discovered area:

> They take and find many pearls in the southern sea of the South, and
> much greater ones on the Island of Pearls that the Indians call Terarequi
> that is in the Gulf of San Miguel, and there have appeared greater pearls
> of more worth than on the other coast of the north . . . This I say as an eye
> witness. . . From this island of Terarequi is a pear pearl of thirty-one carats
> . . . From that isle also is a round pearl . . . got from the sea . . . and
> weighted twenty-six carats. In the city of Panama on the South Sea, I
> gave for that pearl six hundred and fifty pesos of good gold.[9]

The myths were carried by a variety of people, by intellectuals as well
as simple men of action. Every bit as influential as Balboa in nurturing
them was a certain lawyer, Bachiller Martín Fernández de Enciso. This
Enciso had scuffled with Balboa over the government of Darien. He
returned to Spain to lodge complaints against Balboa, leaving the field
open for Balboa to win the historic laurels. Enciso was the man Balboa
referred to when he asked the King to command "that no Bachelor of
Law . . . may pass to these parts of the mainland . . . for no *Bachiller*
comes here who is not a devil, and they lead the life of devils, and . . .
contrive and possess methods to bring about a thousand lawsuits and
villainies."[10]

But it was a forlorn request. Enciso returned with regal consent to
take command, leading to Balboa's downfall and death.

Our concern is with the part Enciso played in the continuation of the
myths. Circumstances gave him a certain case to argue, less as a
villainous lawyer than as a patriotic propagandist in the guise of a
geographer. The situation was this. Under the "Omni-Insular Doctrine" of papal dominion over all islands, the Pope had divided the
Western Sea between Portugal and Spain (page 28). The "Tordesillas
line," 370 leagues west of the Cabo Verde Islands, cut through the
newly-discovered continent of South America. West of Portuguese
Brazil, everything belonged to Spain.

Now comes Balboa's discovery of the Second Sea. "All were agreed,"
in E. G. R. Taylor's words, "that there must be a multitude of islands in
the South Sea which would yield pearls and spices besides the Moluccas
themselves."[11] The Moluccas had been reached by the Portuguese in
1512, when they traveled east around Africa. But now that Spain lay
claim to everything in the great new ocean, the Pope was faced with the
question of exactly where to draw the demarcation line in the Far East.

It was his job to play Solomon. He must halve the world by continuing the Tordesillas line around the globe.

Though Enciso missed the great event of reaching the South Sea, his was the distinction of justifying Spain's claim to everything within and bordering it. The bordering lands included Cathay, Mangi, Ciamba and Loach (variously spelled: Lochac, Locach, and even Beach) on the Asian mainland. The rest of the Spanish claim was for all the known islands of the East Indies archipelago, as well as the "whole width of the newly-discovered South Sea . . . including all the hidden islands and lands which it might contain."

Enciso was just the man to plead Spain's cause. He had direct knowledge of the New World. Being educated as a lawyer, he was well-trained in polemics. His "brief," titled *Suma de Geographia*, was published by Jacobo Cromberger at Seville in 1518. It was read by Roger Barlow, an English merchant in Seville, and "Englished" by him in 1541—with important consequences, as will be seen in Chapter XV. As edited by E. G. R. Taylor, that translation is used here for quotation.

As important as Enciso's work might be for making the Spanish case, it is little more than an old Ptolemaic geography extended to include Polo's Oriental Ocean of the Greater Indies, as featured on the maps in Chapter I. Some of the islands claimed for Spain were real, such as Ciapangu (Japan), Java Major and Minor, and the Spice Islands— which fell ultimately to Portugal. Enciso also speaks repeatedly of Tarsis and Ophir "from where Solomon took the gold for the temple."[12] He claims: "Offir is an island,"[13] yet elsewhere admits "we have no more knowledge of opher and tarsys but it is in the orient."[14]

Nor were the named islands the only ones. "In the gulf of gangica and in the sea be very many islands and all be inhabited and rich." But beyond Categara (another variant spelling) "from thence forward there is no knowledge of more countries for that they have not sailed beyond."[15]

Although Enciso claims to write partly from "our own day to day experience which is the mother of all," he relies heavily on classical and medieval writers. The discovery of the Second Sea had revived thoughts of all the old promises in the ancient texts. Enciso notes that in the unknown lands and oceans of the east "they say should be paradise terrenal where springeth the iiii rivers and after consumeth under ground and come out again by the veins of the earth."

He also makes several mentions of Asiatic Amazons. One reference is to a group of women who had lost their husbands and made arrangements with men of a neighboring tribe to "keep company with them" at a "certain time of the year." Another tells of an Amazon queen "procuring to lie" with Alexander "to have generation of him." But Enciso inclines to reject the belief in the Amazons' prowess and independence on macho grounds. "All is taken for fables, for it is not to be believed that women should continue so long without men, nor that they should be so valiant in arms as it is said by them." Nevertheless, even for this sharp lawyer, all the myths are still in the arena of the debatable, not yet relegated to the midden heap of the preposterous.

Enciso speaks of the benefits Spain might be expected to derive from various islands, including those so rich in pearls in the Gulf of San Miguel. He ends his work with the promise (omitted from Barlow's translation) of even greater things to come:

> There are in the sea of the South side many islands where are much gold and pearls.[16]

Who today remembers Enciso as they do Balboa? Yet Enciso's influence was considerable, especially on the island craze. Via Barlow's translation, his work was even to influence English policies of exploration. By helping to set British interests against those of Spain in the last half of the sixteenth century, Enciso's book would help nurture the Island-of-California myth.

Discovering, taking possession of, and staking a claim to the rich new ocean full of islands was only half the battle. The other half was to get ships onto it to gain control of the new seaways. This was easier hoped than done. For it was now becoming alarmingly possible, as more and more coastline was discovered, that the Americas were a wall of land stretching for many thousand leagues from north to south.

But surely there must be hidden passages through that huge continental barrier that would link North and South Seas—the Atlantic and Pacific. Throughout his Decades, Peter Martyr touches on the fervid competition to find a strait across Central America, perhaps even from the Yucatan, or through Nicaragua.[17] But as more and more probes of that relatively narrow neck of land of Tierra Firme came up blank, hopes began to dwindle of ever finding a strait in that vicinity.

Always the go-getter, Balboa had had ships constructed on the South Sea. After his death, these were used for exploration of the coast. But they were too rotten for venturing far. Many began to fear that the unbroken, endless run of land was nature's way of separating "the end of the east"—or "the beginning of the world"—from "the end of the west," as though there were some determinate alpha and omega of the earth. Even when wishful thinking spurred Magellan to test the insularist belief of a waterway around the south of South America, there were many doubters. This letter by Maximilianus Transylvanus, written in 1522, summarizes that negative view.

> Their [Magellan and Company's] course would be this, to sail westward coasting the southern hemisphere (till they came) to the East. The thing seemed almost impossible and useless, not because it was thought a difficult thing to go from the west right to the east and under the hemisphere, but because it was uncertain whether ingenious nature, which has done nothing without the greatest foresight, had not so dissevered the east from the west, partly by sea and partly by land, as to make it impossible to arrive there by either land or sea travelling. For it had not then been discovered whether the great region which is called Terra Firma did separate the western sea from the eastern; it was clear enough that the continent, in its southern part, trended southwards and afterwards westwards. It was clear, also, that two regions had been discovered in the North, one of which they called Regio Bacalearum (Codfish Land), from a new kind of fish; and the other Terra Florida. And if these two were united on that Terra Firma, it was impossible to get to the east by going from the west, as nothing had ever been discovered of any channel through this land, though it had been sought for most diligently and with great labour. [18]

But the dream was too persistent to be denied. The "insularist" view of the "fourth part" of the world was exceedingly persuasive. Magellan had apparently seen a chart which, like the Paris Green, or the Quirini, globe (see Plate 7), showed a break at the "tip" of South America. Armed with as much information as he could muster, he took up the challenge to seek the passage around or through the southern end of the great obstacle.

As is the frustrating case with so many historic documents of famous "firsts," the notebooks of Antonio Pigafetta, diarist of Magellan's voyage, are lost. But although we miss the minute-by-minute account of this historic episode, Pigafetta's summary, made from his notes on his return home after circumnavigation of the globe, survives in several languages. This excerpt, as translated by Lord Stanley of Alderley, gives a powerful sense of the expedition's desire, frustration, despair, and overwhelming relief and thankfulness at that historic breakthrough by water into the fabled ocean:

> After going and taking the course to the fifty-second degree of the said Antarctic sky, . . . we found, by a miracle, a strait . . . a hundred and ten

leagues long, . . . and . . . as wide as less than half a league, and it issues in another sea, which is called the peaceful sea; it is surrounded by great and high mountains covered with snow.[19]

Detailing the days leading up to this event, Pigafetta goes on:

The greater number of the sailors thought that there was no place by which to go out thence to enter into the peaceful sea. But the captain-general said that there was another strait for going out, and said that he knew it well, because he had seen it by a marine chart of the King of Portugal, which map had been made by a great pilot and mariner named Martin of Bohemia. The captain sent on before two of his ships, . . . to seek for and discover the outlet of this strait, which was called the Cape De la Baya . . . In the night we had a great storm which lasted till the next day at midday . . . The other ships met with such a head wind that they could not weather a cape which the bay made almost at its extremity; wishing to come to us, they were near being driven to beach the ships. But, on approaching the extremity of the bay, and whilst expecting to be lost, they saw a small mouth, which did not resemble a mouth but a corner ["Canton"], and (like people giving up hope) they threw them-selves into it, so that by force they discovered the strait. Seeing that it was not a corner, but a strait of land, they went further on and found a bay, then going still further they found another strait and another bay larger than the first two, at which, being very joyous, they suddenly returned backwards to tell it to the captain-general.

After going forward a few days more, another boat was sent ahead, and returned triumphant:

They told us that they had found the cape, and the sea great and wide. At the joy which the Captain-general had at this he began to cry, and he gave the name of Cape of Desire to this cape, as a thing which had been much desired for a long time . . . We called this strait Pathagonico . . . I think that there is not in the world a more beautiful country, or better strait than this one . . .

Wednesday, the twenty-eighth of November, 1520, we came forth out of the said strait, and entered into the Pacific sea, where we remained three months and twenty days without taking in provisions or other refresh-ments . . .

We ran full four thousand leagues in the Pacific sea. This was well named Pacific, for during this same time we met with no storm . . . And if our Lord and his Mother had not aided us in giving us good weather . . . we should all have died of hunger in this very vast sea, and I think that never man will undertake to perform such a voyage.

After three months on an empty ocean, the expedition reached the

Moluccas, the Spice Islands, the very threshold of Cathay and Ind. It supposedly encountered en route some of the promised marvels such as giants, hairy men, and men with long ears. Pigafetta even heard tell of the Amazons inhabiting an island near Great Java:

> There is an island called Acoloro which lies below Java Major where there are no persons but women, . . . who become mothers by the wind. When they give birth, if the offspring is male, they kill it, but if it is female, they raise it. If men go to that island, they kill them if they can.

But although this historic circumnavigation of the globe (*see* Plate 17) achieved the main goals of the westward thrust, it did not lay the dreams to rest; it stimulated them all the more. Somewhere in that vast new ocean all the rest of the promised myriad isles of Ind lay waiting to be found.

Chapter VI

CORTÉS SEEKS THE ISLES OF IND INCLUDING THE AMAZON ISLE

In the seven years between Balboa's arrival at the Pacific Ocean and Magellan's discovery of a strait by which to enter it, other explorers continued to probe west and south from Cuba. When the Yucatan was discovered just a hundred or so miles away, it was believed to be another island promising dreams of copious gold.

The myths continued to go wherever the explorers went. When Governor Diego Velásquez sent his nephew on an expedition to the Yucatan, in 1518, the Amazon dream was ready to be activated at the slightest stimulus. One of the first experiences of Juan de Grijalva is reported as follows:

> Sailing north we came to a tower on the headland of a certain island and to country places which they say only women haunt after the custom of the Amazons. Yet we could determine nothing for the captain prevented us from going to them.[1]

Another account of the same expedition gives similar details:

> We . . . turned back to the Isla de Yucatan on the north side. We went along the coast where we found a very beautiful tower on a point, which is said to be inhabited by women who live without men. It is believed they are of the race of the Amazons . . . But the captain did not allow us to go ashore.

Henry R. Wagner identified the headland as "possibly the south point of Isla de Mujeres, where ruins are still visible." This Isle of Women is a small island north of Cozumel off the east coast of the Yucatan. Present-day tourists are given an explanation put forward by the sixteenth-century historian Francisco Lopez de Gómara, that it was named for the women-like dolls or idols supposedly found there.[2] But a Spanish map of about 1526–1530, in the August Herzog Bibliothek of Wolfenbüttel, Germany, clearly shows the name "amazonas" beside several small islands just off the north-east coast of the Yucatan—which is itself represented as an island (see Plate 9).

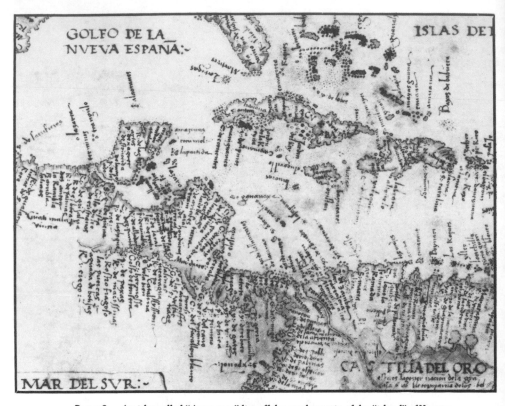

A similar map by the same mapmaker shows not only an island labeled "Amazonas" but an "isla de mujeres." This detail may be related to an account in Peter Martyr playing a variation on the theme of companies of women. A group of vestal virgins are reputed to inhabit one island, a pack of harlot amazons another.

It is not known whether [the Yucatan] is an island or not, but it is believed to be part of the continent . . . A number of . . . islands lie off the coast . . . which are inhabited only by women who have no relations with men. Some people think they live as the Amazons, but others . . . believe they are virgins dedicated to God, who take pleasure in solitude just as those amongst us; or in ancient times, did the vestals of the priestesses of the *Bona Dea*. At certain epochs of the year, men cross to the islands, not to have intercourse with these religious women, but out of the spirit of piety to cultivate their fields and gardens . . . The report is spread however, that there are other islands likewise inhabited by women of bad morals, who from their earliest youth cut away the breast to enable them to draw their bows with greater facility. Men go to these islands to have relations with them, but they do not stop there.[3]

In time, the religious motive and nature of the reputed women would win out over the warlike and promiscuous image of the Amazons. But even four decades later, in this account by Cervantes de Salazar, the old legend is clearly not yet dead:

They crossed over to Yucatan to . . . encircle it . . . They came to a point which extended into the sea on which was a masonry building, which on landing they found to be a temple of great devotion where religious women came to offer prayer and sacrifices. The Captain named this point Punta de las Mujeres. Some were not lacking who said that in that country there were Amazons, although our people never saw any because, as some Indians said, they had gone inland on the arrival of the Spaniards.[4]

These quotations illustrate the vitality of the Amazon myth at the beginning of the subjugation of the vast territory of Mexico. That brutal phase in Spanish expansion can be conveyed here only by a few bare facts as a frame of reference for what is necessarily an abstract of ideas. Suffice it to say that this idyllic dream of a treasure island complete with yielding women was very far from the reality the conquistadores encountered and created.

Although the hostility of the Mayans must have dampened his anticipation, Grijalva took back to Cuba news of extraordinary sights, marvels, and riches. Another more heavily armed expedition was planned. A vigorous, ambitious man by the name of Hernan Cortés politicked hard to have Governor Diego Velásquez give the command to him instead of to Grijalva, and got his way.[5]

Cortés set out on his infamous journey in 1519. He carried with him a long list of instructions. Some of these show that the myths still continued to preoccupy the Spaniards. Item 26 instructs Cortés to find out about "other islands and lands" inhabited by people "with big wide ears, and others who have faces like dogs"—notions straight out of Mandeville's and Polo's work. Cortés is also ordered to find out "where and in what region are the Amazons."[6]

For the next couple of years Cortés was busy slashing his way across the Mayan and Aztec empires, killing Indians by the thousands and plundering their gold. The campaign reached its crisis on the Noche

Triste of June 30, 1520, but it took more than another year to complete the subjugation.

During this period the quest for Amazons was not forgotten. Every so often "news" of them was sent back from the spearhead of exploration, as in this quaint adaptation of the myth:

> They say to the west a quarter southwest, are some high mountains in which live giants of marvellous stature . . . It is affirmed from certain conjectures that beyond this mountain is a great house or monastery of women where there is a principal dame whom the Spaniards call the lady of the silver. They tell such stories about this and I do not write them to your reverence as they are incredible. It is sufficient to say that the lady has so much silver that all the pillars of her house are made of it.[7]

After the fall of the Aztec capital of Tenochtitlan on August 13, 1521, Cortés turned his attention to other projects. As a man of action, he could not rest upon his laurels. He was not the type to settle down to the humdrum job of administration of the territory he had just "reduced."

At this crucial point in his career, he apparently craved new lands to conquer. According to Bancroft, "an idea often uppermost in the mind of the Conqueror . . . was that of western and north-western discovery, the exploration of the South Sea with its coasts and islands, and the finding of a northern passage."[8] This amounted, in Bancroft's estimation, to an idée fixe. Cortés had caught the infectious euphoria of Balboa and Magellan for the fabulous new ocean.

In 1522, Cortés was still demonstrating more than a perfunctory interest in Velásquez' instructions regarding the dream myths. In Cortés' Third Letter to the King, we glimpse his conviction about the existence of the rich, many-thousand isles of Ind. Out there in the vast new sea, those fabulous islands waited to be discovered by a conqueror-hero like himself. Indeed, as he tells the King, he has lost no time in sending a contingent ahead to discover the coast:

> I had obtained a short time ago information of the other sea of the South, and had learned that in two or three directions, it was twelve or fourteen days' journey from here. I was very much concerned because it seemed to me that in discovering it a great and signal service would be rendered to Your Majesty, especially as all who have any knowledge or experience of the navigation in the Indies have held it to be certain that, with the discovery of the South Sea in these parts, *many islands rich in gold, pearls, precious stones, spices, and other unknown and admirable things would be discovered* [italics added]: and this has been and is affirmed by persons of learning and experience in the science of cosmography.[9]

Continuing the narrative in his letter, Cortés tells how he has taken "actual and corporeal possession" of the sea, and that an advance contingent has already sent back samples of pearls and gold—on their way, now, to the King.

But the greatest tidings Cortés had for the King were these: on the newly-discovered coast of the South Sea, ships were already being built, on Cortés' instructions, to go in quest of the longed-for isles:

> As God, Our Lord, has well guided this business, and fulfilled my desire to serve Your Majesty on this South Sea, being as it is of such importance, I have provided with so much diligence that, in one of the three places where I discovered the sea, two medium-sized caravels and two brigantines are being built: the caravels for the purpose of discovering, and the brigantines to follow the coast . . . Your Majesty may believe that it will be a great thing to accomplish this, and the greatest service since the Indies have been discovered will be thus rendered to Your Majesty.[10]

If Magellan hadn't already found a way to take ships through the continental barrier, or if Cortés had subdued Mexico before Magellan found his straits, the building of the ships on the west coast would have been a greater triumph than it now appeared, boosting Cortés' stock still higher. But it could still be used as leverage. Ships launched in the Pacific saved the tediousness, danger, and expense of a long journey across the Atlantic, a time-consuming dip southward, and a hazardous navigation of the straits.

Cortés wasn't backward in blowing his own trumpet. Indeed, his recent triumphs had made him so sure of himself that he had the nerve to draft a petition for a contract with the Crown covering all future expeditions into the South Sea. He dared to spell out to the King the benefits and concessions he expected for himself if his efforts bore fruit.[11]

A Memorial to the King in 1522 details the terms and conditions of Cortés' proposal. Juan de Rivera presented this, on Cortés' behalf, in person to the Court in Spain. He speaks first of the services Cortés is performing:

> He has begun to make, at his expense, bergantines and ships: the bergantines to run along the coast of the said Sea to seek ports, and the ships *to discover islands* [italics added] . . . He is willing to put his person and estate and that of his friends at all risk and danger in the prosecution of it . . . He will navigate, or have navigated . . . the said Sea of the South until his said ships discover continent or islands which up until now have not been discovered nor seen by Spaniards.[12]

In this Memorial, presented by Rivera, Cortés proposes a time limit for the enterprise. Cortés requests exclusive rights to prosecute discovery of the South-Sea islands for six years, running from his own discovery of the South Sea in 1522

In remuneration of Cortés' services, Rivera asks for the conventional powers and spoils of conquest:

> First that of all the land and islands of the said Sea of the South that the said Hernando Cortés has discovered or will discover at his expense and by his industry, he will be governor for all his life and after of his heirs and successors for always . . . In addition, of the gold, silver, pearls, stones and other metals and tribute . . . that will belong to Your Majesty . . . in the said lands and islands of the south, the said Hernando Cortés will have and keep the tenth part.

There is a further request in the petition. This one would bear significantly on the island rage as it relates to the discovery and development of California. Cortés desires an island of his very own, one that he will be free to pass on to his heirs in perpetuity:

> Supposing that the said Hernando Cortés will have discovered or discovers any continent, island or islands in the Sea of the South . . . reaching and discovering up to three islands . . . he will subjugate them, pacify and settle them at his own expense . . . Your Majesty might grant him the favor of one of the said three islands that he might choose, so that it will be his and his heirs and successors . . . In case what the said Hernando Cortés might discover and populate will not be islands but mainland, of three towns . . . one of them shall be his and his heirs.

The letters from the King to Cortés in 1523 show no awareness of this petition, unless the very silence is construed as a reprimand for his effrontery. The King's cédula for June 26, 1523, orders Cortés to seek out the "great secrets and things" in the "sea toward the south of the land" without mention of material reward.[13] Cortés is also ordered to look for a strait between the North and South Seas (the Atlantic and Pacific) somewhere northward of the conquered region. The quest for this strait has very great import for the California story, and will be taken up in Chapter XI.

What concerns us now is what happened to the cocky petition of Cortés. It seems not to have been granted while Rivera was at Court. What was the holdup?

Apparently there was considerable resistance from the Court to Cortés' ideas and claims. Peter Martyr, who made it his business to talk to all visitors from the New World, conveys this in his report of his conversations with Rivera. Martyr makes a case for Cortés' position that there are many more islands in the great vast second ocean than Magellan's voyage had turned up. Martyr cites a private letter he had read wherein "it is stated that it has been learned that the spice islands which also produce gold and silver lie not far distant from the coast." He has also seen a map in Rivera's possession showing "the southern coast ranges, whose inhabitants stated that off the coast lie the islands we have above described as producing an abundance of spices, gold and precious stones."[14]

In defending Cortés' position, Martyr also inadvertently reveals why Cortés might be getting unsympathetic treatment from the Court. In the following quotation, we get some feeling for Cortés' psychology— the intensity of his conviction that the many fabulous isles lay in easy reach of the coastline of New Spain. It sounds as if Martyr is defending Cortés against charges of irrationality:

> Such a great man as Cortés must have . . . sound reasons for his statements. May not other islands . . . exist as well as the Moluccas, equally favored by climate and fructified by the sun's rays so as to produce spices? Why may not such countries have remained unknown until the present time? Do we not likewise know that there exist numerous parts of the ocean and the continent, unheard of until our time? . . . Cortés has accomplished such great things that I cannot believe him to be so wanting in common sense as to undertake, blindly, at his own cost, such an important enterprise as the construction in the South Sea of four ships, fitted out for the discovery of those countries, did he not possess some certitude or at least some probability of success.

From our present vantage point, with wisdom after the fact, we can see that Cortés did indeed suffer a touch of blindness and a lack of common sense about those islands. This would become more and more apparent in the next ten or fifteen years of Cortés' career.

Martyr missed a clue, indeed, in his own report, that Cortés' motivation might not be based on reason but on wishful dreams. Rivera mentioned the Amazons—about which Martyr had always shown a healthy scepticism. Martyr records Rivera's view without editorial comment:

> Rivera told us of having heard something about a region inhabited only by women, in the mountains situated toward the North; but nothing definite. As proof of the veracity of this rumor, he cited the name of Iguatlan, which in the language of the country means "region of women," from "iguatl," "woman" and "Lan," "Lord."

Rivera's comment is of special interest to us for the way the Amazons are relocated "toward the North." This shift in the horizon of that dream location heralds the California segment of the myth.

We are always wishing we had the maps mentioned in these old accounts, such as the map Martyr saw in Rivera's hands. The best we can do is try to deduce it by surveying the maps of the period that have survived.

Some contemporary maps follow Waldseemüller (Plate 6), depicting a post-Ptolemaic-Martellus-Behaim end to Asia, and a single, huge, continuous ocean full of islands, some continent-sized. Peter Apian

PLATE 10.   The concept of the New World as a single huge ocean abounding in islands, some large, some small, continued to attract non-Spanish mapmakers. This 1520 map by Peter Apian follows Waldseemüller. It was copied often in the following decades. (Discussion also on pages 62, 185). *Photograph and permission by the British Library (C.32.m.5.)*

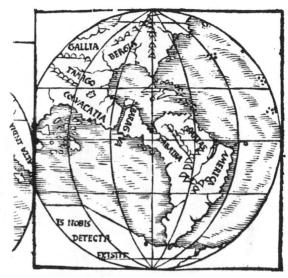

PLATE 11. An imaginary waterway slices through Baragua (Veragua) as though to get to the cluster of islands off the coast of New Spain, on this rough map by Franciscus Monachus, circa 1527. Columbus's belief that he had reached Asia is still thriving— we find Mexico (Colvacatia) joined to "ALTA INDIA." Are the islands meant to represent the rich archipelago in the Indian Ocean and South Sea? Was this an attempt to claim for Spain what was soon to be adjudged in the Portuguese hemisphere? (Discussion also on page 192.) *Photograph and permission by the British Library (586.b.23.[1]).*

carried this vision forward (Plate 10), followed by Sebastian Münster (Plate 32), Gemma Frisius (Plate 33), and Gerhardus Mercator in the next few decades. Such maps were to the taste of the French, British and the Dutch throughout the century.

But in the 1520s, Spanish explorers took the other track, nurturing the Columbian model. Probes for a waterway around Veragua had continued. Those who had crossed overland to the west coast of the isthmus verily believed they were gazing on the Indian Ocean, the South Sea.

That Columbus's ideas were in full vigor is apparent from a map of 1525 made by Franciscus Monachus. On his rough double-hemisphere map he drew an imaginary strait across Mexico, separating "Baragua" from "Colvacatia," and joining the northern part of the New World to "Alta India" (Plate 11).

A fascinating feature of this map is the large cluster of islands in the ocean "sinus" south and west of this mongrel landmass. What islands are they meant to be? The map doesn't name them. The tract doesn't tell us, and the globe which must have accompanied the tract is lost.

Later maps following the same line of thinking provide the answer. A crude manuscript map in the Sloane collection in the British Library

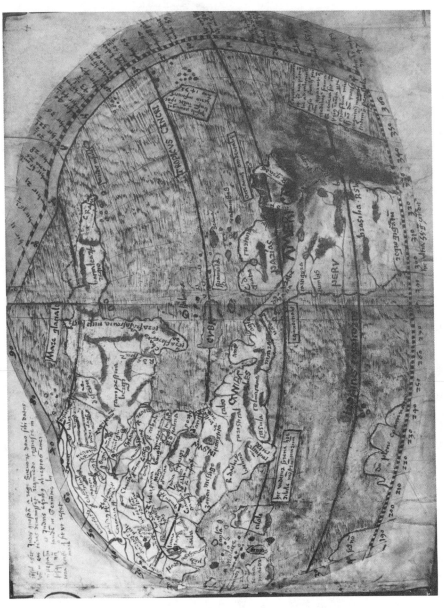

PLATE 12. The islands depicted off the coast of New Spain in this rough manuscript map dated 1530 are bewilderingly named Java Major, "Saylan," and the Moluccas. The mainland has been overwritten in a darker ink with such Asiatic names as "India Superior" and "Mangi." (Discussion also on pages 64-66, 192.) The continent-spanning rivers may have been viewed as hoped-for straits. (Discussion on page 137.) *Photograph and permission by the British Library (Sloane MSS 117, 3v-4).*

(Plate 12), shows a revision in thinking actually taking place. A number of Asian names—India Superior and Mangi, for example— are penned in a darker ink over a sketch-map of New Spain. The New World and Asia are made one and the same thing.

West of this New World-Asia we find again this strange cluster of islands, only now they are labeled—surprisingly with such names as Java and Saylan. All the islands of the Indian Sea, especially the East Indies, are apparently perceived as being close at hand. How such confused illogical thinking could come about is still something to be traced. Perhaps it was that sort of map that Rivera showed to Martyr— yet only if the islands were not named, as on the Franciscus Monachus map. Cortés' rich islands lying "not far distant from the coast" in the passage quoted are specifically classified by Martyr as not the Moluccas or any islands previously known. Martyr could not have bought the notion if they had been identified as islands of the East Indies Archipel- ago. He believed too deeply in a Western antipodean hemisphere equaling that of the Old World in breadth. His preference would no doubt have been for the Martellus-Waldseemüller school of imaging, with its huge group of islands in the Oriental Ocean off Cathay.

The features of the Sloane Manuscript map were crystallized by Oronce Fine (Orontius Finaeus) in a map published first in 1534, and copied over many decades (Plate 13). On such maps the continuous continental mass forming the Americas is labeled with Polo's Asiatic names. And the dense cluster of islands immediately off the west coast continues to be labeled Java and the Moluccas. On the cordiform map they appear up in the top lefthand corner. This reinforces the impres- sion of their lying a brief distance from the coast in the vicinity of what would soon be thought the islands or island of California.

If Cortés' pet ideas about South Sea islands did not influence the making of these maps, perhaps such maps had influenced him. In any event, the resurrection of Polo's Asian identifications suggests that the conquistadores were still in the grip of medieval myths. In view of Cortés' castle-building psychology, this should come as no surprise.

This irrational extrapolation from the Columbian, or "continentalist," concept had wide appeal. Many contemporary globes carried the same features as Fine's maps. Among those which survive are the Gilt Globe, the Vopell Globe and the Nancy Globe. An abstract of the relevant hemisphere of the Gilt Globe is sketched as Plate 14. Again it shows the island cluster just off the west coast. A glance at this will give a hint of

Map labels: Java Minor, Cathay, Mangi, Mare de Sur, Terra Florida, Baccalear, America, Terra Australis, Oceanus Magellanicus

PLATE 13. A host of islands, labeled with East Indies' names, lies just off New Spain—perceived as Asia—in this sketch abstracted from a series of maps originating with Oronce Fine's map, designed several years before its publication in 1534. The cordiform projection adds to the illusion that the islands lie in the area where Baja California would be discovered. (Discussion on pages 87, 64, 192.) *See Rodney W. Shirley, The Mapping of the World, frontispiece, for a facsimile of Fine's map in the Bibliothèque Nationale.*

how important this concept would be in the development of the California island myth.

While Rivera and others were in Spain lobbying for a contract, Cortés continued to pursue his plans. Despite all the other matters that must have absorbed his attention from the Mexican campaign, he sent various probes toward the coast of the South Sea. All were aimed at making preparations for expeditions to the fabled isles once he got the royal nod to proceed on his own terms.

The Amazonian legend remained an integral element in the overall dream. When Cortés sent Gonzalo de Sandoval with a contingent to solve occupation problems on the west coast, the lieutenant picked up this account of the elusive women, as related by Gómara:

Sandoval and his colleagues were led to believe that at ten days' march

PLATE 14.   The islands of the East Indies Archipelago are again depicted immediately off the coast of Hispania Nova-cum-Asia Orientalis in this hemisphere sketch map abstracting concepts of the Gilt Globe of 1528 in the Bibliothèque Nationale. (Discussion on pages 64, 87, 134.) *From a facsimile in Edward Luther Stevenson,* Terrestrial and Celestial Globes (*New Haven: Yale University Press, 1921*).

from there was an isle of Amazons, a rich country; but such women were never met.[15]

Gómara adds that he believes that "the name Ciuatlan, which means land or place of women," gave rise to this rumor. His explanation echoes Rivera's own highly fanciful etymology as reported by Martyr. But it is more likely that the myth impelled a specious semantic exercise than that a real name evoked the myth.

The Fourth Letter, dated October 15, 1524—in which Cortés promises the King "more kingdoms and dominions than all those discovered up till now"—carries an account of Sandoval's expedition:

> He wrote me from there all that had happened, and I ordered him to seek a good site to found a town which he should call Coliman . . . and bring me the fullest reports of the secrets of the country. When he returned, he brought this report, as well as certain samples of pearls . . .

> In his description of these provinces, there was news of a very good port on that coast, which greatly pleased me because there are few; he likewise brought me an account of the chiefs of the province of Ciguatan, who affirm that there is an island inhabited only by women without any men, and that, at given times, men from the mainland visit them . . . If they conceive, they keep the female children to which they give birth, but the males they throw away. This island is ten days' journey from the province, and many of them went thither and saw it, and told me also that it is very rich in pearls and gold. I shall strive to ascertain the truth, and when I am able to do so, I shall make a full account to Your Majesty.[16]

It is possible Cortés is using this as a carrot to get the King to honor his petition with a contract. But from other evidence, belief in the Amazons by Cortés and his men seems to have been deep and earnest. Cortés gave his nephew, Francisco Cortés, these instructions when he sent him to Colima in 1524:

> I am informed that up the coast adjoining this town there are many well-populated provinces where there are known to be some riches, and in a certain part an island inhabited by women, without any men, where they say generation occurs in the manner that the ancient histories tell us of the Amazons. In order to learn the truth about this and other particulars of this coast . . . you will . . . follow the coast.[17]

The mere asking of leading questions of the natives would probably have produced answers that could be interpreted or misinterpreted to fit the dream. Francisco Cortés was able to oblige his cousin-captain to the extent of finding a queen, a widow with a ten-year-old son, ruling in an area in Jalisco:

> Reinaba a la sazón en Jalisco una viuda con un hijo de hasta diez años . . .[18]

Cortés comes through as a man consumed with fantasies in this final phase of his career. Henry R. Wagner, who was deeply steeped in the history of this period, makes this comment about Cortés and the Amazons:

> This story perhaps provided the motive for the efforts of Cortés to conquer the coast of the South Sea as far north almost as the Rio Grande, and for his later voyage by sea farther north. The legend about the women lasted a long time. It became gradually ascribed to regions farther and farther north . . . Although Cortés never writes about his reasons for his persistent attempts to explore the western coast, I am inclined to believe that some such stories were the basis of it.[19]

Cortés' reputed sexual appetite must have given him added interest in this particular myth. Gómara wrote that Cortés was "much given to consorting with women," spending as liberally on them as on war and "fancies."[20]

Accounts of recent times often make it sound as if Cortés' interest was only in the Spice Islands — more or less in the limited sense that we know them today. But Gómara's account makes it clear that it was more than that. In his view, Cortés was driven "to look for the Moluccas and other islands yonder which have spices and other riches . . . and to establish a route in order to go and come from those islands to New Spain, still thinking to find in between rich islands and countries." But, says Gómara, reflecting dryly on this vanity: "He did not discover there what he imagined."[21]

This notion of additional islands between New Spain and the Moluccas suggests that Cortés did not adhere to the concepts of the Sloane Manuscript map, leading to the Oronce Fine map and the Gilt Globe. Perhaps his growing awareness of the vastness of the new ocean on his doorstep propelled him closer to the Waldseemüller camp. That would have reinstated the Oceanus Orientalis with its five to eight thousand more islands in his mind. This must lead in turn to the implication that if the New World *were* attached to Asia, it would have to be by a land bridge further north.

Another passage from Gómara backs this up. The passage is also important to our story for the way it conveys the intensity of Cortés' hunger for those islands. It is given here in an eighteenth-century translation which renders Cortés' imaginative compulsion or fixation as "a conceit"–that is, a fancy, a whim, a vain or freakish notion:

> Cortés imagined by that coast and sea to find another New Spain; but he performed no more than what I have mentioned . . . He was filled with a conceit that there were large and very rich islands between New Spain and the Spice islands.[22]

We glimpse Cortés' disproportionate faith in dreams when Gómara concludes his comment with the quip:

No man ever wasted money on such enterprises with so much zeal.

Still, dreams have a way of keeping things moving; it is their nature to be chased but never caught. Dream locations are always situated over the next horizon, always a few days' journey ahead. Just as classical and medieval accounts placed the realm of the Amazons outside the limits of the then-known world, so in the exploration of the New World the mysterious realm was pushed ever further west and north as the conquistadores spread out.

The persistent pursuit of such a fantasy ultimately yielded the reality of California. The eighteenth-century historian Miguel Venegas shrewdly speculated how this came about as he commented on Cortés' Fourth Letter:

He [Cortés] relates . . . the great efforts he had made for the conquest of the province of Colima near the Sea of the South, and that the lords of it gave notice of an Isle of the Amazons, or women alone, abundant with pearls and gold, ten days' journey to the north of Colima, to which some of the natives had been.

. . . The Isle of the Amazons was as chimerical as another province of them on the River Marañon, which also took the name of them; but the notice of the pearls inclines me to believe that these were the first confused intimations we had of California and its gulf. [23]

In the next chapters we shall see how myth and raw experience intermingle as Cortés takes action to realize his dreams. These actions pushed him to the threshold of California.

Chapter VII

CORTÉS SUFFERS MANY ORDEALS
IN PURSUIT OF HIS DREAM ISLAND

The speed with which Cortés had conquered Mexico must have deluded him into expecting similar success in his South-Sea exploits. But he couldn't get his expedition off the ground. Besides his failure to get the King's cooperation, he was plagued by other problems. Not the least of these was vicious opposition from men with similar ambitions.

One of the bitterest of Cortés' rivals was Nuño de Guzmán. He was the ruthless explorer of the northward territory called New Galicia. Guzmán also believed in the Amazons and wanted to be the first to reach them. To keep the proper perspective we must remember that like all the other explorers he had a host of simultaneous concerns to contend with. The disappointments and headaches of overrunning the mainland probably fanned the yearning for an island paradise in the ocean to the west. Lust undoubtedly motivated Guzmán in his quest for the Amazons as much as did greed for gold, for his lechery and sadism are well-known.

Guzmán's feeling about the Amazons is shown in the letter-report quoted below. The translation is from the work of Samuel Purchas, the man who took over the work of Richard Hakluyt, the sixteenth-century compiler of works of exploration:

> From thence [Aztatlan] ten days further I shall go to find the Amazons which some say dwell in the sea, some in an arm of the sea, and that they are rich, and accounted of the people for goddesses, and whiter than other women. They use bows, arrows and targets; have many and great towns; at a certain time they admit men to accompany them, which bring up the males as these the female issue. [1]

The *Third Relation* of Guzmán's journey to New Galicia also mentions the Amazons:

> At the river of Ciguatan we found eight villages . . . and in them we found some men of war and a great many women very different from those we had seen . . . The few men . . . were said to be from neighboring villages . . . come to defend the lady Amazons. Many of those women

were taken . . . Those women said they had come by the sea, and of old they lived in such a way that they did not have husbands.[2]

As we have seen, Ciguatan, on what was sometimes called the "Rio Grande de Mujeres," was in territory already probed by Cortés. But Guzmán obviously had no compunction about encroaching on his rival's claim, even if only to prove, as the *Fourth Relation* suggests, that Cortés' grapes were sour:

> From here, traveling ten leagues, passing through some warring towns, and pacifying none, we arrived at the town of Ciguatlan, that is the capital of certain towns around it, where we obtained information, and it was said that there were Amazons. In this town and in others that extended around, only women were found and very few or almost no males, and from this it was more presumed they were the women of which notice was brought; and the reason why no males were found among them was because the men were off commanding troops to make war against us on a certain headland.[3]

Cortés' frustration must have been acute with this arch-enemy breathing down his neck in search of the same bounties. We can only imagine what he must have suffered as he marked time, waiting for word from the Spanish Court. Making matters worse, the increasingly powerful Audiencia, set up by the King in 1522, grew ever more hostile to Cortés' desires for South Sea exploration. Their hostility was not from doubt of Cortés' aims, but from desire to further their own interests. The King's own auditor, Rodrigo de Alborñoz, kept his eye on the situation, reporting to his Majesty in 1525:

> The two ships that have been built in Zacatula, and a bergantin, are finished, and will be able to go to explore and follow the route of the Spice Islands, that, according to what the pilots say here . . . are not six to seven hundred leagues from Zacatula, and there is news from Indians who say that on the way there are islands rich in pearls and precious stones, and being on the South side have to have, according to reason, gold in abundance.[4]

Beset by his enemies, ignored by his king, Cortés' authority was increasingly weakened. With his ruling passion thwarted, he must have grown more single-minded by the minute, perhaps becoming almost crackpot in his intensity.

All this couldn't have helped his image very much. Perhaps perceived as a fanatic, and a has-been snubbed by his sovereign, he would no doubt have had to suffer the sneers of sceptics as well as the machinations of cutthroat rivals. His long arrogance would have effectively cut him off from support and sympathy; he would have had to endure all without demur.

All the while, Cortés' enemies continued intriguing to poison the establishment against him. By 1526, no royal concessions and privileges had been granted from his petition of 1522. More than three years had elapsed since Rivera had gone back to Spain to negotiate. Now, in his Fifth Letter, dated September 1526, Cortés was still beseeching the King to "grant me the favors which I asked for." His ships "are ready to start their voyage" to discover "the spice islands and many others, if there be any between Mulaco, Malaca and China." He pleads: "If therefore it pleases Your Majesty that I should undertake this enterprise, concede me all that I have asked."[5]

In the same letter he exhibits an astonishing foolhardiness. His rivals have whispered accusations that he had feathered his own nest at his Sovereign's expense. To put this talk to rest, he offers to share his fortune with the King. The impression is that he wants the King's consent so badly, he is willing to trade anything. Presumably the gesture would have raised rather than quieted suspicions about his prudence and integrity—even his sanity. We can only assume that his inordinate desire had made him blind.

Another couple of years of sweating passed. In 1528, five long years after Cortés had submitted his euphoric proposals, he felt desperate enough to take matters into his own hands. He returned to Spain to plead his cause in person, and to defend himself against enemies currying favor with the court.

But when Cortés finally received an audience, the King turned a deaf ear to his claims to the governorship of New Spain. Cortés received only the marquisate of the Valley of Oaxaca as payment and honor for his conquest of the vast new territory.

But despite generally shabby treatment, there were some important concessions. The King did deign to accord him the rank of captain-general of New Spain and the South Sea.[6] And what is of great importance to the California story, he made a new agreement that Cortés should share in the profits and be made governor for life of any islands and lands he should discover thereafter.

Here is part of the agreement as translated by Robert Ryal Miller:

Since Don Fernando Cortés, Marquis of the Valley, wishing to serve us and for the welfare and growth of our royal crown, has offered to discover, conquer, and settle whatever islands there may be in the South Sea of New Spain . . . and whatever part of the mainland has not yet been discovered . . . we promise to make you our governor for life of all the said islands and lands which you discover and conquer . . . and that you will have civil and criminal jurisdiction in the cities, towns, and populated places in them. . .[7]

Such islands could not have included the spice islands—even then being conceded to Portugal. Cortés must have made a case for a wealth of other islands lying in the South Sea. It cost the Spanish Crown nothing to go along with his conceit.

Cortés returned to the New World more intent than ever on justifying himself by finding the dream destinations he had long pursued. Unfortunately he fell victim to an incredible train of ordeals and disappointments in the sharpest contrast to the "success" of his previous decade. One of Cortés' officers, Bernal Díaz del Castillo, wrote, between 1553 and 1568, his memories of these events. In his *True History of the Conquest of New Spain*—not published until 1632, in Madrid—he has left us a moving account of the decline in Cortés' fortunes. The following nineteenth-century rendering in English reads like a great romantic novel, unfolding the final tragic sequence:

The marquis Del Valle had, previous to his departure for Spain . . . built two vessels . . . The command of these vessels he gave to Alvarado de Saavadra [who] was instructed to shape his course to the Moluccas, or towards China . . . This armament, indeed, reached the Moluccas, and visited several other islands, but suffered dreadfully from heavy tempests, hunger, and disease, and many of the men died.[8]

Díaz continues the catalogue of Cortés' misfortunes:

After his first armament had departed, Cortes fitted out two more vessels . . . The command of these vessels he gave to a certain Diego Hurtado Mendoza, who set sail from Acapulco in the month of May, 1532, for the discovery of islands and new countries. The captain Hurtado, however, did nothing of all this, and durst not even venture far out to sea, so that the greater part of his men at length grew wearied of sailing about to no purpose, refused all further obedience to him, and deserted with one of the vessels . . . Hurtado, in the meantime, continued to sail along the coast, but all at once his vessel disappeared, nor was she or any of those on board ever heard of.[9]

Quite clearly, the second sea was turning out to be far less peaceful than its namer, Magellan, had found it to be. As we have seen, Balboa had experienced its double face from the beginning when he went fishing for pearls in the Gulf of San Miguel. Is it possible that Cortés interpreted the angry ocean as evidence of his dream's existence? He certainly didn't let it daunt him. It is the nature of fanatical idealism to thrive on setbacks. Each dashed hope entrenches a "conceit" more deeply. Each defeat tends to be viewed as ritual trial or ordeal to be overcome before the quest can succeed. It is certain that after the failure of the Hurtado expedition, as Díaz tells it, Cortés bounced right back:

> Cortes was excessively grieved at his loss, yet it did not deter him from fitting out other armaments for the same purpose. He had already built two more vessels at his own expense, which were lying in the harbour of Guantepec, and were manned with seventy soldiers. The command of one of these vessels he gave to a cavalier named Diego Bezerra de Mendoza . . . . Ortuña [or Fortun] Ximenes, of Biscay, a great cosmographer, accompanied this expedition as a chief pilot. Bezerra's instructions were to go in quest of Hurtado; but if he should not fall in with him, he was to steer at a venture for the main ocean in search of islands and new countries; for it was said there were many islands in the South Sea which produced immense quantities of pearls. The chief pilot Ximenes was so confident of the good success of this expedition that he promised the men on board he would steer them to countries where they would all become rich, and many there were who firmly believed what he said.

The pilot Ximénes was clearly as obsessed as Cortés with the dream of island paradises. His greed for gold and pearls produced its own catastrophe, as Díaz goes on to tell:

> Bezerra, who was a haughty and ill-disposed man . . . continued to sail forward, but he soon fell out with the chief pilot Ximenes, who, with his countrymen of Biscay and a greater part of the troops, fell upon Bezerra in the night, and put him to death, with several of the soldiers.

Whether aptly or ironically, this act of greed and violence, itself a product of fanatical persistence, entrained a series of events that brought California out of the realm of dream, into the arena of reality.

Chapter VIII

The Island Craze Leads to
Baja California's Discovery

Ximénes sailed away after murdering his captain, and "came to an island," Díaz wrote, "where, according to all accounts there were fine pearl fisheries."[1] With this event, we begin the story proper, for the "island" Ximénes reached would become known as Baja (Lower) California, often called simply "Baja" by modern Californians. Baja is still a part of Mexico. It would be many moons before the territory that is now a state of the United States entered the picture. But Baja and Alta (Upper) California share a common history for the first three centuries, which explains why they carry the same name, and why, until the nineteenth century, they are treated as a unit.

The mutinous, murderous, Ximénes and his crew have the signal honor of being the first Europeans to arrive at the threshold of California. They crossed or sailed up into the stretch of water we now call the Gulf of California some time in 1533. Whether they landed on an offshore island or on Baja itself we do not know for sure. Ximénes did not live long enough to make a map or write a report. The survivors, however, were able to make it back to the mainland, and they subsequently retraced the voyage to that general area. Here is Díaz' relation of this incident:

> This island was inhabited by a savage tribe of Indians, and they massacred Ximenes with the whole of the men who had accompanied him on shore to take in fresh water. The few sailors who had remained on board put back with the vessel to the harbour of Xalisco, where they related all that had taken place and spread a vast account of the large population and the rich pearl fisheries of the island they had discovered.

Cortés' reaction to this news was mixed. It was another setback to his enterprise. But in this case, land offshore had been discovered. After years of dreaming and sweating, there was hope at last.

It is easy to imagine how the news must have fed Cortés' obsession. The relief of finding anything that would prove him not to be the fool his enemies took him for, must have been tremendous. Instead of putting him off, reports of the hostility of the natives to Ximénes may have suggested to Cortés the fierce defense of a rich paradise. A guard of cannibals and ferocious beasts was often associated with the Amazons. Nothing would do for such a dreamer except to go himself to claim the "island" for which he yearned.

Díaz relates Cortés' reaction from the first moment he receives the ambiguous news:

> These accounts soon reached Mexico, and as may be imagined, were anything but pleasing to Cortes, but as he was a man whose spirits were not easily damped by adversity, he determined in future not to trust similar expeditions to other hands, but to take the chief command himself. By this time three other fine vessels were lying in readiness at Guantepec, with which he proposed to sail out in person, for he felt a great temptation to visit *the above-mentioned pearl island* [italics added], besides that he fully believed there were other large continents to be discovered in the South Sea.

Spurring Cortés on was a report that Guzmán had seized the ill-fated ship from the survivors and was secretly making plans to send settlers to the new discovery. In a letter to the Council of the Indies protesting Guzmán's intent to intrude upon Cortés' claim, Cortés wrote:

> I learned, almost miraculously, about the diligence that Nuño de Guzmán employed in guarding the secret that there had arrived in a port of his jurisdiction the flagship on which Diego Becerra and up to seven of his men had been murdered, and the traitorous pilot [Ximénes] and the others had been killed by the natives of *an island which had been discovered* [italics added]. And because of the good news that they brought from the land, Nuño de Guzmán had taken the ship . . . and [he] was hurrying to send people in that ship to the discovered land . . . I decided to . . . speed up [construction of] ships which I had in the shipyard, and to lift my skirts and go to see this land.[2]

We should notice here for later discussion that Cortés calls Ximénes' discovery an island, and also interchanges the word "land" in speaking of that island discovery.

But to return to Díaz' story:

> As soon as it was known in New Spain that Cortes was going to head the expedition in person, no one any longer doubted of its good success, and of the riches it would produce those who joined it; and so many cavaliers, musketeers, and crossbowmen offered their services, that their number soon amounted to above 380 men, among whom were thirty married men, accompanied by their wives.

These vessels were provided with a copious supply of the best provisions, with all kinds of ammunition, and tools of various descriptions. The most experienced pilots and sailors were hired, who, with the troops, received instructions to repair by a certain route to the harbour of Guantepec, while Cortes, with Andreas de Tapia, several other officers, a few priests, surgeons, physicians, and an apothecary, travelled thither by another road. When they arrived at the harbour above mentioned he found the three vessels in readiness, and immediately set sail with the first body of troops.[3]

Researchers have ferreted out a good deal of information in recent times about when, where, and how Cortés established that first colonizing expedition on what we now call Baja California. Henry R. Wagner provides the following summary of the known facts from his intensive research of contemporary documents as well as a search of the locale:

May 1, 1535, he [Cortés] sighted the coast of California, and May 3 landed and took possession, naming the country "Santa Cruz" in commemoration of the discovery of the Holy Cross on that day. He laid out his settlement on what is now known as Pichilingue Harbor, opposite the island of San Juan Nepomuceno in La Paz bay. No detailed or consecutive account of the enterprise exists, but from numerous incidental allusions to it, it seems that some explorations were made inland.[4]

The outline map (see endpapers) helps us understand where he founded this settlement, though little evidence remains today.

The May 1, 1535, date is confirmed by what Robert Ryal Miller called Cortés' "little-known letter written from Baja two weeks after his landfall" to Cristobal de Oñate in Compostela. The following excerpts are from Miller's translation:

This is only to let you know how I arrived at this port and bay of Santa Cruz, the day of the Holy Cross [3rd] of May, in honor of which this name was given to it.

I sighted land on May 1st, day of the two apostles [Felipe and Santiago], and because there was a range of mountains in the part of land we saw, the name of San Felipe was given to the highest range. On this same day near this land we discovered an island that was named Santiago [later called Cerralvo], and then we saw two others, one was named San Miguel Island [Espiritu Santo], and the other San Cristobal [San José].

I took sixteen days on the crossing because of many calms and foul weather . . .

I do not write to you about the form and condition of this land because I have not gone out . . . When these ships leave, I will go inland . . . on returning will have more news of its secrets . . .

From the port and bay of Santa Cruz, May 14, 1535. At your service.

The Marquis [5]

Reinforcing the details of Cortés' letter is a notarized document recording the formal act of possession:

On the third day of the month of May, 1535, about midday, the very noble lord, Don Hernando Cortés, Marquis of the Valley of Oaxaca, Captain General of New Spain and the South Sea for his Majesty, arrived at a port and bay in a newly-discovered land in the South Sea . . . Upon arrival he went ashore with personnel and horses, and there on the beach . . . in the name of his Majesty he took possession of the newly-discovered land where we were and all the rest adjacent to it and within its limits so that from it as a start, the disclosure, conquest and settlement of it could be pursued, and as a sign and token of said possession, the Marquis named the port and bay "Santa Cruz." Then he walked over the ground from one point to another, threw sand from one place to another, and with his sword he cut some trees that were there, and he commanded those present to accept him as his Majesty's governor of the lands, and he carried out other acts of possession. [6]

Another legal ceremony was conducted on May 10, 1535, to install the Marquis as governor. To confirm his rights, Cortés exhibited the contract which the Crown had made with him during his visit to Spain in 1529. He required each man present to swear "that he accepted the lordly Marquis as governor of this land, in the name of his Majesty"— according to the notarized contemporary account. [7] Such elaborate proceedings were no doubt taken to forfend against attacks upon his title by Guzmán and Antonio de Mendoza, just made Viceroy of New Spain.

But the realization of Cortés' dream was not to be. It was as if (wrote Mendoza later) "God miraculously did hide it from him." [8] At the events which followed, as described by Díaz, even Cortés himself must have felt the weight of doom:

The three vessels then put back for Guantepec to fetch the ladies and the rest of the men who had remained behind under the command of Tapia. This time, however, the passage was not so favorable, for the vessels were driven out of their course by a violent wind . . . Overtaken by another storm, . . . they became separated from each other. There was only one which reached the harbour of Santa Cruz; the second was cast on shore off Xalisco, the men on board narrowly escaping a watery grave and becoming wearied of the perils of the sea, dispersed themselves through New Spain, only a few remaining in the province of Xalisco. The third vessel . . . likewise ran aground, nor were the hands on board able to set her afloat again. Cortes in the meantime was impatiently awaiting the arrival of these vessels, particularly as all his provisions were consumed, for the greater part of the biscuits and salted meat was on board the vessel which had got ashore off Xalisco. As the inhabitants of Santa Cruz are perfect savages, and neither grow maise nor in anywise till the ground, but merely live on wild fruits, fish, and animals, there arose so dreadful a famine among Cortes' troops, that twenty-three of the men died of hunger and disease. The greater part of the remaining troops likewise suffered from ill-health, and they threw out their bitter curses against Cortes, *the island* [italics added], and the whole voyage of discovery. Cortes, determining, if possible, to put an end to their disaster, ran out with the vessel which had arrived, in search of the two others, taking with him fifty men, two smiths, and several shipwrights. On arriving off Xalisco he found one of them lying on a sand-bank, quite deserted, and the other he discovered jammed between the coral rocks. By dint of the utmost exertions he succeeded in setting them afloat again; and, after the carpenters had properly repaired them, he arrived safely with two vessels and their cargoes at Santa Cruz. Those of the troops who had not tasted any nourishing food for so long a time ate so ravenously of the salted meat that half of them died of a violent dysentery.[9]

Even so, Cortés would not give up. His obstinacy and pride would hardly have permitted him to admit defeat:

As Cortes was so weary he was wishing to get back to New Spain, however, through obstinacy, so that they should not charge him with having expended great numbers of pesos de oro without finding any new lands of value, and having no luck in matters to which he put his hand, and on account of the soldiers, he did not go.[10]

But at last, the emotional appeals of his wife, supported by the new Viceroy's gentle commands, allowed him to return home without loss of face:

At that very same time, as the Marquesa Dona Juana de Zuñiga, his wife, had received no news of him, and more than that one ship had gone ashore on the coast of Jalisco, she felt very anxious, thinking that he might be dead or lost, and she promptly sent two ships in search of him; one of these was the ship in which Grijalva, who had sailed with Bezerra, had returned to New Spain, the other a new ship which they had just finished building in Tehuantepec, and these ships were laden with all the provisions which could be obtained at that time.

She sent as Captain of one of them a certain Fulano [Francisco] De Ulloa, and wrote most affectionately to the Marquis, her husband, praying him to return at once to Mexico to his estate and Marquisate, and to remember the sons and daughters he possessed, and cease to contend any more with fortune, but be content with the heroic deeds and the fame of his person which had spread everywhere. Thus, too, the most illustrious Viceroy Don Antonio Mendoza wrote to him most charmingly and affectionately, begging him to return to New Spain.

After a favourable passage these two ships arrived where Cortes was stationed, and as soon as he saw the letters of the Viceroy and the entreaties of his wife the Marchioness and his children, he . . . at once embarked and came to the port of Acapulco, and going ashore after a favourable journey he reached Cuernavaca where the Marchioness was living, which caused great rejoicing.

Cortés was so hooked on his "conceit" that after his return he sent out still another expedition, as we'll see below. But the aborted Santa Cruz experiment was really his last exploit. Concluding his account of the Marquis's career, Díaz sadly observes:

If we think of it, in nothing at all did he [Cortés] have any luck after we had conquered New Spain.

True, he may have done nothing further to advance his career of bloody conquest. But in terms of the island myth that we are tracing, his final efforts hold considerable importance. By carrying the myth to the threshold of California, he significantly shaped her destiny in the early years.

Chapter IX

CORTÉS BELIEVES BAJA CALIFORNIA TO BE AN ISLAND

The land where Cortés tried to found his colony is a peninsula. The endpaper map shows Baja California as a long finger of land over one thousand kilometers long, running more or less parallel to the mainland in a northwest to southeast direction. Its width varies roughly between one and two hundred kilometers, as does the Gulf separating it from the mainland. At the crotch, where peninsula and mainland join, the Colorado River "flows" into the Gulf of California.

But our interest is not so much in the objective facts themselves as in the way preconceptions were handled in confrontation with experience. We are not primarily concerned with what Ximénes and Cortés actually discovered, but rather with what they *thought* they discovered, and how and why they thought it.

When the explorers came across Baja, what they *thought* they found was an island. Díaz has already been quoted as saying that Ximénes "came to an island," and the word is used repeatedly in his narrative of the episode.

True, Díaz wrote his memoirs many years after the event, but there are many contemporary statements telling of the island nature of Ximénes' discovery. Cortés' letter to the Audiencia objecting to Guzmán's proposed encroachments has been quoted above (page 100). The excerpt shows that Cortés had heard and accepted the island report— enough to act upon it. He speaks plainly of "an island that has been discovered," and of Guzmán's and his own intention to visit this "discovered land."

Perhaps Cortés used the word "land" as homologous to "island" in order to suggest a significant size and entity of the new discovery. Cortés confuses the issue in later documents by raising the possibility that the Bezerra-Ximénes landing may have been on one of the smaller islands:

> I sent another armada . . . with two ships in claim of that land, of which the captain was Diego Becerra, and one of the said ships arrived . . . at the said land, or an island bordering on said land . . . I went in person in claim of the said land to conquer and settle it, and arrived in port at the said land or island where the said ship had been.[1]

In any event, whether Cortés viewed his new discovery as "continent" or "island," the distinction that has to be made is whether or not he viewed it as a separate "tierra"—a land unattached to the mainland of New Spain. Díaz touches on Cortés' varied expectations in the excerpt quoted on page 100. There he speaks of Cortés' "great temptation to visit the above-mentioned pearl island." More than that, Cortés "fully believed there were other large continents to be discovered in the South Sea."

In the squabble between Cortés and Guzmán, many documents were filed. Excerpts from a couple of these will suggest how the island notion was reinforced by this litigation. The first example is from a "Transcript of a Provision of the Audiencia of Mexico," dated 1534, deciding between Cortés' and Guzmán's claims to possession of *la dicha isla*, "the said island." Indeed, the very title of the Traslado speaks of the aim "to pacify and settle a certain island of the South Sea." Clearly it is no small affair, but an island important enough to fight over who was going to pacify and settle it. The document details Guzmán's handling of Ximénes' crew, and rules against him:

> The said ship came . . . to a port of your jurisdiction, and . . . you have seized the said ship and endeavored . . . to equip it to go to pacify and settle the said island . . . We order you to hand over the said vessel to the said Marquis or to he who might have his authority.[2]

Guzmán's version of the Ximénes episode, in a document dated 1540, has this reference to the "island" which the Marquis failed to colonize:

> Pursuing his course, Ortun Gimenez fetched up with that point of the island which they say became Santa Cruz by name.[3]

Soon after this, Guzmán would change his tune, calling the island inference a misconception, as quoted below.

Of even more interest and force is what Cortés must have inferred from direct experience when he led his colonizers across the Sea of Cortés—the Gulf of California as we know it today. Nothing he saw on the voyage could have called into doubt the island theory. The facts were that he and his party sailed many leagues for many days across a body of water from the mainland of New Spain. They then came upon some small islands and a great chunk of land with extended coastline to north and south. Given the lie of the land with respect to the mainland, as we see on the modern map (*see* endpapers), they were justified in concluding that their discovery was detached from the mainland. The anonymous narrator of the Second Relation of Guzmán's itineraries suggests how the misconception could occur:

> From this sierra is made the *ancon* which comes to end the point . . . where Ortun Jimenez—the captain who rebelled against the marquis— died, which land they called island, because as one went forward through that gulf and entered on the sea, it appeared to them that it could not be firm land, until after they went to it.[4]

The deduction that Baja was an island is illustrated on Plate 15. This map is believed contemporary with those events. It was found among the papers of one of Cortés' law suits, and is said to have accompanied

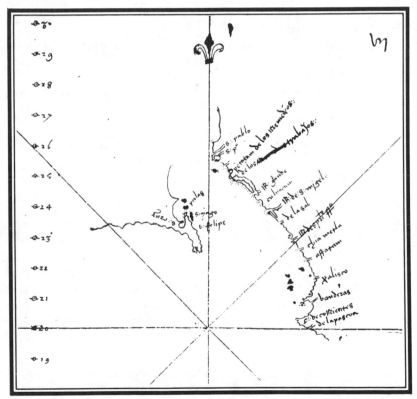

PLATE 15.   That Baja California was originally perceived as an island may be inferred from this map, made between 1535 and 1537, found amongst Cortés' legal papers. S. Cruz is written upside down. *Photograph and permission by Archivo General de Indias, Sevilla.* (M. 6. — "*Se publica con autorización del Archivo General de Indias, el cual se reserva los derechos de sucesivas reproducciones y publicaciones.*")

Cortés' Act of Possession of his Santa Cruz settlement. Wagner, how-ever, believes it was drawn a bit later than that.[5]

As we have seen, there were strong psychological reasons why the explorers would have wanted to believe Baja an island. The report of rich pearl fisheries no doubt triggered the island dreams from Polo and Mandeville, fetching more than three hundred volunteers from all walks of life to follow Cortés' leadership.

The following testimony of Juan Fernández de Ladrillero, in Wagner's translation, suggests the powerful attraction of the dream material. The testimony was given in 1574 about a voyage of 1541, many years after the event, yet a sense of the mythic isles of Mandeville and Polo is very strong. Even the yarns of huge pearls worn by natives who had no idea of their value are echoed and remembered.

> Asked, if he [Ladrillero] knows or has any information whether, on the said islands where this witness has gone and has made discovery, there is any gold, or silver, pearls or precious stones, or other things of value and esteem, that he should declare what he knows particularly about this matter, or has heard about it; he [Ladrillero] answered that in California this witness set foot on land in the port of San Lucas and went inland two or three leagues with six men with their arms, and came to a rancheria where they found fifteen or twenty Indians who were fishing; the said Indians had pearls hanging from their hair about the size of a finger; . . . as these Indians had these pearls, and as he saw many oyster shells and oyster deposits in the sea, this witness considers it certain that there is a quantity of oysters and pearls along the coast which this witness has navigated; these pearls are found in some places more than in others; the same is true of *these islands which this witness says he saw and went around* [italics added].[6]

Of course, one could come across *tierra firme* with the same kinds of bounties. But islands had special benefits in the way of clearer title, and were thus more to be desired. The question of what distinguished an island from a continent had continually absorbed explorers. Peter Martyr discussed Columbus's dilemma on discovering the north coast of South America:

> It is evident that this coast is too extended to belong to an island, and yet, if one takes it altogether, the whole universe may be called an island.[7]

The geographical attributes of a territory had political implications. A continental territory could generate problems from those having claims to areas on the same landmass. The usual disputes about boundaries, and other resentments and hostilities, could arise from adjacent settlers. But if the geographical and political-legal limits coincided, no such problems could develop once the territory was subdued. The optimum situation was an island-continent that had not been previously discovered or claimed by "civilized" men. It should be large enough to bring one wealth and stature, but not so large as to make one's holding of it tenuous. Baja appeared to fit these specifications.

When it came to politico-legal documents of possession and settlement, the word *tierra*, "land," was customarily used. This explains why Cortés' Act of Possession does not make reference to an island. *Tierra* carries the sense of a territorial possession. Its geographical nature wasn't then the focus of attention.

Many who went to Baja on that ill-starred expedition, believed, and seemed to go on believing, that Baja was an island. This is demonstrated by various *relaciones de servicios* made by men who were with Cortés. By the time they testified, the popular view had swayed toward a theory of the territory's peninsularity, so it is all the more remarkable that they would speak of it as an island. Wagner summarizes these affidavits:

> In the fifty-six that referred to the expedition of Cortés himself to California, we find . . . that nearly one-half of the explorers referred to it as the *isla*.[8]

These old soldiers were no doubt the last remnants of the troops who, Díaz said, "threw out their bitter curses against Cortés, the island, and the whole voyage of discovery" back in 1535.

Cortés had even more than the general interest in Baja's being insular. His long-standing dreams to discover rich islands had become, as we have seen, an idée fixe. The long period of waiting for the King's response to his petition, which had both tarnished his image as a conquering hero and frustrated him, had made him compulsive about his dreams. Add to this, diminishing energies and dread of approaching age, and we see that his need to reach his ideal destination must have grown desperate. It is not hard to understand why he jumped to conclusions on hearing "the good news," as he put it, and why he tried to make his experiment work despite all adversity.

Then there were practical political reasons for Cortés wanting to believe the new discovery an island. As already noted, he had been, in his view, dispossessed of the territory of New Spain by being passed over for the governorship. The King chose to appoint the Royal Audiencia (later, Antonio de Mendoza as Viceroy) over his head. This snub couldn't have been easy for an arrogant man to take. He would have wanted to find his own country to rule as soon as possible. In his petition of 1522, he had asked the King to grant him "lordship and jurisdiction" over one of three islands he might discover. And hadn't the King, in 1529, given him license to "discover, conquer and settle any islands in the South Sea of the said New Spain, that are in its locale," and promised to make him governor "for all the days of your life" of those islands and lands?[9] The chance to extricate himself from his shameful predicament would have made Cortés rush to put the best construction first on the news, then on the experience of his expedition.

The very bitterness of his political rivalries points to his believing that he was going to an island-continent—a piece of land totally distinct from areas already conquered. Given his enmity with Guzmán, he certainly wouldn't have wanted land contiguous with territory that Guzmán held. In fact, his contract with the Crown had clearly spelled out that he could only discover, conquer, or settle any island or mainland that had not been provided with a governor. Even more particularly, the contract stated that he could not explore and settle anything which fell within the limits governed by Guzmán and Narváez, specified by name.[10]

Cortés would hardly have "picked up his skirts to go himself" to an area whose title could be at all uncertain or ambiguous. Much less would he have mustered an ambitious party of married couples, surgeons, and skilled artisans for the purpose of colonizing it. There were all kinds of unexplored regions on the mainland where he could have more easily done that.

Then there were the elaborate ceremonies: the Act of Possession, and the second event installing him as governor, all according to the King's contract, which he waved at all assembled. In retrospect these make a laughingstock of him. He surely wouldn't have put on all that fanfare if he didn't think his title unassailable.

Cortés went on fantasizing it as an island realm even after his return. Bancroft has noted how deep must his obsession have been that he could go on accepting "the new discovery as an island even after a fruitless attempt at occupation and finding riches."[11] In 1538, the notion still buzzed as loudly as ever in his bonnet. He signed an agreement with Juan Castellon to fit out another ship for yet another expedition up the Sea of Cortés. As Wagner summarizes it:

Castellon . . . was to go as captain and pilot of the ship to the new land named Santa Cruz, where Cortés had been, and survey all the *ancon* between the "island" and the mainland . . . in order that it might be settled with Spaniards.[12]

Wagner points out that in that period, *ancón* could mean one body of water connecting with another, not simply an enclosed bay.[13] The name "Sea of Cortés," instead of "gulf," speaks to the same effect.

A letter from Cortés to Castellon, in March 1538, suggests that Castellon is being sent to a territory of distinct and separate jurisdiction: "I can tell you that I have received much good news about the country where you are going."[14]

The agreement with Castellon was later broken by Cortés' substitution of Francisco de Ulloa as captain of the expedition. This expedition will be dealt with at length in Chapter XI. What interests us here is the reference to the island nature of the new discovery in a breach-of-contract suit brought by Castellon against Cortés in 1541. Wagner comments on his research of this document:

> None of the numerous witnesses examined in the ensuing suit gave any account of the voyage. The only remark of any importance to us was made by one of the Franciscan friars, Fray Antonio de Meno, who, in speaking of the demand on Ulloa made by Castellon at Santa Cruz, referred to the "Isla de California." . . . This, and another use of the word *isla* by Cortés himself, seems to indicate plainly enough that the peninsula was supposed to be an island.[15]

A facsimile of Friar de Meno's reference, with his signature, appears on Plate 16.

In speaking of this Castellon-Ulloa expedition, Díaz again suggests the new territory was an island:

. . . y le mando Cortes al capitan que corriese la costa adelante y acabasen de boxar la California . . .[16]

. . . and Cortes commanded the captain to run along the coast further and finish sailing around California . . .

The Maudslay translation for the Hakluyt Society renders this "to finish the circumnavigation of California," the Spanish word *boxar* or *bojar* conveying that sense.[17] This expression, in turn, implies a belief in California's insularity.

Later, when Cortés forwarded to the King the accounts of the Ulloa voyage (discussed below), Cortés would continue to refer to Baja as "the new land."[18]

PLATE 16. "La ysla dela California" on lines three and four above is possibly the first record of the name California given to the supposed island of Baja discovered by Cortés. H. R. Wagner found the reference in the 1541 testimony of Father Antonio de Meno, one of three Franciscans who accompanied Ulloa up the Mar de Cortés or Mar Vermejo—the Gulf of California. (Discussion on pages 111, 123.) *From a facsimile of the original in the Archivo General de la Nación, México. Photograph by the Bancroft Library.*

Cortés and his company of would-be colonists were not alone in regarding Baja as an island. His enemies also accepted this as the geography of the new discovery. We have already seen that Guzmán originally shared this view. Viceroy Mendoza speaks of an island discovery at the very moment he is cataloguing Cortés' follies and failures several years after the event. Richard Hakluyt, the sixteenth-century British compiler of travel works, translated the following statement by Mendoza from the Italian compiler Giovanni Battista Ramusio. We note in passing—for development in Chapter XX—that Hakluyt marginally annotates Mendoza's mention of the island: "This was the Port of Santa Cruz, in the Isle of California."

Mendoza summarizes:

> . . . The Marquis de Valle Hernando Cortes' sent a captain with two ships to discover the coast; which two ships and the captain perished. After that he sent again two other ships, one of which was divided from her consort, and the master and certain mariners slew the captain and usurped over the ship. After this they came to an *Island* [italics added], where the master with certain mariners going on land, the Indians of the country slew them and took their boats; and the ship with those that were

in it, returned to the coast of Nueva Galicia, where it ran on ground. By the men which came home in this ship, the Marquis had knowledge of the country which they had discovered: and without seeking any further intelligence of the state of that *Island* [italics added], he set forward on that voyage with three ships . . . which fell out so contrary to his expectation, that the most part of the people which he carried with him, died of hunger. And although he had ships, and a country very near him abounding with victuals, yet could he never find means to conquer it, but rather it seemed that God miraculously did hide it from him; and so he returned home without achieving ought else of moment.[19]

There are other instances in the record of the Viceroy regarding Baja as an island. He refers to the new discovery as "Isla de Marqués" in his instructions to Zuñiga to explore the South Sea and the islands of the west in 1541:

No. 7: Having received the fleet . . . and made sail from Navidad, you will follow the coast of New Spain . . . Look for the outside point of the Isla de Marqués . . .[20]

Another reference to the Isla de Marqués occurs in a letter by Viceroy Mendoza dated March, 1542.

Mendoza did not merely accept Cortés' word; he had his own independent source of information—as he thought. In 1538, he issued instructions to a Friar Marcos de Niza to explore northwards up the mainland on the east side of the Sea of Cortés. Niza brought back "news" of the mythical kingdoms of Cibola, Quivira and the Seven Cities, which he had gone to seek. His report also "confirms" the island nature of Cortés' discovery:

There came to seek me certain Indians from the Island where Fernando Cortés the Marquis of the Valley had been, of whom I was informed that it was an island and not firm land, as some suppose it to be. They came to the firm land upon certain rafts of wood: and from the main to the island is but half a league by the sea, little more or less. Likewise certain Indians of another island greater than this came to visit me, which island is farther off, of whom I was informed that there were thirty other small islands, which were inhabited, but had small store of victuals, saving two which have maize or corn of the country. These Indians had about their necks many great shells which were mother of pearl. I showed them pearls which I carried with me for a show, and they told me that there were in the islands great store of them.[21]

Niza goes on to say:

I determined to stay there until Easter to inform myself of the Islands . . .

And so I sent certain Indians to the Sea . . . to bring me some Indians of the Sea-coast and some of those Islands . . . who returned unto me upon Easter day, bringing with them certain inhabitants of the Sea-coast, and of two of the Islands. Of whom I understood, that the islands . . . were scarce of victuals . . . and that they are inhabited by people, which wear shells of pearls upon their foreheads, and they say that they have great pearls and much gold. They informed me of four and thirty islands, lying one near unto another: they say that the people on the sea-coast have small store of victuals, as also those of the islands, and that they traffic one with the other upon rafts. This coast stretcheth northward as is to be seen.

Cortés called Niza a liar in making this report, but not because the substance was inaccurate. In a Memorial to the King of June 25, 1540, Cortés charged that Niza did not get his information from actual experience but from having learned it all from Cortés' own lips:

At the time I came from the said land the said Fray Marcos spoke with me . . . and I gave him news of this said land and discovery of it, because I had in mind to send him in my ships to follow up the conquest of the said coast and land, because he appeared to know something about navigation; the which said friar communicated to the said Viceroy, and with his permission it is said he went by land in claim of the same coast and land that I had discovered, and that was and is of my conquest; and since he returned, the said friar has announced, it is said, that he arrived in sight of the said land; the which I deny him to have seen or discovered; but rather, what the friar states to have seen, he said it and says it only from the report I have made to him of the information I had from the indians that I brought from the said country of Santa Cruz, because all that the said friar states is the same as the said indians related to me. [22]

Cortés' accusation carries an important implication for our story. If Niza picked up everything he knew from Cortés' lips, then he must have picked up the purported island nature of Cortés' discovery from him as well. The combination of Niza's statement and Cortés' Memorial ties Cortés ever more closely to the island view.

This episode may also suggest why the Viceroy could be content to let Cortés have his "island." In the first place, the colonizing fiasco had proved it a white elephant. In the second, if Cortés' discovery was insular, it could not then be contiguous with the mythical cities Niza promised. Cortés could not lay automatic claim to them. The Viceroy's interests would be well served by promoting the concept of the "Isla de Marqués."

Francisco Vásquez de Coronado was sent by Mendoza in quest of the mythical golden cities after Niza's supposed probe. Coronado also contributed to the story of off-shore islands. In a section which Hakluyt has annotated "Seven or eight Isles, which are the Isles of California," Coronado notes:

> The Indians of the Sea coast came unto me: which told me, that two days sailing from their coast of the Sea, there were seven or eight Islands right over against them, well inhabited with people, but badly furnished with victuals, and were a rude people.[23]

More will be said about Coronado's expedition in Chapter XII.

Belief that Cortés had discovered islands was certainly the official view back at the Spanish Court. In 1542, the Royal Cosmographer Alonso de Santa Cruz was given the job of producing an *"islario,"* a study of islands, for the King. Such a study was in the tradition that had produced the *Insularium Illustratum* of Henricus Martellus Germanus (*see* page 30). Mappings of islands continued to be popular in fifteenth- and sixteenth-century Italy, such as the *isolarios* of Sonetti and Bordone.[24] But now the power over islands invested in the Pope under the "Omni-Insular Doctrine" has clearly passed to Caesar in all concerns except the spiritual mission of the universal church.

Alonso de Santa Cruz's *Islario General de Todas Las Islas del Mundo* naturally includes all the newly discovered islands since Columbus. It also includes many debatable ones, such as the Yucatan, and the "Amazonas" off its coast.

The passage of most interest in California's story occurs at the end of a section titled "Islas de los Golfos de Panama, Nombre de Dios:"

> Turning to the coast that goes from the province of Panama towards that of Nicaragua to Guatemala, . . . all of them are full of many islands, most without names and uninhabited and of no use . . . Near the province of Nicaragua there is a gulf called San Lucas full of unpopulated islets, and in another bay in the same province called Fonseca there are many others and so for all the coast as far as New Galicia and up to a gulf of the sea which Don Hernando Cortes, the Marques del Valle, discovered a short time ago in which there are some islands great and small that were thought until now to be unpopulated.[25]

The area is illustrated in the beautiful Atlas accompanying the text. The map, however, seems based on later reports than the brief mention quoted above. What we now call the Gulf of California is shown as a rounded bay, but the lower half of Baja is an island (*see* Plate 18). This

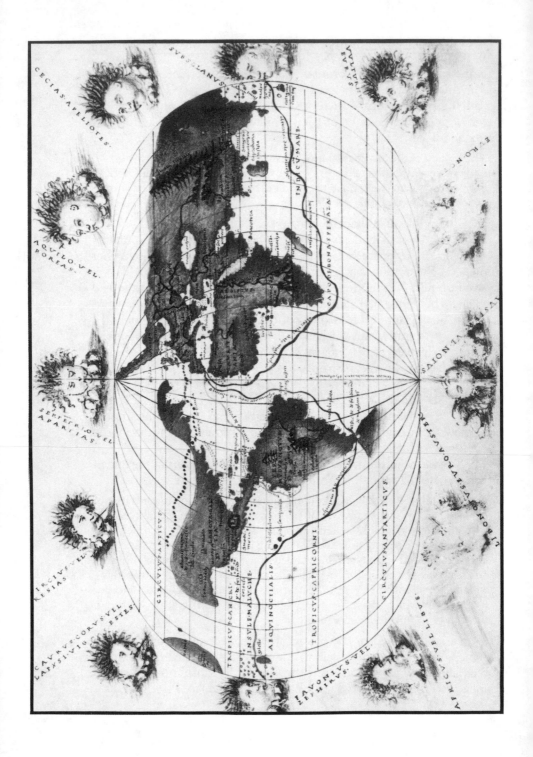

configuration seems to reconcile conflicting views about the Sea of Cortés—whether it was the South Sea proper, washing around islands off the mainland, or simply a bay or gulf without any exit to the north. This difference in interpretation will haunt the California story from here forward.

The configuration found in the *Islario* occurs again in a famous map now in the Royal Library in Stockholm (*see* Plate 19). On both maps we find the legend in Spanish: "The island which the Marques del Valle discovered," describing the island, and: "The land that Don Antonio de Mendoza sent [explorers] to discover," describing the land north of the bay. These legends capture the bitter rivalry of the Marquis and the Viceroy, their conflicting hopes and views. Both maps are dated 1542.

The insular concept is shown in a different way on another map in the

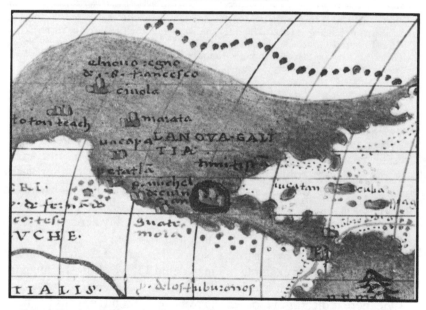

PLATES 17a & b.   California was first conceived to be a group of islands, as seen on map 17a (left) by Battista Agnese, c. 1541. On the detail, 17b (above), a circular archipelago (perhaps reminiscent of that feature on the Paris Map) is labeled "y. de fernãdo cortese." (Discussion on pages 118, 232, 240, 305.) This concept was the source of the name "the Californias" persisting into the eighteenth century. The map also illustrates the concept of the Sea of Verrazzano. Verrazzano's route, depicted by a dotted line, is shown penetrating the east coast straight into the South Sea! (Discussion on pages 135, 185.) Magellan's route is also shown. *Photograph and permission by Kungliga Biblioteket: the Royal Library—National Library of Sweden, Stockholm.*

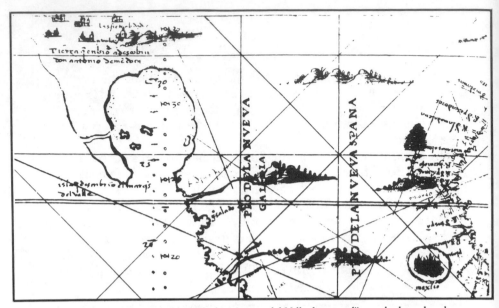

PLATE 18. The "island which the Marques del Valle discovered" says the legend at the southern tip of an islanded Baja California. The map is from an official *islario* by Alonso de Santa Cruz, dated 1542. (Discussion on pages 115, 117.) *See D. Antonio Blazquez,* Islario General de Todas Las Islas del Mondo por Alonso de Santa Cruz *(Madrid, 1918). Photograph from a facsimile, by the Library of Congress.*

Royal Library, Stockholm (*see* Plate 17). This map by Battista Agnese, was probably done in 1541–2, earlier than the two above. It depicts a *group* of islands in the vicinity of the present-day Baja. They are labeled: "y. de Fernando Cortes," island(s) of Fernando Cortés. This notion of a group of islands conforms more closely with the text of the *Islario* than Santa Cruz' own illustration. From this we understand why in subsequent accounts reference was so often made to "las Californias."

Maps of a few years later begin to show some ambivalence or uncertainty about Baja's configuration. Such a map, dated circa 1545, by an unidentified cartographer, is in the National Library of Austria, Vienna (Plate 20b). Another example is a map dated 1554 by Lopo Homem in the Instituto e Museo di Storia della Scienza, Florence (Plate 20a).

One more indicator of Cortés' island belief is found in what the new discovery was called. This will be demonstrated at length in the next chapter when the link is traced to the age-old tradition of mythic island destinations and to the medieval spirit of *romanticismo insulare,* the romance of islands.

By the time many of these references and maps were made, Cortés had gone back to Spain, never to return. This lag suggests that his island concept had taken firm root in the collective imagination. Indeed, it would stubbornly resist all efforts to eradicate it totally for the next two hundred years.

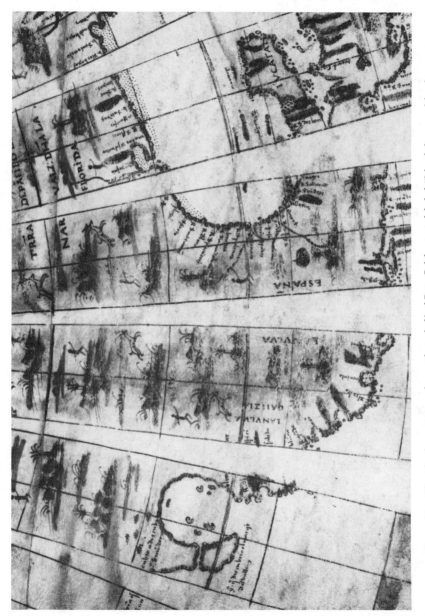

PLATE 19. The island comprising the southern half of Baja California is labeled "Island discovered by the Marques del Valle" on this portion of a gored map attributed to Alonso de Santa Cruz, dated 1542. Above the circular head of the Gulf with symbols of the seven cities occurs the legend: "Land which Don Antonio de Mendoza sent to be discovered." (Discussion on pages 117, 141, 155, 305.) *Photograph and permission by Kungliga Biblioteket: the Royal Library—National Library of Sweden, Stockholm.*

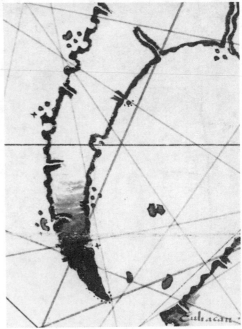

PLATE 20.   Two expressions of uncertainty about Baja's topography are seen in: (a) Lopo Homem's planisphere of 1554. *Photograph and permission by the Instituto e Museo di Storia della Scienza, Firenze (Florence).* (b) An anonymous planisphere, 1545. *Photograph and permission by Österreichische Nationalbibliothek, Wien—the National Library of Austria, Vienna.* (Discussion on page 118.)

Chapter X

THE NAMING OF CALIFORNIA
REFLECTS THE ISLAND MYTH

The very name "California" suggests that Baja was thought to be an island at the time of its discovery. But the facts of the naming process need to be established before the derivation is discussed.

No clear account has come down to us about how the name was chosen, where, when, or by whom. All we have to date are tantalizing scraps of information. Some of these are unreliable since the manuscripts may have been amended after they were written. Another problem is that accounts recorded long after the events took place could have been distorted by material generated in the interim, between happening and recollection.

What *do* we know about the christening process of Ximénes' discovery? Díaz associated the name with Cortés. But since Díaz wrote thirty years after it all happened, we must read him warily. In a puzzling passage, Díaz says Cortés left the suffering colonists in Santa Cruz, "went to discover other lands, and then struck up with California."[1] With the construction we now place upon the name, this sounds as if he sailed from his island to another place. But it is more likely that on Baja he sent scouts out to explore the hinterland, and so discovered the southern limits of his "island." From other evidence unfolded below, it may be that the name was applied first to the southernmost point, or to no more than the surrounding regions of the southwest "corner."

The naming has also been attributed to the voyage of Ulloa of 1539 (to be discussed in Chapter XI). Ramusio's version of that exploration of the Gulf contains three mentions of "California." Twice the reference is to "Isola California;" the third reference seems to designate the southern point of Baja. Ramusio's translation into Italian was made from a journal by Francisco Preciado, who was on the second ship of the expedition. Preciado's original is now lost. We therefore have no way to assure ourselves that the name was used on the voyage, or at least penned by Preciado. H. R. Wagner and Alvaro del Portillo believe the name was interpolated by Ramusio.[2] The account was published in the third volume of the *Navigationi et Viaggi* of 1556. An account by Ulloa, which came to light only in the twentieth century, does not carry the name.

The Bolaños expedition is often said to have first used the name. This took place, according to Wagner, "sometime subsequent to the year 1540." In describing a map of 1545 bearing the name P. de California, Amando Zugarte Cortesão dismisses this association as an inference "based on mere supposition." Mention of the name occurs in the testimony of Juan Fernández de Ladrillero about the Bolaños voyage (page 157). But that testimony was given in 1574. The same caution must apply to Ladrillero as to Díaz about placing reliance on statements made long after the facts.[3]

The name California appears on Domingo del Castillo's map of 1541. It is spread across the bottom half of Baja (*see* Plate 21). Both the extended area and a difference in script raise questions of the name having been added. This could have happened when Francisco Antonio Lorenzana had the original copied in the eighteenth century—the only version we now have.

The name also appears in the narrative of an expedition led by Juan Rodriguez Cabrillo with the pilot Ferrelo in 1542. But again this provides us with no certain information about the naming. We do not know for sure how soon after the expedition the narrative was written, and the logs that might tell us more have disappeared.

The Cabrillo narrative confirms that the name was first applied to the tip of Baja. But the following quotations raise questions of the exact designation. It is not clear whether *Punta de la California* means "Point California" localized to the headland, or whether it is a point of land at the end of a wider area called "California."

> Sunday, July 2, had sight of California, having been delayed in crossing almost four days on account of the winds which were not very favorable. On Monday, the 3d, they cast anchor at the Punta de la California . . .
>
> . . . They went sailing on the same course along the coast up to 28 degrees, where they anchored under the shelter of a point where there are some trees, the first seen since leaving the Punta de la California . . .
>
> In 33 degrees . . . all the country from California here has beaches of sand.[4]

Shortly following this date, several maps designated a "Punta de California," including Antonio Pereira's map discussed by Cortesão.

The earliest and most reliable mention of an *Isla de California* seems to be that made by Friar de Meno quoted on page 111 and reproduced in facsimile as Plate 16. Wagner comments on this:

His evidence was given in March 1541, and this seems to be the earliest contemporary record of the use of the name.[5]

Meno's mention occurs in sworn testimony in a suit brought by Castellon against Cortés for breach of contract of 1538. It therefore refers to the Ulloa expedition of 1539 (to be discussed in the next chapter). So whether Cortés used the name himself or not, it is tied clearly enough to his activities of 1535 to 1539.

But how does the name support the claim that Baja was perceived as an island? To answer this we must find out where the odd name came from, and why it was given to the land of Baja. Here again, no ready-made answers have come down to us. It is still true, as Wagner stated in Volume I, Number 1 of the *California Historical Society Quarterly*: "Almost everything connected with" the discovery of California is "a matter of conjecture."[6]

The fact that California is not a saint's name, or otherwise connected with the religious calendar, makes it, in Carlos Pereyra's words, a "*merla blanca*," a white crow among Spanish names, hence especially curious and mysterious.[7] To find explanations for its choice we must trace a scholarly exploration every bit as interesting in its own way as the story of the exploration of California itself.

Early diarists and historians strained to understand the reasoning behind the selection of the name. They attempted to derive it from Indian words or Latin roots. But these games of speculative etymology didn't produce any theories that sounded convincing.

Then one day a scholar made an interesting connection of two stray facts in his vast store of information. The connection attracted various other scholars, and a fascinating chain of imaginative inference began. This led to a deduction that was so plausible and compelling that it has never been challenged since.

In the middle of the nineteenth century, Harvard Professor George Ticknor discussed in his *History of Spanish Literature* (1849) a Spanish romance of the fifteenth century called the *Amadís de Gaula*. The first four books are a translation by Garcia Ordoñez de Montalvo of an older Portuguese romance. In a fifth book, Montalvo added his own sequel called *Las Sergas del muy esforzado caballero Esplandian, hijo del excelente rey Amadís de Gaula*—"The exploits of the very powerful cavalier Esplandian, son of the excellent king Amadís of Gaul." The total work is a fanciful rehash of the struggle between Christians and Moslems during the Crusades.

George Ticknor thought the sequel inferior to the *Amadís*, a view originating with Cervantes in *Don Quixote*. The curate and the barber toss the *Esplandian* in the bonfire, while keeping the *Amadís* in Don Quixote's library. In the course of his adverse critique, Ticknor deplored the license Montalvo had taken with "real history and geography":

> All reference to real history or real geography was apparently thought inappropriate, as may be inferred from the circumstances that a certain Calafria [sic], queen of the island of California, is made a formidable enemy of Christendom through a large part of the story.[8]

Ticknor got his dates confused. He himself notes that (in his day) "the oldest edition of the Esplandian now known to exist was printed in 1521." In thinking that the land in the romance was named after the west coast territory, he forgot that Baja California wasn't even discovered by Europeans until 1533.

It was not until 1862 that the nature of the link Ticknor had perceived between fact and fiction was accurately stated. The connection, as Edward Everett Hale was the first to see, had to be the other way around—the actual land was named after the fantasy:

> In the winter of 1862, I read for the first time the Spanish romance of the "Sergas of Esplandian" . . . I saw at once that here was the origin of the name of the State of California . . . At the next meeting of the American Antiquarian Society, I called their attention to this derivation of the name . . . The romance of "Esplandian" is now so rare that I translated for the Atlantic Monthly [March, 1864] all parts which relate to the Queen of California, and I now republish them.[9]

Although the evidence is circumstantial, we feel as certain of Hale's view as if we had come across a sworn statement of the source in the Spanish archives. Now that the earliest edition is known to have preceded Balboa's discovery of the Second Sea, the flash of recognition is all the stronger when we read the relevant excerpts.[10] (The translation is literal to capture the clumsiness of Montalvo's style.) The story is at a point where the infidel Sultan, embattled by Esplandian, receives support from unexpected quarters:

> Now I want you to know the strangest thing that could ever be found in literature, or in any case in the memory of people, where the city was at

the point of being lost, and how from there where the danger came, came its salvation. Know that to the right hand of the Indies was an island called California, very near to the region of the Terrestrial Paradise, which was populated by black women, without there being any men among them, that almost like the Amazons was their style of living. These were of vigorous bodies and strong and ardent hearts and of great strength; the island itself the strongest in steep rocks and great boulders that is found in the world; their arms were all of gold, and also the harnesses of the wild beasts, on which, after having tamed them, they rode; that in all the island there was no other metal whatsoever. They dwelt in caves very well hewn; they had many ships in which they went out to other parts to make their forays, and the men they seized they took with them, giving them their deaths, as you will further hear. And sometimes when they had peace with their adversaries, they intermixed with all security one with another, and there were carnal unions from which many of them came out pregnant, and if they gave birth to a female they kept her, and if they gave birth to a male, then he was killed . . .

On this island, called California, there are many griffons . . . and in the time that they had young these women would . . . take them to their caves, and there raise them. And . . . they fattened them on those men and the boys that they had borne . . .

Any male that entered the island was killed and eaten by them . . .

There ruled on that island of California, a queen great of body, very beautiful for her race, at a flourishing age, desirous in her thoughts of achieving great things, valiant in strength, cunning in her brave heart, more than any other who had ruled that kingdom before her . . . Queen Calafia.[11]

This amazing recycling of the ancient, oft-repeated myth contains the obligatory four elements: (a) the realm of exotic, free-loving, though formidable women is (b) near the most delectable place on earth, the Terrestrial Paradise, but (c) the place is hard to penetrate by virtue of being a remote, rockbound island, guarded by vicious creatures, though (d) its vast wealth (coupled with the women's sexual favors) would make the ordeals and trials involved in invading it worthwhile.

Romance writers felt even freer than oriental travel writers to give their imaginations rope. Montalvo has reworked elements of the traditional Amazon stories and other fabulous tales from various versions. He has also integrated yarns brought back from the New World by the turn of the century when he wrote his sequel. His Amazons do not belong to the Christian or Caucasian world. They are Saracen or

Moorish, as called for by his fiction, since they go to the aid of the embattled Sultan in the strife between Mohammedans and Christians.

Montalvo may have taken his lead from an implication in a version of Prester John's Letter circulating around 1500: "Do not think that it [the Great Feminie] is in the land of the Saracens, for the one we are talking about is in our country."[12] Montalvo could have drawn on non-Caucasian accounts like the Tartar Amazons in Johann Schiltberger's Reisebuch printed in 1440.[13] Those Mongol female warriors were giants led by a vindictive princess resembling Montalvo's "queen of great body," Calafia.

In describing his California Amazons as "mujeres negras" Montalvo was following the color prejudices of the period. In his time, and in some places still, black describes any complexion other than white, including the coloring of dark Caucasian. Mandeville describes a tribe neighboring his Amazons as "black enough and more than black . . . and they be clept Moors."[14] The Moors who invaded medieval Spain were of mixed Arab and Berber descent, spreading from the Middle East along the North African coast.

When the explorers met the inhabitants of what they believed was "Ind," they lumped them automatically into the dark-skinned category of their crude "we/they" classification. Attitudes from the New World, the Crusades, and the invasion of the Moors were fused in Montalvo's Californian Amazons.

Montalvo's placement of his Amazons in "well-hewn caves" also comes both from classical accounts and the explorers' tales. Columbus's Amazons on Matinino were said to take refuge in subterranean caverns (page 46).

The griffins of Montalvo's island of California are also a mixture of old and new fable. Griffins were related to the fabulous birds of Arabia, as in Sinbad the Sailor. Prester John's Letter tells of "birds called griffins who can easily carry an ox or a horse into their nest to feed their young." He himself claims to have been carried across the uncrossable Sandy Sea by them, just as Alexander had been carried to the enchanted castle.[15] Griffins are found in Polo's and Mandeville's accounts on neighboring islands to the Amazons, and are described on neighboring pages.[16] But stories of griffins were also coming back from the New World. According to Ferdinand Columbus's account of the fourth voyage of Columbus, there were people living in trees between Veragua and Puerto Bello. They did so "out of fear of the griffins that are in that country."[17] During Cortés' campaign in Mexico, claims were made of griffins in high sierras four or five leagues from the village of Tehuacan. The population of the neighboring valley was said to flee in terror of being eaten by these creatures.[18] The great condors must have flourished in substantial numbers in the Andes and mountains of Central America when the explorers first came to the New World. They were understandably identified as griffins.

In the traditional literature Amazonia was often an island very hard to get to, as already discussed. Or it was a remote wilderness on the edge of the known world. Montalvo's island is the strongest, most rock-bound island on earth. It is as forbidding as Columbus's island, which, according to Peter Martyr, is unapproachable because of the north wind (see page 46).

Montalvo's Amazons retain their most appealing attribute—their abundant wealth. Their armor is of gold, the only metal they possess. Their island, moreover, is "very near to the Terrestrial Paradise." As mentioned previously, the four rivers that flowed from there were laden with precious gems. Prester John's "Great Feminie" was girdled by such a treasure-laden river flowing from paradise.

The warlikeness of Montalvo's Moorish Amazons seems far more sinister than the tradition. Their steeds, the griffins, were fattened on the men seized on their forays. No man was allowed inside their island fortress on pain of death. Their carnal unions took place only in the countries of the adversaries during temporary truces. Male offspring were killed and fed to the griffins—none of that civilized courtly nonsense found in Santisteban's *Dom Pedro* (see page 41). The Christian conception of the Infidel, the Spanish conception of the marauding Moors, and stories of New-World cannibals, seem to merge in Queen Calafia's ladies.

What grounds are there for believing that Cortés and his company named that offshore territory at the farthest reaches of New Spain after the imaginary island of Montalvo's Amazons? The mere coincidence of such a strange name appearing in two diverse contexts and nowhere else is highly persuasive of a link. If it could be shown that the Spanish explorers were acquainted with the romance literature, the case for the connection would be compelling.

Early in the twentieth century, the scholarship of George Davidson and Ruth Putnam showed that the romances enjoyed a great vogue in Europe at the end of the fifteenth and beginning of the sixteenth centuries.[19] The recently-invented printing press afforded wide circulation of these popular entertainments to an eager audience—a phenomenon equal only to the emergence of film and television in the twentieth century. These romances were recyclings and weavings of all the most wondrous, marvelous, gory, dramatic, extravagant and hair-raising bits of myth and history the authors could lay hands on. There was a lot of borrowing, translating, expanding and rehashing of older works, including the eastering travel literature.

Voluminous "good reads," these rambling romances were just the thing for long boring voyages across the wide oceans that were being explored. Magellan, for example, presumably had a recent best-seller in his cabin, *Primaleon of Greece* (Castile, 1512), for he named the land through which his southwest straits meandered after the monster, the Grand Patagon, captured by the hero Primaleon, and transported to the homeland as a curiosity.[20] Nature imitating art, Magellan captured a "giant" of his own, intending to take him back to Spain, but the poor creature died on board.

In Bernal Díaz' work there are references to the *Amadís de Gaula,* as when he tells of first seeing the native towns: "We were amazed, and said it was like the enchantments they tell of in the legend of Amadís."[21] So in considering the naming of California—on an expedition at which Díaz was present—we do not have to stretch too far to imagine Cortés or his soldiers making the new *descubrimiento* the namesake of Montalvo's mythic island. After all, Cortés had been seeking Amazonia for many years. He so much wanted this island to be it.

These scraps of evidence become stronger when we learn that in 1510 Jacob Cromberger of Sevilla published a large edition of *Las Sergas de Esplandian,* to which he had obtained the rights for its sale in the Americas.[22] Irving A. Leonard has assembled evidence to show that the House of Cromberger, with large inventories of romances, continued to supply the colonial market until Juan Cromberger, the son, contracted to set up a printing press in Mexico City in 1539. He received from the Viceroy of New Spain an exclusive privilege for the sale of books there.[23] This date of 1539 is significant as the year in which Cortés launched his last expedition to "sail around" California.

In choosing an obviously fictional name, the naming process may have involved imaginative analogy as much as naive literalism. Bancroft strongly suspected that "the name was applied in derision" by the disgusted colonists.[24] Ruth Putnam also suggested that the historic christening was no more than a humorous, ironic comment on the gap between reality and dream—between the poor, hostile offshore land, and Montalvo's newest version of Amazonia.[25] If the name was given, as Díaz states, during the horror of the Santa Cruz experiment, this view could hold water.

But the Californian historian Charles E. Chapman reminds us that:

> The name was applied before the Spaniards had any clear knowledge of the country, and thus represented their beliefs and hopes rather than disappointment . . .[26]

And Nellie Van de Grift Sánchez contends that the name was given "rather in hopeful anticipation, almost in a spirit of prophecy of the riches and wonders to be found there." For as she points out, the conquistadores "were not looking for green trees and babbling brooks, but for the yellow gold, and none knew better than they that the precious metal was more often found in such bare, desolate land."[27]

This echoes an opinion in a work printed in 1540 called *Pyrotechnia*. There, the author Vannuccio Biringuccio describes how gold is produced in nature:

> You shall understand that it is engendered in divers kinds of stones in great and rough mountains, and such as are utterly bare of earth, trees, grass, or herbs.[28]

He advises the explorers to start looking for it in the worst terrain:

> You shall see the aspect of such mountains to be rough, sharp, and wild, without earth or trees. Or so that if there be a little earth found upon the same with a small vein of herbs or grass, you shall preceive the greenness thereof to be faint and in manner withered and dried.

The belief that gold could grow only under the hottest sun would surely have made desert islands in the Torrid Zone appealing.

Given our knowledge of Cortés' obsession, and his desperate need of an island territory to call his own, it is reasonable to conclude that he thought himself on the threshold of his grand and ultimate ideal. The last of the series of setbacks he had suffered might well have been viewed as the obligatory ordeal demanded of the questor of a long-desired goal. An unwelcoming threshold, consistent with the hostile, rockbound island of Amazon stories, could even have enhanced his hopes. Any sense of irony would have come only after repeated disappointment had finally punctured those grandiose dreams, after Cortés returned to Spain.

If the name California stood for dreams, it must also have been imbued with dread—perhaps contributing to the delay in California's development. Associations with Montalvo's sinister viragoes may have deepened the torments of the barren country and its reputed cannibalistic native inhabitants. Paradoxically, the dream itself (its negative components) could have hampered its realization.

Once it was agreed that California was called after the name of Montalvo's Amazon realm, scholars wondered where he got it. George Davidson offered the far-fetched theory that the name Calafia for the Queen, and the name California, were concocted from *Kalli*, the Greek root for beauty.[29] Hale, however, had been on a more reasonable track when he made his historic connection:

> In ascribing to the *Esplandian* the origin of the name *California*, I know that I furnish no etymology for that word. I have not found the word in any earlier romances. I will only suggest that the root *Calif*, the Spanish spelling for the sovereign of the Mussulman power of the time, was in the mind of the author as he invented these Amazon allies of the Infidel power.[30]

Ruth Putnam returned to Hale's theory, and added more:

> Calafia is nothing more than a female caliph. What more natural appellation for a sovereign queen, an ally to the heathen Turk? From that, "California" was coined.
>
> There is, however, another possible explanation for the origin of the word "California" which transfers the responsibility of actual invention from the shoulders of Montalvo to that of the unknown author of *La Chanson de Roland*—the great epic of the eleventh century or earlier. When Charles the Great (Carles li reis) laments the death of his nephew Roland on the field of Roncevaux, he enumerates the foes who will attack him when they know that the valiant warrior is gone—the Saxons, Hungarians . . . those of Palerne and of Affrike and those of Califerne.[31]

The passage Putnam quotes is given here in the Oxford text and English translation by Gerard J. Brault, published in 1978:

> "Morz est mis niés, ki tant me fist cunquere.
> Encuntre mei revelerunt li Seisne
> E Hungre e Bugre e tante gent averse,
> Romain, Puillain e tuit icil de Palerne
> E cil d'Affrike e cil de Califerne.
>
> My nephew, through whom I conquered so much, is dead.
> The Saxons will rebel against me,
> The Hungarians, the Bulgars, and so many infidel peoples,
> The Romans, the Apulians, and all the men of Palermo,
> The Men of Africa and those of Califerne.[32]

Putnam then continues her argument:

> Editors either pass over the word in silence or say that it cannot be identified, although it is probably *the calif's domain* . . .

Here the conjecture is possible that Montalvo had this very country in mind, this calif's heathen land, while the different vowel in the word he actually introduced into his novel was either due to intention, to suit the requirements of the maiden queen's remote island, or to one of the chance misprints not unknown to the modern press. And then the changeling held its footing precariously until it climbed upon the map.

Chapman adds the following comment to this discussion:

There can be no question but that a learned man like Ordoñez de Montalvo was familiar with the *Chanson de Roland,* especially since it was cognate to the material that he himself employed. Certainly the cycle of tales about the knights of the round table at the court of King Arthur was very well known to Ordoñez and the other romancers, for the heroes of those stories appear frequently in the novels of chivalry. The appearance of "Califerne" in this list of peoples and lands, of which several were certainly not Christian, might well have caught Ordoñez's attention, when he himself was making a similar catalogue of the nations. "California" is a perfectly natural Spanish form for "Califerne," especially since "e" and "o" have not infrequently changed from one to the other in the history of Spanish words. This derivation of the word "California" can perhaps never be proved, but it is too plausible—and it may be added too interesting to be overlooked. Thus does the name "California" become linked with one of the greatest poems in history, and the date of its origin is placed four centuries earlier. One wonders, indeed, if there might not have been some long past Moslem realm so-called, at least by peoples of Europe, carrying the name far back to the great days of Bagdad and Damascus.[33]

Imaginative speculation is an important part of scholarly exploration. Many people have played with this possible link between Montalvo's name *California* and the other *Califerne* of romance, sometimes going overboard. One person suggested that the realm of Califerne derives from a Berber confederation in Algeria during the tenth and eleventh centuries, called Ifrene, in combination with the word *Kalaa,* meaning "stronghold." Another wondered if the name is compounded of the rivers Chalus and Ferne, forming the region of Aleppo in Syria. Still another suggestion is that Califerne is a corruption of the Persian Kar-i-farn, which in Iranian mythology is the "mountain of Paradise," where dwelt many griffins. This latter theory is the most interestingly plausible.[34]

Antecedents for the name of Queen Calafia have also been researched by scholars such as Donald C. Cutter for the light that might be thrown on the name California.[35] The white Amazon queen in the *Libro de Alexandre* (*see* page 40) bears the name Calectrix and Calestres in the two versions that are extant. Cutter argues that Montalvo may have rung the changes on this name for his Moorish queen. Cutter also wonders whether Montalvo had in mind a virago mentioned in the *Siete Partidas* in 1265. There, a ban on women serving as advocates is based on the alleged brazen conduct of one Calfurnia, with whom the judges could do nothing. In a still earlier German work this shrill advocate is called "Calefurnia." But it would be more likely, if it happened at all, that Montalvo would have drawn his inspiration directly from the shrew in the Alfonsine code of Hispanic law set down in the *Siete Partidas*. The prototype of Calefurnia, we are told, was a woman called Caja Afrania described in the writings of the Roman Valerius Maximus.

Whatever the source of "California," these fascinating exercises deepen the sense of the beautiful, the exotic, the mysterious, and the romantic, kindled by the name. California is thereby connected to the Moslem world, to the Middle East and Africa as well as to Rome, Greece and medieval Europe generally. By curious chance the reverberations and resonances fittingly symbolize the intercultural diversity which has characterized Californian society increasingly over the centuries. And for this great diversity of people California often represents the single, simple, common ideal of a dream island, epitomized in the name.

Chapter XI

ULLOA PROBES THE SEA OF CORTÉS FOR STRAITS

In the three or four years following the fiasco of Santa Cruz, Cortés didn't act like a man who was the least bit chastened by his negative experience. He was a man with a mission, and the myths taught that trials and ordeals prefigured success.

On his return to Oaxaca in 1537, he set about planning new expeditions to determine the extent of California, and whether it offered more hospitable stretches than the hinterland of Santa Cruz. He may also have wanted to check out talk of his "island" being joined to Guzmán's territory. From the Niza episode (see pages 113–14), we know he sought the mythical kingdoms of Cibola, Quivira and the Seven Cities, too.

As we have seen, Cortés contracted with Castellon for preparing an expedition up the *ancón* between the mainland and the "island." However, he finally chose Francisco de Ulloa—who had relieved him at Santa Cruz—to lead the exploration in 1539.

Díaz has very little of any consequence to say about the affair, except to state that its purpose was to "finish the circumnavigation of California":

> Within a few months, when Cortes was already somewhat rested, he despatched two other ships well supplied both with bread and meat, as well as other sailors and sixty soldiers and good pilots; and Francisco de Ulloa . . . went with them as captain . . . They sailed from the Port of Natividad in the month of June in the year fifteen hundred and thirty odd, (this matter of the years I do not remember), and Cortes ordered the Captain to follow along the coast and finish the circumnavigation of California, and endeavour to search for Captain Diego Hurtado, who never appeared again.
>
> Ulloa occupied seven months on the voyage in going and coming, and I know he did nothing worth recording. [1]

The voyage is too important in the history of California for us to dismiss it with equal casualness. It becomes a crucial episode in the unfolding of the island myth when rounded out with more information from the records. This requires us to return to some events that would seem, on their face, to have little relevance to the expedition.

We backtrack sixteen years to 1523, when the King of Spain wrote Cortés to be on the lookout for a strait somewhere to the north of New

Spain (*see* page 82). Now that Magellan had discovered the southern passage, the hunt was on for a northern one to correspond with it. Nations not yet in the swim of things were especially interested in finding it. From now on the story of exploration would involve action and reaction among several national competitors, becoming a tale of rumor and intrigue.

In the 1520s, the late-starting French and English were beginning to cast calculating eyes on the New World. While the Spaniards still favored variants of the Columbian model, the French and English grabbed onto Waldseemüller's more hospitable geography. Their thinking illuminates the dynamics of geographical mythmaking. French/ English need was for a configuration of shrunken land areas in the north, with plenty of open ocean and huge waterways connecting the Atlantic and Pacific. Only thus could Spain's adversaries hope to join the race for the fabulous isles of Ind. Theirs was a problem of means as well as ends, of routes as well as destinations. They clung to any theory that might reinforce the insularist vision portrayed on the various globes of the early Schöner school (*see* the Paris Green globe, Plate 7). They needed to believe that the Fourth Part of the world could not possibly be continental in the sense of being joined to the other three joined parts or continents.

For the Spaniards, on the other hand, it suited them to rest on some variation of the Columbian model. Cortés and company were standing right there on the west coast of Mexico, their full attention fixed on the riches of the South Sea. It gave a feeling of great security to know that Asia and their new mainland discoveries were somehow of a piece. This wishful thinking allowed them to believe that the South Sea was blocked by land to the north, rendering their sphere impenetrable from that direction by the French or British (*see* the Paris Gilt globe, Plate 14). So when rumors of secret plans to find a northern passage were passed along by the Spanish Court, Cortés showed only a perfunctory interest in response.

In general, the rumors were about the talk in France and England concerning further exploration for a strait leading west from the Bacallaos (variously spelled). This area of the northwestern Atlantic had been probed for England by John and Sebastian Cabot shortly after Columbus's discoveries. The name described the teeming fish there, hence the English name "the Codfish Sea."

More precise plans were being laid in France, as may be judged by events of 1524. Giovanni da Verrazzano set sail under French colors "to reach Cataia and the extreme eastern coast of Asia." He expected that the new land "would not lack a strait to penetrate to the Eastern Ocean." Instead, Verrazzano ended up exploring a good deal of the eastern coast of North America.

The bit that interests us about Verrazzano's voyage is his "deduction" about the coast south of Cape Hatteras. In his view, the long spit of land that encloses the body of water of Pamlico and Albemarle Sound was an isthmus separating the Atlantic Ocean from the Pacific. This is offhandedly annotated in the margin of the only contemporary surviving manuscript, dubbed the Cèllere Codex, now in the Pierpont Morgan Library, New York:

> We called it "Annunciata" from the day of arrival, and found there an isthmus one mile wide about two hundred miles long, in which we could see the eastern sea from the ship . . . This is doubtless the one which goes around the tip of India, China, and Cathay. We sailed along this isthmus hoping all the time to find some strait . . . or real promontory where the land might end to the north, and we would reach those blessed shores of Cathay.[2]

The map on Plate 17 depicts the "route" of Verrazzano as though he had accomplished what he claimed and hoped. The dotted line passes right through the line of the east coast into a huge sea. Similarly, Münster's map (Plate 31b) shows a sea dipping far southward from northern waters into the heart of the continent. In the following decades this imaginary concept would produce all kinds of distortions in the overall image of North America, as mapmakers attempted to make sense of it. It would also sidetrack and confuse explorers. In 1534, Jacques Cartier set out to explore "the backside of Newfoundland . . . to seek out the passage . . . into the Eastern Indian Sea, otherwise called the Passage to Cathay." He found instead the mouth of the St. Lawrence. Yet on his map he continued to depict the Verrazzano Sea, even providing a convenient entry to it through the isthmus above Florida.[3]

The concept would prove particularly attractive to the English. "Insularists" jumped at anything that offered a lot of water and breached the wall of the New World. The figment would have its strongest influence on English geographers later in the century (*see* Chapter XIX), and would loom large in the thinking of the doomed colonists of Roanoke, Virginia.

Cortés, on the other hand, if he heard about the Verrazzano Sea in 1524, would not have been too much concerned about such a curious hypothesis—though he would have shared his King's vexation that a

Catholic country would dare flout the Pope's allocation of the world to Spain and Portugal. He would also have understood the King's alarm that a northern strait might indeed exist. Since Magellan's ordeal, straits tended to be viewed as hidden phenomena, as secrets difficult to ferret out. But it would have taken much more of a scare than this to deflect Cortés from his primary purpose: the discovery and conquest of islands of the South Sea. It may, indeed, have added to its urgency.

Nevertheless, he must respond obediently to his sovereign's commands if he was to win the favors he asked in his Memorial of 1522 (*see* pages 81 ff). In 1524, in his Fourth Letter, he promises to search "toward the North as far as the Bacallaos:"

> For it is believed absolutely that there is a strait on that coast which leads to the South Sea . . . And should it please God, our Lord, that the said strait be found there, it would open a good and short passage from the spiceries to the dominions of Your Majesty, quite two-thirds shorter than that which is at present followed.[4]

But Cortés planned more than this east coast exploration. Thinking, no doubt, to kill two birds with one stone—seek his islands and the strait at the same time—he offered to send ships up the South-Sea coast, "in search of the same strait:"

> For if it exists it cannot escape those who go by the South Sea and those who go by the North [Sea] . . . Thus on one side or the other we cannot fail to discover the secret.

We must bear in mind, however, that at that early date Cortés would not have imaged anything like a northern North Pacific Ocean in offering this plan. Under the Columbian model, any outlet of a strait into the South Sea would have been envisaged as only a few hundred leagues north of the Mexican territory conquered to that date. In fact, his notion of a "northern" strait seems to have been of something joining the Gulf of Mexico to the South Sea. He sent Cristoval de Olid out from Veracruz in 1524 to search for it from the North Sea side.

But our main interest is in Cortés' execution of his promise on the side of the South Sea. In his letter to the King of September 2, 1526, he reports this probe up the west coast:

> I despatched a captain to the town of Coliman, which is on the South Sea . . . ordering him to follow the coast, for a hundred and fifty or two hundred leagues, for the whole purpose of learning all about it, and of discovering if there were any ports. He executed my order, penetrating

one hundred and thirty leagues inland, and bringing me an account of many ports he had found on the coast . . . His account also described a very large river, which the natives told him was ten days' march from its source, and about which, and the people inhabiting its banks, they told me many strange things. I am about to send him again with a larger force and better equipment, so that he may explore the secrets of that river, which, judging from the size and importance the natives attribute to it, I would not be surprised if it turned out to be a strait.[5]

Pagden translates this significant fragment: "To explore that river, which, to judge by the reports of its width and great size, will most probably turn out to be a strait."

What we are reading about here is probably the first European contact with the delta of the Colorado River. But the prospect of its being a strait is the operative factor for our story at this time. Though Cortés may only have tossed in the comment to placate the King, it would become an important element in the Island-of-California myth.

Nobody could really mix up a river with a strait—at least, not in real experience if one got close enough. The two waterways are such distinct phenomena, even to think of confusing them is absurd. Yet in that period the river-strait alternative was a characteristic expression of wishful thinking indulged by frustrated seekers of the elusive northern waterway between the Atlantic and Pacific. If you couldn't find a strait, you had to hope you could find two rivers easily linked by portage. On the map they could be made to look awfully much like the continuous waterway you longed to sail.[6] At worst, a continent-spanning network of rivers, even when innavigable, would provide life-supporting leading-strings across deserts and wilderness. But such realistic attitudes were still some distance in the future.

The trompe-l'œil of wishful thinking informs the Sloane Manuscript map (see Plate 12). Great rivers are shown discharging into the oceans both to east and west. Their headwaters almost "join" in the middle of the continent. The myths themselves encouraged the confusion: the river flowing from Paradise, for example, girdled Prester John's Great Feminie like a sea.

When Cortés wrote the King in 1526 about the river-that-might-turn-out-to-be-a-strait, he might have had a map, at least in his mind's eye, featuring something like the river-strait concept as we see it in the Sloane manuscript.

By 1529–30, news of the huge water prompted Nuño de Guzmán to set out in quest of it. Not news of the river alone, but its access to the fabulous Seven Cities, rich in gold and silver, is what had pricked his greedy ears. The narrator of the Second Relation of his journey states:

> The order that we carried when we went to discover this river was the Seven Cities, because the governor Nuño de Guzmán had news of it, and of a river that went out into the Sea of the South, and that was four or five leagues in width, and the indians had a chain of iron which crossed the river to hold back the canoes and balsa rafts. . .[7]

But to get back on the track where this chapter began, we leave the flashback and come forward again to the year 1539. What has all that background to do with Cortés sending Ulloa and Castellon to explore the Sea of Cortés and "sail around" California?

Since he wrote that letter in 1526 about a river-that-might-turn-out-to-be-a-strait, Cortés had found and failed to settle his new discovery at Santa Cruz. In 1539 he might have reasoned that such a waterway might run between his "island" and the mainland before heading off across the continent toward the Bacallaos or Florida. Perhaps it had branches forking to both the North and South Seas—the Atlantic and Pacific. And surely such a strait must take them to the golden cities about which he had told Niza (see page 114). Cortés insisted that they rightfully belonged to him—he having been the first to hear about them from the Indians.

Niza's betrayal, and Mendoza's move to usurp Cortés' powers as Captain of the South Sea, made the investigation of the strait an urgent matter.

We turn now to the narratives of the voyage to determine what was discovered at the nook of the Gulf of California, as we now call it. Ulloa's own narrative was found in the Archivo General de Indias only in the twentieth century. In the preceding centuries the only known narrative was that made by Francisco Preciado—and then only in its Italian translation by Ramusio, or the Englished version of Ramusio published by Hakluyt. The original is lost.

Ulloa has very little to say about what he found at the head of the Gulf. It is as though he was being deliberately reticent. In Wagner's translation, part of Preciado's account is inserted to supplement the deficiency. Perhaps Ulloa was reluctant to spell out in detail information that he thought his Marquis would not want to hear about his findings at the crotch:

> We commenced to find the water white, like river water, and as we sailed

through this water, we saw land to the southwest, eight or nine leagues from us. Thinking that it was an island, we went to it to see it . . . The nearer we came to it, the less depth we got, to such extent that we found ourselves in four or five fathoms, and the sea all reddish and turned to mud. Because the water was shallow where we were, and the water turbid, we anchored, to find a way to draw nearer that land. We did not find it, nor could we get nearer than we were, which was more than two leagues away. Therefore, this same day, it being then late, we turned back to the mainland, to see if between it and this other land we might find deep water, in order to continue on.

We found a channel two leagues from the mainland, eight fathoms deep, into which its two tides flooded every twenty-four hours, in their order, flood and ebb, without falling off a jot, and with a flood and an ebb current so strong it was marvellous. When the tide ran out it left dry, and when it flooded it covered, more than two leagues . . .

The next day, Monday, September 28 . . . it being low tide, we saw the whole sea where we must pass, between one land and the other, closed with shoals . . . and . . . saw . . . many summits of mountains . . . Since, for these reasons, we could not go ahead, I landed on a sand bar nearby, and took possession for your lordship.[8]

The undesirability of this report from Cortés' point of view may explain why Díaz dismissed it as of little worth. Although Ulloa was careful to confine himself to facts, he did appear to be telegraphing negative findings to the Marquis, as this further excerpt from the narrative suggests:

Seeing that these people and those whom we had seen previously were all of one kind, and that this land and the Bahia de Santa Cruz were also all one, to judge by the appearance of the people and the trend of the land and its appearance, and finding ourselves so near it and thinking it likely that between it and where we were there could not be anything of any more account, we stood away from there on a southward course, running in and out, as the contour of the coast required.

We weighed from Pasaje de Belen on October 13, and arrived at the Puerto y Bahia de Santa Cruz on the 19th.

As it turned out, Ulloa did not have to face the music. He sent his narrative home with his second ship while he continued his quest on the outside coast. His return is wrapped in obscurity.[9] But it didn't matter. By 1540, Cortés had left for Spain to argue his grievances against Mendoza. He was never to return to the New World.

Francisco Preciado, on the other hand, was in the second ship that was sent back early to home port. Whether or not this had anything to do with it, Preciado's account was a good deal fuller on the crucial question. More to the point, it was written in such a way as to leave the theory of a strait and island unresolved. It is of great interest to this study that Preciado's account was the one that got circulated and translated, first by Ramusio, then by Hakluyt. Indeed, the English version of it may have helped nurture the Isle-of-California myth to a second flowering, as we shall see in Chapter XX.

Preciado's narrative reveals the crew's interest in the possibility of a strait extending north from the nook of the Sea of Cortés. In the following quotations, Preciado reports that the men debated the nature of the land that lay to westward as they sailed northward up the Gulf. This was the land where many of them had taken part in the Marquis's aborted settlement of Santa Cruz. The crew wonders whether the huge water of the "Sea of Cortés" was the main ocean with some kind of exit to the north. The divided issue is expressed in such alternative terms as "island" versus "firm land" or "mainland;" "strait/outlet" versus "river/ mouth;" and "sea" or "arm of the sea" versus "bay" or "gulf". Such a discussion of alternatives implies that determination of this question was indeed a purpose of the mission.

As the expedition got under way, the debate commenced:

> We began to be of divers opinions, some thinking that this coast of Santa Cruz was a firm land, and that it joined with the continent of Nueva Espanna, others thought the contrary, and that they were nothing else but islands, which were to the westward. And in this sort we proceeded forward having the land on both sides of us, so far, that we all began to wonder at it . . .[10]

Hakluyt highlights this section with an annotation in the margin: "Some take the land of California to be nothing but Islands."

Still traveling toward the northwest, they "saw another land which stretched Northwest, and was full of high mountains," straight ahead. This was possibly the first glimpse of land lying within the present boundaries of the State of California.

Soon the expedition approached the nook:

> And still continuing this course we searched very diligently to see if there were any passage through between both the lands, for right forward we saw no land. And thus sailing we always found more shallow water, and the Sea thick, black, and very muddy, and came at length into five fathom water . . . and we perceived the Sea to run with so great a rage into the land, that it was a thing much to be marveled at, and with the like fury it returned back again with the ebb . . .

With the wisdom of hindsight, we know that the force they encoun-tered was the tidal bore: the force of ocean waters meeting the waters of the Colorado River pouring from its delta into the Gulf.

Although the narrative sticks closely to unfolding fact, we feel preconception pressing to be recognized and proven true. The narrative continues:

> The day following the captain and the pilot went up to the ship's top, and saw all the land full of sand in a great round compass, and joining itself with the other shore, and it was so low, that whereas we were a league from the same we could not well discern it, and it seemed that there was an inlet of the mouths of certain lakes, whereby the sea went in and out. There was divers opinions amongst us, and some thought that the current entered into those lakes, and also that some great river there might be the cause thereof . . . And when we could perceive no passage through . . . the captain went . . . to take possession thereof. The same day with the ebb of the sea we fell down from the other coast from the side of Nueva Espanna, though always we had in sight the firm land one side of us, and the other islands on our left hand on the side of the port of Santa Cruz situate on the western shore.

The conclusions to be drawn from this experience clearly brought anxiety to some members of the crew. Perhaps they feared the effects their failure might have upon the Marquis, as suggested here:

> Here from this day forward we began to be afraid, considering that we were to return to the port of Santa Cruz; for it was supposed, that all along this mighty gulf from the entrance in at Culiacan until the returning back unto the said haven, was all firm land, and also because we had the firm land always on our right hand and it goeth round circle-wise unto the said haven; but many thought and hoped that we should find some mouth or outlet, whereby we might pass through unto the other coast. What our success was we will declare in the relation following.

The statement "many thought and hoped" is a revealing glimpse of the power of island-dreaming in the imaginations of the mariners—and perhaps the fear of disappointing Cortés' hopes. Incidentally, the term "circle-wise" no doubt explains the gulf's shape on such maps as those of Plates 18 & 19.

There was nothing else for it but to follow the coast south along the California side. Some of the crew were beset with a sense of failure as they "drew near to the port of Santa Cruz"—the present-day La Paz:

> Whereat we were sorry, because we were always in good hope to find some outlet into the main Ocean in some place of that land . . . and that we

had committed a great error, because we had not certainly sought out the secret, whether that were a Strait or river, which we had left behind us unsearched at the bottom of this great sea or gulf . . .

To find Preciado still teeter-tottering between the river/strait and sea/gulf alternatives after the expedition had been to the head of the gulf is of great interest in this study of ideas. That indecision contradicts claims that California's peninsularity was definitively established by the Ulloa voyage.

There are several reasons for this vacillation. In the first place the expedition was, apparently, not given carte blanche to discover what it would. Preconceptions were at stake; the mission had the delicate task of measuring dreams against reality. Smart men would dodge adverse conclusions like the plague.

Secondly, Magellan's experience warned against jumping too hastily to conclusions. To all seekers of straits he provided a model of patient persistence. His ships had had to weave perilously in and out of numerous channels for many days, never sure that they would make it through.

Thirdly, close inspection of the area beyond the shoals had not been possible with the crude sailing ships built on the west coast; and the primitive state of navigation in that period intensified the risks.

Finally, Preciado and others of the crew may have been among those who, for one reason or another, wanted to keep the dream alive. Because a strait hadn't yet been found, didn't mean there wasn't one. Not proving a theory isn't the same thing as disproving it. In the absence of negating evidence, the question remained open. Diehards could ignore even a strong presumption against a "Strait of California" until all the evidence was in.

This label, "Strait of California," is, incidentally, a useful shorthand term to describe the imaginary concept in the unfolding of events. It appears in Antonio de Herrera y Tordesillas' Index to his *Historia General de los Hechos de los Castellanos*, published in 1601. The term bears clear witness to the prevailing concept, even though Herrera skeptically qualified his "Estrecho de California" as "incierto" at the time he wrote.[11]

Once again, when the Ulloa expedition enters the haven of Santa Cruz, Preciado's account returns to the same niggling question. Regret is expressed that the head of the Gulf was presumed closed without the crew having made an adequate investigation:

We were come near unto the haven of Santa Cruz, which is all firm land except it be divided in the very nook by some strait or great river which parteth it from the main, which because we had not thoroughly discovered, all of us that were employed in this voyage were not a little grieved. And this main land stretcheth so far in length, that I cannot well express it; for from the haven of Alcapulco, which standeth in seventeen degrees and twenty minutes of latitude, we had always the coast of the firm land on our right hand [sailing north] until we came to the great current of the white and red sea; and here (as I have said) we knew not the secret of this current whether it was caused by a river or a strait: and so supposing that the coast which we had on our right hand [sailing west] was closed up without passage, we returned back again, always descending southward, until we returned to the said haven of Santa Cruz.[12]

Certain names given to the head of the Gulf may have some bearing on our tracing of the myth. Ulloa declares in his account:

This inlet and reddish sea are in 34 degrees. We named it the Ancon de San Andres and Mar Bermejo, because it is that color and we arrived there on Saint Andrew's Day.[13]

Wagner has pointed out that the application of the word *ancón* did not resolve the Gulf's topography once and for all:

The word *ancon* is usually translated as "bay" in the modern dictionaries, but in the sixteenth century it was not used as synonymous with bay, but rather meant a tidal channel connecting one body of water—the sea for example—with another.[14]

Nevertheless, the name "Mar Vermejo" used in conjunction with the word *ancón* would have been likely to settle the meaning in the sense of "bay." Ulloa gives a simple descriptive rationale for the choice of "Red Sea": the purported color of the water at the crotch of the Gulf. Yet can it be doubted that in the on-going debate, someone had surmised a likeness to the Red Sea between Africa and Arabia? Both "seas" would have seemed close enough in size, shape, and bearing to suggest a plausible parallel.

In support of this view are the manuscript maps of the world made by Battista Agnese in the 1540s, such as Plate 22. On these the Californian and Arabian gulfs (the Mar Vermejo and the Red Sea) are made to resemble each other. On medieval *mappae mundi* (like Plate 1), the Red Sea was traditionally painted vermillion. Agnese highlights the comparison by coloring both.

Such a derivation for the name crops up from time to time in later years. Cornelius Wytfliet, for example, wrote in 1597:

California is joined to Granata toward the west, being separated, the one from the other, only by an arm of the sea, which comes from the South, and enters into its lands more than two hundred Italian leagues, the same as does the Arabian, or the Red Sea, which divides Asia and Africa; which occasioned those who first discovered it to call this water the Red Sea, because they resembled each other. [15]

This view still had currency in some writings of the eighteenth century, as, for example, when Father Luís Sales attributes the name to a "resemblance to the Gulf of Arabia." [16]

In 1539, the name might have done more than suggest geographical similarities. It would also have evoked the mythic overtones of the wealth of Solomon. The Red Sea had proved the only waterway out of the closed system of the Mediterranean to the fabulous East. Through it, Solomon had sent ships for gold and precious gems to adorn his temple. These riches were found, so the legend went, in Ophir and Tarsis in the great Oriental Ocean, now lying to the west. The effect of the name Mar Vermejo would therefore have been to hint at the disappointing truth of the land's topography while still nurturing the myths.

But for Ulloa the evidence was not all in. He had only failed to find a northern passage from the side of the Sea of Cortés. The next step was to return through the southern "boca" (the mouth of the Gulf), sail around the Punta de California, and try to find an outlet from the outside (South Sea) coast. This phase of his voyage will be taken up in Chapter XIII.

Chapter XII

Viceroy Mendoza's Men Cast Doubt on Baja's Insularity

Antonio de Mendoza, the man appointed first Viceroy of New Spain, began at this time to intensify his rivalry with Cortés. This excerpt from Ramusio, via Hakluyt, summarizes their dissension:

> The right honourable Don Antonio de Mendoça being sent by Charles the Emperour to be viceroy of Mexico and Nueva Espanna, and having understood that Don Ferdinando Cortez had sent many ships along the coast of Nueva Espanna to discover countries, and to find out the Isles of the Malucos, began himself to desire to do the like, as viceroy of Nueva Espanna; and hereupon they fell out: for Cortez said that he was general and discoverer of the South sea, and that it belonged to him to set forth those voyages. On the other side, the lord Don Antonio alledged that it belonged to him to make that discovery, as being viceroy of Nueva Espanna. So they fell at great variance.[1]

Viceroy Mendoza was as anxious as Cortés to know what was up the Sea of Cortés. Friar Marcos de Niza had tattled about Cortés' confidences (*see* page 113), including "news" of fabulous cities to the north. Mendoza dispatched the friar to test these rumors. Niza went up the mainland coast in 1538.

Among Mendoza's instructions to Niza was the following:

> Enquire always if there is any information about the proximity of the North and South Seas, for it may be that the continent grows narrower and that an arm of the sea penetrates to the interior.[2]

In addition, the friar was asked to "discover the end of the firm land."

Friar Marcos was the first of a string of credulous padres to cloud an understanding of California's true topography. Among the strange bits of "information" he brought back was this:

> I learned that the coast turns west very abruptly, for up to the time of entering this wilderness which I crossed, the coast extended always to the north. Since the turning of the coast is very important, I wanted to verify it, and so I went in search of it, and I saw clearly that at a latitude of thirty-five degrees it turns to the west.[3]

Niza's geography was way off base. The 35th parallel is north of Needles, where the present-day California state line leaves the Colorado River. Moreover, Niza apparently believed the eastern coast of the Gulf was the outside coast and that it continued on after its westward turn. The mainland coast was the only coast in his implied opinion. Offshore was the Marquis's discovery, one of many islands that the natives had described (see page 113 & 114).

Upon Niza's return, Mendoza immediately organized a two-pronged expedition to seek the promised fabulous cities. Hernando de Alarcón was to sail north in the *ancón* to probe its "secrets" to 36 degrees—that is, beyond where Niza said it turned to the west. At this point Alarcón was to make contact with the other prong trekking north from Culiacan and Sinaloa. That overland expedition toward the present-day Arizona and New Mexico was led by Francisco Vásquez de Coronado.

It is generally maintained that Alarcón determined at this time that Baja California was a peninsula. But there is no clear-cut statement for or against any such geographical proposition in Alarcón's own narrative. Alarcón simply states, in Hakluyt's translation, how "at the very bottom of the Bay" he found "a very mighty river." He calls the river (now the Colorado) "Rio de Buena Guia," purportedly after Mendoza's emblem. He penetrated the interior a considerable distance up this river. He did not make contact with Coronado, but, as bidden by Mendoza, erected "a very high cross . . . whereupon I engraved certain letters to signify that I was come thither . . . if by chance any of the people of general Vasquez de Coronado should come thither."[4]

This part of the story meshes roughly with a narrative made by a Pedro de Castañeda. In this we are told that Alarcón's marker was found by an advance party of Coronado's men. Melchior Díaz led the small contingent. It had branched off from the main expedition, heading "toward the north and west . . . in search of the seacoast."[5] This contingent reached the Colorado River, which was given still another name, the Rio del Tizón, Firebrand River. The name derives from a native custom of carrying flaming brands from shore to shore.

Castañeda reports:

> It is a very great river and is more than 2 leagues wide at its mouth; here it is half a league across. Here the captain heard that there had been ships at a point three days down toward the sea. When he reached the place where the ships had been, which was more than 15 leagues up the river from the mouth of the harbor, they found written on a tree: "Alarcon reached this place; there are letters at the foot of this tree." He dug up the

letters and learned from them how long Alarcon had waited for news of the army and that he had gone back with the ships to New Spain.

These letters have unfortunately not survived to tell us whether Alarcón figured out California's peninsularity. Castañeda's account tells us that he did so, but that account is not totally reliable. It was written some time after Coronado returned "shamefaced" to Mexico. Further, the manuscript, in the New York Public Library, is only a copy dated 1596. There is no knowing what the copier may have interpolated for "clarification" more than half a century after the events. The copying was done when aged participants of the early expeditions were being closely questioned about their knowledge of the region. Memory was inevitably alloyed by opinions developed subsequent to events, and copiers had no compunction about altering a record. The Castañeda narrative is plain enough, but can we count on it?

> He [Alarcón] was unable to proceed further, since this sea was a bay, which was formed by the Isle of the Marquis, which is called California, and it was explained that California was not an island, but a point of the mainland forming the other side of that gulf.

This was the view propounded in the Second Relation of Guzmán's activities, quoted on pages 106–07. But though current in Alarcón's day, it was then only advanced as an alternative possibility.

The narrative contains other passages re-evaluating the Gulf's topography:

> Captain Melchior Diaz crossed the Firebrand river on rafts, in order to continue his discoveries farther in that direction . . . After they had crossed the river they went ahead in search of the coast, which in that region turned south or southeast, for the arm of the sea extends straight to the north and the river, flowing from north to south, empties into the head of the gulf.

Later in the same chapter, these details are made clearer, but whether by the original narrator or by the copier of 1596 we do not know:

> On the coast of this province there begins the gulf which extends north to the sea and inland 250 leagues and ends at the mouth of the Tizon river. One point of this land lies to the east; the point to the west is California. The width from point to point, as I have heard from men who sailed this gulf, is thirty leagues, for, having lost sight of land on one side, they begin to see the other. They say the gulf is 150 leagues wide from shore to shore. Moreover, from the Tizon river the coast turns to the south, forming an arch as far as California, where it turns to the west, forming the headland

which formerly was thought to be an island. It is a low and sandy land, inhabited by savage, bestial, naked people who eat their own excrement, and where men and women couple like animals, the female placing herself publicly on all fours.[6]

These comments on the behavior of the California Indians will be seen to resemble a *History* written by Baltasar de Obregón (*see* page 177).[7] Since Obregón's work is dated 1584, we wonder again about the status of the Castañeda narrative: Is it an unadulterated record of impressions contemporary with the events described? Or were later opinions interpolated by the copier or transcriber?

Yet even assuming the narrative's dependability, there are other statements making grist for the mill of rumor to keep alive the strait and island myth. What would readers have made of this:

In order to turn west . . . in search of India, one should follow the route taken by the army, because even though one might wish to take a different route, there is none. It is hindered by the arm of the sea that enters this coast inland toward the north . . . . This might be overcome by building a fleet that would cross this gulf.[8]

Reference here may be to the huge "sinus" between Asia and America — which were believed by the "continentalists" to be joined by a land bridge. But some, undoubtedly, would have confused it with the Californian gulf. The obstacle (and hope) of such an arm of the sea would figure in the narratives of the New Mexico explorers around the turn of the century. Materials for building ships would even be packed to the interior to permit a crossing of this gulf when it was reached.

Melchior Díaz and his patrol could not have conclusively established the absence of a strait. When they reached the head of the Gulf there was another kind of "sea" to bar the way. Their strange experiences may even have encouraged the myths. An account is found both in Castañeda and Obregón, again suggesting a pooling of ideas. Subtitling it "Waste Land at the Tizon River," Obregón relates:

Melchior Diaz . . . found the country sandy, windy, and full of great sand dunes which move repeatedly from one place to another. The strong and constant winds make them grow or decrease to big or small dimensions. Thus necessity and the danger of being lost compelled him to return.[9]

That adverse experience was reinforced by still another along the river:

They came to some sand banks of hot ashes which it was impossible to cross without being drowned as in the sea. The ground trembled . . . so that it seemed as if there were lakes underneath them.[10]

Such experiences might have put the credulous in mind of the mythic Sandy Sea featured in the *Letter of Prester John*. This was so impassable that Alexander had had to be transported across it by griffins, the huge beast-birds which figured prominently in Montalvo's story of Queen Calafia and her island of California.

In Henry R. Wagner's view, Alarcón's expedition did not conclusively rule out the existence of a strait in that confusing area. Wagner notes:

> There is some indication that some of Alarcon's party had discovered the depression west of the Cocopa Mountains which is occasionally, at times of very high water in the Colorado, filled by the overflow passing around the lower end of the Cocopa Mountain. The channel through which the water flowed was evidently discovered at that time and very possibly also the lake, now known as the Laguna Salada, which might have been at that period full or partly full of water from a previous overflow . . . It seems certain that he heard of Volcano Lake and probably also of the Salton Sea, which may have been filled with water at that time. Volcano Lake discharged through what is known as Hardy's Channel into the main river just above Montague Island, and it may be that Alarcon did not recognize this branch as one of the outlets of the Colorado, but thought that it connected with some other body of water west of the Colorado. At any rate there seemed to be a notion current at the end of the century that west of the Colorado there was some body of water which might be supposed to be the main gulf extending to the north.[11]

Wagner says further:

> Evidently while Alarcon was away, the Santa Catarina, one of the vessels, made a reconnaissance of the California coast . . . This expedition . . . discovered the channel which connects at high water the delta of the Colorado with the Laguna Salada, as appears from the name "Brazo de la Laguna."

The "Brazo de Lagunas"—the "arm of lakes"—appears on a map made by Domingo del Castillo in 1541 (*see* Plate 21). Castillo was with Alarcón; his name appears in the narratives. His map has been used to clinch the case that Baja's peninsularity was determined at this time. Yet the map shows clearly that the "secret of the gulf" was not conclusively unlocked. The Río de Buena Guia or the Tizón River is not the only opening at the crotch. Castillo shows two open-ended "arms." The "arm of the lakes" evokes the possibility of a strait branching from the Ancón de San Andrés to join the South Sea on the northwest coast. And perhaps the other, the "Brazo de Miraflores," suggests a transcontinental strait. Wagner reminds us that with Spanish and Portuguese

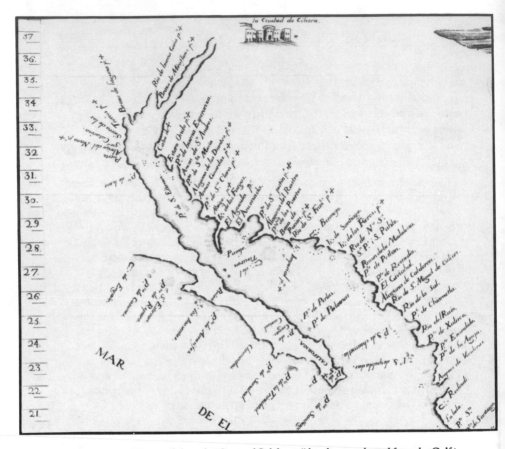

PLATE 21. The possibility of a "Strait of California" heading northward from the Gulf is fostered by the opening of two *brazos* (arms or branches) separate from the mouth of the Rio de Buena Guia (now the Colorado River) in this map made by Domingo del Castillo in 1541. The Brazo de Lagunas seems headed toward the Pacific; the Brazo de Miraflores toward the Atlantic. (Discussion on pages 149, 122.) *From a copy made by Francisco Antonio Lorenzana in* Historia de Nueva España *(México, 1770), p. 328. Photograph by the British Library.*

cartographers "it was a principle of their mapmaking not to show anything but actual discoveries."[12] These uncompleted arms suggest inlets needing investigation in further explorations—thus keeping open the question of California's possible insularity.

Battista Agnese used this device liberally on his many maps through the 1540s and 50s (Plate 22). Unresolved openings all along his coasts denote unexplored bays and river outlets. We therefore know enough not to place too much weight on his open channel at the head of the Gulf. But the legend in Spanish points to special circumstances: "The

Red Sea, where in the channel at high tide there are 11 fathoms, and at low tide 8." This information jibes with the Preciado-Ulloa narrative:

> We perceived the Sea to run with so great a rage into the land . . . and with like fury it returned back again with the ebb; during which time we found 11 fathom water, and the flood and ebb continued . . .[13]

For those who wanted to continue their belief that a strait existed, these tides could be interpreted as the surging of water into a narrow channel betokening not a river but an arm of the sea.

In the above quotation about Alarcón's possible experience at the nook, Wagner speaks of the Salton Sea. This extensive body of water, whose level has fluctuated widely over the centuries and millenia, lies in a huge depression along a geologic fault. The fault bears the same name

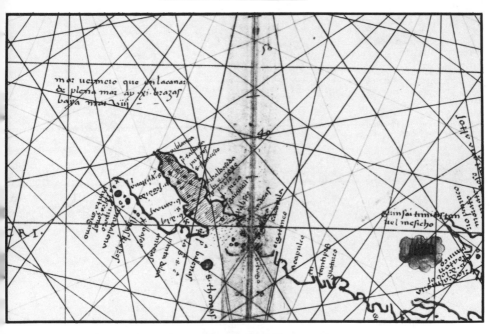

PLATE 22.   The opening at the head of the Gulf was Battista Agnese's way of indicating that further exploration was needed before conclusions could be drawn. But believers in straits and channels may have found comfort in the legend written high above the opening: "the Red Sea where in the channel at full tide are eleven fathoms, and at low tide eight." The Gulf, however, is painted red, paralleling the Red Sea of the Old World. (Discussion also on pages 143, 170, 178.) *Photograph and permission by the Huntington Library (HM 10, c. 1550, folio 4).*

as the *ancón*, San Andreas—though this is no more than a fascinating coincidence. The fault is said to be named for a lake in the fault zone south of San Francisco.

It was along this fault line running northward from the crotch that the "Strait of California" was imagined to lie. The trough may have suggested a continuation of the Gulf, as we now recognize it potentially to be. Modern studies in plate tectonics tell us that along the Gulf and the San Andreas fault the North American and Pacific plates converge. Geologists say that a northward drift has been separating Baja from the mainland for many eons. All the land west of the fault will be detached and propelled northward toward Alaska over the next many million years (*see* Plates 52a & b).

Thus may ancient myths turn into prophecies.

Chapter XIII

Ulloa and Cabrillo Seek Straits on California's Outer Coast

The first investigations of Baja were naturally of the coastline inside the Gulf, opposite the mainland. But Cortés had instructed Ulloa in 1539 to "sail around" the " island." By implication, then, the call was also for information about the outer coast giving onto the main ocean, the South Sea.

Since the shoals at the head of the Gulf had inhibited further investigation in that confusing area, Ulloa might have reasoned that he would do better to retrace his steps and seek answers on Baja's exterior littoral. The nature of the new discovery could be proved just as well by looking on the far side of the "island." If a strait running to and from the Ancón de San Andrés did indeed exist, he might find its other end more easily.

But this proved to be a major ordeal. Preciado's account of "doubling the point"—the southern extremity of Baja—is tense with drama. This portion of the narrative begins with the return from the crook of the Gulf to present-day La Paz bay:

> We determined to take in fresh water at the haven of Santa Cruz, to run along the outward western coast, and to see what it was, if it pleased God . . . The nine and twentieth day of October, being Wednesday, we set sail out of this haven . . . directing our prows to the main sea, to see whether it would please God to let us discover the secret of this point. [1]

They were met with such baffling winds and life-threatening storms that they were filled with superstitious dread:

> Whether it pleased not His goodness, or whether it was for our sins, we spent eight days from this port before we could double the point by reason of contrary winds, and great rain, and lightning and darkness every night. Also the winds grew so raging and tempestuous that they made us all quake and to pray continually unto God to aid us.

Out in the vast ocean, the storms continued:

> On one of these nights, which was very tempestuous with wind and rain, because we thought we should have perished, being very near the shore,

we prayed unto God that He would vouch-safe to aid and save us, without calling our sins to remembrance. And straightaway we saw upon the shrouds of the Trinity as it were a candle which of itself shined, and gave light, whereat all the company greatly rejoiced . . .

During these terrors, is it possible that inflamed imaginations recalled stories of the inaccessibility and sinister aspects of the Amazon isle? Suggestive of the matrix of ancient legend and mythology out of which the Amazonian story grew were reports in the narrative of giant Indians.[2] A sierra running along Baja still bears the name Sierra de la Giganta, perhaps deriving from such beliefs. The name California for the land they were trying to circumnavigate would seem all the more apt for these frightening experiences.

Altogether it took the Ulloa expedition five months to sail only as far as Cedros Island. Hardship forced the return of one of the ships. But Ulloa pushed on in the flagship, feeling, as his own narrative states, "that it was regrettable to have spent so much time and labor without accomplishing what your lordship so greatly desires."[3]

If Ulloa kept any journal of the final phase, northward of Cedros, none has been found. Francisco Lopez de Gómara briefly mentions the episode in his *Historia de la Conquista de Mexico* (1552). Despite its tantalizing brevity, it has the merit of having been written when the event was still fresh. Gómara says Ulloa sailed north from Cedros Island "until level with the Ancón of San Andrés"—*hasta emparejar con el ancon de San Andres*. That means, presumably, until he reached roughly the same latitude as the nook of the Gulf. Ulloa named the last point he rounded "el cabo del Engaño," the Cape of Deceit, or False Point, and then turned home. Here, in translation, is the paragraph entire:

> From the Ancon of San Andrés, continuing to the other coast, they arrived at California, doubled the point, placed themselves between the land and some islands, and went until level with the ancon of San Andrés. They named that point the Cape of Deceit, and they turned around for New Spain, on account of encountering very contrary winds and running out of provisions. They were on this journey an entire year, and did not bring news of any good land: more was the noise than the nuts.[4]

Was the name Cabo del Engaño given to the headland in disgust at again finding no opening of a strait? Did the name symbolize the last straw of the compounded frustrations and disappointments endured by the crew in this yearlong quest? Perhaps history is silent on this episode because Ulloa would have been reluctant to report, and Cortés would have been reluctant to heed, such a lack of success.

But the result of Ulloa's voyage must have circulated via the grapevine. His Cabo del Engaño appeared on several maps following this expedition, written in varying locations along the outer coast. It appears on the Castillo map of 1541 as the last location shown at the end of the mapped coastline. Though not "on a level with" the Ancón, it lends support to Gómara's summary.

The exact location of Cape Deceit is still unclear. The description of Punto del Engaño in the Cabrillo narrative suggests the present-day Punta Baja near El Rosario. But perhaps Cabo de San Quintín was the disappointing headland where Ulloa and his men finally gave up.

As suggested in Chapter XI, Ulloa's unsuccessful quest did not put speculation totally to rest. Once again, failing to find an outlet was not the same as proving no strait existed. Ulloa may not have been looking in the right place, or neglected to check out some likely inlet.

In Bancroft's opinion:

> Ulloa's voyage left some doubt whether there was a strait just above Santa Cruz separating the southern end of the peninsula.[5]

The maps on Plates 18 and 19 express this version of a smaller "island of California." So, indirectly, does the legend inscribed off the coast of Baja on Map No. III of Plate 49, referring to an unexplored gulf of great depth in that vicinity. The fact that that map is dated 1700 demonstrates the survival power of the myth.

The failure of Ulloa's expedition to find a strait from the inside or outside coasts of Baja, coupled with the experiences of Mendoza's men, led to a presumption of Baja's peninsularity in the next few decades. But the failure to prove the negative proposition would cause the island myth and the theory of a Strait of California to resurface on and off for two more centuries. This lingering of the myth was probably aided by the fact that the most widely circulated narrative of these explorations was Preciado's ambiguous account. It was this version translated by Ramusio and Hakluyt that was to influence non-Spanish thinking greatly in the last part of the century.

Even before the disappointing outcome of Ulloa's voyage could have been known, plans for another survey of the outside coast were already in the works. This impetus for a more concerted assault on the "secrets" of the South Sea littoral came from a former lieutenant of Cortés—but not at Cortés' bidding, nor in his interests. The faithless Pedro de

Alvarado made an agreement with the King and Viceroy Mendoza in 1540 to explore the South Sea in ships of his building.[6] This became part of the Viceroy's policy to probe the mysteries to the north and west in direct competition and conflict with Cortés.

Cortés' star was now really in decline. A death blow was inflicted on his fortunes when the King appointed Alvarado as "Captain of the South Sea." Such action was in direct contravention, Cortés believed, of the King's Agreement with him of 1529.

Cortés protested this violation of his rights, but his quirks and failures had deprived him of any clout. In 1540, once more he "returned into Spaine to complain unto the Emperour."[7] Given a negative reception at the Court, he was forced to live out his remaining years in retirement in Spain.

Thus did the dreamer depart the scene. Without him, California would soon slip back into the shadows of what Bancroft calls the "Northern Mystery," becoming again the stuff of imagination, myth, and unrealized dream for two more centuries.

But the candle would flare for another year or so while Mendoza's men made one final effort to pierce the veil.

Alvarado's aims were no different from Cortés'—to discover rich islands and find out what was up the coast. In a letter written to the King dated March 28, 1541, Alvarado states:

> It is expedient to the service of Your Majesty that it [the fleet] be divided in two parts, since there is enough for all, and the one [part] should go to the Islands of the West . . . and the other should run along the coast of the mainland so far as to see the end and secret of it, and the turn that it makes.[8]

If the "insularists" were right, the coastline would turn east, where, in the historian Gómara's words, "it closes the country [America] as an island at Labrador or Grunlandia."[9] But since most people in New Spain had conceptualized the New World as being, if not part of Asia, at least joined to Asia by a land bridge, they expected the north-bearing coastline to turn west—at worst punctuated by a river-straight bearing eastward or northeastward.

Plans were for Alvarado to command the coastal expedition, and for Ruy Lopez de Villalobos to lead the voyage to the Philippines. But there were hitches, and the evidence is sketchy about what actually occurred. This is hardly surprising considering that intense rivalry would call for super-secrecy.

Apparently, Mendoza sent a voyage up the coast in 1541. This,

however, was under the command of Francisco de Bolaños. The information comes from a mention in the testimony of Juan de Ladrillero
made in 1574, more than thirty years after the event. In that testimony,
Ladrillero refers to Bolaños as the general to whom Mendoza had a fleet
of three ships delivered "in the Puerto de Navidad . . . to go on the
voyage of discovery of this coast *and of the strait* [italics added]." On
account of bad weather they "did not finish their voyage."

The affidavit goes on to say:

> They remained in California and sent from there to advise the viceroy,
> Don Antonio de Mendoza, who ordered them to return, as at that time
> Villalobos was going to sail for the Islas de las Malucas and it was
> necessary for him to take the ships in which this witness and others had
> sailed to carry the people he had to take to the said islands to the west;
> that so it was that the said ships served for that voyage, and the discovery
> of the strait remained as it is up to today.[10]

As this passage and other documentation make clear, the plan for
Villalobos to lead the westward expedition was carried out. But a map
exists indicating that he may also have taken part in an expedition
along the coast of what we now call California. If the map is taken at
face value, he must at least have coasted north before heading west.

The map is in the Kohl collection in the Library of Congress (*see*
Plate 23).[11] Kohl copied this map by Juan Freire, dated 1546, in two
parts, from the original in a Portuguese portolano possessed at that time
by Santarem. Kohl notes that Lower California follows Domingo del
Castillo's map of 1541, though the names are garbled.

But of greatest interest to us in this present context is the copied
section labeled "Upper California." It bears the legend *Esta costa he aqui
descubrio ho Vilha Llobos per mandado de emprador*—"This coast was
discovered by Villalobos by order of the emperor."

Kohl wonders whether the map could be fictitious. In considering
this, he first asserts the presumption of Freire's reliability:

> The Portuguese Freire has . . . always laid down his maps after true
> history. I know of no other instance of fictitious maps made by him.

Moreover, although the map displays no identifiable names or specific
locations, Kohl judges it to be an authentic rendering of what it
purports to be:

> The coast of California is well represented in the main, its great uniform-
> ity, its stretching out in one long not much broken line, without large
> peninsulas, without spacious bays, and without great islands before it.

Only sometimes is it interrupted by rivers. The coast seems depicted so, as if it had actually been seen, perhaps also only from far. It recedes always more to the north, though it in the same time advances much too far to the West. *But this latter was a common error of all the early maps of California.* It was always believed that the coast of California conducted to the West.

But there is one significant feature of the map that is indeed fictitious—a feature upon which, surprisingly, Kohl did not comment. It is a feature of great importance to our present story: an *Estrecho de Islas*—a "Strait of Islands." The label is written in large letters across an inlet full of islands. The inlet tapers to many small open-ended branches, perhaps evocative of the maze of Magellan's Strait. On one side of the inlet is *Entrado dell estrecho.* On the other *Entrado del Streito*, as though to make sure it is understood.

If Villalobos was given the charge of seeking a strait, he seems obligingly to have "found" one. The implication is that he explored it some distance beyond its entrance to have rendered it in so much detail.

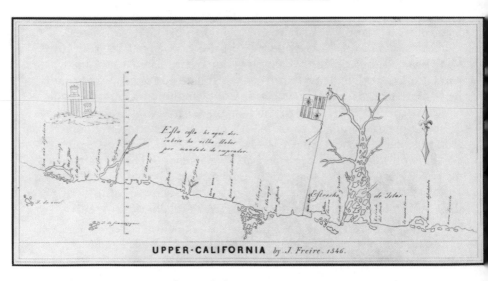

UPPER-CALIFORNIA by J. Freire. 1546.

PLATE 23. The "Estrecho de Islas"—The Strait of Islands—is a strange figment of imaginary geography in this map of the coast of Upper California purported to be by Juan de Freire, 1546. The map is a copy made by J. G. Kohl from a Portuguese Portolan he once saw in the library of the Visconde de Santarem. What kind of strait did the mariners think they had discovered? (Discussion on pages 157-59.) *Photograph and permission by the Library of Congress (The Kohl Collection, No. 278).*

Since this could not have been, we have to wonder what was the maggot of the idea, the name, and its depiction. Perhaps the instruction was to seek the waterway that would prove Baja an island or group of islands. As is the way with folk transmission, the term could have been redefined literally to put islands into the imagined strait.

Wagner commented on this map that "Kohl got his sketches mixed," and that the map actually "portrays the discovery of Ortiz de Retes." Wagner also declares: "The map is a curiosity as an example of imaginary geography, but as a cartographical document it has no value."[12] For purposes of this study, the clouding of the source in no way affects our interest in the figment. And it is precisely as imaginary geography that it has value here.

It is clear that Villalobos carried out more than his share of Mendoza's plan. Not so Alvarado. Retribution caught up with him. He died in an engagement with outraged Indians before he could launch his expedition.

Alvarado's commitment passed to his second in command—Juan Rodríguez Cabrillo, with his pilot by the name Ferrelo.

So began the first chapter of the history of Alta (Upper) California. The name California, however, applied at most to the lower part of Baja then. More than another half a century would elapse before the name came to embrace the entire coastline sighted on this voyage. How the name expanded to cover so large an area will be developed in Chapter XXIV.

The single narrative that has so far come to light doesn't tell us what the Cabrillo expedition was charged to do. In those jealous days, when one rival dared not let the others know what he was up to, speculations tended to remain secret until discoveries could be confirmed, and the proper rites of possession performed to nail the claim. But it seems likely that Cabrillo took over Alvarado's intentions with his mission. The inevitable quest for rich islands was confirmed as the goal long after the fact, when Cabrillo's son sued in 1560 for the restoration of his father's property. In an official interrogation, Francisco de Vargas testified, somewhat exaggeratedly:

> If Cabrillo had not died he would have discovered the great country of spices and the Moluccas, which they were on their way to find, and perhaps would have gone even farther . . . [13]

Vargas even claims:

> They discovered the island named "Capitana" and according to the latitude which the pilot calculated, they were very near the Moluccas and the spice country and in the neighborhood of China . . .[14]

But, in fact, it was Alvarado's complementary goal that was pursued by Cabrillo with the greater assiduousness. This was the promise that Alvarado had made to determine "the turn that the land makes" (*la vuelta que haze la tierra*) when reconnoitering the coast.

Cabrillo's quest for the "turn" was prompted partly by Spain's continuing fears of France's penetration from the east. Defense was now the vital reason for exploration of the "back side" of the emerging northern continent, to test the geographic claims of Spain's competitors. As discussed on page 135, the concept of a Sea of Verrazzano mightn't hold much water—especially with Coronado's trek to the interior. But the English concept of a northern passage was something else. If it existed, better it be found by Mendoza's men. As Bancroft suggests, its discovery "would be no benefit but a positive disadvantage and menace to Spain." But it must be found in order that "in possession of Spain it might be closed to the navigators of other nations."[15]

Because the "continentalist" view prevailed in New Spain, the fear was not so much of a northern sea as of a "river-strait" spanning the northern continent. Ulloa's failure to find any outlets meant only that Cabrillo should continue the search beyond the point Ulloa reached.

The records are slender, but there are several hints that Cabrillo was seeking the mouth of a great river. In historian Antonio de Herrera y Tordesillas' account of the expedition comes this statement:

> Saturday, the 11th, they went on along the coast with a south-east wind, always looking for the Rio de Nuestra Senora, but they did not find it.[16]

Coronado's men had recently discovered a river that they named Our Lady. It is described in "An Account of what Hernando de Alvarado and Friar Juan de Padilla Discovered Going in Search of the South Sea." Winship identifies this river with the "Tiguex," the present Rio Grande.[17] That was the river Cristoval de Olid investigated when sent by Cortés to find a strait running from the Gulf of Mexico to the South Sea (*see* page 136, and the Sloane Manuscript map, Plate 12). Coronado's men continued the hope of that transcontinental waterway for quite practical reasons.

Perhaps Cabrillo was charged to seek its South-Sea outlet. His narrative (rendered in the third person) contains some hints of this:

> Monday and Tuesday, the 31st, the eve of Todos Santos, they went tacking about endeavoring to reach the mainland in search of a large river on the other side of Cabo de Galera [Point Conception] of which they had information, and because on the land there were signs of rivers. They

did not find any, however, nor did they anchor there because the coast was very bold.[18]

Then again:

It seemed to them that there is a very large river, of which they had heard much, between 42 degrees and 43 degrees, as they saw many indications of it . . . This day in the afternoon they sighted Cabo de Pinos [Point Reyes], but on account of the high seas they could do nothing but run down the coast in search of a port. They endured much cold.[19]

More insight into what Cabrillo and Ferrelo were seeking comes from a memorial written by Andrés de Urdaneta about twenty years later. Urdaneta speaks of searching for Cabrillo's "big water," and determining whether it was salt or fresh.[20] Perhaps Urdaneta had access to some other now-lost narratives of the Cabrillo voyage in which a lot more was made out of the concept of the elusive river described above. Urdaneta's views will be more fully explored in the next chapter.

But to finish our discussion of Cabrillo from the only narrative extant, we note the strong empirical emphasis of the voyage. A survey of the coast was made as close into land as possible. Yet the experience may, like Ulloa's, have fed unbridled imaginations, and added fuel to the Amazonian myths. Dreadful storms held the ships offshore most of the time. Equally forbidding were the snow-topped coastal ranges ending in towering cliffs and palisades. Might not these, and the treacherous, rocky, surf-plagued coastline, have evoked the inaccessible rockbound fortress of Montalvo's Amazons?

Certainly all the ingredients, including superstitious fear, were there. During the voyage Cabrillo died from an accidental wound that turned gangrenous. This may have been read as a warning omen to keep away from the mysterious region, whose bounds no man knew.

All the way through the narrative are mentioned the hostilities of weather and coastline. South of the Isle of Cedros they made the same poor progress as had Ulloa "on account of the vile winds." Along the coast they found "some very dangerous reefs of rocks called *Abrejo* which only appear when the surf breaks on them," and noted the sierras as "very high and rugged."[21]

The greatest trouble with the weather occurred around Cabo de Galera, known today as Point Conception:

A south-southwest and west-southwest wind with rain struck them, and they saw themselves in trouble as it was an on-shore wind, and they were near land . . . That night they held out to sea . . . and . . . went beating

about in one direction and another with contrary winds . . . The coast
was very bold . . . They found the weather . . . very cold in the mornings
and afternoons and with great storms of rain, heavy clouds, great darkness, and heavy air.

Wednesday at midnight, November 1, while standing off, a heavy north-
northwest gale came up which did not allow them to carry an inch of sail.
At daylight it came so much fresher that they could do nothing but run
back to shelter . . .

Running north, with the Santa Lucias on their right, they experienced
still more bad weather:

All the coast followed this day is bold, without shelter, and a range of very
high sierras on which the sea breaks runs along all of it, as high at the sea
as inland. Four hours after nightfall, while lying six leagues from the
coast, waiting for daybreak, with the wind in the southeast, such a
rainstorm and heavy clouds . . . came up . . . they could not carry an
inch of sail. They had to run before it all that night with a small piece of
sail on the foremast, with great labor, and on the Sunday following the
storm became much more violent, lasting that day and night and until
Monday at midday . . . Saturday night they lost sight of their consort
. . . They turned toward land in search of their consort, praying God to
succor her, as they very much feared that she would be lost . . . They
came to reconnoiter . . . in a very high country and then went along close
to the coast looking for a port where they could take shelter. The sea was
so high that it was frightful to see; the coast was bold and the mountains
very high.

Of the area we now call Big Sur, the narrative recites:

All the coast passed this day is very bold: there is a great swell and the land
is very high. There are mountains which seem to reach the heavens, and
the sea beats on them; sailing along close to land, it appears as though
they would fall on the ships. They are covered with snow to the summits.

The adverse weather made them decide to lie over for the winter in
the offshore islands, the one presently called San Miguel affording them
the greatest shelter. This is where Cabrillo succumbed to the infection
caused by his earlier injury, and in his memory the crew named the
island after him—a naming that did not survive due to the oblivion
into which his work was cast.

Cabrillo's dying request that Ferrelo take one more swing north
before going home points again to the expedition's having a definite,
vital mission. But Ferrelo did not find the "turning of the land" nor the

mouth of any large river. Driven up and down the coast, prey to "vile weather, wind and snow," he and his crew were continually in life-threatening predicaments:

> . . . The wind shifted and came from the southwest with great fury, the seas coming from many sides, which molested them very much or broke over the ships. As these had no covered decks, if the Lord had not aided them, they could not have escaped. As they could not lay to, they had to run before the wind to the northeast in the direction of land. Considering themselves lost they commended themselves to our Señora de Guadalupe and made their vows. So they ran until three o'clock in the afternoon with great fear and travail as they saw that they were about to be wrecked. Already they saw many signs of land, which was near, such as birds and fresh logs, which came out of some rivers, although by reason of the great darkness land could not be seen. At this hour the Mother of Our Lord succored them with the grace of Her Son, and a very strong rainstorm came up from the north, which made them run before it towards the south with lower foresails all night and all the following day until sunset. As there was a high sea running from the south, each time that it assailed them on the bow it passed over them as if over a rock. The wind shifted to the northwest and to the north-northwest with great fury, forcing them to run before it to the southeast and east-southeast . . . with such a high sea that it set them wildly crying out that if the Lord and His Blessed Mother did not miraculously save them they could not escape . . . They also passed through hardships on account of the food, as they had nothing except some damaged biscuit.

Enough was enough. They turned south for home.

Failure, misery, superstitious dread, obviously outweighed the positive aspects of this expedition. Officialdom had no interest whatsoever in the West Coast's potential as a realistic paradise. Totally ignored were glimpses in the narrative of the bounties of fertile coastal plans and sheltered harbors like the "very good closed port" at the site of the presently-named San Diego:

> While in this port a great tempest passed over, but nothing of it was felt as the port was so good.

Sailing north from San Diego, the Cabrillo expedition "saw many valleys and plains," until they came to the present San Pedro/Long Beach/Los Angeles area:

> It is an excellent harbor and the country is good, with many valleys, plains, and groves of trees.

Of the area now named Oxnard and Ventura, the narrative gives this account:

> The country within is a very beautiful . . . inland in that valley there was much maize and food. Beyond this valley some high, very broken sierras were visible.

This expedition also discovered and described the presently named Monterey:

> This ensenada . . . is full of pines down to the sea, and it was named the "baia de los Pinos."

Cortés might have jumped at such opportunities to found new colonies. But he was gone. The new Spanish establishment wasn't interested in distant pastoral Edens to be achieved by settlement and cultivation. The gentle Indians would be left unmolested to enjoy their lovely lands for another couple of centuries.

Chapter XIV

The Isle-of-California Myth
Goes into Remission

The return of the survivors of the Cabrillo expedition marked the end of the first short but action-packed chapter of California history. For the next fifty years, no further exploration of the region was attempted. The horror stories told by survivors of Cortés' Santa Cruz experiment discouraged further contact with Baja. Only a handful of pearl fishers had any continuing interest in the Gulf. As for the outside coast, reports by the scurvy-ridden remnants of the Cabrillo voyage made it clear that it was far too formidable a challenge for the then-prevailing state of navigation.

The ensuing neglect of the region was due also to changes in the cast of principals. Gone now were the powerful spurs of Cortés' obsession, and Guzmán's ferocious rivalry. All exploration was placed firmly under viceregal control. The islands in the far west looked like far better bets for producing wealth than the territory closer to hand. The trade route to the Philippines became the focus of official attention. All available ships and personnel were diverted to that end.

The mystery of California's topography was still unsolved when the first chapter closed. No definitive conclusions about the lie of the land at the nook of the Gulf were forthcoming from the records of the explorations of 1539–1542. But an impression had been gained that Baja was more likely to be a peninsula than an island. This became the prevailing view. Maps made after 1542 reflected the general opinion that the Sea of Cortés was indeed a Mar Vermejo, a closed gulf. The river-that-might-turn-out-to-be-a-strait was a river after all.

Yet the California island myth was never quite extinguished. Those who had followed Cortés in both thought and action tended to accommodate to the alternative theory without relinquishing the island view completely.

Bernal Díaz, for example, as a soldier with Cortés, shared his captain's predilection for the island theory. But when he came to write about the California experiment thirty or so years later, he had to allow for information that had gained currency in the interval. In the following quotation, the expression "or bay" sounds like an interpolation acknowledging the alternate view. It seems to serve as a rough abbreviation for the newer theory that Cortés' discovery was the western arm of a vast bay:

> All the soldiers and captains who had remained on those islands or bay which is called California came back . . . [1]

Another reading for "or bay" might be a simple reference to the Gulf of California itself, that being the newer name for the Sea of Cortés. But either way the statement reflects the two contrasting concepts.

Persistence of the myth in popular rumor is also revealed by Antonio de Herrera y Tordesillas, in a section dealing with the events of 1550. He lists the provinces "Culiacan, Copala, Chiametla, and further ahead, California . . . first reached by the Marquis and named by him" then comments:

> The land is not very wide, because the sea cuts into it with a huge bay or gulf that makes the turn of the north of such great size that some think that it reaches very close to the place of the Bacallaos where there is a strait to go out to the other sea near the islands of Ireland and England; but this is an imagined opinion: but however that may be, the same coast gives a great turn toward the south leading to the West . . . China . . . the Philippines. [2]

From the clear description of the territory, we can be sure the "imagined opinion" refers to a strait running northward from the Gulf. Moreover, his index entry "Estrecho de California, incertio," (see page 142) refers to the page bearing this passage. Ironically, Herrera gives standing to the "Strait of California" while recording it as a doubtful phenomenon.

From time to time curiosity flared up about "the Northern Mystery." Among the documents pertaining to the opening of the Philippines and Ladrones, various statements by Andrés de Urdaneta are of interest to this present study. Plans for his own voyages to those islands—and "many other islands if there are any"—included mapping a course that would permit him to test Cabrillo's theories. As noted on page 161 above, Urdaneta had probably read the now-missing journals of Cabrillo's voyage, which must have included statements about a "big water" needing further exploration. Urdaneta's memorial to the King of Spain, written in 1561, speaks of alternative suggestions for the expedition to accomplish that end:

> If it should turn out that we cannot leave the coast of New Spain some time in January to sail toward the south as just stated, we should wait until

the month of March or later, until we have good winds with which to sail on the side of the Arctic Pole or north, following the coast of New Spain, which trends toward the west-northwest. Given propitious winds for this purpose we should sail, although perhaps somewhat distant from the coast, up to the latitude of 34 degrees or more, where we should endeavor to examine the country on the coast which Juan Rodriguez Cabrillo discovered. Taking what was necessary of what might be found on that coast and having communicated with the Indians, although only by signs, about a big water beyond toward the land side, of which they had given information to Juan Rodriguez Cabrillo, we should follow the coast in search of it . . .[3]

This reference to Cabrillo's "big water" puzzled Henry R. Wagner. He remarked: "There is nothing in the account of Cabrillo's voyage to indicate that he had heard anything about a large body of water. The only statements in his narrative which might be considered to relate to one are a reference to a river in the north."[4]

But given the confused wishful thinking about rivers and straits and gulfs and seas, it is highly likely Cabrillo's huge river *was* the phenomenon at issue. Urdaneta goes on to show that Cabrillo's "big water" could be anything—fresh or salt, even a sea:

We should follow the coast in search of it [a "big water"] in order to see if that water might be sea and if the end of this land be there. We should soon know if it is salt or fresh water and if God should be pleased that we discover what it is, we should take the direction from there toward the west on a southwest course down to 37 degrees or 35 degrees of latitude, sailing directly west from this point and discovering what there is between this land and China, to a point close to the Islands of Japan, if we should not discover something sooner of such importance that we would be contented with it.

The latitudes offered for Urdaneta's suggested side trip are quite consistent with the two passages quoted from the Cabrillo narrative (page 160). Cabrillo's first mention of the river is in the vicinity of the Santa Barbara channel, in the latitude of 34 degrees—the very latitude where Urdaneta thinks the exploration should begin. The second mention of a river in the Cabrillo narrative is between 42 and 43 degrees. Urdaneta presumably meant to navigate as far north as that since he spoke of dropping back "on a southwest course to 37 degrees" after determining the nature of the "big water."

Such an interest by Urdaneta almost twenty years after the Cabrillo expedition illustrates the grip exercised by the dream of straits. Cabrillo's failure to find an outlet had been seen by many not as the negation of a theory, but as a temporary failure to find proof of it. Despite empirical intimations to the contrary, the theory survived.

Out of Urdaneta's curiosity about the Northwest Coast and the North Pacific emerged the discovery of the belt of westerlies that would carry return craft eastward between the Philippines and Mendocino. Thereafter, this became the standard return route of the Manila galleons. A new surge of island-dreaming generated a crop of mythic islands in this region: the Isla del Armenio, the Rica de Oro, and the Rica de Plata.

As a consequence of interest in Cabrillo's "big water," Urdaneta's name became associated with modifications in the coast's imaginary geography. Anecdotes circulated about him having discovered and traversed a west-to-east transcontinental strait. Rumor also had it that around Mendocino he had entered the "rear entrance" of the "Strait of California," emerging from it at the head of the Gulf. With this, the seed of a huge island of California was planted, to germinate later in the century (see Chapter XXIV). Just as the "bottom" portal of the Strait of California had been linked with a possible west-east fork in Cortés' day, so the "top" portal was tied to the west-east passage Urdaneta was supposed to have navigated.

The figment of the Cabrillo-Urdaneta "estuary-outlet" or "big water" would survive for many years. In its wildest form it appears in apocryphal tales carried on the winds of rumor about straits sailed by men of several nationalities. Many of these are cited and quoted throughout the works of Bancroft and Wagner.[5]

The figment keeps cropping up in the otherwise sensible reports of French explorers. Jacques Cartier would believe that he had discovered in the St. Lawrence the gateway to the Orient. Père Marquette set out in 1673 to find a "Big Water," hoping to "reach the gulf of California, and thence the East Indies."[6] La Salle had similar expectations, and the Sieur de Vérendrye planned "to discover the Western Ocean" through a series of lakes and rivers which "must discharge above California."[7] This turned into "La Mer de l'Ouest" on the Buache map (Plate 51). There, one of the linking bodies of water in the west is "Grande Eau," once more reminding us of Urdaneta and Marquette. So tenacious was this transcontinental freshwater concept that belief in such a super-river endured into the mid-nineteenth century, until John Charles Frémont stated: "It has been constantly represented . . . that the bay of San Francisco opened far into the interior by some big river, on which

supposed stream the name of Rio Buenaventura has been bestowed . . .
Our observations . . . show that this neither is nor can be the case."[8]

We shall see an interesting manifestation of the "rear entrance" of
the Strait of California in the form of a "Rio de Los Estrechos," a "River
of the Straits," on a map of Abraham Ortelius in 1587 (*see* Plate 37).
This feature would play a part in British thinking toward a revival of the
Isle-of-California myth (*see* Chapters XIX and XX).

But in the interim following Cabrillo and before the myth's reflowering,
cartographers in general came down heavily on the side of the theory
that the land called California was the western arm of a huge bay. The
Ortelius map just cited represents that view. Nevertheless, continuing
awareness of the island-theory alternative is exhibited in a number of
maps. By charting ambiguous features, some mapmakers seemed to keep
their options open.

Various devices were used for this. The map of Diogo Homem, dated
1568 (Plate 24) employs the traditional method of unfinished openings.

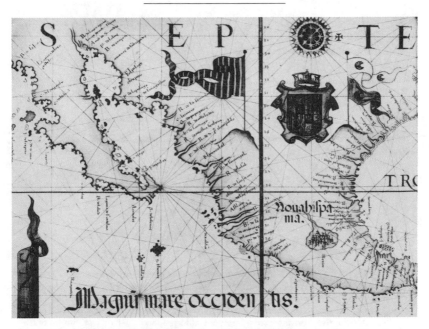

PLATE 24. Unfinished inlets at the nook of the Gulf and along both coasts of Baja kept
alive the possibility of straits in this Diogo Homem map of 1558. *Photograph and permission
by the British Library (ADD. MSS. 5415-A).*

The opening at the crotch could be either the mouth of a river or the outlet of a narrow strait. An unfinished opening on the outside coast of Baja at the Cabo del Engaño corresponds with one on the inner coast, suggesting a smaller island. Similarly, Battista Agnese continued to show an opening at the north of his red-colored Mar Vermejo (*see* Plate 22).

A useful fence-sitting device was to create a river on paper with a little *trompe-l'œil* to allow it to suggest a strait. Giacomo Gastaldi's map of 1546, favoring the "continentalist" view, depicts a huge river rising on the Asian side of the landbridge, and flowing broadly all the way to the Gulf of California (*see* Plate 25a). So huge and wide a river suggests a strait. A mere jog of the hand could turn California into an island. One way of doing this is shown in a seventeenth-century "doctored" version in the Bibliothèque Nationale (*see* Plate 25b).

In 1561 Gastaldi revoked his former "continentalist" persuasion by

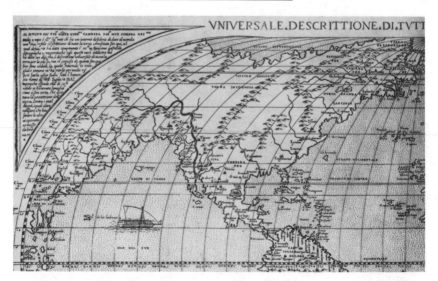

PLATES 25a & b.   This huge, imaginary waterway is yet another expression of uncertainty about what lay north of the head of the Gulf. 25a (above) is a version of Giacomo Gastaldi's map of 1546 (made by Paolo Forlani in 1560). 25b (at right) is a copy modified in the seventeenth century to insert a Strait of Anian between Asia and America, demonstrating how readily the river converts into a Strait of California, and the land to westward of the river into a huge island of California. *Photographs and permission by the British Library (K. Top. 4.6.) and the Bibliothèque Nationale (GE D 12287. BIS), respectively.*

showing a small separation between Asia and America, named the Strait of Anian. This new concept will be discussed in Chapter XVII. What interests us here about his new map is how Gastaldi appears to hedge his bets about California's topography. One branch of the big river emptying into the Gulf has its source very near the northwest coast. A confusion of the curves of the river with the curves of the pictorialized mountains invite the reading of a "Strait of California" (*see* sketch map, Plate 26). There is a second possibility when another branch flowing south into the Gulf lines up with a river flowing north into some northern sea. A short stroke would join the two. At the very least, easy portage is suggested between the heads of these paired rivers. Zaltieri's map of 1566, and Paolo Forlani's map of 1574 copy these features.

Ortelius's heart-shaped map of 1564 also presents the source of the Gulf's river as very close to the northwest coast (*see* Plate 27).

None of these maps remotely resembles the course of the real Colorado River. They are figments of imagination fabricated out of lingering dreams.

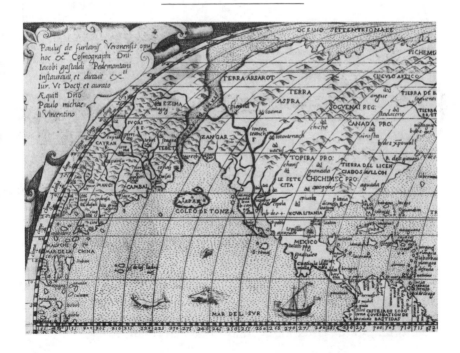

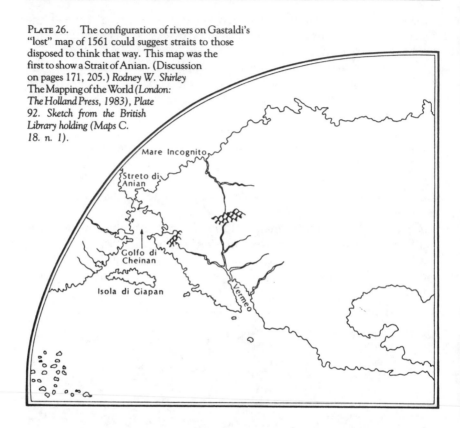

PLATE 26. The configuration of rivers on Gastaldi's "lost" map of 1561 could suggest straits to those disposed to think that way. This map was the first to show a Strait of Anian. (Discussion on pages 171, 205.) *Rodney W. Shirley* The Mapping of the World (*London: The Holland Press, 1983*), *Plate 92. Sketch from the British Library holding (Maps C. 18. n. 1).*

Yet another way of keeping options open was to feature a tremendously long Gulf of California (Plate 28). Johann Honter's "continentalist"-style map of 1561 depicts a gulf reaching vaguely far into northern latitudes. Another accommodation is found on the "insularist"-style map of Michele Tramezzino, dated 1554. Here, California is shown as a long, thin appendage dangling by a mere thread from the mainland. The long Gulf falls just short of being a "Strait of California" outletting into the North Pacific Ocean, which merges with the insularists' wide northern sea (Plate 29).

A world map of 1570 by Jehan Cossin shows two open arms at the head of the Gulf. One points toward an open arm from the Septentrional Sea. The other all but meets an open arm from the outside coast of California, so the latter looks almost islanded (Plate 30).

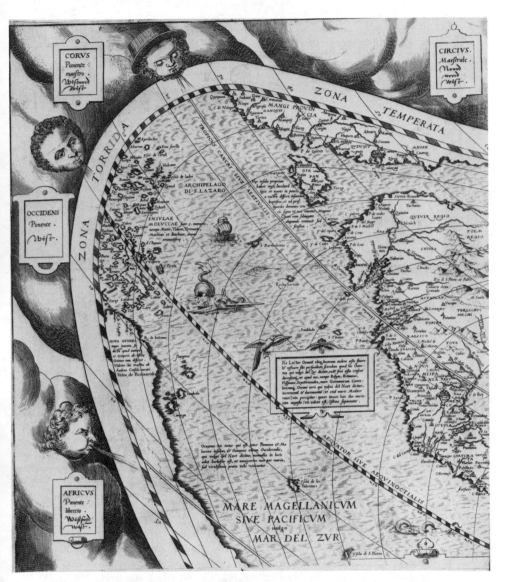

PLATE 27. An imaginary branch of the Colorado River rises close to the northwest coast in Ortelius's map of 1564. Strait-of-California enthusiasts must have been tempted to complete the line to the coast. (Discussion on page 171). *Photograph and permission by the British Library (Maps C.2.a.6.).*

PLATE 28. The long Gulf, stretching beyond 50°, on Johann Honter's map of 1561, is another imaginative conjecture about the waterway between California and the mainland. (Discussion on page 172.) *Photograph and permission by the British Library (C.74.a.14).*

PLATE 29. California is a hair-breadth short of being an island on this portion of Michele Tramezzino's map of 1554. (Discussion on pages 172, 224.) *Photograph and permission by the British Library (Maps K Top IV.2.).*

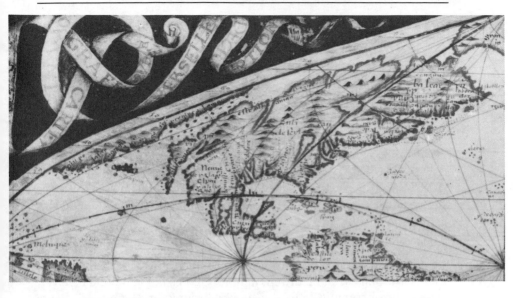

PLATE 30.   An opening at the head of the Gulf is level with an opening on the outside coast to suggest that Baja could be quickly converted into an island, in this portion of a 1570 map by Jehan Cossin. (Discussion on page 172.) *Photograph and permission by the Bibliothèque Nationale (Rés GE D 7896).*

Another way to test the tenacity of a geographical myth is to consult the opinions of those living closest to the region. The pearl fishermen in the Gulf were the most acquainted with the area. Indeed, in this long hiatus, they were virtually the only Spaniards from the mainland keeping first-hand contact with the Gulf and Baja. They were, however, simple men; there is little on record recounting their activities and views. We must rely, therefore, on a general history, and one that was written after this period of quiescence began coming to a close. This is the *Chronicle* or *History* of Baltasar de Obregón, despatched to the King in 1584.

Obregón gives a fascinating glimpse of the thinking of the period's pearl fishers. This glimpse is based on personal memory. Apparently sometime before the year 1564, as dated by Wagner and others, Obregón went pearl-fishing along the Gulf coast with Antonio de Luna, his father-in-law.[9] On the basis of his experience, Obregón declares that the Tizon River (the present Colorado River) drains into "the arm of the sea called *ancón.*" He states that, as Cabeza de Vaca and Coronado had discovered, east and north of the *ancón* "all this coast is firm and participant with [joined to] Quivira, Cibola, Tibuex, New Mexico and Florida." But speaking of the west side of the gulf he describes Baja as "la Isla de California."[10]

Obregón's fishing trip occurred almost a quarter of a century after the Ulloa and Alarcón expeditions were supposed to have pushed the bias toward peninsularity. His account calls, therefore, for particular attention. He asserts:

> I have been an eye witness of some of the things of which I am giving account to your majesty, especially of those in the region along the coast from Acapulco to the Tizon River and California, where I went to serve your majesty in the company of Don Antonio de Luna, my father-in-law.[11]

In the next sentence in this account, he defines California unequivocally as an island:

> He went to that island to fish for pearls.

In an earlier section, California is given the same geographic status, though the name is garbled. This jumble, George P. Hammond believes, "was an error committed by the copyist." Hammond's translations are used here:

> I came from the trip which I made to the island Cardena de la Carniferia. I was accompanied by my father-in-law, Don Antonio de Luna.[12]

The Isla de Cardon, or Isla de Cardonas—perhaps meaning "isle of teasel or thistle" in description of the cactus there—was the name sometimes given in early *relaciones de servicios* by Cortés' followers.[13]

But to return to the section that speaks clearly of the island of California (correctly spelled), Obregón continues his account of his excursion there with his father-in-law:

> In three days he [Antonio de Luna] obtained a large number of oysters through the help of the native divers of the island. Among these people were found large quantities of misshapen, burned, and unbored pearls damaged by fire. The marquis found one which he valued at more than five thousand ducats; and many others of high value were secured by the soldiers whom he took along . . .[14]

Clearly, the Marqués del Valle has not been forgotten, nor his harbor, his settlement, his soldiers, or his "island." The great romantic elements out of the Mandeville and Polo tradition are "proven" here: the giant pearls of great price, and the ignorant natives who cook their oysters with the pearls still inside them.

In the following section, bearing the subtitle "Spring of Water on the Island California," the Marquis is again remembered:

> Those who may go to this island should provide themselves with fresh water. Within two harquebus shots from the shore in front of the harbor of the marquis Don Hernando Cortes is a spring which flows into the sea. Its water must be drawn when the tide is low.

Reading Obregón's account, we can imagine the simple fishermen regaling each other with stories as they steered their fishing boats up the uncertain Gulf. Obregón describes his "island" of California with several details suggestive of the Amazon myth. It is a hostile island, guarded by warlike, bestial people. This description is given the subtitle "Quality of the Island California and Its Inhabitants:"

> In California are high bare mountains. It is a thorny and craggy island inhabited by naked cannibals, the most primitive, immodest, dirty, vile, and wretched people ever seen or known in the Indies. Besides eating their own excrement they do not act with propriety, nor do they consider it immodest for the women to place themselves on all fours and have intercourse with the Indians before one another and the Christians at any hour of the day like mere animals. They wear their hair long, stretching to the waist. They are warlike from pure bestiality. They are wonderful divers and practise that activity in finding pearl-bearing oysters in water from fifteen to twenty fathoms deep. This is their ordinary food. [15]

What is an Amazon-style island without gold, as well as pearls? Obregón states gold will be found further north along the Island's coast. There, "it is possible that they are clothed people who possess gold and silver."

Since Obregón was writing in 1584, he would have had to take account of the contending views of peninsularity and insularity of California. In a syntactically problematic passage, Obregón appears to offer an ingenious method to reconcile the conflict. Literally translated, the passage suggests that low and high tides join or detach California to or from the mainland by turns:

> It goes down (or diminishes?) to the *island* of California when the tide is up; and when the tide is out, it becomes mainland with that of Quivira and Florida. (*Baja a la isla de la California cuando es creciente y cuando es menguante queda hecha tierra firme con la de Quibira y Florida.*) [16]

The tidal theory of transitory "islandness" may owe something to the reports of Ulloa and Alarcón about how the tides rushed in and out of the nook of the Gulf. Such behavior of tides rising several feet in a

channel at the nook is recorded on the Agnese map (Plate 22). If
Obregón was thinking of that phenomenon, he was not thinking of any
small island such as the one sometimes postulated at the southern end of
Baja. Rather, he would have been led to envisage a much larger island
extending north of the latitude of the Ancón de San Andrés.

Another passage, again somewhat cryptic, suggests that he indeed
was thinking of islanded territory of a considerable size:

> The mountain chain of the island is ranged along the route of the
> Philippine ships [or the voyage from the Philippines] for more than six
> hundred leagues. (*Va encadenada la sierra de la isla el viaje de las Filipinas mas
> de seiscientas leguas.*)

The galleons from Manila arrived off the California coast near Mendocino.
They caught the California Current flowing south along the coast all the
way to Cabo San Lucas, before crossing the *boca* of the Gulf to
Acapulco. If Obregón perceived the mountain range of California as
running along much of that route, then the island he conceived was
very large indeed.

Obregón's theory of a tidal island could not have been derived from
actual experience. What we have in his report are tantalizing glimpses
of folk memory. They indicate that Cortés' dream conceit was still
clinging to life in the cultural subsoil. It had survived intact through the
decades of the forties to the eighties, passed from one person to another,
as from Luna to Obregón.

Evident here is the psychology of straddling. Some imaginations
spawn hybrid rationalizations to avoid deciding between questioned
myth and experience-generated hypothesis. Among the causes and
motivations are timidity, romanticism, fear of conflict, and an overrated
or sentimental respect for harmony, compromise, and reconciliation.
Another example of straddling is on pages 318–19.

Such references as Obregón's to the island myth would surely have
triggered many recollections of views prevailing forty-odd years earlier.
Seventy-year-old survivors of the explorations of 1533 to 1542 would
have brought the myth out of the attic of their memories and dusted it
off. It wouldn't have taken many of these nostalgia trips for the island
theory to start enjoying a new vogue.

What was it that stirred these memories? What could have stimulated
a revival of Cortés' beliefs?

Obregón's Chronicle was dispatched to Felipe II in 1584. Answers to
our questions must be sought in the events preceding the writing of the
Chronicle. Part II of this study is an attempt to account for not only the

revival of those memories, but for a full-blown second manifestation of the island myth that grew from it.

Before grappling with the causes of that second flowering, we should note that the phenomenon is not unanimously perceived as a rein- statement. A difference of opinion exists among historians of its rela- tionship to the earlier belief. Hubert Howe Bancroft saw a definite connection between the two occurrences. Speaking of Cortés' accept- ance of his discovery as an island, Bancroft comments:

> The idea that it was an island was soon abandoned, only to be revived for a longer life in later years. [17]

Elsewhere, however, Bancroft comments on the second manifestation:

> The real source of the new geographical idea . . . has not been known to modern writers.

He did not probe the possible connection he had earlier perceived.

Henry Raup Wagner sees no affinities in the double incidence. He warns his readers that the conception of an island of California in the seventeenth century "must not be confounded with the similar one entertained when California was discovered." In his view, "the two conceptions were totally distinct, and had no historical connection."[18] And he repeats this statement elsewhere:

> This [seventeenth-century] conception had no connection, historic or geographic, with the idea which arose when California was first discovered, that it was an island. That opinion disappeared after the voyages of Ulloa and Alarcón and all the maps in circulation from about 1545 to 1625 display California in its true form, as a peninsula. [19]

Despite this statement, Wagner recognized that the first phase of the island myth never quite died out:

> Nevertheless, during all that time the views held about the configuration of the upper part of the Gulf of California and about the rivers flowing into it were extremely hazy. The idea continually crops up that the gulf did not end where the Colorado River enters it, but extended northward to the west of that river.

Wagner comes closer to Bancroft here. And Bancroft's hunch is the more appealing. It seems too much of a coincidence for the same notion to spring up twice in the same context without being connected. It is far more likely that a single myth should flower a second time. We know from modern studies and experience that myths are persistent and resistant. The tenacity of astrology through the ages is a case in point, as are the more recent myths of Big Foot and UFOs.

Later chapters will trace the regrowth of the myth from the time it started putting out new shoots to its fruition (and ultimate decline). At the same time an attempt will be made to demonstrate how this second growth is connected both to Cortés' conception and to the whole ancient and medieval tradition of the romance of islands. But to do this we shall have to leave the threshold of California for a while, and pick up some new threads of the story.

PART TWO

Chapter XV

Tudor England Catches South-Sea-Island Fever

To put it baldly, it was the British who would reactivate the dormant concept of a Strait of California in the Spanish consciousness during the 1570s and 80s.

But how this came about is a long and involved story. We need to shine the spotlight on England for a chapter or two. What was going on in Tudor Britain while Spain was feathering her nest in the New World?

The British, no less than the Spanish, believed in the myriad isles of Ind. The Englished versions of *Mandeville's Travels*—such as the one used for quotation in this study—as well as other travel works and treatises on geography, circulated these exciting dreams. In the decades before Columbus sailed, Bristol mariners had searched the northern part of the Atlantic for such legendary islands as Hi Brasil, perhaps as way-stations for a longer voyage. Then, in the mid-1490s, the Cabots sailed northwest to seek "islands and lands" for the King of England. The "Newe Isle," or the New Found Land, is what they reached. But after the Spanish discovery of the "other ocean," the north became, in imagination, less an end than a means; rather than a destination, a route to the South Sea.

The romance of islands and the appeal of Vespucci's voyages inspired the setting of Thomas More's *Utopia* in 1515. Other fans of exploration under Henry VIII were some young West-of-England men who had close trade contacts with the Spanish and Portuguese. These English merchants had residences in Seville as well as in London and their home port of Bristol. This international set, trading in wines and oils and other exotic commodities, included the Thorne brothers, Robert and Nicholas, their representative, Emanuel Lucar, Roger Barlow, Henry Latimer or Patmer, John Bridges (who became a Lord Mayor of London), and the Ostrich kin, one of whom married Sebastian Cabot's daughter, so tightly knit was this circle.[1]

Robert Thorne's father had been associated with John Cabot when he made his historic landfall. As a child, Thorne had thrilled to stories of the voyage. All his life he cherished dreams of further explorations in the northwest in order to find the passage to Cathay and Ind. He himself may, on health grounds, have only been able to enjoy his dreams vicariously. This he did by financing voyages and choosing surrogates to participate. That is what happened in the case of Sebastian Cabot's voyage intended "for the discovery of Tharsis, Ophir and Eastern Cathay," via the Magellan Straits, the Southwest Passage, in 1526. Thorne put up a considerable sum of money for two friends, Roger Barlow and Henry Latimer, to take part in the expedition.

Of course there were other motives besides burning curiosity and pure enthusiasm for Thorne's generous backing. As a Bristol-Seville merchant, he stood to benefit materially from opening new trade. But his main desire was to have his two friends pick up some experience in navigation and gain access to confidential Spanish charts. They were also to determine, if they could, whether the Pacific Ocean was open in the north—that is, whether "insularist" maps were closer to reality than were "continentalist" maps. Thorne had a secret reason for wanting to know that.

While Cabot and Barlow were exploring the east coast of South America, Robert Thorne met Henry VIII's almoner, Dr. Edward Lee. Lee was on a diplomatic mission to Seville, in part to collect a debt owed by the Emperor to the King. Thorne was called on to provide banking services for transmission of the funds. Lee may also have asked Thorne's opinions about whether Henry should make a bid for the "Spiceries"— later sold to Portugal in 1529.

Thorne seized the opportunity to interest Lee—and through him, Henry VIII—in a pet project he had nursed for many years. Thorne put it all down in his famous letter of 1527. This letter survives in manuscript in the British Library.[2] The printing by Hakluyt in his *Divers Voyages* of 1582 is used for quotation below.

Perhaps in answer to questions from Lee, Thorne discusses the Pope's division of the world between Spain and Portugal, and their quarrel over title to the rich spice islands. This gives Thorne the excuse to deliver a short geography lesson. His thoughts about the spherical world provide a perfect preface for arguing his pet project. He seizes the opportunity to propose that England seek a route via the North Pole to get down into the South Sea. Finding the shortest, most convenient, route to Cathay and the isles of Ind, would give England a decided edge:

> Nowe then, (if from the sayde newe founde landes the Sea bee Navigable), there is no doute, but sayling Northwarde and passing the pole, descending to the equinoctialle lyne, wee shall hitte these Ilandes, and it should bee much more shorter way then eyther the Spaniardes or the Portingales have . . .[3]

Thorne's belief in a polar passage is based on a conviction that "up there" it was all open ocean. He is squarely in the camp of the "insularists." In this he had been influenced by the claim of Sebastian Cabot. This report comes down to us through Ramusio as translated by Hakluyt:

> Having sayled a long time West and by North beyonde these Ilandes unto the latitude of 67 degrees and an halfe under the North Pole, and at the 11 day of June, finding still the open Sea without any manner of impediment, he [Cabot] thought verily by that way to have passed on still the way to Cathaio, which is in the East.[4]

Thorne's enthusiastic faith in the prospects of his project is generalized into this statement of supreme optimism:

> There is no lande unhabitable nor sea innavigable.[5]

This slogan would animate British expansionism throughout the sixteenth century.

The polar route advocated by Thorne was one aspect of the dream to find what came to be called the "North-West Passage." The name comes from the direction taken by English ships when they left English ports to seek the elusive waterway across the north of America. It came into use to differentiate it from English sailings to the northeast around mid century, when the main quest was for a North-East Passage, across the "top" of Russia, down into the South Sea.

At the time when Thorne was making his big pitch about a polar route, the "continentalists" in New Spain and elsewhere were joining America and Asia. That concept might even have been given extra play to dampen English and French enthusiasm for a northern passage. Such a continuity of land between Asia and America would present an impossible obstacle for those dreaming to reach the South Sea from the north.

But the English were such dogged "insularists" nothing would daunt them. Their vision of the New World remained a collection of islands and wide waterways. When Thorne was presenting his theory, maps like Peter Apian's (Plate 10) represented the many-islanded New World championed by the insularists.

Indeed, the English eagerly welcomed every new theory that kept North America small and surrounded by water. The Verrazzano-style maps and globes (Plates 17, 32, and page 135) were particularly dear to them. These depicted the incursion of the South Sea as far east as an

"isthmus" north of Florida near Cape Hatteras. Such a map, now lost, was given to Henry VIII.[6]

Henry secretly got together an exploring party of his own. John Rut was sent to make "a certain exploration toward the north between Labrador and Newfoundland." As may be expected, his ultimate mission was to "go and discover the land of the Great Khan."[7] Rut carried with him Henry's Verrazzano map, or a copy of it.

Rut did not, of course, fulfill his charge. He was forced to turn south after meeting "many large islands of ice." Then he sailed all the way down the coast to the Caribbean, searching for a way to get to those "islands that we are commanded by the grace of God, as we were commanded at our departing."

Rut set sail in 1527. That was the same year as Thorne's letter. There was apparently no direct connection between the two events, except that both, like the Verrazzano voyage, demonstrate accelerating interest in seeking a northern waterway.

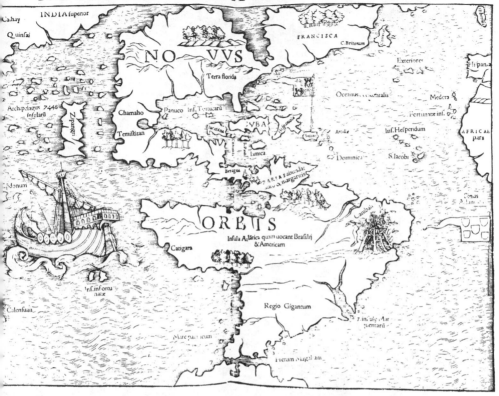

PLATES 31 a & b.   Insularists delighted in Sebastian Münster's maps of 1540-41, one titled "New Islands." The following features are notable:

1.   Islands numbering 7448 (Marco Polo's estimate) in the South Sea shown on both maps. (Discussion on pages 26, 85.)

2.   The name "Insula Atlantica," the Island of Atlantis, marked across what had already been named (South) America. (Discussion on pages 196, 200ff.)

3.   An open seaway across the north, which became the "North-West Passage." (Discussion on pages 189, 200ff.)

4.   A huge bay scooping southward between "Terra Florida" and "Francisca," representing the Verrazzano Sea. (Discussion on page 135.)

Photographs and permission by the British Library (Maps C.1.c.2.).

Through the 1530s and 40s, blind faith in a northern waterway would be expressed in many maps by non-Spanish Europeans. Sebastian Münster, in 1540, featured not only Marco Polo's 7448 South-Sea islands; he promised a strait to get to them. *Per hoc fretū iter patet ad Molucae*— "By this strait the route is open to the Moluccas"—he wrote across the north (Plates 31 and 32). Equally favored by the insularists were globes like the one depicted in Hans Holbein-the-Younger's paint-

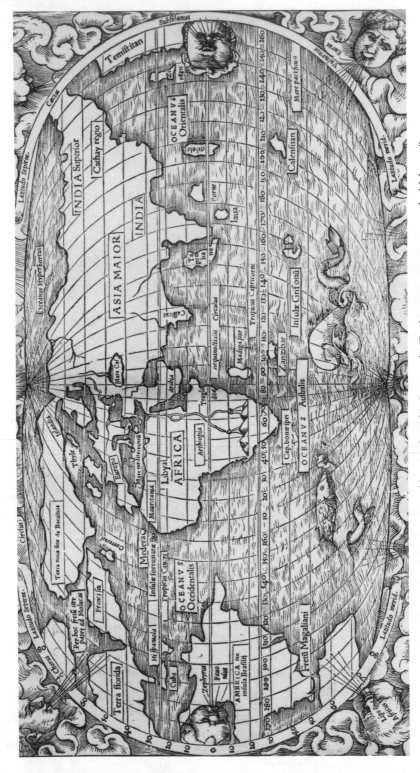

PLATE 32. On Münster's world map, a legend in Latin reads: "By this strait a way is open to the Moluccas," suggesting a strait from the Bacallaos into the open northern sea. (Discussion on page 187.) *Photograph and permission by the British Library (Maps C.1.c.2).*

ing "The Ambassadors," and the similar "Anonymous Globe Gores" now in the New York Public Library. The maps of Gerhardus Mercator continued this school of imaging.

A glance at the Gemma Frisius-Peter Apian map (Plate 33), will explain its appeal to the insularists. Along the "top" of a skinny North America is a wide ocean. From the narrow North Sea entrance at the Bacallaos the coast turns in a smooth curve west to southwest down to the Pacific coast of New Spain. From the point of view of an English mariner, once the fretum or strait at the Codfish Sea had been penetrated, it would be plain sailing along the Septentrional (Northern) Sea. This was not quite the over-the-pole route Thorne had envisaged, but both would bring one out into the wide waterway between Asia and America, thence down into the South Sea or Pacific ocean. There was one burning question shared by all: where exactly was this magic gateway to the Orient on the Atlantic seaboard of the New World?

These figments of straits and open northern seas dominated the thinking of the British throughout the century. As they moved from armchair exploration to the real thing in the last half of the century,

PLATE 33.   A wide seaway washes the north of the "island" of America in this 1540 map by Gemma Frisius, first published in Peter Apian's *Cosmographia* of 1544. It expresses the typical "insularist" view of easy access to the South Sea's rich islands. *Photograph and permission by the British Library (from Gregor Reisch's 1583 edition of the* Margarita Philosophica, *Basle).*

these preconceptions would bear upon the reburgeoning of the island myth of California.

So far we have looked only at the theory of routes in Robert Thorne's pet project. His letter also promises unusual destinations never yet discovered. Like everybody else, he is preoccupied with islands. He has the rich-South-Sea-Island dream. But he does not intend for England to trespass on known Spanish and Portuguese preserves. It turns out that the islands he is interested in promoting are not precisely those of the "spicerie of the Emperour" that "are fertile of cloves, nutmegs, mace and cinnamon," . . . or "other there about" which "abounde in gold, Rubies, Diamonds . . . and other stones and pearles."[8] He claims there are a host of *new* islands, with exactly the same bounties, waiting to be found:

> And though wee went not to the said Ilandes, for that they are the Emperours or Kinges of Portingale, we should by the way, and comming once to the line Equinoctiall, finde landes no less riche of Golde and spicerie as all other lands are under the said line Equinoctiall: and also should, if wee may passe under the North, enjoye the Navigation of all Tartarie.

He says he doesn't include many islands on his accompanying map only for "lacke of roome" and because "there can be no certification how they stand." On a map attributed to him, the imaginary islands of Solomon's Ophir and Tharsis do, however, appear. As discussed in Chapter V, South-Sea-island status had been given to these legendary places by Martin Fernández de Enciso in his *Suma de Geographia.* Thorne would have seen this work when it was published by Jacobo Cromberger in Seville in 1519. His acquaintance with the work will be apparent when we come to discuss Roger Barlow's further contributions on pages 192–93.

Exactly what new islands Thorne had in mind for the polar voyagers are located by his comparing various routes through the South Sea. Once over the pole, the voyagers would have three choices. The first would be this:

> For they being past the Pole, it is plaine they maye decline to what parte they list. If they will goe towarde the Orient, they shall injoy the regions of all the Tartarians that extende towarde the midday, and from thence they may goe and proceede to the lande of ye Chinas, and from thence to the land of Cathaio oriental which is of all the mayne lande most orientall that can bee reckoned from our habitation. And if from thence they doe continue their navigation following the coaste that returns towarde the

occident, they shall fall in Melassa, and so in all the Indees which we call oriental; and, following that way, may return hither by the Cape of Bona Speransa: and thus they shall compasse the whole worlde.[9]

The second option would be this:

And if they will take their course after they be past the pole towarde the occident, they shall goe in the backe side of the new found lande, which of late was discovered by your Grace's subiectes, untill they come to the backside and South seas of the Indees occidentalls. And so continuing the viage, they may returne thorowe the Straite of Magallanas to this countrey, and so they compasse also the worlde by that way.

But those are the provinces of the Portuguese and Spaniards. Here is England's special objective:

If they goe this thirde way, and after they bee past the pole, goe right toward the pole Antartike, and then decline toward the lands and Ilands situated between the Tropikes and under the Equinoctial, without doubt they shal find there ye richest lands and Ilands of the worlde of Golde, precious stones, balmes, spices, and other thinges that we here esteeme most: which come out of strang countreys, and may returne the same way.

Thorne was an armchair explorer of visionary rank. He had a practical imagination that enabled him to think in terms of a globe. He could visualize going over the "top" of the world into the South Sea. Coming from the north he could steer in any direction that he chose. He could see himself heading southwest to Cathay and Ind, thence home around Africa via the Cape of Good Hope. Or he could sail southeast and touch the back side, the Pacific coast, of New Spain, thence continuing south to the Straits of Magellan and homeward across the Atlantic on a northeast course.

But the bit he really liked envisioning was coming over the pole into the South Sea and taking a course due south until he reached the tropical belt. There he would find a host more of the rich islands which had never hitherto been discovered. After claiming these for England, he could then sail back over the north pole, only having to "travell halfe of the way that other doe, wich goe round about as aforesaid."

Thorne did not cut this dream of many undiscovered islands out of whole cloth. Enciso's book would have given him the general picture. Also, this was the time when Cortés was lobbying the Spanish Court for a contract. Cortés wanted royal permission and concessions to go in search of the islands he believed to be not far off the coast of New Spain. Peter Martyr had interviewed Rivera, Cortés' delegate to the Court, and broadcast it. Thorne would certainly have known about all that. When Thorne told Dr. Lee he had "discovered the secret" of the Spanish map-makers, the hoped-for islands off the coast of New Spain may have been what he had in mind. Around this time (1527), the cluster of islands appeared on Franciscus Monachus' map (Plate11), and later, on such maps as the Sloane Manuscript map of 1530, and the maps of Orontius Finaeus (see Plates 12 and 13)—where they are confused with the Malay Archipelago. We may surmise that a desire to pick up scuttlebutt about these islands could have been another good reason that Thorne had paid Barlow's and Latimer's passage on the Cabot expedition. Thorne's excitement at the prospect of the English being the first to reach them arose out of his belief that the route "over the top" would take them swiftly there and back.

Apparently Dr. Lee suggested that Thorne should write a proper address to the King once the outcome of Sebastian Cabot's voyage was known. As it turned out, Cabot didn't make it into the South Sea; he got only to the River Plate. Barlow returned in 1529. Political hostility between Spain and England led him to leave Spain with Thorne around 1530.

These men had not lost any enthusiasm from Cabot's difficulties. After all, their faith was firmly staked on the polar route. They worked on the declaration to Henry VIII to make their case and solicit support, though apparently it never reached the King. But Thorne was heavily committed to the enterprise. Even before he left Spain, he had bought a Bristol-built vessel on the Spanish market, called the *Saviour*. [10]

But suddenly all plans came to an end. Thorne died in 1532 at the age of forty. Barlow did not have the resources to continue alone. He married a Bristol woman and settled down to raise a family. Using his connections, he parlayed the prestige gained from the Cabot expedition to acquire and develop an estate in Pembrokeshire over the next ten years.

By 1540, now a prosperous squire, Barlow decided to have another stab at the dream project. He did this by writing a work that E. G. R. Taylor titled a *Brief Summe of Geographie* for purposes of publication. This work is not much more than a translation of Martin Fernández de Enciso's 1518 publication adapted to Barlow's purposes by some additions and slight changes. The last pages of the manuscript—to be seen in the British Library today just as it came from Barlow's hand—are almost a repetition of Thorne's Declaration. Taylor thought that the

Address to the King was that which was written, but undelivered, in 1530.

The vital passage concerning the third direction to be taken once over the north pole to reach the secret islands has been slightly changed:

> And if in passing the pole articke thei will saille streite toward the pole antarticke, thei shall enclyne to the londes and ilondes that have ther situacion betwene the tropicons and under the equinoctiall, which without dout be the most richest londes and ilondes in the world, for all the golde, spices, aromatikes and pretiose stones, with all other thinges that we have in estimation, from thens thei come. [11]

The Privy Council debated Barlow's proposal. Cabot was standing by. But no expedition resulted. Nor were any commands given to honor Barlow's request to have his book "put forth in print." The *Brief Summe of Geographie* would have done much to raise the popular consciousness to awareness of new geographical theory. But it remained in its single original manuscript form until the Hakluyt Society published it in the twentieth century.

The Wotton Manuscript, written by a family member about the Barlow family in the eighteenth century, says this:

> Had not King H. ye 8th death prevented it, he [Roger Barlow] was to have undertaken ye discovery of ye northern passage to ye East Indies with three of his Majesty's ships from Milfordhaven, where he purchased a fine estate of Harry ye 8th. [12]

Even after Henry's death the expedition was still being weighed. Secret intelligence to the Dowager Queen of Hungary in 1550 reported "that the English are seeking a road to the Indies" and that "the king intended to send a few ships towards Iceland by the northern route to discover some island which is said to be rich in gold."[13] The same source reported in 1551 that "certain Englishmen experienced in navigation who have been with Cabot" are "to go to discover some islands, or seek a road to the Indies, taking the way of the Arctic Pole."[14]

Barlow was appointed Vice-Admiral of the coast for Pembrokeshire in 1549, but he died in 1554 without having taken part in any polar expedition.

As yet, mid century, England posed no threat to New Spain. But the seeds planted by Thorne and Barlow would bear much fruit in the following half century.

Chapter XVI

THE BRITISH DREAM UP A
NORTH-WEST PASSAGE TO SOUTH-SEA ISLES

A new crop of believers and enthusiasts took over where the Thorne-Barlow circle left off. This group, though London-based, was still largely composed of West-of-England men and some of Welsh extraction, both having strong seafaring traditions. It was a much larger group of people than the Thorne group, with more diverse interests and abilities. They did not form a close circle. But many had more than a nodding acquaintance with one another, and among them were numerous deep friendships and close family and business relationships. This loose constellation of enthusiasts pursued their interests over the second half of the sixteenth century, for the duration of Elizabeth's long reign.

This group falls into subgroups of men with special talents and interests, though there were a number of all-rounders. Among the men of ideas were researchers and translators. They brought works of exploration from Spanish, Portuguese and Italian sources to the clerisy, the literate public. Richard Eden pioneered such publications just after mid century. Then, in the last two decades of Elizabeth's reign, Richard Hakluyt the Younger executed that vital task. Hakluyt's importance may be judged from the many times this study has had recourse to his work. Samuel Purchas continued Hakluyt's work into the seventeenth century.

By contrast, another kind of scholar was not concerned with publication and popularization of exploration literature. John Dee and Richard Hakluyt the Elder served rather as advisors to the cognoscenti. They built great private libraries of maps and manuscripts for consultation.

Among or behind the scholars was a sympathetic cadre from the establishment élite. These were the people with the power to make things happen. The names that come up in the politics of Tudor expansionism include Lord Burghley, the Dudleys, the Sidneys, Sir Francis Walsingham, Sir Christopher Hatton, Robert Beale, besides the Queen herself. There were also financial backers from the rich merchant class. These banded together to form joint stock companies, such as the Muscovy Company, to fund ventures into the South Sea.

And finally there were the doers, among whom were Gilbert, Willoughby, Chancellor, Frobisher, Davis, Raleigh, Grenville, Hawkins, Cavendish, and Drake.

There is no room here to follow their exciting voyages. Our concern is with the intellectual background of British exploration. Shortly before Elizabeth came to the throne, Richard Eden was the chief purveyor of ideas. As an associate of William Cecil, later Lord Burghley, Eden waved the torch for exploration by the British. He exhorted his countrymen to renounce their "inexcusable slothfulness." He urged them on first by serving as a conduit for such works as Münster's *Cosmographie*, Pigafetta's *Voyage of Magellan*, and Peter Martyr's first three Decades, all published before 1555. More than that he expressed personal views in prefatory letters to the reader. Echoing Thorne and Barlow, he took up such matters as the islands of the South Sea, especially Ophir and Tarsis, and the need to seek "the passage by the North Sea into the main East Sea"—whether that turned out to be via the northeast ("above" Russia), or the northwest.[1]

Eden gave a special fillip to the insularist persuasion by the selection of a certain excerpt in his compilation. This excerpt occurs in a section "Other notable things . . . out of the writings . . . of Francisco Lopez de Gomara and Sebastian Cabot." After the quotation of Seneca's prophecy of the discovery of a great new land, Plato's opinions are discussed under the heading "Of the Great Iland which Plato called Atlantica or Atlantide":

> The Philosopher Plato writeth in his Dialogues of Timeus and Cricia, that in the old time there was in the sea Atlantike over against Affrica, an Ilande called Atlantide greater than Affrica and Asia: affirming that those lands are from thence continent and great . . . But that in a certain great earthquake and tempest of rain, the Ilande sunk and the people were drowned: Also that there remained so much mud of the drowning or sinking of that Ilande that that sea Atlantike could not be sailed. Some take this for a fable: and many for a true history . . . But there is now no cause why we should any longer doubt or dispute of the Iland Atlantide, forasmuch as the discovering and conquest of the west Indies do plainly declare what Plato hath written of the said lands . . . We may . . . say that the Indies are either the Ilande and firm land of Plato or the remnant of the same: and not the Ilandes of Hesperides or Ophir, or Tharsis, as some have thought of late days . . . As concerning Ophir and Tharsis, it is not known what or where they be.[2]

Although, as Gómara points out, Columbus had himself considered this Platonic theory, it played more into British predilections. It worked very nicely to back up the British desire for islands and resultant waterways in the north of the New World. It tied in both with inundation legends associated with King Arthur, and with the lore of Arthur's island conquests in northern climes, named by Geoffrey of Monmouth as Iceland and the "Six Islands of the Ocean Sea."[3] Belief in these Arthurian islands was revived in the sixteenth century through such works as William Lambard's *Archaionomia* of 1568. A mysterious, anonymous text called *Gestae Arthuri*, "Deeds of Arthur," had the hero discovering and colonizing Arctic and American islands — a view beloved by John Dee, who decreed the Tudors of Arthurian lineage.

These Arthurian claims were, perhaps, bolstered by resonances of Viking island-hopping to Iceland, Greenland, and Vinland in the tenth century, and by a purported fourteenth-century voyage of the Zeno brothers from Venice to the Arctic, reported by Ramusio.[4] In any event, Sebastian Cabot gave a big boost to the lore of northern islands over the "top" of the New World, when he communicated to Ramusio that he had "sailed beyond those Islands" into an open seaway to the Orient (page 185). Ramusio's preface to the third volume of *Navigationi e Viaggi*, 1556 (as translated in Hakluyt), where he mentions Cabot's view, captures the efforts of non-Spanish Europeans to image North America:

> Lands [situated in 50 degrees of Latitude to the North] are not thoroughly known, whether they do join with the firm land of Florida and Nova Hispania, or whether they be separated and divided all by the Sea as Islands; and whether by that way one may goe by Sea unto the country of Cathaia.[5]

The theory of Platonic islands would possess the imagination of the British throughout the century.

Through the sixties and seventies the most important ideamongers were two scholars of a different style and stripe: Richard Hakluyt the Elder, and John Dee.[6] Like Eden and Cecil, these were men with Welsh and Border ancestry. Both were highly educated, but did not direct their gifts toward publication. Almost nothing of the elder Hakluyt's writing has come down to us. Although surviving manuscripts tell us that Dee wrote a great deal, a surprisingly small percentage got into print. For this reason they remain somewhat shadowy figures.

Indeed, to their contacts in high places, the elder Hakluyt and Dee functioned as what, in today's jargon, we would call consultants. They operated as a kind of "think tank" of two to the policy makers, the backers, and the men of action. In a sense, they were brokers, bringing together the thinkers, the dreamers, the schemers, and the doers. It was their job to make available their vast collections in their private libraries, to digest the ideas that came their way, and to deliver opinions.[7] They had an international network of resources. Dee's professor had been Gemma Frisius. Frisius's assistant, the brilliant cartographer Gerhardus Mercator, was Dee's close friend. Hakluyt and Dee were in touch with Oronce Fine and Abraham Ortelius.

Doubtless, as counselors, they would not think of broadcasting the advice they gave. Elizabethan England was alive with spies and informers trying to breach national security. Moreover, knowledge was viewed as a special trust in the Welsh bardic tradition, only to be passed orally to initiates. So when Dee did commit to writing, he wrote obliquely, arcanely, hintingly, avoiding names. He apparently wrote in a great rush of inspiration quoting copiously from the many languages at his command. The poet-courtier Edward Dyer, Dee's fellow occultist and friend at court, "decoded" him for the Queen. Dee let her read his "Secret Book" when she visited him at his Mortlake Library. Perhaps the most vital quality Dee provided was imaginative fervor—a high state of excitement that everything was possible. The same sort of spirit possessed Robert Thorne and Eden, and inspired the literary creativity of Shakespeare.

Dee and the elder Hakluyt played a crucial role in the great quickening of national spirit in Elizabethan England. The development of this spirit is important to our story for the way it alarmed the Spaniards. In stimulating English voyages, it would eventually pose real threats to New Spain.

Many of the Queen's subjects—Christopher Hatton, Humphrey Gilbert, Richard Grenville, Drake, Hawkins, and so on—owned their own ships. Their love of the sea, their skill and prowess at navigation, helped contribute to a sense of the burgeoning of England as a maritime power. But there was a growing feeling that the country should have its own naval force. Dee wrote an unpublished pamphlet on this need in 1566. Then, in 1576, in an intense, creative outburst, Dee began a four-part magnum opus. The first part, his *General and Rare Memorials Pertayning to the Perfect Arte of Navigation,* is a passionate advocacy of a "Pety Navy Royall." He allowed it to be published in a limited edition.[8]

Various references, such as "my instructor doth wish and advise," give this the flavor of an "inspired writing" intended for the guidance of his superstitious Queen. His message was delivered in the best tradition of Welsh prophecy. The Queen is counselled to build a navy not only to secure England's boundaries and her fishing rights, but also to aspire to greatness in pursuit of commerce and discovery.[9]

As a Welshman, Dee disdains to use the words English and England. He harks back to a nomenclature more ancient and aboriginal than that which the invading Anglo-Saxons used when they dubbed the natives "Welsh"—that is, foreigners. By using the terms "Briton," "Britain," and "British," Dee supplies a greater authenticity to the Tudor title, the Tudors themselves being of Welsh stock through Henry VII. Indeed, in another work in his four-part magnum opus, Dee validated the Queen's title to all of North America based on voyages there of her Welsh ancestors in the Middle Ages. Although this work was destroyed, the details of the claim are preserved on the back of Dee's famous map of North America of 1579–80, in the British Library.[10]

For good or ill, the term "British Empire" is owed to Dee. And in the same vein, he preferred the even more ancient name of "Albion" for "this Incomparable Islandish Impire" of Britain. This he derives from such sources as *Historia Regum Britanniae*, written by the twelfth-century Welshman Geoffrey of Monmouth. In the dispersion following Troy's destruction, Bryttus (Brutus) sailed to an island called Alban or Albion, "which in kymraec [Welsh] is called y wenn ynys [the White Island] . . . And then Bryttys desired to call the island by his own name, and that the race inhabiting it should be called brytanniaid; . . . And from that time on, the language of that people was called brytanec."[11] Hence Dee's fervent little outburst: "O Albion, O Britain, O England, and I say thrice times over, O Brytan yet again."[12] We may imagine the chilling of Spanish blood when the English corsair, Drake, used Dee's jingoistic terminology to name his West Coast claim "New Albion." But more of that in Chapter XIX.

This surging imperialism was coupled with talk of voyages having a new practical kind of destination. Dreams of rich islands of gold, pearls and spices might be as strong as ever. And Dee himself nourished a desire for a secret "commodity" of the East, one "passing all earthly treasures," that is, occult knowledge.[13] But what struck fear into the Spanish was the elder Hakluyt's pet objective—to plant colonies. This was to begin with a fort-and-supply station on the North-West Passage. It would have the additional advantage of providing an honorable living for "such needie people of our Countrie, which now trouble the common welth." These sentiments were repeated in such works as George Best's *True Discourse*, the younger Hakluyt's Dedicatorie of *Divers Voyages*, and again in his *Discourse on Western Planting*.[14]

But our central interest is in how this Spanish fear of the British stirred the old Isle-of-California myth. And here Dee's theories about routes for British voyagers to the New World had great influence. At first, in the middle decades of the sixteenth century, Dee's advice was concentrated on those who staked everything on a North-East Passage across the "top" of Russia. But by 1565, so many gallant seamen had been sacrificed, so much money had been lost, that the Muscovy Company became disenchanted.

The North-West Passage buffs rushed immediately into the vacuum. Humphrey Gilbert petitioned the Queen in 1565 "to make tryall" of it in his own ship from his home port of Plymouth. The elder Hakluyt and Dee helped him develop arguments. Gilbert debated his position before the Queen and her Privy Council. But to no avail.[15]

Ten years later, in another attempt to sway the Queen, Gilbert allowed those arguments to be published in his name by the poet George Gascoigne. Although Gascoigne's preface says "it commeth forth without his consent,"[16] Gilbert has been given all the credit for this book titled A Discourse of a Discoverie for a New Passage to Cataia, of 1576.

Actually, most of the intellectual supporting arguments had come from the elder Hakluyt and Dee. Chapter IV, for example, copies arguments from Hakluyt's letter to Abraham Ortelius of 1566. Ortelius's heart-shaped map of 1564, that Hakluyt had requested to show the open waterway across the north of the New World, is reproduced in rough without credit (Plate 34).

Gascoigne does give a sop to John Dee in his preface: "A great learned man (even M. Dee) doth seeme very well to like of this Discoverie and doth much commende the Author." Dee himself had to set the record straight elsewhere by pointing out that he had "almost ten years since set down in writing" at Edward Dyer's suggestion, a pamphlet "to the self-same purpose"—a gentle charge of plagiarism?[17]

This unpublished pamphlet by Dee had actually been called "Atlanticall Discourses." The adjective refers to the theory of Atlantis rather than to the Ocean (though that is of that provenance). Dee believed profoundly in the Platonic theory of the New World's genesis, as disseminated by Münster and Eden (Plate 31b, page 196). Dee considered the name "America" a misnomer—though not for reasons we now hold, that Columbus, not Vespucci, should have had the honors. Since America was really Atlantis, it should be called just what it was. In his Great Volume, Dee always applies the name Atlantis in speaking of America. For example, he comments on the relationship between America and

Asia: "Great doubt of the Periplus of Asia north-east quarter, and of Atlantis north-west corner."[18]

We find Dee's whole Platonic argument in the Gilbert-Gascoigne "Discourse." It should therefore be viewed rather as a "committee report," prevailing opinions of the best minds of the time. Gascoigne has merely licked it into shape as promotion literature for Gilbert's pet scheme "to make tryall of" the North-West passage. We see a public-relations touch in the crude reproduction of Ortelius' map.

There is a naive quaintness to the Atlantis argument. Chapter I launches right into it:

> The fourth part of the world, commonly called America . . . I found to be an island environed round about with sea . . .
>
> Plato in Timæo, and in the Dialogue called Critias, discourseth of an incomparable great island then called Atlantis . . .[19]

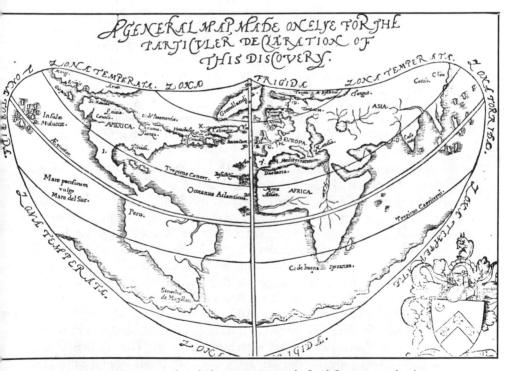

PLATE 34.   British optimism about finding an easy way to the South Sea is expressed in this simplified version of Ortelius's map of 1564 with its wide northern waterway. The map was published in Sir Humphrey Gilbert's A Discourse of a Discoverie for a New Passage to Cataia in 1576. Photograph and permission by the British Library.

Further authorities are cited to reveal what happened to this island:

> This was . . . thought . . . to be overflown and swallowed up with water, by reason of a mighty earthquake, and streaming down of the heavenly floodgates. . . . The . . . calamity happened unto this Isle of Atlantis 600. and odd years before Plato's time.

The conclusion is then drawn:

> In these our days there can no other main or island be found or judged to be parcel of this Atlantis, than those Western Islands, which bear now the name of America: countervailing thereby the name of Atlantis, in the knowledge of our age.

What promise this legend gave of a North-West Passage. To start with, the original insular nature of Atlantis guaranteed a passage to the north. But more than that, when it was partially submerged, the water had flowed into the valleys leaving the mountain tops as so many islands, thus creating many additional waterways to Cathay:

> Then, if when no part of the said Atlantis was oppressed by water, and earthquake, the coasts round about the same were navigable: a far greater hope now remaineth of the same by the Northwest, seeing the most part of it was, since that time, swallowed up with water, which could not utterly take away the old deeps and chanels, but rather, be an occasion of the inlarging of the old, and also an inforcing of a great many new: why then should now we doubt? . . . seeing that Atlantis now called America was ever known to be an island, and in those days navigable round about, which by access of more water could not be diminished.

Following publication of the *Discourse,* insularist ideas bloomed riotously in a hothouse atmosphere between 1576 and 1583. They inspired the three voyages of Frobisher, in 1576, '77, and '78. Though these voyages turned up no North-West Passage, the assumptions were unshaken. A captain who was with Frobisher, George Best, could still write in his "True Discourse . . ." of 1578: "America an island is included . . . on the north with Frobisher's Straights."[20] This name is used to label the wide waterway along the "top" of America on his accompanying sketch map. It is all wishful thinking.

Humphrey Gilbert finally got the royal nod and set off in 1583, only to lose his life in the attempt. The interest of this voyage for our present study lies in the map he carried with him (Plate 35). The original, or the only surviving copy, is now a treasure of the Philadelphia Free Library. Titled "Sir Humfray Gilbert his chart," it bears Dee's personal symbol, as well as the unique, unmistakable, stamp of Dee's strange ideas. Could a similar chart have illustrated Dee's "Atlanticall Discourses" in 1566?

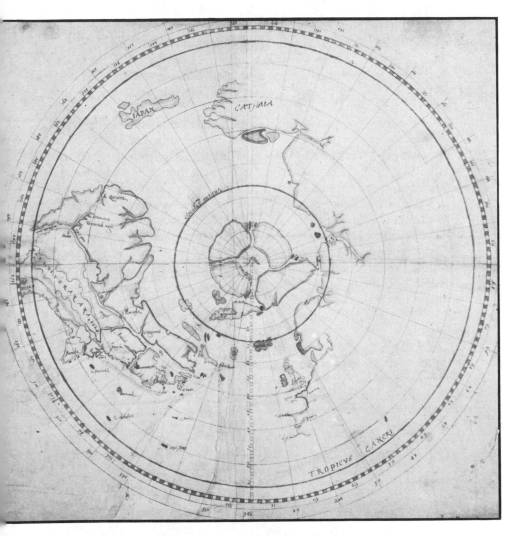

PLATE 35.   Water, water, everywhere, is the way John Dee, the Elizabethan Welsh scholar,
conceived of the New World in this map which surfaced in 1583. No bottlenecks occur
across the north or into the South Sea. His Atlantis, as he called North America (shown on
the left side of the map), is carved into many islands by transcontinental waterways. A
strait runs from the mouth of the St. Lawrence to the head of the Gulf of California. An
extraordinary Verrazzano Sea runs from Virginia to outlet in Mexico. (Discussion on page
204). California is well on the way to becoming conceptualized as one of Atlantis's many
islands. (Discussion on page 223). *Photograph and permission by the Rare Book Department,
the Free Library of Philadelphia.*

The map is visionary. It is a collection of possibilities, of conjectures, rather than a representation of established fact. It is based on Dee's own theory of Atlantis, and on numerous scraps of information of "might-be-so's" garnered from his wide reading. The polar projection shows a wide seaway north of Atlantis giving into the South Sea. Atlantis is carved into islands by several waterways. First the St. Lawrence "river" slashes the continent to emerge at the nook of the Gulf of California, where sixty or so years before, Cortés had expected a river-that-might-turn-out-to-be-a-strait. Still another continent-spanning waterway is an unusual Verrazzano Sea running all the way from Virginia to the mouth of the Gulf of California. It joins the South Sea on the coast of New Spain opposite La Punta de California or Cabo San Lucas. There are additional links of water between these waterways. One strait connects the St. Lawrence-to-Gulf of California waterway with the Verrazzano Sea. Another with the Atlantic Ocean about where the Penobscot River flows, making New England an island. And yet another auxiliary strait connects with the great ocean to the north. Florida and other bits are made to look like islands, too. Altogether, a partly inundated Atlantis is presented here.

Of very special interest to our story will be how Dee fits California into his vision of Atlantis on this map of 1583. This will be discussed in chronological order in Chapter XIX. But first there are more threads to follow in the complex tapestry of Tudor England's story of exploration. Other dramatic events of the seventies bearing on California's destiny are outlined in the next two chapters.

Chapter XVII

BRITONS PLOT TO RAID THE PACIFIC VIA MAGELLAN'S STRAIT

Not everyone in British exploration circles was equally enthusiastic about making an attempt on the North-West Passage. Some doubted it could even be traversed. It was especially feared that a certain strait called Anian might not give the ready access into the Pacific that the maps promised.

What exactly was this Strait of Anian? It will be recalled that in the 20s and 30s some "continentalists" had "rejoined" Asia to America while keeping them distinct. According to that view, a land bridge blocked access from the northern ocean passage—if that ocean did indeed exist. Among the Spanish, a comforting belief in this impenetrable obstacle persisted until well past mid century.

At last the unshakeable conviction of the British in a northern passage must have won out over the other view. In 1561, Jacobo Gastaldi separated Asia from America by a narrow strait, "allowing" passage between the Pacific and the Septentrional (Northern) ocean (*see* sketch map, Plate 26). At this time the strait was almost certainly hypothetical. It would be a long time until the Bering Strait was actually discovered.

Meanwhile, as the breadth of the Pacific had become increasingly appreciated, the "insularists" had begun to concede a northwest "corner" to the American landmass. Mercator, Ortelius (Plate 37), Jode, and Plancius, among others, "stretched" their North America very widely across the top. Their northern seaway was narrowed as it was lengthened to correspond. When Gastaldi's Strait of Anian appeared, they incorporated it as the west-end gateway from that northern ocean passage down into the South Sea. With these accommodations on both sides, continentalist and insularist positions drew closer to each other.

Dee identified the source of the name Anian as Polo's *Book*. In his fourth volume, *The Great Volume of Famous and Rich Discoveries*, Dee declares Polo to be so full of "contradictions and repugnances" on the subject of Anian, that a sensible chart could not be drawn from his descriptions. "What a damp may . . . fall on some men's minds" to discover that Polo uses the name to describe firm land! But Dee believes that when voyagers bring back their reports: "I nothing doubt of it upon my former discourses and evidence to be such as will be favorable to Ania Straits; but with small cause called straits, if we hear of no straiter girding in of the sea by the land approaching than by two dayes sayling over." Dee reaffirms his insularist position. The Strait of Anian wouldn't prove to be the bottleneck that maps like Gastaldi's made it appear.[1]

Dee's interest in the Strait of Anian was prompted by the rise of a faction disenchanted with the North-West Passage. These skeptics argued that it would be folly to embark on the hazards of a northern voyage without first ascertaining the nature and location of the Strait of Anian, and even its existence. But how could this information be obtained? By taking the tried and true southern route via the Straits of Magellan, and sailing all the way up the South Sea to take a look at the "back side" of New Spain.

An undated, unsigned, document of the period argues the case convincingly. It is titled: "A Discourse concerninge a Straighte to be discovered toward the Northweste . . . with a Confutacion of their errour that think the discoverye ther of to be moste convenientlye attempted to the Northe of the Baccalaos."[2] It begins by granting that open ocean lies to the north. The real straits—the truly difficult section of the northern passage to the South Sea—must be at the "straights that disjoynethe Asia and America of Gerardus Mercator and other moderne cosmographers . . . called the Straights of Anian." The argument continues:

> Now let us consider which were the more conveniente waie to discover the said straighte, either passinge under the congeled Artike circle, for so highe the maine of America rechethe, or by passinge the straighte of Magilianus to ascende from the equinoctiall alonge the westerne course of that Atlanticall Ilande, as Plato semethe in his Timæo to terme it.[3]

The piece goes on to argue that although this southern voyage would, in distance, be longer, it would, in terms of time, be shorter, since they would be "passinge altogether by seas knowen and already discovered." By contrast northern voyagers would be beset by wind, ice, fog, storm, a confusion of islands and coastal indentations, among other perils and impediments along an unknown course.

Who can have written this "Discourse . . . with a Confutacion?" No attribution was given when the Hakluyt Society published it with a kindred discourse in 1867. However, the manuscript in the British Library is endorsed, in Burghley's hand, "Mr. Grenfeylde's voyage."[4] This is Sir Richard Grenville of Virginia fame. He was a cousin of

Humphrey Gilbert and Sir Walter Raleigh. On March 22, 1574, Grenville and Gilbert asked the Queen to allow an enterprise of discovery of "sundry ritche and unknowen landes" via the southwest passage of Magellan. This request was made in a "Petition of Divers Gentlemen of the West Parts of England . . ."[5] It was as supporting arguments for this Petition that the "Discourse . . . with a Confutacion" and its kindred document "A Discovery of Lands Beyond the Equinoctial" must have been written.[6]

As his cousin Humphrey Gilbert did in researching the North-West Passage, so, apparently, did Grenville in researching the South-West route—he consulted the famous brain trust for a feasibility study. In the documents described above, the hand of the elder Hakluyt has been suspected by A. L. Rowse. Dee's input is indicated in the reference to his pet theory of Plato's "Atlanticall Island."

Grenville's plan may have begun as a rivalry with Gilbert. Perhaps it was a serious attempt to turn Gilbert aside from a potentially disasterous northwest voyage. There is an urgency about the closing argument almost as though Grenville foresaw the price Gilbert would pay for his foolhardy idealism. He predicts harsh consequences for whoever would attempt the North-West Passage without first finding out about the Straits of Anian:

> . . . He shall proceade to the shame and dishonor of him selfe, to the destruction and ruyne of his 'countrey' companye, and to the utter discouradgmente of this nation further to adventure in this gainful honeste honorable enterprise. And reporte me to the judgment of the wise, these reasons before alleaged well weyed.[7]

Grenville may have had some temporary success in turning Gilbert toward what he believed to be a safer alternative—Gilbert's name is joined with Grenville's to the Petition for a southwest voyage. But the Queen did not consent to it until 1577. And by that time the North-West voyages were under way, with Gilbert deeply committed to that preference.

What cause had Grenville to think the southern passage any less perilous than the northwest? The Plymouth mariners, Hawkins and Drake in particular, had been trading (and fighting) with the Spanish in the Caribbean. They would have learned how seldom used was the Strait of Magellan, how ignorant of it were the younger Spaniards and how neglectful the older order of its defense. Indeed, when a few years later Spain rushed to rectify this lapse, Pedro Sarmiento de Gamboa had practically to rediscover it.

Moreover, in the 60s England had begun to chafe under the absurdity of a papal policy that had halved the world between Spain and Portugal. Why should this be binding on a nation that had shrugged off papal domination in the days of Henry VIII? Cecil had told the Spanish ambassador in 1562 that the Pope had no right to partition the world. This position is expressed again in the document "A Discovery of Lands Beyond the Equinoctial," where the French example is applauded:

> Albeit they acknowledge the Pope's authoritie in suche thinges as they grant to perteine to him, yet in this universall and naturall right of traffique and temporall dominion they have not holden them bounde by his power.

If the French, a Catholic nation, felt like that, then how much more justified was Protestant Britain in going her own way. England was fast becoming the world's greatest maritime power, and the Queen was reminding everyone that the sea, as the air, was common to all.[8]

The route wasn't the only novelty in the Petition and the two "position papers" of the Grenville plan. There were novel destinations, too. In addition to the already known "innumerable ilandes of incomparable ritches and unknowen treasure" abounding in that "riche and bountifull sea," *new* dream destinations are envisaged.[9] The Petition speaks of "sundry riche and unknowen landes South of the equinoctial line." The "Discourse . . . with a Confutacion" identifies a new area of the South Sea for discovery:

> The waste occeane to the Southe . . . cannot but be replenished with numbers of Ilandes, the leaste whereof mighte abundantly suffice to furnishe our navie with the forenamed commodities, if gemmes, turkesses, rubies, and other precious juells sholde not be there fownde, whereof there cannot but be greate aboundaunce in some of them.

The view that precious metals and stones "grew" only in the torrid zone was being challenged in this period.[10] The change of view, indeed, had permitted Frobisher to believe he had discovered gold in northern climes.

The belief that the "waste occeane to the Southe" should be exploited by the British is spelled out more fully in "A Discovery of Land Beyond the Equinoctial," as the title indicates. A voyage via the Magellan Strait would have as one of its objects:

> The discoverie, traffique and enjoyenge for the Quenes Majestie and her subjectes of all or anie landes, islandes and countries southewardes beyonde the equinoctial, or where the Pole Antartik hathe anie elevation above the Horison, and which landes, islandes and countries be not

alredie possessed or subdued by or to the use of anie Christian Prince in Europe as by the chartes and descriptions shall appere.[11]

This renewed interest in South-Sea islands, now postulated in southern latitudes, may have been stimulated by reports of Spanish activity in that area. That activity followed Urdaneta's and Legaspe's rediscovery of the Philippines in 1565. A document in the Archives of the Indies states:

In the year 1567 one Pedro Sarmiento gave to the Licentiate Castro, Governor of Peru, information concerning many isles and continents which he said existed in the southern ocean and offered personally to discover them in the name of his Majesty.[12]

Apparently the governor sent his nephew Alvaro de Mendaña to conduct the search. Mendaña had express instructions "to steer for the rich islands . . . and form a settlement."

Mendaña did find some "western islands in the southern ocean" and called them "the Isles of Solomon" either believing, or wanting others to believe, that they were "the isles of Ophir and Tarsis from whence Solomon fetched gold to adorn his temple at Jerusalem." According to Lopez Vez, Mendaña was stopped from settling them "so that the English . . . might have no succour" there while prowling the South Sea.[13]

We know the British got wind of the Isles of Solomon. Henry Hawks, an English resident in Mexico, mentioned Mendaña's discovery in his account of 1572.[14] For the Grenville party this may have given substantiation to the airy theories Dee would have been venting.

For Dee the whole Pacific offered new prospects. To the travellers via the north he promised "divers wonderfull Isles of the Northern, Scythian, Tartarian and Most Northern Seas, and neare under the Pole." But the dream destinations of the southern voyage were even more exciting. He hints slyly at an expedition about "to enter and proceed upon the further discovery of that part which is least known to Christian men," yet an area "most apt for the Brytish wisdom, manhood, and travail to be bestowed on henceforwarde."[15] Presumably Dee had in mind some southern lands in temperate to frigid zones. The first seven chapters of his *Great Volume of Famous and Rich Discoveries* dealt with these promised lands. Although these chapters are now lost, we know from references in Purchas that they contained Dee's calculation of the time taken in Solomon's day for the journey to Ophir and Tarsis.[16] He figured that his countrymen would do it in a third the time.

Dee was instrumental in a revival of interest in Robert Thorne's letter of 1527, and his Address to Henry VIII. Dee no doubt knew the Address—if only from its inclusion in Barlow's *Geography*. He had Cyprian Lucar, whose father had been Thorne's assistant and executor, bring him a copy of the original letter. In both these documents Thorne had postulated three routes home for voyagers once they were over the Pole and down into the South Sea (pages 190–91). A mistaken construction of the third alternative in this fifty-year-old material may have increased interest in the South Pacific. Thorne had written:

> And if they go this third way, and after they bee past the pole, goe right toward the pole Antarticke, and then decline toward the lands and Ilands situated between the Tropikes and under the Equinoctial, without doubt they shal find there ye richest lands and Ilands of the worlde of Golde, precious stones, balmes, spices . . .[17]

Thorne's words "goe right toward the pole Antartike," or Barlow's "saille streite towards the pole antartike"—could they have been read not as a direction in which to head, but as a destination to be reached?

Besides the promise of a new batch of rich islands, there was hope of new continents such as Sarmiento had detailed. The huge southern continent, Terra Australis, a persistent figment of imagination from classical times, was having a new innings. It appeared on the maps of Ortelius and Mercator of the late sixties and seventies. Dee also revived interest in Marco Polo's Loach, Locach, or Beach—as Dee called it. In resurrecting this region of golden report, he associated it with Ophir and Tharsis in his *Great Volume of Famous and Rich Discoveries.*

The Grenville Plan came to fruition in 1577. An expedition was organized in secret. It was to be led by Francis Drake. The Queen was privy to the plans. She gave her blessing and a small subscription.

Hearing the "slender news," Dee ferreted out the Latin text of Maximilianus of Transylvania on the subject of Magellan's voyage. In his *Great Volume of Famous and Rich Discoveries*, he hints arcanely at its purpose:

> How aptly I have here placed this record of Magellan his strait finding, as well to answer our Mexico passenger withall, as to be an advice to all discoverers upon such a purpose to be very circumspect, patient, and constant, till the uttermost search be made; and that perfectly and not imperfectly.[18]

What is meant by the "Mexican passenger?" Not a passive traveler in the modern sense, but the person who is about to pass through the passage (the strait) leading into the Mexican sphere—a cloak-and-dagger code for one whose name must not be mentioned, nor his secret enterprise revealed. Invited or not, Dee was making sure Drake got the benefit of his accumulated knowledge by collecting texts of the Magellan voyage.[19]

There was much coming and going to Dee's Mortlake library during this period, so most of the advice was probably delivered orally. The nature of it may be deduced from various comments Dee scribbled in the margin of the Maximilianus text. Dee had copied the text at length into his manuscript in the original Latin.[20] Among Dee's marginalia is a comment on the incident of one of Magellan's ships giving up after three days' scouting for the strait:

> Let the Mexican passenger learn here to be circumspect, before he report passages of two dayes sayling over to be rivers and not straits of the Ocean.[21]

Where Maximilianus's text gives information concerning variations of width of the Straits, Dee jots:

> Note here you man of Mexico against your next passage or return.

There is an interesting sidelight on Dee's annotated text of Maximilianus copied into his *Great Volume*. Cited as an illustration of his work, it turned up in print in a collection of materials from Glastonbury compiled by Thomas Hearne in the eighteenth century.[22] How did this section copied from Dee's Book, find its way to Glastonbury? Drake is known to have had on board a copy of Magellan's account, as did Winter in the second ship.[23] Is it possible that the Glastonbury segment was a copy made by Dee for Drake's famous voyage? Where now is that manuscript copy that Hearne printed?

There are hints that Drake's copy of Magellan's voyage was indeed Dee's annotated text of Maximilianus. Coincidences between Dee's marginal advice and Drake's actions are provocative. Where Maximilianus's text details Magellan's ruthless treatment of his mutinous crew in St. Julian's Bay, Dee tips his "Mexico Travailer":

> You may read it, and it is worth the reading.[24]

Could this passage and comment have influenced Drake in his decision to execute the troublemaker Doughty—in sight of Magellan's gibbet —before embarking on the dangerous navigation of the Straits?

Similarly, Winter's desertion could have been aided by another of Dee's comments. Maximilianus' text tells of the desertion of Magellan's nephew, who let his ship be "carried back by the tide . . . to the very place where they entered the gulf." There, Dee wrote in the margin:

> Note by these words . . . that a ship that entereth from the easterly parts, may also come back again the same way; which is a great secret.

It was a secret Winter certainly took advantage of when he turned tail.

We may deduce another tie between the insularist Dee and Francis Drake. We know Dee had a copy of Robert Thorne's letter of 1527 brought to him in 1577 by Cyprian Lucar, the son of Thorne's executor. We may assume that in discussions, probably at Dee's Mortlake library, Drake would have been shown this letter. But we have more to go on than assumptions. Drake had clearly in mind the three routes Thorne had postulated for getting in and out of the South Sea (*see* Thorne's quotations on pages 190–91). Testimony of this was given by the captain of a Spanish ship seized by Drake off South America. According to the record, "in the city of Panama, the 16th day of March, 1587," there appeared before the Royal Audiencia of Panama one "Saint John de Anton, master and owner of the Bark our Lady of Conception." He deposed that, while courteously detaining him, Drake showed him a map of the world, and told him that:

> There were three ways to go forth of these seas of Sur: the one way by the Cape of Bone Esperance which is toward the Country of China. The other is by the Chylle, by the way that he came. But as for the third way he would not tell him.[25]

This is the translation given in the British Library manuscript dubbed "Mr. Dee's Booke,"—where a copy of Thorne's letter also appears. These circumstances again suggest a connection between Dee and Drake. Pedro de Sarmiento's account of the same testimony speaks of four ways home—the fourth via "Norway."[26] That was Dee's North-East route from Britain, over the "top" of Norway and Russia into the South Sea.

When Zelia Nuttall turned up San Juan de Anton's actual deposition in 1908, she translated the pertinent passage this way:

> When deponent [San Juan de Anton] asked him [Drake] by what way he thought of returning to his country, the said captain showed him a map of the world and sea chart on which he demonstrated that there were three ways by which he could do so. One was by the Cape of Good Hope, via China; the other by way of Chile, by which he had come. He would not tell which was the third way.[27]

Fifty years of British schemes against Spanish claims to South-Sea treasure islands are wrapped up in this scrap of testimony.

Chapter XVIII

THE SPANISH TAKE ALARM
FROM THE BRITISH THREAT

The classified top-secret status of the Drake mission was well justified. Throughout the sixties and early seventies, the Spanish ambassador to Elizabeth's court had built an active network of informants. Scraps and rumors about various British imperialistic enthusiasms and undertakings were duly transmitted to King Philip. The King, in turn, informed the Viceroy of all matters touching New Spain.

From the midsixties on, the activities of the British privateers in the Gulf of Mexico had roused Spanish fears that they might penetrate the South Sea via the much-touted North-West Passage. The talk in Mexico revived recollections of the former quest for straits. Old experiences were reprocessed. At his Mexican listening post, Henry Hawks provided valuable intelligence to his countrymen to this effect. He wrote in 1572:

> There is another port town which is called Culiacan, on the south sea, which lieth west and by north out of Mexico, and is 200 leagues from the same: and there the Spaniards made two ships to go seek the strait or gulf, which as they say, is between the Newfoundland and Greenland; and they call it the Englishmens strait: which as yet was never fully found. They say, that strait lieth not far from the main land of China, which the Spaniards account to be marvelous rich.[1]

The quest of a strait, mentioned in this quotation, could not have been—we know from the record—any new activity. The garbled gossip he picked up must have referred to the voyages of Ulloa, Alarcón and Cabrillo in 1539–1542. The words "strait or gulf" seem to echo the old question of whether a Strait of California led from the Gulf or Mar Vermejo and connected somehow with a continent-spanning strait to the Bacallaos. The strait that "lieth not far from the main land of China" is the Strait of Anian—the other end of the North-West Passage from the Bacallaos. Hawks seems to be compressing a complicated system of imaginary waterways into one package.

It was only a matter of time before these fears began to be projected by the nervously excited Mexicans. Alarms that the English might penetrate into the Pacific inevitably brought reports of sightings of their ships. Impressionable residents on the west coast of New Spain "saw" flotillas of them in 1573 off Compostela and Vandera.

The Mexican authorities were disturbed in 1574 by new word from London that "an English gentleman named Grenfield, a great pirate," was "going to the Straits of M [agellan]" probably to "lie in wait for the ships from the Indies and other merchantmen."[2] Reports of sightings of flotillas were treated with new urgency. An official investigation was launched in Guadalajara in 1574.

Franciscan Friar Juan de Luco testified to having seen the ships.[3] He believed them to be French or British. However, he knew nothing about *el estrecho del yngles*—the Englishmen's Strait—through which these ships were thought to have entered the South Sea. Another witness testified to seeing a light far out to sea, like a bundle of burning fodder. It stayed lit about as long as it took to say the Apostles' Creed. This witness had heard it said that they were ships of Juan de Achis'—John Hawkins. Hawkins had come to get satisfaction for damages inflicted at San Juan de Ulloa.[4]

For information on the Strait, the investigators had to rely on those who had participated in the explorations of thirty-five or so years earlier. Old salts were still around who remembered the quest for the "Strait of California," and for the opening of a wide river-strait on the northwest coast. Juan Fernández de Ladrillero, an old-timer, whose memory was well laced with imagination, must have really put the wind up his investigators with his testimony:

> Asked, if the witness knows or has heard in any manner that by this strait there have passed any ships from the North Sea to the South sea . . . he answered . . . that it is about a year and a half, more or less, since he heard it said by many people in these kingdoms of New Spain and New Galicia that there were going about in the South sea twenty-seven ships which it was believed had entered by the said strait, which they call that of the Bacalaos; that they were English or French; . . . and this witness understands and considers it certain that by the said strait the said ships could enter, and many others, and could make fortifications in the said strait and in other places in the South sea, where they could fortify themselves and make settlements, and from there come down to all the ports and bays in all the South sea . . . where they could do great damage to his majesty; and the South sea could not be navigated with the same freedom as up to the present; and those who came in by the strait would become masters of all the South sea without encountering resistance; . . . and if it should be necessary he will go to the strait, and will do away with the doubt whether any settlements or people are in the said strait . . .[5]

As we have seen, since Gilbert's Petition of 1565, the elder Hakluyt had advocated the establishment of a supply-station-cum-fort-cum-colony on the South-Sea end of the North-West Passage. But it is not certain from Ladrillero's testimony whether he fears settlements there or closer to home, somewhere along the Mar Vermejo. He goes on to tell how he acquired his information about straits. He apparently was on the little-known Bolaños expedition of 1541, which had barely started out before it was diverted to the Philippines (see page 157):

> This witness and the others who were with him had the intention of discovering a strait which this witness understands exists between the South sea and the North sea, and which, according to his information, disembogues where the English go after codfish; and if this witness had been alone with the ship and the people who were in it, he would have gone in search of this strait and would have sailed until he had seen it, but on account of the contrary weather which they encountered, and the bad treatment of the ships, they returned as related above, and did not finish their voyage . . . and the discovery of the strait remained as it is up to today; and that this witness is certain that there is such a strait and that it is eight hundred leagues more or less from Compostela.

The jumpy residents of New Spain soon had a live Englishman to question in the shape of John Oxenham. And what a catch he was. So much so, indeed, that he seemed the embodiment of all their previous fears. He was a buddy of Drake. He had been with that master mariner on a scheme in 1572–73 to deprive the Spanish of their treasure as they transported it eastward across the Isthmus of Panama, from the Pacific to the Caribbean.

Later, Oxenham had dreamed up a new strategy for plunder. In 1576 he crossed the Isthmus and built a pinnace on the South Sea to accost the galleons.[6] He may even have had a plan to rendezvous with Drake. But he was captured with the loot, and imprisoned by the Inquisition.[7]

Early in this century Zelia Nuttall turned up Oxenham's deposition made in Lima in 1579, before they hanged him at an auto-da-fé. It reveals Spain's awareness of the Grenville Plan and of Britain's professed intentions to found settlements. Oxenham tells of Grenville's application "to the Queen for a licence to come to the Strait of Magellan and to pass to the South Sea, in order to search for land or *some islands* [italics added] where to found settlements, because, in England, there are many inhabitants but little land."[8]

Questioned on Drake's plans, Oxenham deposed:

> The witness thinks that if the Queen were to give a licence to Captain Francis Drake he would certainly come and pass through the Strait,

because he is a very good mariner and pilot, and there is no better one than he in England who could accomplish this . . . The said Captain Francis had often spoken to witness saying that if the Queen would grant him the licence he would pass through the Strait of Magellan and found settlements over here in some good country.

Oxenham hastened to protect the Queen by telling his inquisitors:

The Queen will not, as long as she lives, grant the licence, but . . . after her death, there will certainly be some-one who will come to the Strait.

Even as Oxenham spoke, his sovereign and Drake had made a liar out of him.

The Spaniards questioned Oxenham about the further objective of the Grenville Plan—the quest for the Straits of Anian, and Drake's instructions and intentions with regard to it:

Questioned whether they had discussed how, and by what route, they were to return to England after having passed through the Strait [of Magellan], he said that it seemed to him that some said that it was to be by the same Strait, but others said that there was a route through another Strait that passed into the North Sea, but nobody knows this for a certainty or has passed through it.

The reactions of the Spanish to the British offensive may be easily imagined. They were outraged that their sphere was threatened with invasion via their own strait. They were alarmed that quest for the Strait of Anian might mean that penetration of the North-West Passage was imminent. They were terrified at the prospect of Britain attempting to establish an empire in the southern area of the South Pacific—an empire that properly belonged to them, and that they were on the fringes of discovering.

Already at this time, the authorities in New Spain had been put on the alert that Drake was on his way. Panic inflamed the imagination of the Spaniards, leading to a new wave of geographic speculation in the next few decades.

Chapter XIX

DRAKE'S VOYAGE REACTIVATES THE STRAIT-OF-CALIFORNIA MYTH

It is not the job of this chapter to retell a story that has been told so well so many times—the exciting voyage of Francis Drake in the *Golden Hind*.[1] The focus of our interest here is the part played by Drake in triggering a new growth of the Strait-of-California myth. What do his motives, his goals, and his actions tell us about this?

Drake's zeal to achieve *his* dream-conceits almost equalled those of Balboa and Cortés. The contemporary historian William Camden gives us a vivid glimpse of the young sea-captain's ambition. While Drake was sacking the Isthmus of Panama in 1572, he was invited "to see at once the two seas" as Balboa had done:

> He discovered from the top of high mountains, the South Sea; hereupon he was so inflamed with a desire of glory and wealth, that he burned with an earnest longing to sail into those parts; and in the same place, falling upon his knees, he heartily implored the Divine assistance to enable him, that he might one day arrive in those Seas, and discover the secrets of them; and to this, he bound himself with a religious vow. From that time forward, was his mind night and day troubled, and as it were excited and pricked forward with goads, to perform and acquit himself of this Vow.[2]

Drake's zeal sprang from more than acquisitiveness, ambition, and an adventurous spirit. It sprang also from revenge. He had a score to settle with the Spaniards for their treachery, and for the losses he and his relative Hawkins had suffered in the Caribbean in 1568. Having learned in 1572 of the extent of Spanish treasure carried by Spanish shipping on the South Sea, Drake intended to do more than merely get even. As already noted, he may have planned to link up with Oxenham at the back of the Isthmus of Panama to raid the galleons.

But he must have had more than these purely personal goals when he went to realize his dream to sail upon that sea of "such golden reports" in 1578. No doubt he had also been asked to check out the two objectives of the theorists of the southwest voyage—the lands and islands of the southern South Pacific, and the Strait of Anian in the north.

The logs of this famous voyage have never turned up. They were apparently suppressed by Elizabeth to keep the Spanish guessing in her game of cat-and-mouse. The first account did not appear until ten years after the events. This was the "Famous Voyage" appended by Hakluyt to his 1589 edition of *The Principall Navigations*. It was based on an account identified as the "Anonymous Narrative." A further account was published almost forty years after the events described. But that later account, called *The World Encompassed*, added little to the earlier narratives on the California episode. As A. L. Rowse said of his study of Grenville: "It is a region of obscure inference and fascinating surmise that we are working in."[3]

Drake certainly did go south after clearing the Magellan Straits, perhaps to 57 degrees. But this doesn't prove a serious intent to survey the area. Huge winds had given him no option, beating the *Golden Hind* southward for a month or so.

From her study of Drake's Draft Plan (mutilated by fire), Taylor believed Drake was expressly commissioned to go in quest of non-Spanish southern lands.[4] Certain statements in what little record remains of such events do sound, indeed, as if Drake was seeking answers to specific questions. He anchored at what he believed to be "the uttermost Iland of terra incognita, to the Southward of America." For the sake of theorists in London, he pronounced that "there is no maine nor Iland to be seene to the Southwards, but that the Atlanticke Ocean and the South Sea, meete in a most large and free scope."[5] A sad little comment sums up these tidings: "It hath beene a dream through many ages, that these Ilands have been a maine."

While the Queen's name was being carved on a raised stone, Drake sought out the most southerly headland with his compass. There he indulged in these histrionics:

> He . . . cast himselfe downe upon the uttermost poynt groveling, and so reached out his bodie over it. Presently he imbarked, and then recounted unto his people, that he had beene upon the Southernmost knowne land in the world, and more further to the Southwarde upon it, then any of them, yea, or any man as yet knowne.[6]

Perhaps Drake, the arch opportunist, was merely turning calamity to profit. He was given to making thespian productions out of history-making moments, perhaps to fix them in the record. If exploring southern latitudes was one of his commissions, his perfunctory efforts would loom large in memory.

The question of whether Drake was to undertake the other objective of the Grenville Plan—to seek the Strait of Anian—has been hotly debated. The mutilated Draft Plan of Drake's voyage is not much help. Rowse believes he made an effort to find both the southern lands and the northern strait: "The two attempts, even if they were no more than feints, may be regarded as passing tributes to Grenville's scheme."[7]

What we do know is that Drake plundered his way along the coast, and at southern Mexico headed into mid ocean. Striking the trade winds, he sailed to the northwest. Here is how the "Anonymous Narrative" tells it:

> Drake watered his ship & departed sailing northwards till he came to .48. gr. of the septentrional latitude still finding a very large sea trending toward the north but being afraid to spend long time in seeking for the strait he turned back again still keeping along the coast as near land as he might, until he came to .44. gr. and then he found a harbor for his ship where he grounded his ship to trim her.

Incidentally, these latitudes, long thought erroneous, were recently assumed accurate, sparking a claim that New Albion is Whale Cove, Oregon.[8]

Little more is learned from the later account, *The World Encompassed,* except that the trimming of the ship is put prior to the quest for the Northern Passage:

> Considering also that the time of the year now drew on wherein we must attempt, or of necessity wholy give over that action, which chiefly our General had determined, namely, the discovery of what passage there was to be found about the Northern parts of America, from the South Sea, into our own Ocean (which being once discovered and made known to be navigable, we should not only do our country a good and notable service; but we also ourselves should have a nearer cut and passage home; where otherwise, we were to make a very long and tedious voyage of it, which would hardly agree with our good liking, we having been so long from home already, and so much of our strength separated from us), which could not at all be done if the opportunity of time were now neglected; we therefore all of us willingly harkened and consented to our General's advice, which was, first to seek out some convenient place wherein to trim our ship, and store ourselves with wood and water and other provisions as we could get, and thenceforward to hasten on our intended journey for the discovery of the said passage, through which we might with joy return to our longed homes.[9]

But whether Drake was or was not commissioned to seek the northern strait from the Pacific side, or whether he did or did not go seeking it, is not our present concern. Our interest in the matter is what the Spanish *thought* Drake did, long before the accounts came out. The authorities in New Spain formed their judgments from statements by their own witnesses. We have seen San Juan de Anton's testimony of Drake's hints of a North-West passage home (*see* page 212). Clearer testimony came from the Portuguese pilot, Nuño da Silva. He was detained by Drake to lead the English ships through the Straits of Magellan, and was released before Drake headed north. This man swore to the Spanish authorities, even under torture, of Drake's intention to seek the northern straits:

> Many times he told me . . . that he had to return by the Strait of Bacallaos which he came to discover. [10]

The Viceroy of New Spain was naturally suspicious that the Portuguese pilot might have been released by Drake solely to spread alarm. But the prevailing view among the Spaniards was that Drake not only sought, but would find the strait, as this excerpt from the narrative of Pedro Sarmiento de Gamboa reveals:

> From the month of March . . . to September it is summer and the hot season, up to Cape Mendocino in 43 degrees by which he [Drake] has a short and easy route to return to his country from this sea. This route, although it is not known by the pilots around here because they do not sail ordinarily in that region, is known to the cosmographers, especially to the English who sail to Iceland, the Bacallaos, Labrador, Totilan and Norway . . . The high latitude does not frighten them. This Corsair . . . will not shrink from undertaking this route. [11]

Sarmiento repeats this view:

> Having arrived at 43 degrees, that is, Cape Mendocino . . . he would continue sailing . . . toward the east to the land of Labrador which is in the neighborhood of England.

We note the precise locating of the strait at Mendocino, where Urdaneta was said to have entered it returning from the Philippines.

The belief that Drake was headed for the northern strait is again expressed in a letter to the King from Mexico in September 1579. The writer, Don Luis de Velasco, discusses measures that might be taken to capture the *Golden Hind*:

> Some results could be obtained by following the coast towards the port of Navidad, Colima, the coast of Chiametla, Culiacan and California . . . where it can be presumed that the Corsair would go, in search of the new strait of which they say he talked so much, saying that this was his route.

This carries the implication that Drake might be expected to course between the mainland coast and California. It suggests that Velasco had in mind the old Strait-of-California theory. The statement by Antonio de Herrera quoted on page 166 bears similarity to Velasco's words, and throws light on them.

It was H. R. Wagner's belief that Drake's voyage certainly fueled the notion of a strait heading northward from the Gulf:

> An opinion seemed to exist in Mexico that in some way Drake was responsible for placing on the map the extension of the Gulf of California to the Straits of Anian.[12]

Even raising the name "California" in conjunction with Drake's exploits appears to have fanned fears that English ships would thereafter come sailing down through the gateway of the Gulf to terrorize the mainland. In his discussion, Wagner points out that this notion was helped along by a story whose origin is unknown. A Spanish or Portuguese pilot named N. de Morera was supposed to have steered Drake through the Straits of Anian. Some substantiation of such a character was given by the Mayor of Guatalco, Gaspar de Vargas, who testified that "the name of the pilot of the ship (the Golden Hinde) is Morera."[13] Hearsay imputed to Morera the claim that he had been put ashore at some harbor on the Strait of Anian. He had then wandered for several years and many hundred leagues down a "brazo de mar." That arm of the sea was described as running north to south and dividing New Mexico from a great western land. This story gave credence to the notion of a channel running all the way from the Strait of Anian to the Gulf of California. The story was not recorded, apparently, until the account of 1626 quoted below, but the chain of hearsay is reported, too. These credulous transmitters will be discussed later (page 259). Our interest now is with the association of Drake's name with a long north-south waterway connected to the Strait of Anian:

> A foreign pilot, named N. de Morera, who steered the Englishman from the North Sea to the South Sea by the Strait of Anian, gave this account . . . When Captain Francisco Draque was returning to his country, leaving through the Strait, this pilot who was accompanying him was very ill and was more dead than alive. And thinking that perhaps the climate on land would bring back his health, and like something dead, they cast him ashore. In a few days he recovered his health and traveled through the land over a period of four years; he came out at New Mexico . . . After telling . . . at length of his many wanderings, he told . . . that the aforementioned Englishmen, Francisco Draque, in a stop at the Strait of Anian, had put him on land . . . and that after he had recovered his health he traveled through different countries and provinces for more than 500 leagues on mainland, until he reached a place where he caught

sight of an arm of the sea that divides the lands of New Mexico from another very large land which is to the west . . . This pilot said that this arm of the sea flowed from north to south and that *it seemed to him that it went on to the north to join the port where the Englishman had put him ashore* [italics added].[14]

The degree of truth in this story is not at issue. We know that espousers of imaginary concepts garble true anecdotes or else spawn self-deceptive fictions as needed to shore up their case. Such fictions are our facts in a study of the evolution of ideas. The Morera story is another sign of the stirring of the old Strait-of-California conceit.

A statement made by Josephus d'Acosta in 1590 in his *Historia Natural y Moral de las Indias* seems to speak to this growing belief in the Gulf as the gateway to the Englishmen's strait. His meaning is no less vague and ambiguous than other statements. But we shall find that the following passage was read by contemporaries as a reference to the Strait of California merging with the North-West Passage:

> Some will say that Drake had knowledge of this Straight, and that he gave occasion so to judge, whenas he passed along the coast of new Spain by the South Sea. Yea, they hold opinion, that that other Englishman, which this year 1587, took a ship coming from the Philippines, with great quantity of gold and other riches, did pass this straight, which prize they made near to the Californias, which course the ships returning from the Philippines and China, to new Spain, do usually observe.[15]

Such obliqueness possibly derives from the subject matter being so well known as not to need repeating. The underlying assumptions were probably patent to most readers. But for us today, who can only work by inference, the passage is a puzzle. How could the Manila galleons have come sailing down the Gulf—if the Gulf is intended? We can only make comparisons with other tantalizing scraps on the same subject. In this case, we recall hints elsewhere of Urdaneta finding a "rear entrance" to the Gulf around Mendocino when he was returning from the Philippines (*see* pages 166 to 168). Mendocino figures as an entry in stories of both the west-to-east and north-south straits, perhaps as an elbow joint in a continuum.

Several unusual maps helped reinforce this Spanish notion of the Gulf as the gateway to a strait used as a homeward route by Drake. They were produced in Britain just after Drake returned in triumph from his circumnavigation. In the great buzz of excitement, British imaginations naturally worked overtime.[16]

First there was John Dee's visionary map of "Atlantis" (*see* Plate 35).

Given Dee's secretiveness, we do not know when this was actually conceived. But Dee listed it under the year 1583, when a copy of it was taken by Sir Humphrey Gilbert on his ill-starred voyage to the North-West Passage. As we have seen, this polar map sports a huge open seaway across the north of the New World. Besides this, the North American continent is traversed by two completed waterways: the first, a St. Lawrence-to-Gulf of California "river-strait;" the second, a "Verrazzano Sea" more eccentric than the original claim, being channel-like and outletting at the Gulf of California.

It remains for us now to notice what Dee has done with his California. A long inlet is depicted northwestward from the crotch of the Gulf or Mar Vermejo. This all but meets another inlet running to the southeast from the vicinity of Mendocino. Together, these inlets create a line suggestive of a "Strait of California" to those programmed to admit the concept. This impression is helped along by the brown line which outlines California as a single entity. This brown line invites the eye to "complete the dotted line" between Gulf and Mendocino inlets. Dee had made Florida and New England into islands. There would be nothing extraordinary in hypothesizing California as another island in his partially submerged Atlantis complex.

In appearance, Dee's California owes something to Ortelius's rendering in his heart-shaped map of 1564 (Plate 27). And there may have been yet another map made by Ortelius that inspired Dee's. Hakluyt refers to this when writing to Raleigh:

> I am fully perswaded by Ortelius' late reformation of Caluacan and the gulfe of California, that the land on the back part of Virginia extendeth nothing so far westward as is put down in the Maps of those parts.[17]

On that map, the Verrazzano Sea must have been depicted as cutting from the Gulf into Virginia.

Putting together Dee's maggot of a Strait of California with the feature of his transcontinental river-strait outletting at the mouth of the St. Lawrence in the east, and the nook of the Gulf of California in the west, we are reminded of Cortés' conception. Cortés' river-that-might-turn-out-to-be-a-strait might have been a similar figment of forked straits, one prong slanting northeast or east across the continent toward the Bacallaos, or Florida; the other northwest or north to outlet into the Pacific or the Septentrional Sea.

Much of Dee's library was burned by a mob fearful of his being a conjurer. We can therefore only guess at the basis of his speculations.

But certainly some of the old ideas were floating around the whole British exploration circle. According to statements of the younger Hakluyt, the "olde excellent mappe" that "master John Verazanus . . . gave to King Henrie the eight" was having a new vogue. In 1582, it was "yet in the custodie of Master Locke."[18] Michael Lok made, or had made, a "copy" which Hakluyt published "annexed to the end of this boke"—his *Divers Voyages* (Plate 36).

Lok's "Mare de Verrazano of 1524" (as he labels it), resembles the original as it relates to the east coast. Like Münster's map (Plate 32), it flows into a great northern sea joining Atlantic and Pacific. But when it comes to the west side of the continent, Lok is as idiosyncratic in his way as Dee. In a wild flight of fancy, he depicts a huge Gulf of California reaching almost to 45 degrees. An equally huge California is joined to the mainland by a narrow neck of land. A slip of the pen would make it an island, the Gulf becoming a strait. This neck occurs where the northern ocean meets the South Sea at a group of mountains called "Sierre Nevada." The elder Hakluyt had wanted Gilbert to plant a colony or way station at such a point. All in all, this map by Lok could have scared the Spanish half out of their wits.

Lok's map reminds us of the Michele Tramezzino map of 1554 (*see* Plate 29). There, too, California is an appendage (though much smaller) dangling by a thread. Did Lok deliberately pick up this ambiguous feature which had kept a Strait of California within the realm of possibility?

Lok's map gave particular momentum to the association of Drake's name with an extension of the Gulf of California. It was the first map to make reference to the English navigations in the legend "Anglorum— 1580." This appears directly above the geographical oddity.

A map with kindred notions to Dee's conception is Ortelius's map of 1570 as amended in 1587 (Plate 37). As noted earlier (page 169), a "Rio de los Estrechos" had been added. Its course suggests an incipient linkage with the head of the Gulf as Dee's inlet had done. The estuary-outlet of Ortelius's River of the Straits appears near his "Cabo Mendocino." This was where Cabrillo and Urdaneta had searched for a "big water." Ortelius's map also depicts a continent-straddling waterway of two rivers almost "joined" at their respective sources. Dee had gone one step further and made them one.

The archives of Spain, comments Wagner, "are full of documents . . . illustrative of the panic into which the Spaniards were thrown by Drake's boldness in venturing into the South Sea."[19] Indeed, the panic

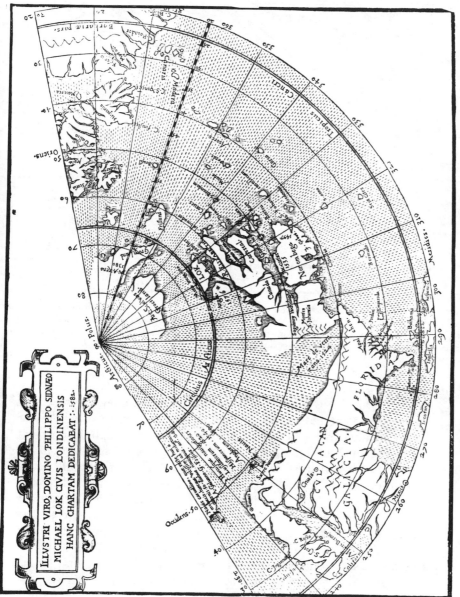

PLATE 36.   Only a small neck of land joins California to the mainland at the end of a huge Gulf in Michael Lok's map of 1582. This is the first map to make claim to an English presence at the South-Sea end of the North-West Passage in the legend: "Anglorum 1580." *Photograph and permission by the British Library (from Hakluyt's Divers Voyages, 1582).*

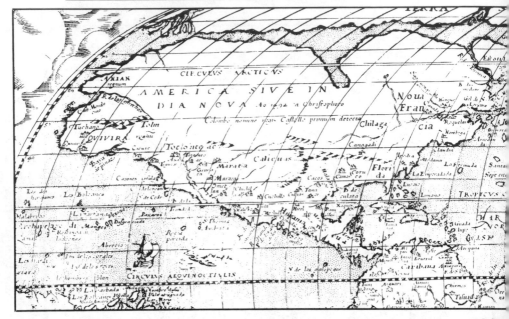

PLATE 37. A "Rio de los estrechos" (River of the Straits) discharges into the South Sea between Cabo Mendocino and Anian—an amendment made in 1587 to Ortelius's famous map. The course of the "Rio de los estrechos" suggests continuing preoccupation with a waterway between Mendocino and the head of the Gulf. (Discussion on pages 169, 224, 294.) *Photograph and permission by the British Library (from Hakluyt's* The Principall Navigations, *1589).*

made the Mexicans irrational. Although they well knew the routes by which Drake entered and left the South Sea, rumors persisted that he had gone home by the new route in record time—through the portal of the California Gulf presumably. The renaming of his ship the *Golden Hind* may have helped to mix things up. Frobisher's simultaneous expedition to the North-West had a ship of the same name. Of course, both ships were dubbed in honor of their patron, Sir Christopher Hatton—whose emblem bore the golden hind. But it is interesting to speculate whether a contributory motive in Drake's change of names was a desire to confuse the Spanish. Inasmuch as superstitions of ill luck attached to such renaming, there had to be a powerful rationale for it.

The arrival of Thomas Cavendish off the coast of California in 1587, and his seizing of the galleon the *Santa Ana*, added fuel to this rekindling myth of a Strait of California. The corsairs lurked in Pichilingue (Freebooter) Harbor, just inside the *boca de California*. When they darted out after their prey, the impression was given to the credulous that they had just come down the Gulf out of the strait.

The Hollanders soon began to be as much a menace as the British in South-Sea waters. The Netherlands had seized freedom from Spain in the 1570s, quickly becoming a force to be reckoned with in world

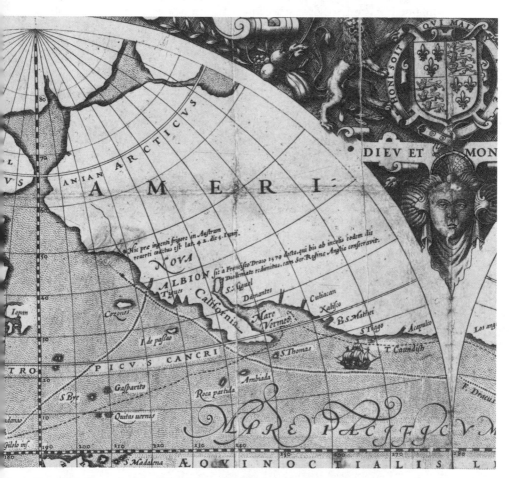

PLATE 38.   The concept of a Strait of California may have been helped along by the open-ended Mare Vermeo on this portion of a map by Jodocus Hondius of c. 1595. The dreaded names of "Francisco Draco 1579" and "Nova Albion" above the opening could have reinforced the illusion it was Drake's way home—despite his real return route across the Pacific being clearly shown. (Discussion on page 228.) *Photograph and permission by the British Library (Maps MT.6.a.2.).*

exploration. Oliver van Noort invaded the Pacific and circumnavigated the world in 1598–1601.

The Dutch spread alarm not only through the prowess of their mariners. The maps coming out of Amsterdam bore features hinting at a Strait of California. Early in the 1590s Jodocus Hondius produced a map showing the circumnavigations of Drake and Cavendish (Plate 38). At the head of the Gulf of California is an unfinished opening. Just above it, "Nova Albion" is printed in very large script, with a legend about Drake's discovery of it. The association is provocative.

Later, in his map of 1611, Hondius seems to be trying to figure out the other end of that open arm he drew in 1590. He revived the Verrazzano Sea, muddling it in with the Septentrional Ocean, now depicted as forming the north boundary of Virginia. This bizarre coastline, continued to the west, trails off half way across the continent, as though Hondius couldn't quite puzzle out its connection to the Gulf (Plate 39). He takes another stab at this on his 1613 globe in the National Maritime Museum at Greenwich.

The sum of these "proofs" of their worst fears so spooked the Spanish that in due course Drake would be credited entirely with the Strait-of-California theory. A hundred years after Drake's death no memory would remain of Cortés' initiation of the myth. Around 1700, in the course of challenging the concept, Father Eusebio Francisco Kino would attribute the whole thing to Drake's own thinking:

> After the English pirate and pilot, Francis Drake, sailed on these seas . . .
> he, seeing then the many currents of the Gulf of California, concluded
> and proclaimed as a certain thing that this California Gulf and sea had
> communication with the North Sea.[20]

Here, Drake is charged with deducing the strait's existence, not with actually using it. It had obviously not made a scrap of difference that the records had later shown he did not use that passage home. He was still saddled with it in the Spanish consciousness.

The next chapter will continue combing the records of the three decades following Drake's voyage to see what more contributed to the genesis of that belief.

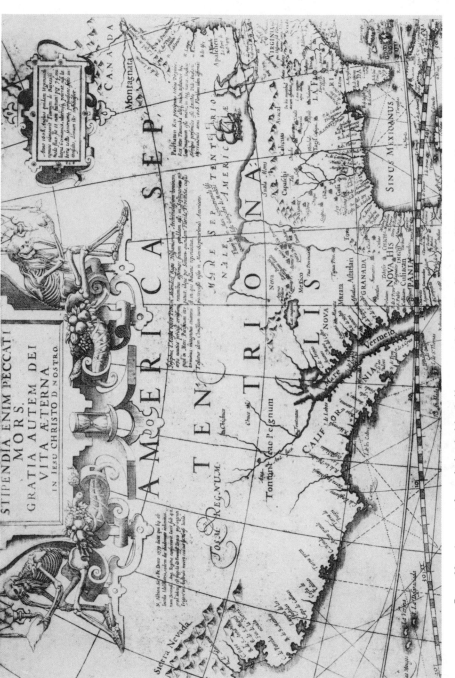

PLATE 39. An open inlet at the head of the Gulf appears on Jodocus Hondius's map of 1611, together with a tentative, unfinished, Verrazzano-style sea stretching from Virginia to New Mexico. Was Hondius trying to figure out if they were connected? (Discussion also on page 279.) *From a facsimile by Edward Luther Stevenson and J. Fischer, S. J., of the original in Schloss Wolfegg. Photograph by the British Library.*

Chapter XX

THE SPANISH THINK DRAKE'S "NEW ALBION" IS AN ISLAND

The flip side of the "Strait of California" is the "Isle of California." This yin-yang configuration is important to our story. For Cortés, the island was the central concept. Before and after Drake's incursion into the Pacific the major emphasis was on the strait.

As we have seen, Spanish fears stirred memories of the expeditions of Cortés and Mendoza. Investigations into the possible routes of "Lutheran" corsairs necessarily revived the mythos of the island, since the concepts went in tandem. Testimony such as that given by Ladrillero, and accounts written by such as Obregón, naturally gave new life to the island myth.

In the years following Drake's voyage, the emphasis began to shift. Drake's name became associated with the island aspect as much as with the strait. He began to be credited less with finding the strait than decreeing that California was an island. Looking back from a century on, Kino would believe that Drake "delineated it [California] as surrounded with seas and as an island (which would have been the greatest in the world)."[1] Kino went even further, believing that Drake had invented the strait in order to support the island myth:

> Drake, in order to carry his point that California was an island, would feign another Strait of Anian with another much-talked-of Sea of the North over here above California.

The idiosyncratic maps of Dee and Lok could have helped clinch Drake's identification with the Island of California as the years went by. The strong possibility that those maps did influence the second flowering is suggested by the hugeness of the almost-islands. Size is a major difference between the first and second manifestations of the island myth.

Drake's association with an island actually developed as a notion quite independent from the Strait-of-California revival, rather than as an obverse, or corollary of it. It was more a product of Spanish speculations about his destinations and stopping places near New Spain.

The idea that Drake discovered an island in the South Sea may have begun with Oxenham's deposition to the Inquisition. He testified that

Grenville had petitioned the Queen to search the South Sea for "some islands where to found settlements." The Spanish would have put their own construction on what that might mean.

The notion may also have derived from a conjecture made by the Licentiate Valverde from Guatemala. Like Viceroy Velasco, he proposed sending ships to the Golfo de Bermejo. In his letter to the King in 1579, he bases his proposal on this speculation:

> The great probability is . . . that the Corsair has wintered on the coast, in the region of the Californias.[2]

Wagner has commented that the "use of the term 'Californias' at that period is very curious." It can hardly have contained the idea of an Alta and Baja California, or New and Old California. The use of those appellations was a long way in the future.[3] Valverde must have been harking back to the notion of a cluster of fabled pearl islands associated with Cortés (see Agnese's map, Plate 17). The reference would have conjured up their romantic and mysterious aura and all the wealth they represented. For Drake to have careened his ship on one of those islands, preparing to take the northern passage home, would have added insult to injury. For him to claim possession of it would be like stealing a pearl from the Spanish crown.

The Spanish alone dreamed up this blow to their security. In the long-delayed reports, there was nothing to tie Drake to any island. The "Famous Voyage" says only this:

> The .5 day of June, being in 43. degrees toward the pole Arctike, we found the air so cold, that our men being grievously pinched with the same, complained of the extremity thereof, and the further we went, the more cold increased upon us. Whereupon we thought it best for that time to seek the land, and did so, finding it not mountainous, but low plain land, & clad, and covered over with snow, so that we drew back again without landing, till we came within 38. degrees toward the line. In which height it pleased God to send us into a fair and good Bay, with a good wind to enter the same. In this Bay we anchored . . .[4]

Likewise in the "Anonymous Narrative" we are told only of Drake's "keeping along the coast as near land as he might, until he came to .44 gr. and then he found a harbor for his ship where he grounded his ship to trim her."[5] Nor is there anything in The World Encompassed to suggest the location was an island, though there is plenty to suggest a natural paradise waiting to be settled:

From the height of 48 deg. in which now we were, to 38 we found the land by coasting along it to be but low and reasonable plain: every hill (whereof we saw many, but none very high) though it were in June, and the sun in his nearest approach unto them, being covered with snow . . . In 38 deg. 30 min. we fell with a convenient and fit harbor, and June 17 came to anchor therein: where we continued till the 23 day of July following . . .

After that our necessary businesses were well dispatched, our general with his gentlemen, and many of his company, made a journey up into the land . . . to be the better acquainted with the nature and commodites of the country . . .

. . . The inland we found to be far different from the shore, a goodly country, and fruitful soil, stored with many blessings fit for the use of man: infinite was the company of very large and fat deer, which there we saw by thousands, as we supposed, in a herd: besides a multitude of a strange kind of conies, by far exceeding them in number.[6]

The only mention of islands in this context occurs *after* the stopover to trim the ship. Depending on one's theory of Drake's harbor, this could have been the Farallones:

Not far without this harbor did lie certain islands (we called them the Islands of Saint *James*) having on them plentiful and great store of seals and birds, with one of which we fell July 24, whereon we found such profusion as might competently serve our turn for a while. We departed again the day next following, viz, July 25. And our general . . . with consent of all, bent his course directly to run with the Islands of the Moluccas. And so having nothing in our view but air and sea, without sight of any land for the space of full 68 days together, we continued our course through the main ocean . . .

Drake's teenage cousin John may inadvertently have had a hand in developing Drake's association with an island. John had been on the *Golden Hind*. He was captured on a subsequent journey to South America. He made two depositions to the Inquisition. John's youth and fear may have made him suggestible to Spanish preconceptions of an insular discovery, when grilled about Sir Francis' exploits.

Here is an excerpt from his first deposition at Santa Fe in Argentina in 1584. In the usual third person synopsis, John's description details Drake's movements after his leaving southern Mexico:

They put to sea, making for the NW and NNE (?), and sailed during the whole of April and May and half June from Aguatulco . . . On the way

they met with great storms: the whole sky was obscured and covered with
clouds; they saw five or six islands, to one of which Captain Francis gave
the name St. Bartholomew and to another St. James. These islands were
situated in forty-six and forty-eight degrees. Captain Francis gave to the
land which lies in forty-eight degrees the name of New England. They
remained there a month and a half, taking in wood and water and
repairing the ship.[7]

There is no necessary relationship here between mention of the six
islands and the land he named New England, except for the shared
forty-eight degrees of latitude. However, John's second deposition,
quoted below, taken by the Inquisitors at Lima on January 9, 1587, does
suggest that an island was what Drake discovered. This is clearly implied
by the statement that Drake's landfall was in "the Californias." The
location of these islands in so high a latitude as 48 degrees is, however,
bewildering :

> From there they sailed in a N.W. and N.N.W. direction and covered a
> thousand leagues as far as 44 degrees, always on the bowline, then the
> wind changed, so they made for the Californias, and found land in 48
> degrees. They disembarked and made huts, remaining there a month and
> a half to repair the ship . . . The country is temperate, cold rather than
> hot: a very rich country to the eye. They repaired their large ship . . .[8]

It is unlikely that the term "the Californias" would have sprung
spontaneously, uncoached, from John. It could have cropped up in a
leading question by the inquisitors, or been added by the reporter
—since the responses are summarized.

There are two details in these depositions that might have, inadvertently, added to the island notion. The first is the description of Drake's
claim as temperate and rich—suggestive of ideal islands from the
dreamstock. The second is the naming of the claim "New England,"
promoting associations with the island nature of Drake's homeland.

These associations could only have been deepened by the following
statements from the account in Hakluyt, when it appeared in 1589:

> Our General called this country Nova Albion, and that for two causes:
> the one in respect of the white banks and cliffs, which lie towards the sea:
> and the other, because it might have some affinity with our country in
> name, which sometime was so called.[9]

"New Albion" even more than New England would have evoked in
Spanish minds the concept of an island. Dee's *Pety Navy Royall* (*see*
page 199) had resurrected the old name of the "Isle of Britain" as more

appropriate to the stature of "this Incomparable Islandish Impire." To be reminded of Dee's imperialist stance could only have compounded the dismay in Mexico.

When Drake set up his brass plate and named his claim, the "affinity" he intended to draw was probably no more than the kind conferred through the christening of a namesake. But the Spanish may have jumped to the conclusion that the affinity was in a shared attribute, namely insularity. In the quotation above from the "Famous Voyage," the "because" suggests a prior cause. *The World Encompassed* changes the "because" to "that"—meaning "so that" or "in order that"—better reflecting Drake's intention to create a relationship, rather than to describe a pre-existing one.[10]

A sense of separateness may have been suggested, too, by the statement made to fix the claim more surely:

> It seems that the Spanish hitherto had never been in this part of the Country, neither did ever discover the land by many degrees to the southwards of this place.[11]

Reverberations of ideal islands from the dreamstock would also have been set in motion by the assertion:

> There is no part of earth here to be taken up, wherein there is not a reasonable quantity of gold or silver.[12]

Antonio de Herrera's *Historia General del Mundo* put the official stamp on the belief in Drake's island discovery:

> He [Francis Drake] sailed towards the northwest and the northeast two months, encountering great storms and a sky obscured with many fogs, until he reached a latitude of somewhat more than 45, with the purpose of seeking the strait which has been referred to.

> Francis Drake, on this journey, saw five or six islands of good land. He called one San Bartolome, one San Jaime, and another which seemed to be the largest and the best, Nueva Albion. Here he remained a month and a half, repairing the two ships.[13]

The belief that Drake discovered an island would survive as a debatable issue into the eighteenth century. But by then the Isle-of-California myth had bloomed anew, and it and Drake's island had elided into one. We have seen Kino's views on this. Kino's colleague, Father Luis Velarde, reveals the misconception by "correcting" it.

> In my poor judgment, that pilot [The Englishman, Sir Francis Drake] . . . did not sail around California by this gulf where he said he entered with

his ships . . . Being so careful, he should have verified this statement before letting it be published. He wanted to be made famous by the assertion that he had gone around the great California.[14]

Another statement by Kino makes clear that in the century between Drake's voyage and Kino's arrival in the New World, California and New Albion had completely coincided in the popular imagination. Ernest J. Burrus translates notes "written in great part by Kino and published in Latin by Scherer with the 1685 map" as follows:

California is the first and principal island of the entire world and also the largest. It is separated from New Mexico by the narrow Red Sea . . . The renowned English captain, Francis Drake . . . also touched at this island, calling it New Albion, that is New England, inasmuch as England of old was called Albion. Thus, as far as is known, Drake was the first to go to California.[15]

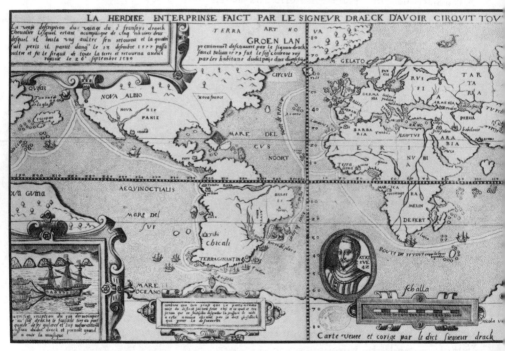

PLATE 40. Giving credence to the Spanish notion that Drake trimmed his ship on an island is this map showing two clusters of islands on Drake's route—one off the point of California, the other off the northwest coast. On this "French Drake Map"—by Nicola van Sype (c. 1583)—"Nova Albio" is not, however, any small island, but an extensive claim running from east to west coasts. *Photograph and permission by the British Library.*

Indeed, the Island of California and the Island of New Albion became so totally identified as to expire simultaneously. Gregorio García wrote in 1729:

I do not believe that la Nueva Albion, which Drake discovered . . . is an island, but continent.[16]

Several maps about Drake's voyage may owe something to the tales associating him with an island. The "French Drake Map" (Plate 40), and the "Dutch Drake Map," depict two clusters of islands, one off the point of California, another off the northwest coast. Both clusters are on Drake's route as shown on the map. We might notice, however, that "Nova Albio" is on the mainland. So extensive is the claim, its boundaries are drawn to include California *and* Florida.

Although the British had no actual plans to make "plantings," they would have made noises of pressing their claim if only to give one more tweak to the Spanish beard. So we have to wonder if the Spanish pushed the island notion as a way to keep English paws off their mainland. Insularists by persuasion, the British would have had no trouble buying the Spanish notion. They were eager to see islands anywhere.

Indeed, the younger Hakluyt may himself have contributed to the Drake island fallacy. He did more than publish Lok's provocative map, and Ortelius's map showing the Rio de los Estrechos. It is likely that the Spanish materials he was making available to British readers fanned his zeal for islands. These materials included documents then close to half a century old. Among them were the accounts dealt with in Part I revealing belief in the Isle-of-California myth originating with Cortés. Their very publication at this time no doubt stimulated the revival of that myth. The myth then rubbed off on Drake because of his association with the quest for straits.

Whether deliberately or inadvertently, Hakluyt helped fuel the myth by emphasizing it in marginal annotations to his collected texts (*see* examples, Plate 41). Next to a letter by Antonio de Mendoza about Cortés' settlement, Hakluyt notes:

This was the port of Santa Cruz in the Isle of California.[17]

The captions accompanying the translated narratives of Niza read:

A great island and 30 small islands which seem to be the new islands of California, rich in pearles.

and:

where Fernando Cortez the Marques of the valley had bin, of who an island, & not firme land, as some suppose it to be. They came to y of wood: and from the maine to the island is but halfe a league by s certaine Indians of another island greater then this came to visit m whom I was informed that there were 30. other smal islands, whi store of victuals, sauing 2. which haue Maiz or corne of the country. necks many great shels which were mother of Pearle. I shewed with me for a shew, and they told me that there were in the Island very great: howbeit I saw none of them.   I followed my voya

The island of Saint Iago.

A great island, and 30. small islands, which seeme to be the new islands of California rich in pearles.

---

captaine with 2. ships to discouer the coast: which 2. ships sent againe 2. other ships, one of the which was diuided f taine mariners slue the captaine, & usurped ouer the ship. the Master with certaine mariners going on land, the In their boat: and the ship with those that were in it, returr it ran on ground. By the men which came home in this

This was the Port of Santa Cruz. in the Isle of California.

---

turne of my messengers which I had sent vnto the Sea, who re- p, bringing with them certaine inhabitants of the Sea-coast, and m I vnderstoode, that the Ilandes aboue mentioned were scarce fore, and that they are inhabited by people, which weare shelles of and they say that they haue great Pearles, and much Golde. They tie Ilandes, lying one neere vnto another: they say that the peo- all store of victuals, as also those of the Ilandes, and that they on raftes. This coast stretcheth Northward as is to bee seene.

Great pearles and much gold in the Isles of California, which are 34. in number.

PLATE 41.   A reviving belief in California's island nature became apparent at the end of the sixteenth century when Richard Hakluyt published translations of the Spanish expeditions of 1535 to 1542 for British readers. Hakluyt's marginal headings in *The Principall Navigations* (1589) identified California both as a great island and as a group of islands. (Discussion on pages 237-39.) *Photographs and permission by the British Library.*

Great pearles and much gold in the isles of California, which are 34 in number.

Annotating the Coronado narrative, he states:

Seven or eight isles, which are the isles of California.

The Ulloa narrative carries the marginal comment:

Some take the land of California to be nothing but islands.

Hakluyt made it his business to pass on any new information that came his way about "the rich Isles of California." These tidbits entrenched the myth in English imaginations ever more deeply. He offered to his reader, for example:

An extract of a Spanish letter written from Pueblo de los Angeles in Nueva Espanna in October 1597, touching the discovery of the rich Isles of California, being distant eight days sailing from the main.

This letter, which Hakluyt presents indirectly in synopsis, seems to summarize the history of Baja from Ximénes' discovery and the Marqués del Valle's aborted settlement:

We have seen a letter written the eighth of October 1597, out of a town called Pueblo de los Angeles situate eighteen leagues from Mexico, making mention of the Islands of California situate two or three hundred leagues from the main land of Nueva Espanna, in Mar del Sur: as that thither have been sent before that time some people to conquer them: which with loss of some twenty men were forced back.

In 1597, the dream island stories of gold and pearls are still intact, for the letter-summary continues:

After that, they had well visited and found those islands or countries to be very rich of gold and silver mines, and of very fair Oriental pearls, which were caught in good quantity upon one fathom and a half passing in beauty the pearls of the Island Margarita.

The letter goes on to tell of efforts to "conquer" the islands. But we cannot be sure from the sketchy information whether this refers to the original aborted expedition, or to more recent activity, possibly to an expedition by Sebastian Vizcaíno into the gulf of California, to be discussed in Chapter XXII:

The report thereof [of gold and pearls] caused the Viceroy of Mexico to send a citizen of Mexico with two hundred men to conquer the same. Therein also was affirmed that within eight days they would sail thither from the main.

Assuming the authenticity of this letter, we can point to it as the clearest evidence so far uncovered of the resurgence of the island myth—at least in one of its earliest Cortésian forms. In his *Islario* of 1542, Alonso de Santa Cruz, the royal cartographer, had described such a group of islands "great and small," and Battista Agnese had depicted them on the map now in the Royal Library at Stockholm (Plate 17). And as we have already seen, at least one Spanish official, Licentiate Valverde of Guatemala, had had such a geographical concept in mind when he feared Drake had "wintered on the coast, in the region of the Californias" (page 232). De Acosta echoed this concept (page 222).

A cluster of islands great and small is a long way from the huge single island of California that would soon develop in the myth's full and final flowering. But in this fashion, increment by increment, we see the myth moving to reinstatement. The stages in that development are detailed in the next two chapters.

Chapter XXI

Spain Contrives to Keep Foreigners Out of the South Sea

The speed with which Drake returned to England persuaded the Spanish that he must have gone home via the North-West Passage. Drake deliberately played up these fears by feeding disinformation to Spanish informers around the Court. On October 16, 1580, Bernardino de Mendoza wrote Philip II that the Queen's councillors were very cagey about the voyage:

> They are very particular not to divulge the route by which Drake returned, and although as I wrote to your Majesty, Hatton's trumpeter had said that the road home had been by the Portuguese Indies, Drake himself signifies to the contrary.[1]

Mendoza added that Drake's men were gagged:

> They are not to disclose the route they took on pain of death. Drake affirms that he will be able to make the round voyage in a year, as he has found a very short way.

Worse news yet, Mendoza reported:

> He is arranging to return with six ships . . . At present there is hardly an Englishman who is not talking of undertaking the voyage, so encouraged are they by Drake's return.

The British must have hoped the Spanish would make the kind of deduction expressed here by Gerhardus Mercator to Ortelius in a letter of December 1580:

> I am persuaded that there can be no other reason for so carefully concealing the course followed . . . other than that they may have found very wealthy regions never yet discovered by Europeans.[2]

In response to this continuing threat, Philip of Spain began to work out defensive policies with the Viceroy in Mexico. A three-pronged action was discussed. The first prong involved a survey of the outside coast, the second, a survey and settlement of the Gulf. The third prong related to explorations into the interior of the mainland called "New Mexico."

The official rationale for the first prong, the exploration of the outer coast, is given in this letter by Fray Andrés de Aguirre to the Archbishop and Viceroy of Mexico in 1584:

> The voyage of discovery which your lordship orders to be made, as well for the purpose of gaining a knowledge of the coast and harbors, and the quality of the land and condition of its people, to the present time discovered to the westward of this New Spain in the South Sea, as for the further prosecution of the exploration of that coast and region beyond the forty-first degree of latitude, is of great importance and very necessary both in connection with the return voyage of vessels from the Philippines and all parts of the west, and for the purpose of understanding and knowing the lay of the land and its qualities and those of its people and of *the islands of great importance which are understood to lie near that coast* [italics added]. Although the ships which come every year from the west to the port of Acapulco make a landfall on that coast and sail within sight of it for more than five hundred leagues, to the present time it is not known what harbors or stopping places it has. It is very important to know this, so that ships which come needing to stop, after reaching that coast from a distance of two thousand leagues, without touching anywhere, may stop and provide for their needs.[3]

This passage takes up the three major concerns raised by Drake's audacity: (1) What harbors could give shelter to the weary galleons and serve as boltholes when the corsairs stalked the area? (2) Where were the "islands of great importance" among which, presumably, might lie the one Drake claimed? (3) What were the "secrets" of the northwest coast above Mendocino, "which some say joins on to the main land of China while others hold that it ends at the strait called Anian which leads to Ireland"?

On the question of straits, the greater fear may have been for an entry running north from the Gulf of California. The King wanted quick action on that second prong of policy—the survey and settlement of the Gulf to fortify it against future predators. However, in 1585, a new Viceroy tried to dissuade him from this course:

> From the reports of the voyage to the Californias made by the Marques del Valle and the expedition of Francisco Vazquez Coronado to the cities of Cibola, Your Majesty has learned that the greater part of the people on that coast is a savage people eking out a scanty living by fishing; and, as it might be inconvenient to make settlements there just now, while from not having done so no inconvenience has arisen, there is no need, for the present service of Your Majesty, to treat of that matter.[4]

This advice made little impression on the King. Royal pressure to protect the Gulf would continue into the next century.

The Viceroy was supposed to coordinate the coastal survey with activities on the New Mexico frontier. This constituted the third prong of recommended policy. "New Mexico" was the vast, indeterminate interior, running from what today we call northern Mexico, through Arizona and Texas on toward the north and west. It was hoped that the overland explorations to New Mexico could be helped by the projected sea-going exploration. If a strait were discovered, it might prove to be the long-sought waterway through New Mexico, providing a less costly route for settlement:

> In addition . . . by this route, and at a less cost than by land, communica-
> tion might be had with New Mexico, on its being settled, as may be
> understood from the statement on this subject that had been made by
> Antonio de Espejo.

Espejo was one of the first explorers since Coronado to penetrate that interior. He was persuaded of the existence of a great river, many leagues wide, and connecting both oceans.[5] This echoed river-straits that had lured Cortés, Coronado and Guzmán, and the maker of the Sloane manuscript map. Most recently, Obregón had described such a continent-spanning figment, a Rio Salado, a salt river, in his *History*.[6] Francisco Díaz de Vargas also told of a great river traversing New Mexico. He contended it might be "el estrecho de los bacallaos"—the Codfish Strait. He also described "an arm of the sea where one could enter from one or another coast."[7] Perhaps the "big water" of Cabrillo and Urdaneta came into play again, depending on whether an outlet was envisaged on the outside coast above Mendocino, or at the Ancón de San Andrés in the gulf.

As a matter of policy, then, New Mexico explorers would continue their quest for the huge waterway, to follow it to its outlets. This would coincide with the mariners' quest for an outlet along the coast.

The Viceroy speaks to this subject in his letter of 1585, perhaps to temper his sovereign's urging. The Viceroy takes note that "it is yet unknown whether" this "midland" or "between-seas" region (New Mexico) "communicates with the North Sea, or is closer to the South Sea."[8]

In terms of this study, this third prong of official policy to find a strait would prove the most influential of the three. The New Mexico explorers would play a crucial role in the revitalization of the Strait-of-California myth.

But for the moment we must follow the first prong of the post-Drake policy—the exploration up the outer coast. This was set in motion before 1584. Special ships were supposed to be built for the purpose. But as Obregón expressed it: "This expedition would cost less and require less time if carried out from the Philippine Islands."[9] Always happy to save money and speed things up, the then-Viceroy saw the merit of combining trade and exploration—private and public sectors we would say today. He would call on one of the captains plying the Manila-to-Acapulco route to do the job.

The decision seemed to make a lot of sense. The route of the Manila galleons was down the very coast needing closer scrutiny. Returning from the Philippines, they sailed the Japan Current into the North Pacific Drift, between 40 degrees and 50 degrees, driven east by *los vendavales*, the strong southwesterlies. About Cape Mendocino, they caught the California Current and were carried southward to Cabo San Lucas, then to Acapulco.

A galleon captain was selected and subsidized to make the survey. He was Francisco Gali or Galli, or Gualle—as he is called by Richard Hakluyt, whose translation of the narrative is used below. In his report, Gali speculated on the change of currents encountered by the galleons off the California coast in the latitude of Mendocino. These, said Gali, must imply the existence of a strait between America and Asia:

> Running thus east, and east and by north about three hundred leagues from Japan, we found a very hollow water, with the stream running out of the north and northwest, with a full and very broad sea, without any hinderance or trouble in the way that we passed: and what wind soever blew, the sea continued all in one sort, with the same hollow water and stream, until we had passed seven hundred leagues. About two hundred leagues from the coast and land of New Spain we began to lose the said hollow sea and stream; whereby I most assuredly think and believe, that there you shall find a channel or straight passage, between the firm land of New Spain, and the countries of Asia and Tartaria. Likewise all this way from the aforesaid seven hundred leagues, we found a great number of whale-fishes and other fishes called by the Spaniards atuns or tunnies, whereof many are found on the coast of Gilbraltar in Spain, as also albacoras and bonitos, which are all fishes which commonly keep in channels, straits, and running waters, there to disperse their seed when they breed: which maketh me more assuredly believe, that thereabouts is a channel or strait to pass through.[10]

Gali's deduction of a strait as he approached Mendocino would have, in the next decade, as much bearing on the Strait-of-California myth as on the Strait of Anian.

But Gali gave only a superficial inspection of the coast. More than this was really not to be expected from the captain of a galleon. Although the sighting of the Coast Ranges, and the catching of the southward current, must always have been a matter of rejoicing for those battered, weary, scurvy-ridden mariners, no one wanted to get too close. The dread of shipwreck on the rocky, surf-lashed, fogbound shore must have evoked something like the old ambivalence toward the Amazon island. It was the custom of the galleons to keep well clear of the mysterious, treacherous land, and sail right past.

Superstitious avoidance of this coast over many decades may explain why all record or memory of the Cabrillo-Ferrelo voyage seems to have disappeared in the intervening forty or so years. The excellent anchorages of San Diego, San Pedro, and the sheltered coves of the offshore islands are no longer known or recognized. Gali's account manifests no awareness of Cabrillo's precise descriptions; it deals rather in vague generalities:

> Being by the same course upon the coast of New Spain, under seven and thirty degrees and ½, we passed by a very high and fair land with many trees, wholely without snow, and four leagues from the land, you find thereabouts many drifts of roots, leaves of trees, reeds; . . . there likewise we found great store of seals: whereby it is to be presumed and certainly to be believed, that there are many rivers, bays and havens along by those coasts to the haven of Acapulco.

> From thence we ran southeast, southeast and by south, and southeast by east, as we found the wind, to the point called El Cabo de San Lucas, which is the beginning of the land of California, on the northwest side, lying under two and twenty degrees, being five hundred leagues distant from Cape Mendocino.

> In this way of the aforesaid five hundred leagues along by the coast, are many islands: and although they be but small, yet without doubt there are in them some good havens, as also in the firm land, where you have . . . good havens . . .now lately found out.

Once again we have a glimpse of a real paradise awaiting exploration. Yet however promising the coast and havens might appear through a spyglass, only extreme emergency would persuade those merchant mariners to put ashore.

It was therefore through accident that the first on-land information was gathered in this period. A perilous voyage from "China" in 1587

forced Pedro de Unamuno to land somewhere north of Point Conception, in the vicinity of Morro Bay. He was relieved to find that the basic
needs of his suffering crew were well supplied:

> In this port there is an unlimited quantity of fish of different kinds, trees
> suitable for masts, water, firewood and abundant shell-fish, with all of
> which a ship in need could supply itself.[11]

He also noted; "The land of this coast is well suited for wheat and
maize." Only an encounter with resenting Indians offset these advantages.

It finally took a shipwreck of another galleon to produce hard information. Sebastian Roderiguez Cermeño was assigned the job of again
trying to survey the coast on his way south. His galleon, the San
Agustín, came in sight of Mendocino at the beginning of November,
1595:

> We encountered cloudy weather, a calm sea and a favorable wind. By
> night I did not sail as we were near the land and feared running ashore,
> and kept casting the lead continually until Saturday morning, the 4th of
> November, when the land . . . appeared . . . We came within a league of
> land, which appeared mountainous and heavily forested with trees . . .
> Among them were many pine trees growing very thickly near the sea and
> inland . . . We went coasting along near the shore where there might
> possibly be found conveniences and a safe port to enter and make the
> launch to prosecute the reconnaissance.[12]

Cermeño anchored off what we now call Point Reyes. They called the
bay the Puerto de San Francisco. The galleon was wrecked there in a
storm. The launch that they were building for exploration of the coast
became their only vessel. As they limped south, they were reduced to
living off the land. They discovered, as Drake had done, that behind
the inimical coastline there lay excellent country:

> The land seems fertile as far as three leagues inland, according to what I
> saw and what the other Spaniards saw whom I took with me to seek food,
> of which there was need on account of the loss of the ship. The soil will
> return any kind of seed that may be sown, as there are trees which bear
> hazelnuts . . . and fragrant herbs like those in Castile. There is also near
> where I went to seek food a branch of a river which runs into the sea, and
> near the camp are other arroyos of fresh water about two musket-shots
> from the sea. There are also in the country a quantity of crabs and wild
> birds and deer, with which the people maintain their existence. And this
> is as put down in the declaration, and I have knowledge of it as a person
> who twice went inland to seek food as we had none.

But there was no sudden recognition of the birth of a new kind of promise. The sole concern of the crew was to reach the Mexican mainland in one piece. As they proceeded down the coast they were impressed more by inhospitable features of the land than by its potential bounties:

Sailing close to the land and at times within a musket-shot of it, one could see it plainly, and that it was bare, like rough broken country, although above on the mountains there were some pine and oak trees.

They discovered a large bay, probably Monterey, without exploring it. South of that the coastline was "rough and with ravines, and the hills, although very high, are bare, without trees." Only in the vicinity of San Luis Obispo, as we know it now, did they have time to note that "the land seemed to be good, as it was covered with trees and verdure." There the Indians brought them fish and a seal. On another occasion the mariners themselves "went fishing with lines and caught some thirty fish like *cabrillas* [sea bass]—which we soon ate on account of our great hunger."

Relying on wild fruits and grasses—often gifts of the helpful Indians—on fish, and on chance arroyos of fresh water, the crew managed, with much suffering, to pass beyond the Point of California, and reach the populated mainland of New Spain.

Cermeño was probably the first European to demonstrate by actual experience that the unprobed territory to the north was capable of supporting colonists. He inadvertently revealed some likely natural havens, first at Puerto de San Francisco then at Monterey. One more testimonial had been added to those of Cabrillo and Drake that this region gave promise of being a realistic paradise once the impediments of natural hazards and superstitious fear were overcome.

But from the point of view of those trying to shape a defensive policy, the use of the galleons for coastal exploration hadn't been too smart an idea. They had failed to find the strait, and lost valuable cargo in the process. It dawned on the Viceroy that perhaps he was expecting too much of crews exhausted by so many gruelling months at sea, and in vessels so heavily laden. After the Cermeño fiasco the Viceroy wrote the King on April 19, 1596:

Touching the loss of the ship, San Agustín, which was on its way from the islands of the west for the purpose of making the exploration of the coasts of the South Sea . . . while the sufferings they underwent after the ship was cast away elicit compassion . . . the intention of Your Majesty has not been carried into effect. It is the general opinion that this enterprise should not be attempted on the return voyage from the islands and with a laden ship, but from this coast and by constantly following along it.[13]

It was all very fine to propose a coastal survey starting in the south and coasting north. But the northward voyage involved running against the current, a far more difficult affair. Who had the skills to undertake such a challenge? The Viceroy could only look to those who had been trying to execute the second prong of his defensive policy—the surveyors of the Gulf.

This second prong of action had been as improvised an affair as the coastal exploration. It was hurriedly put together in reaction to the King's fears that the corsairs might again come sailing out of the North-West Passage down the "Strait of California" into the Gulf. The authorities had cast around for a way both to keep the area patrolled and to probe the nook of the Gulf to find out what was up there. The only men who could fill this bill were the men who wanted to fish the Gulf for pearls. There weren't too many candidates. In the forty years between Cortés' final gambit and Drake's advent, only a handful of casual independent operators had dared face the perils of the Gulf. A primitive craft was no match for its winds and storms. And the hostility of the Indians—some of whom were reputed to be cannibals—made camping on California hazardous. We have seen from the *History* of Baltasar de Obregón that the pearl fishers were often simple, superstitious men. Their adverse experiences with the Gulf kept alive the stories of the fabled isles. The instinct to keep clear of the strange island was often stronger that the lure of pearls.

The way to attract private entrepreneurs to serve public policy was to give them a monopoly. Hernando de Santotís was granted a license to fish for pearls in return for a survey of the Gulf. He set about building ships to achieve his commercial and official objectives. But, ironically, when his ships were still under construction in the slips of Navidad, in 1587, the English privateer Thomas Cavendish entered the port and set fire to them.[14]

Nothing could better have demonstrated the need for vigilance in the area. The incident increased the panic, and the panic increased the belief that the corsair had sailed down the Gulf from the Bacallaos. This was at a time when Spanish informers in London were reporting that British optimism ran very high. John Davis had just returned to England from the North-West Passage saying: "The passage is most probable, the execution easie."[15] It was a time, too, when England was trying to colonize Virginia, under the leadership of Raleigh and Grenville. And the tension between Spain and England was building rapidly to the showdown of 1588, when Drake, the arch-enemy, would emerge in gloating triumph from his engagement with the Armada in the English Channel.

Ironically, as the need grew for investigation of the Gulf and the region generally, Santotís became less able to comply. His heavy losses prevented him from ever fulfilling his contract with the Crown.

It was now more than a decade since Drake's incursion into the South Sea. So far the anti-corsair policies of the Spanish were a dismal failure. It was as though California obstructed every effort to penetrate her secrets. A replacement for Santotís must be swiftly found.

Chapter XXII

Vizcaíno Sails to Solve
the Secrets of the Straits

In 1593, a man named Sebastian Vizcaíno, together with some business associates, applied to have Santotís's monopoly license transferred to him. Vizcaíno was prepared to survey the Gulf in consideration of the exclusive right to fish for pearls.[1]

Of special interest to our story is Vizcaíno's conjecture of the existence of a "Strait of California." A petition made by Vizcaíno, dated "between 1593 and 1596," mentioned the possibility that the "arm of the Sea of California" penetrated the interior to connect with another ocean:

> It could be that the arm of the sea of California opens into the ocean sea
> as it is understood that it goes to New Mexico.[2]

This surmise could only have applied to an opening heading north, northwest, or northeast from the crotch; it was self-evident that the *boca* of the Gulf joined the ocean at the south. Such utterances must have been the tip of concepts so well known, they needed no spelling out.

Both Philip II and the Viceroy leaned to this appealing view. The license was transferred to Vizcaíno on condition that he give threefold service to the Crown. He must build a fort to protect against the invading Lutherans, give succor to the galleons, and find a faster, cheaper, route into New Mexico.[3]

When, at last, Vizcaíno crossed to California in 1597, the myths were certainly on the minds of members of his crew. His boatswain betrays knowledge of the association of the Amazon legend with California in this way:

> We came upon a large haven, which was called the Bay of La Paz . . . and
> an island at the mouth which was called the Island of Women, who were
> without men, none passing over to them except in summer on rafts made
> of reeds.[4]

During this 1597 expedition, Vizcaíno honored the clause of his contract requiring him to go up the Gulf. But he was unable to test his theory of a "Strait of California." His luck was hardly any better than that of Santotís. He was plagued by a host of problems. Besides the usual furious northwest winds and hurricanes and ferocious Indians, he had the loss of some of his men to contend with, and the destruction by fire of his small colony at La Paz. In his narrative of the expedition, he reported that he had ascended the Gulf only to 29 degrees, "and although it was my wish to go on farther, for the reasons I have set forth, I could not do so." He promises his Majesty that the next time he would "undertake the discovery of the whole inlet and Gulf of California."[5]

He then goes on, in George Butler Griffin's words, to make "a very wild statement" about California:

> I note also that the land is of twice the extent of this New Spain, and is preferable for its latitude and situation; because commencing at Cape San Lucas, which is in latitude twenty-one, and going towards the northwest, there are more than a thousand leagues of mainland; and this I have seen.[6]

Here we have the germ not only of a separate, but of an extremely large, California. We are reminded of Baltasar de Obregón's similar suggestion that the sierra of the "island" went ranging along the route of the Manila galleons for six hundred leagues (see page 178). Clearly, Vizcaíno's experience dispelled the notion of a cluster of islands such as Hakluyt reported from a Mexican letter of 1597 (page 239).

Bad luck had again dogged the new company of pearl fishers. The Viceroy had to face up to the failure of his second prong of policy at a time when he had already had to admit what a poor job the galleons were doing on the first prong—exploration of the outer coast. Having advocated a change of policy on the first prong, the Viceroy now had to put forward a revision of the second. In a letter of November 26, 1597, he wrote the King that in his opinion no further expedition to the Gulf "with intent to subject and settle it, should be attempted, but one for the purpose merely of ascertaining definitely what was there." That much was necessary in order that "greater light may be thrown on what related to the defense and security of these realms and the ships which make the China voyage"—implying that the galleons came down the Gulf.[7]

By this time it had become abundantly clear that commercial interests could not adequately serve the public weal. The survey of both the outer coast and the Gulf of California required a singleness of purpose by men chosen strictly for the job.

But when it came to finding a public-spirited captain to perform the dual expedition, there was not much choice. Vizcaíno was the obvious conscript. Instead of being relieved of his commission for having failed to perform his obligations to the Crown, he could be drafted with good cause. The Viceroy wrote the King: "This Vizcaíno will do sufficiently well." He judged him "a man of even disposition, upright, of good intentions . . . of medium yet sufficient ability . . . with energy to make himself respected."

Vizcaíno expected to have to explore "both the region of Cape Mendocino and the Gulf of California," which might suggest a search for a Strait of California at both ends. For it was now generally believed, as a later Viceroy would observe, that the enemies of Spain "have always been hunting for new ways, always looking for a strait or passage above Cabo Mendocino or by the opening (*boca*) of the Californias."[8] The emphasis, however, was now to be upon the outer coast. Vizcaíno is commanded to inspect it, as far as Mendocino, in Number 22 of the Instructions of March 18, 1602. Weather permitting, he might venture further northward as far as Cabo Blanco. But if the coast ran toward the west, he was to reconnoiter it for no more than a hundred leagues. Presumably a westward-trending coast would suggest a land bridge to Cathay, but an eastward-trending coast, a strait, or a Septentrional Sea.[9]

Two weeks prior to these instructions, Vizcaíno had been told to leave the Gulf alone. But now, in Instruction 23, this order was modified. He could explore the Gulf on his return trip, if weather and supplies allowed. He was, however, warned to go no further than where the Gulf made its supposed turn toward east or west at 37 or 38 degrees. This is several degrees higher than the nook of the Gulf was then believed to reach. All this suggests that the Viceroy accepted the concept of a Strait of California:

> Having reached the cape of San Lucas and made the discovery you bear as your charge, you will judge the weather . . . and having supplies [sufficient] to undertake the entrance of [the] Californias, you will do it, coasting along the land from the cape, reconnoitering the ports and bays . . . inspecting the quality of the land and the climate of it, and the people . . . until you reach thirty-seven degrees or as much as thirty-eight degrees, unless the sea, for ten or twelve leagues before that, has given indication of turning east . . . or west . . . In such a case . . . you will turn about and seek shelter on the coast of Navidad.

The quest for straits was a hush-hush affair. This alone would account for the lack of overt mention in the documents. In his final letter of May 31, 1602, the Viceroy expresses hope not only for the discovery of a good port for the "ships from China." He alludes obliquely to "other news of importance."[10]

Such hints of a "Strait of California" led ultimately to the revival of the island myth—the version that was to receive widespread acceptance throughout the seventeenth century. That extraordinary revival is often attributed to this voyage of Vizcaíno. But contemporary records made during or immediately upon return of the expedition are silent on the question.

Though paradise peeps through the pages of Vizcaíno's own report, it is a realistic, not a mythic, paradise that he describes. The following passages are rooted in experience. They disclose natural bounties of climate, landscape, flora and fauna:

> This place is very pleasant, for it has a large valley surrounded by lagoons in which are many fish, duck, and heron, and a grove with hares and deer. The climate of the land is the best in the world, for the night dews last until ten o'clock in the forenoon.[11]

Fine harbors were discovered, suitable for immediate settlement to assist the Manila galleons and benefit from their trade:

> We arrived . . . at this port of Monterey on the 16th of . . . December . . . The day having cleared, there having been much fog, we found ourselves to be in the best port that could be desired, for besides being sheltered from all the winds, it has many pines for masts and yards, and live oaks and white oaks, and water in great quantity, all near the shore. The land is fertile, with a climate and soil like those of Castile; there is much wild game, such as harts, like young bulls, deer, buffalo, very large bears, rabbits, hares, and many other animals and many game birds, such as geese, partridges, quail, crane, ducks, vultures, and many other kinds of birds.

Yet, following this voyage, nothing further happened. This huge and promising region, the focus of so many dreams, would lie dormant, isolated, untapped, shrouded in mystery, for another century and a half. Why?

Among the reasons given by historians are: the decline in Spanish power throughout the world, too thin a colonial population to colonize so vast a territory, and the reduction of the threat from foreign powers.

It is likely, too, that, as on the Cabrillo voyage, the miseries endured by the crews cancelled out the affirmative findings. The narrative poignantly relates a long catalogue of misfortunes: vile weather, hunger, scurvy, and high mortality. And again the coastline presented all too often an inimical face.

That night a south wind came up, with a heavy sea oblique to the place where we were—which was in a depth of six fathoms—while near us were the breakers. Seeing our great danger, and that if the wind increased it would drive us on the coast, the general consulted with the cosmographer, chief pilot, his assistant, and experienced seamen as to what should be done to escape the peril which we were in and it was agreed that in the morning we should sail, because at present the fog was so thick that we could not see each other.

Again:

God willed that the new moon of January should begin with so furious a south wind, together with so much rain and fog, as to throw us into great doubt whether to go forward or to turn back, for it was as dark in the daytime as at night. The seas were very high, so that we could neither run nor lie by at sea.

Complicating the dangers of weather and coast was the condition of the crew:

All the men had fallen sick, so that there were only two sailors who could climb to the maintopsail.

The fine bay of Monterey could not be adequately explored:

In view of the fact that we had so many sick, that the pilot of the admiral's ship and his assistant were very ill, that there was a shortage of sailors for going forward, and that the supplies were becoming exhausted because of the length of time we had spent in coming, it seemed to the general impossible to complete the exploration . . .

Nevertheless, they continued north toward Mendocino, still battling weather and scurvy:

January 21, 1603: A wind storm came up from the southeast which made us very cold. Worse than this, on the day of San Anton, the 17th of the said month, at eight o'clock at night, when lying by at sea, the ship was struck by two seas which made it pitch so much that it was thought the keel was standing on end, and that it was even sinking. The pitching was so violent that it threw both sick and well from their beds and the general from his. He struck upon some boxes and broke his ribs with the heavy blow.

This trouble continued until the 20th of the said month.

Their predicament was now extreme:

We returned, as has been said, from Cape Mendocino, . . . and on the 25th of the said month we had come as far as the port of Monterey, where the Indians signalled us with smoke. We did not enter it because the state of our health was so bad and the sick were clamoring, although there was neither assistance nor medicines nor food to give them except rotten jerked beef, gruel, biscuits, and beans and chickpeas spoiled by weevils. The mouths of all were sore, and their gums were swollen larger than their teeth, so that they could hardly drink water, and the ship seemed more like a hospital than a ship of an armada. Affairs were in such a condition that anyone who had ever in his life been at the helm steered, climbed to the maintopsail, and did the other tasks, and all who could walk assisted at the hearth, making gruel and porridge for the sick. Above all, we were greatly distressed because the frigate, the *Tres Reyes*, did not appear, for we feared that she had been lost in the past storm; but our need was so great, as had been said, that we could not wait for her.

Not to be tedious, I do not tell of the hardships which the general endured on land, or of his ruined health . . . For lack of necessities the greater part of the men who came on that ship died . . .

Did these physical ordeals evoke the superstitious terrors of the myth? Did they talk about them at each unprobed inlet that might turn out to be a strait? The official records do not record such gossip, but the subject of the straits must have been in the forefront of their thoughts.

The voyagers returned, of course, without any hard information on an entrance about Mendocino. That did not mean their preconceptions were now laid to rest. Indeed, Vizcaíno casually drops the name of Anian as though it were a given, not something to be proved:

When the storm abated . . . we found ourselves in 42 degrees, for the currents and seas were carrying us rapidly to the Strait of Anian.

The second ship, the *Tres Reyes*, was separated in bad weather from the admiral's ship. It was driven beyond Mendocino toward Cape Blanco. Somewhere there, an inlet was discovered, and believed to be the entrance to a strait. The *relación* of the boatswain states:

Further on, in latitude forty one degrees, near Cape Mendocino, we reached a very large bay, and into it entered a copious river that came down from the north side. There flowed such a great force of current that . . . we were not able to enter it more than two leagues.[12]

This account was submitted to Vizcaíno by the remnants of the crew that survived to reach home port. A summary is given in Juan de Torquemada's *Monarquía Indiana*, where the phenomenon is unabashedly equated with the "Strait of Anian," and the locus is placed further north:

And on the 19th of January, the pilot Antonio Flores, who went in the frigate, found himself at a height of forty-three degrees, where the land forms a cape, or point, which is called Cape Blanco, from which the coast begins to run to the northwest, and close to it they happened to find a river, very full and deep . . . and wishing to enter it, the currents did not give way to them . . . Alferez Martin de Aguilar decided that having sailed further north than their instructions laid out, they should return to Acapulco . . . They understood that this river . . . is the Strait of Anian, which the ships that discovered it, traversed, and passed from the North Sea to the South Sea. [13]

Once more that hippogryph—a river-strait.

The principals mentioned in this account perished on the voyage south. But enough weight was given to the notion that, thereafter, an inlet above Mendocino was often labeled: "Entry discovered by Martin d'Aguilar." An example of this will be found on a map (Plate 50) dated more than a century after its supposed discovery.

This claim still does not answer the question of how the second flowering of the island myth of California was attributed to the Vizcaíno voyage. So what does H. R. Wagner have to say about the matter? He hazards this answer:

Who cut the connection between the Gulf of California and this strait [of Anian] remains to be determined, but there is every probability that Father Antonio de Ascension was the man. [14]

Who was Father Antonio de Ascensión? He was one of the padres designated by the Viceroy to accompany the Vizcaíno expedition. His assignment was to serve not only as a religious advisor, but as an assistant cosmographer.

He had little qualification for the latter role. He was totally unconversant with the region, having been sent to the New World only a couple of years before by the Barefoot Carmelites. He was not only inexperienced, but naive and poorly educated. He compensated for these deficiencies, as we shall see, by an oversized and overactive imagination.

The reason for Wagner's reservation in attributing to Ascensión the final snip is this very curious fact: Ascensión's writings containing such claims are dated several years after the voyage was completed. No statements immediately following the expedition express the island view, to tie it to the voyage itself.

There is actually nothing in Ascensión's record before June 18, 1608, that even points in that direction. On that date, five years after his return from the voyage, Ascensión wrote a letter to the King. In it he makes mention of a possible strait running northward from the Gulf. [15]

An examination of its text shows how limited are his claims here compared to later statements.

This letter of 1608 is actually a contribution to the discussion about where to establish the first settlement on California. Vizcaíno had argued for Monterey. Ascensión thinks a place he calls San Bernabé at the southern tip of California would make more sense. He maintains that the port would be close to mainland supplies, a first stage for advance northward. It would give shelter to the galleons at the very place where they were most vulnerable—where the enemy pirates lay in wait inside the mouth of the Gulf. Still another point in favor of his recommendation would be its closeness to New Mexico. This would afford support to Governor Juan de Oñate's explorations and activities.

His final argument is that from such a settlement, investigation of the Gulf could be achieved. The possibility of a strait running from the crotch to meet the Sea of the North could then be tested:

> With this settlement it will be possible with ease to discover where the Gulf reaches . . . because there is a presumption that it crosses to the sea of the north, and if it happened to be so, and that through this strait it were possible to sail the ships of Peru and all the South Sea, they would be able to go from here to Spain with more facility than from Havana . . . to carry to Your Highness all the riches of Peru and China, and of this land, with much less expense and more convenience . . .

Clearly this letter expresses no more than what has been hypothesized in the previous twenty years since Drake's incursion into the South Sea. The "Strait of California" is still a mere "presumption," no more than a possibility. There is no mention of the obverse of the strait, an island of California. However, Ascensión's preference for the designation "Regno de California" may suggest a separate entity, but the concept is still latent here.

So if in 1608, so long after the Vizcaíno voyage ended, an Isle of California has not yet taken shape in Ascensión's imagination, why should it suddenly burst forth a few years later? The full answer must await more evidence. But a clue lies in a statement in the letter itself—in the reference to Juan de Oñate in the same context as a possible strait. It is an important pointer to the way the island myth could have been nurtured in Ascensión's imagination.

Oñate was the leader of the expedition to New Mexico. This brings us to the third prong of Spanish anti-corsair policy. That segment of our story is the topic of the next chapter.

Chapter XXIII

New Mexico Explorers "Discover" the Strait of California

Spanish plans for exploration of the Gulf and coast in the post-Drake period involved the New Mexico frontier. The Viceroy's letter of 1585 (*see* page 243) had intimated that a sea-going expedition might yield a bonus—a waterway by which the inland colony could be supplied. By the same token, explorers in the interior might come across the quested strait and follow it to its South Sea outlet.

We have seen that the New Mexico explorers carried with them the accumulated lore of a huge waterway cutting through that "midland," "between-seas," or "mediterranean" territory. The concept of a trans-continental east-west river-strait from the explorations of 1538–1542 had been talked up more recently by Espejo and Vargas (*see* page 243). They thought it integrated somehow with the north-south strait, fueled by the apocryphal story of Drake's supposed pilot, N. de Morera, walking all the way down an arm of the sea from the Strait of Anian (*see* page 221). Consistent with the ways of myth, that bit of wishful thinking apparently surfaced where it mattered most—the threshold of the terra incognita of New Mexico. Rodrigo del Río y Losa, later governor of New Vizcaya, was supposed to have been the first to "hear" it.[1] Giving extra impetus to the view that the Boca de California might be the gateway to that strait was the hope that it would serve New Mexico.

It is important to our story to note—as Wagner points out—that there is no contemporary account of this tale. It was not until 1626 that it was written down—by Father Jerónimo de Zárate Salmerón. And where did Zárate Salmerón get it? From Father Antonio de Ascensión, whose role as compiler of these tales will soon be seen:

> Fray Antonio de la Ascension, discalced Carmelite religious, one of the three who went with Sebastián Vizcaíno on the exploration of Cabo Mendocino, gave me this account as a true fact, and that is why I write his name here.[2]

In the course of his transmission of Morera's story, Zárate Salmerón passes along earlier links in the chain of hearsay. Apparently the story got started when Morera "came out at New Mexico." He then "went searching for Rodrigo del Río . . . and told him the following: . . ."

However the story happened to evolve, it certainly influenced Rodrigo del Río. In advocating more exploration in New Mexico, he accepts as fact the existence of an open arm of the sea claimed by Morera. According to Rodrigo del Río's statements, colonization of the interior was necessary in order to prevent invasion by the "Lutherans"—the Protestant Dutch and English—down such a waterway. Indeed, he was so certain the New Mexico explorers would have to navigate a "brazo de mar" as they moved west from the interior, he recommended that they carry with them the materials for building ships.[3]

This third prong of Spanish policy—overland exploration into the interior—assumed increasing importance after the galleons' failure to find the strait, and the pearl-fishers misfortunes in the Gulf. In 1595, Juan de Oñate petitioned to lead an expedition to New Mexico. He received the official blessing, though a changeover of viceroys clogged the wheels for several years.

Among the aims which the establishment redefined in 1599 was a westward probe by Oñate to the South Sea:

> The discovery of harbors [on the South Sea] would be the best thing that could happen, both to facilitate Don Juan's conquest and the benefits that would result for the ships and fleets trading with the Philippines.[4]

This passage suggests how vague was the perception of the region's true geography. Harbors useful to New Mexico would have to lie on the eastern, mainland, side of the Gulf, close to sources of supply. The galleons, on the other hand, needed harbors on the outside coast south of Mendocino. If the Viceroy envisaged the same harbors doing double duty for these different needs, he must have perceived the mainland coast inside the Gulf as continuous with the outside coast, as though no long peninsula of California intervened. The Viceroy's view thus implied a separated Baja California.

The Oñate expedition got under way. In 1599, a push to the west was made from the interior. This was led by one of Oñate's relatives, Vicente de Zaldivar. But his "plan to discover the South Sea" was thwarted by the mountainous terrain and the exhaustion of his horses "only three days from the sea."

The account goes on:

> When the governor [Oñate] was informed of the above . . . in view of the importance of discovering the South sea, he determined to go in person to make this discovery . . . He is getting everything ready, and will set out

during the month of April of this year, 1601, with carts, artillery, munitions, musketeers, and all things necessary for war and for building ships. According to reports, ships could be built and could be sailed between the North and the South seas . . .

But that excursion was delayed. The King apparently pressed for a northern exploration to address the matter of an east-west waterway in the unknown territory "from Cape Labrador to Cape Anian." The Viceroy warned the King not to hold out "great hopes of wealth or the presence there of any great empire" if the King "should decide to spend something in solving this mystery and should choose Don Juan de Oñate to undertake the task."

There was only one hope for that forlorn New Mexico expedition to redeem itself from being a white elephant. Oñate must make a discovery of the South Sea along some waterway from the interior. In 1603 Oñate mustered his forces and followed the Colorado River to its delta.

The stark facts of hindsight tell us that, in 1604, he reached the head of the Gulf. But how did he perceive it? Luckily some records have survived. A barefoot friar, Father Francisco de Escobar, made a diary of the expedition. What actually remains is the *relación* he made of that diary in 1605.

The account makes astounding reading. Instead of confining himself to making a realistic record of day-to-day events, Escobar indulges in the most flagrant flights of fancy. He is yet another in a string of impressionable padres who liven the story of the Isle of California. He is as naive as Friar Marcos de Niza had been before him, and as Brother Antonio de Ascensión would turn out to be.

The relation reveals an extraordinary predisposition to place store by inherited myths at the expense of empirical evidence. Mandeville's and Polo's influence is as strong as ever. Escobar repeats their incredible fictions as serious reportage of his own. He is a throwback to the Middle Ages. The spirit of Columbus is alive and kicking.

Escobar claims the Indians as his source. He was either ribbed unmercifully, or "heard" what he preconceived. He tells how one Indian told to "a great multitude in my presence" that "between the Buena Esperanza [his name for the Buena Guia, Tizón, or Colorado River] and the sea" lived many monstrous "nations." One tribe had "ears so large that they dragged on the ground, and big enough to shelter five or six persons under each one."[5]

Here, in Herbert Eugene Bolton's translation, is more of Escobar's "report":

Not far from this nation, there was another whose men had virile members so long, they wrapped them four times around the waist, and that in the act of generation the man and woman were far apart . . .

Likewise, we learned from the Indian and the others that near the foregoing people there was another nation with only one foot . . .

They told us of another nation, not far from the last, who lived on the banks of a lake in which they slept every night entirely under the water.

There is another nation that sleeps in trees.

Another nation . . . sustained themselves solely on the odor of their food prepared for this purpose, not eating it at all, since they lacked the natural means to eliminate the excrements of the body.

They told of another nation . . . which did not lie down to sleep, but always slept standing up, bearing some burden on the head.[6]

And where these fabulous creatures appeared, there had to be Amazon-like women—at least a weakened manifestation. A small remnant of that legendary race of female warriors survived on an offshore island:

Here we learned from all these Indians what we had learned . . . from many others, great and small, that the principal person obeyed by the people who lived on the island was a woman called Ciñaca Cohota, which signifies or means "principal woman" or "chieftainess." From all these Indians we learned that she was a giantess, and that on the island she had only a sister and no other person of her race, which must have died out with them.

Escobar struggles with his own credulity:

It appears to me doubtful that there should be so many monstrosities in a short distance . . . But . . . it seemed yet more doubtful to remain silent about things which, if discovered, would result, I believe, in glory to God and in service to the King our Lord; for although the things in themselves may be so rare . . . to any one who will consider the wonders which God constantly performs in the world, it will be easy to believe that since He is able to create them He may have done so, and that since so many and different people, in a distance of two hundred leagues testify to them, they cannot lack foundation, being things of which these Indians are not the first inventors, for there are many books which treat of them, and of others even more monstrous and more wonderful.

In the tradition of the oriental travelogues, where there were monsters and Amazons there would be riches, too:

We learned from this Indian . . . by showing him some buttons of silver or iron, that, not far from here toward the west . . . this metal was to be found . . . They gave us to understand that they dug this metal from a mountain on the other shore of the sea in front of an island five days from where we were, toward which they pointed in the west . . .

We also learned . . . that near there . . . there was a lake on whose banks lived people who wore on their wrists yellow manacles or bracelets . . . of gold and of brass . . . from which it is to be inferred that there is yellow metal in this country . . .

Where there was gold and silver, pearls must also "grow." Escobar notes many white and green shells "from which some of the Indians to whom we put the questions said that they were accustomed to obtain large pearls."

But above all, Escobar gave tidings that the Gulf extended beyond the point that he and Oñate reached. At the delta of the river, at the nook of the Gulf, he notes:

On this coast the sea runs east and west, and makes a turn behind this mountain chain toward the north and northwest according to the assertions of the Indians, none of whom know its terminus.

And again:

This Indian told us of all the people who live on the Buena Esperanza River, clear up to its source, showing this to be close to the sea, toward the northwest, as did many others likewise, all asserting that the Gulf of California makes this complete turn.

Escobar summarizes the findings of the expedition with an optimistic note. The region's riches can be quickly verified. So can the extension of the Gulf with its promise of a strait joining the two oceans:

It does not seem to me that the way to their verification or to that of the other reports, of riches and of the communication of the seas, is very difficult. If perchance they [North and South Seas] do communicate, by the favor of heaven, with less than one hundred men it will be possible to verify the truth of all these things, both of the silver and the tin, or whatever metal it is on the island; of the gold, copper, or brass bracelets or handcuffs worn by the Indians of the Laguna; of the coral; of the pearls which the Indians declare are contained in the shells which we found, and which the Governor and so many Spaniards declare there are in the Gulf of California; and of the turn which the Indians say the Gulf makes toward the north and northeast, not a person being found who knew its terminus; as well as of the monstrosities reported by so many Indians . . .

Apparently Escobar's narrative was given to the Viceroy in 1605. Oñate had sent Escobar back to Mexico with news of discovery of the

South Sea. Oñate hoped thereby to pry more funding out of the establishment. But the Viceroy was negatively impressed by what he'd heard. This is how the Viceroy put it in his letter to the King of October 28, 1605:

> From his [Escobar's] signed report and from four witnesses who returned with the friar I cannot help but inform your majesty that this conquest is becoming a fairy tale. If those who write the reports imagine that they are believed by those who read them, they are greatly mistaken. Less substance is being revealed every day . . .[7]

The Viceroy warns the King against pouring more money into such a suspect enterprise, with one exception. Further probes along the South Sea should be supported:

> As I understand it, the greatest benefit that we could hope for is the discovery of the South sea. . . . At the most appropriate place . . . a small fort should be built and garrisoned . . . A ship should be built at the site where they say the sea was discovered, and another in the province of Sinaloa, New Vizcaya, which is already conquered territory; they should sail at the same time, one following the coast to the right and the other to the left . . . until they meet. In this manner we should learn what there is all along the coast. If a harbor is found that could be used for the Philippine ships, they should take possession of it and seek the best means of fortifying it.

The reference to Sinaloa makes it plain that the Viceroy is speaking of the coast along the east side of the Gulf of California. He does not seem to grasp how the coastline followed by the Philippine ships relates to it. His words carry implications that the Sinaloa coast runs directly northwest (with no interrupting peninsula) all the way to Mendocino. The proposed strategy of the two ships was supposed to show if the coast was broken by the entry to a strait, and generally to clarify understanding of the region.

This mental geography again relegates Baja to the status of an offshore island. This time we are not left to infer it. In the Viceroy's letter there is an explicit statement that brings into play again the old myth of the Isle of California. To his argument for a fortified harbor he adds this advantage:

> If it should prove to be an appropriate place, it might be possible to explore from there the interior ["New Mexico"] or *island of the Californias* [italics added], which has always been so much sought.

We should pause here for a fanfare. At last, after more than two decades of toying with the concept—ever since Drake's entry into the South Sea—we have an overt pronouncement that the land to the west of the Gulf is indeed an island. And this by the highest authority, yet. So casual an observation suggests that such a "fact" was taken for granted, at least echoed unquestioningly from the New Mexico men.

For purposes of this investigation into the resurgent myth, it is important to observe that the Viceroy's letter antedates the 1608 letter of Ascensión (page 257) by nearly three years. Moreover, Ascensión's letter makes no mention of an island; he speaks only of a possible strait. It should also be noted that the Viceroy's letter raises the question of a fortified harbor, while Ascensión's letter, in effect, offers a response, suggesting the location for such a settlement.

All in all it seems fair to say that the revival of the island myth should be credited more to the New Mexico explorers than to the Vizcaíno voyagers. This is made even clearer when Ascensión later on takes up the cause of the Island of California. To make his case he quotes one of the New Mexico narratives at length.

The relation he quotes is by Captain Gerónimo Marqués, whose name crops up a number of times in the Oñate papers. Marqués' account is not extant except as quoted by Ascensión. But other contemporary references to it give confirmation that it did exist.[8] Ascensión introduces it as follows:

> The conquerors of New Mexico under the command of the Governor, Don Juan de Oñate, once went from where they were settled to discover the land towards the west. Captain Gerónimo Marqués, a person very competent, truthful, and worthy of all credit, and well-versed in the affairs of the provinces of New Mexico, accompanied him. He wrote an account of this expedition which he made with the General to discover the country and the Sea of California, which I append here in his own words.[9]

Remarkably, this soldier-narrator is just about as high in cloudland as his fellow traveler, the superstitious friar, Escobar. The account contains many of the same ingredients. But there are distinctions in expression having profound implications for our story. We cannot be sure of when Gerónimo Marqués wrote his narrative, or whether Ascensión edited it to fit his own predilections. But we shall consider it here, independently of the Ascensión arguments, as part of the New Mexico sequence.

As in Escobar's account, Marqués is euphoric at the prospect of a rich

pearl harvest. Pearls "as large as good-sized hazelnuts" were promised by
the shells they saw. Also, as in the other account, Marqués' report
comes complete with the whole myth of the Amazons. Now the word
"Amazon" is actually used:

> They also made signs that in an island nearby in the middle of the sea
> there was a noted large town, of which an Amazon Indian, half giantess,
> who wears on her breast a very precious plate of pearls and who is
> accustomed to take them ground up in her drinks, is queen. These
> Indians said there were many pearls in all that sea, pointing to the south,
> and that these and the pearl beds extended towards the north for a matter
> of thirty-five leagues, but that beyond that there were none, the greatest
> quantity being found around the island of the Amazon Queen.

In drinking a potion of ground pearls, this Amazon queen resembles a
dark-complexioned queen of history, the Egyptian Cleopatra. In being
a dark giantess, she resembles Montalvo's Queen Calafia of the Moorish
California. Calafia, we recall, was "*negra*" and "*muy grande de cuerpo*"—
black or dark, and very great of body. She, too, wore precious armour,
being valiant in battle. The queen's breastplate, made of pearls in
Marqués' account, brings to mind the fabulous pearl necklaces described
in the oriental travelogues. The Middle Ages still had a strong hold on
the New World.

With the pearls and the Amazons there is gold, easy gold. Such
legends as the fabled lakes of oriental travel lore echo through Marqués'
narrative. And silver, too, that "exists in the island of the amazon, or
giantess:"

> They say that the Amazon Queen possesses it, and that they bring it from
> the coast to the west in some boats they have, in which they navigate
> from one place to another. From this it appears that they bring it from the
> land of California.

In this context of "news" of pearls, gold, silver, and an Amazon
queen, it is hardly remarkable that California would once more be
viewed as insular. The components of *romanticismo insulare* were so
intertwined that to fetch up one was to conjure all. Indeed, in the above
quotation, Marqués makes an even clearer statement than Escobar that
the "coast to the west" on the opposite side of the Gulf—this "land of
California"—is detached and separate from the mainland, accessible
by boat alone.

Marqués' narrative must have accompanied that of Escobar in Oñate's
appeal to the Viceroy. In turn, the narratives must have prompted the

Viceroy's mention of the "island of the Californias" in his letter of 1605. Even as the Viceroy was discrediting these reports as "fairy tales," he was swallowing the largest one—the island myth—hook, line, and sinker.

This is how Marqués' account (as transmitted by Ascensión) treats of the "new" geography:

> The sea which we looked at seemed to be very wide, as we saw neither land nor mountains on the other side, not even the island where the queen lived, about which the Indians told us. We considered the sea to be beyond all doubt the same as that of California, because its whole coast runs from northwest to southeast . . . .

As in Escobar's account, the Gulf continues north, making a turn behind the mountains north and east, its terminus unknown:

> . . . The Indians also told us that the seacoast makes a turn [in the north] around the land towards the east, as they sketched it as entering the land. They do not show any end to it, but say that it is very wide and that they do not know how to place any end to it.

But in a bold leap, Marqués pronounces this hypothetical continuation of the Gulf a "Sea of California" separating California from the mainland, in no uncertain terms. More than that, the imaginary fabrication of the system of the straits, theorized since Cortés' day, is now announced as fact. The imagined south-north "Strait of California" joins with the Ocean of the North by the imagined west-east "Strait of Anian:"

> We consider it certain that this is the Sea of California, which runs on between the two lands of California and New Mexico to a communication with the ocean of the north by the strait which they call Anian.

Three quarters of a century had passed since Cortés discovered his "island," and tried to probe his "river-that-might-turn-out-to-be-a-strait." Now another bunch of wishful thinkers have, by fiat, given verbal substance to his dream, considerably enlarging and embellishing it.

Chapter XXIV

ASCENSIÓN FUELS THE REKINDLED ISLAND-OF-CALIFORNIA MYTH

Father Antonio de Ascensión's quotation of Marqués' narrative occurs in his "Relation of the expedition made by General Sebastian Vizcaíno for the discovery of the Californias in the year 1602." This manuscript, now in the Ayer collection of the Newberry Library, Chicago, is—as H.R. Wagner has noted—not a diary of the voyage *per se*. Wagner thought that it was written "long enough after the return to give him time to become obsessed with the idea of a Strait of Anian and the extension of the Gulf of California to a connection with it." Wagner felt "it would not be amiss to conclude that Ascensión compiled it for Torquemada, who completed the first volume of his works about the end of 1611."[1]

Juan de Torquemada published a good deal of this "relation" by Ascensión in his *Monarquía Indiana* in 1613. Ascensión's last two chapters are not, however, included in that work. Yet, as it turns out, these last two chapters hold great significance for our present study. It was in these final chapters that Ascensión delivers himself of his startling epiphany: the realm of California is an island—no ifs or buts.

From our previous analysis, we know the resurgence of the island myth did not come from anything in Ascensión's own direct experience. He had not himself found any inlet above Mendocino, and he had never been up the Gulf. As John Leighly has remarked, Ascensión "indulges in a flight of fancy that goes well beyond the observations made on the expedition."[2] The conjectural posture of Ascensión's letter of 1608 makes it unlikely that he penned any such bold opinions during or immediately after the voyage of 1602.

It must be, then, that in the critical two years following this letter, his imagination became powerfully stimulated by the New Mexico narratives, as his quotation of Marqués' report suggests. Brothers of his own order, including Escobar, had accompanied Oñate. Stirred by Torquemada's prompting for material for his history, these credulous friars and soldiers must have fed each other's brain storms. Ascensión would have used the New Mexico "findings" to "reinterpret" and "update" his own experiences and deductions on the Vizcaíno voyage. As discussed above, "credit" for the reinstatement of the island myth goes to the New Mexico contingent. Ascensión simply seized the ball and ran with it. He had, however, been training a long time to execute that spectacular play.

We should digress a moment to note that Ascensión was not alone in elaborating the Strait-of-California theory at this time. In 1609, Lorenzo Ferrer Maldonado presented a memorial to the King of Spain propounding claims similar to those of Juan de Fuca of 1592–96, that he had passed through a northern strait stretching from Labrador to Anian. Maldonado urges the King to make every effort to control the Strait against the Lutherans. He recommends that a fort be built at its exit into the Pacific. This exit, being no more that a few leagues in width, should be blocked by a chain across its mouth.[3]

Was the exit Maldonado had in mind the Ancón de San Andrés in the Mar Vermejo? It was in this vicinity that the building of forts had been proposed since the New Mexico explorers had "confirmed" the existence of a Strait of California—indeed, since Vizcaíno went up the Gulf in 1597. The suggestion of a chain across the narrow entrance is echoic of statements made by Nuño de Guzmán's men when, in 1529, they explored that "river that went out into the Sea of the North," across which "the Indians had a chain of iron" (page 138).[4] The "river-that-might-turn-out-to-be-a-strait" theory is obviously thriving.

But to return to our examination of Ascensión's "relación," he begins his discourse with just such stories of continent-spanning straits. His introduction is notable, however, for setting out reasons for the Vizcaíno expedition that are not in the official instructions. Though he mentions the need to find harbors for the galleons, he seems to contend that the voyage took place mainly to satisfy the King's desire to find a strait. This desire was inspired by some sort of communication discovered in the papers of Felipe II when he died in 1598. Perhaps this was the account of Juan de Fuca, who claimed to have made his apocryphal penetration in 1592. Ascensión gives this account:

> Having at his charge this new world and the other kingdoms which his father left him, he [Felipe III] found among his father's secret papers a sworn declaration that some foreigners had given him in which it is stated that they had seen and discovered some notable things, on passing through the Strait of Anian, where they were driven in a ship by the great

force of continual winds from the coast of the Bacallaos in what we call "Tierra Nova." In this they relate how they passed from the North Sea to the South Sea by this strait, and that, while searching for shelter from the storm, they entered a copious river on which they came in sight of a populous and rich city named Quivira . . . in the latitude of 40°, almost on the same parallel and in the same neighborhood as Cabo Mendocino, which the ships come to sight in sailing from the Philippines to New Spain.[5]

This revelation certainly explains why Felipe II kept harassing his Viceroys to search and fortify the Gulf in the last years of his life.

Ascensión gives a further reason for the Vizcaíno voyage not in the official orders. The new king had information regarding the old dream-conceit of California—its separateness apparently implied:

His Majesty was also advised that there was information that the King-dom of California, that is the land from the Cabo de San Lucas called "la Punta de la California" to Cabo Mendocino, was a long country . . . and contained great riches in pearls, silver, gold and amber.

By these statements the rebirth of the Island of California (and a huge one, at that) is tied to some narrative in the royal files, and to Felipe III, who put enough faith in it to want it checked out. These references to the King's requests could hardly have been among Ascensión's inventions, though corroborating evidence is still lacking. However, interpretation and expression are Ascensión's, and the rest of the account reveals the quality of those.

Ascensión makes the first connection for a long time between California and Cortés. He has clearly boned up on California's discovery:

The Marques del Valle, Don Fernando Cortes, after having conquered Mexico and its provinces, had gone to the Californias in the year 1535 with the intention of conquering and pacifying that country for the purpose of enjoying its reputed riches. As he had news that Don Antonio de Mendoza had come to New Spain as Viceroy, and in order to settle the matter of his status, he had returned to Mexico with his force without accomplishing anything, his preparations for the conquest having cost him a great amount of money.

Ascensión is sympathetic to Cortés. The campaign to pacify and settle "the Californias" was aborted through no fault of Cortés' own, but by politics.

Ascensión goes on to show that others, directed by Mendoza, fared no better than Cortés in attempting to subdue the fabulous country:

The Viceroy afterwards endeavored to accomplish the same thing at his own expense, and placed his plan in operation, but it did not have the desired effect, because of the great difficulty of sailing along that coast on which the northwest winds are continuously contrary. Those who went therefore returned to New Spain with their ships broken and with great loss, without having settled any matter of importance.

The effect of this historical snapshot is to give reasons other than worthlessness of the territory for its neglect. Ascensión's review of Cortés' island claims must have clinched his acceptance of the New Mexican beliefs.

The main body of Ascensión's narrative presents a day-to-day account of the Vizcaíno voyage, comparable to official accounts, but with personal touches that reveal a sweet but credulous and superstitious nature. But our interest in this study is chiefly in passages making claims that could not possibly have come from direct experience. These must be interpolations, indicating that Ascensión worked over his journal, making alterations to fit his new hobby-horse. For example, in Chapter III, he makes a bald assertion about the existence of a Strait of California that he had handled as an open question just a couple of years earlier:

> Here, in the Kingdom of Galicia on the coast which belongs to New Spain, begins the entrance to the Sea of California, which continues to Sinaloa and Culiacan, and runs on to the provinces of New Mexico, to finally reach the Kingdom of Quivira and the Strait of Anian, by which one can find passage and navigation to Spain, as will be related in its place.[6]

With this flat, undemonstrated proposition, Ascensión clears the way to play his final variation on the island myth of California later on in his account.

Considerable editing of his diary after the fact is also apparent from the way he integrates the experiences of the other ships into his Relación. Ascensión was on the *Almiranta* going north, and when it was sent home with a load of sick and dying, he transferred to the *Capitana*, the lead ship, to continue on with the expedition. Therefore his account of the activities of the third ship, the *Tres Reyes*, in Chapter IX, is all hearsay. This was the ship of Martin de Aguilar, who was said to have discovered in 43 degrees "a copious and deep river," later reported by Juan de Torquemada as leading to the Strait of Anian (pages 256–57). Ascensión did not agree with this identification—but not from any sudden burst of common sense. He refers us to his own theories of this river-strait in a chapter omitted by Torquemada.

That astounding chapter is entitled: "Chapter XV, in which is treated of how the Kingdom of California is not connected with that of New Mexico, and in which the reasons are given to prove it."[7]

The chapter begins with a discussion about the lack of important rivers draining into the Pacific from the realm of California. From this he spins a web of "reasoning" and draws an unwarranted inference:

> If perhaps no river of size enters the sea by such ports, it must be that they do so in other places. As they do not find a passage because of so numerous and such high mountains, they naturally seek lower valleys and through them run to the sea. As the mountains towards the Sea of California are lower, I consider it certain that they empty there. Thus ancient maps and even modern ones now in use display a large ensenada of the Sea of California and copious rivers flowing into it at its end and along its sides, but they do not give any place to the Strait of Anian as I pretend to do between the lands and kingdoms of New Mexico and the Californias.

Ascensión is now ready to deliver himself of his grand illumination:

> I hold it to be very certain and proven that the whole Kingdom of California discovered on this voyage, is the largest island known or which has been discovered up to the present day, and that it is separated from the provinces of New Mexico by the Mediterranean Sea of California, which some call the "Mar de Cortes" because he was the first to discover it, and is between such great kingdoms.

At this juncture, Ascensión quotes the authority of Gerónimo Marqués, discussed on pages 265-67. Ascensión then takes the argument to its ultimate "conclusion":

> From all related in the account which this Captain gave me, you can easily understand that California is an island and that the sea which separates it from the land of New Mexico is the same as the Boca de la California and a continuation of it, and goes on to communicate with the ocean of the north by the Strait of Anian, and with the sea which surrounds the country of Cabo Mendocino.

Ascensión then discusses the inlet discovered by Martin de Aguilar, and decides that it is not the same as the transcontinental river of which Felipe II and III had news. Ascensión interprets Aguilar's inlet as being the north end of the Sea of California where it joins the ocean sea. Both then give onto the Strait of Anian to connect to the Atlantic:

Quivira is in the region corresponding to New Mexico, and not in the Californias, and furthermore . . . the River . . . which the Fragata reached in 43°, as related in Chapter XI of this account where I said that the land and the seacoast turn to the northeast, is a very different one. That is the proper direction for the coast to trend, making a turn to come and join the inside coast of the Kingdom of California and to be the same thing. Thus the two seas come to join, and together enter by the Strait of Anian to communicate with the North Sea, through which one can sail to Spain.

The northern end of the strait in this imaginary geography being above Mendocino, the envisaged island was enormous. The name California, designating an island from the days of Cortés, had naturally to "stretch" to cover this vast extent. We have already noted that the secret paper of Felipe II (if Ascensión's introduction is to be believed) speaks of a "long country" between Cabo San Lucas and Mendocino. Moreover, we have seen that Obregón and Vizcaíno had made comments suggesting the extraordinary size of California some years before this new manifestation of the island myth emerged. The incipient concept has now come to fruition.

Those who knew Lok's map of 1582 and John Dee's "chart" of 1583 (Plates 36 and 35) must have regarded the huge California they depicted as confirmation of these claims—even though each was a tad short of being separated from the mainland.

Now that the name California covered so vast a territory, the sub-labels of Baja (Lower) and Alta (Upper) California (and, later, "old" and "new" California) would soon come into use—giving a new sense to the term "the Californias."

Father Antonio ingrained his belief in the Island of California by repeated tellings. His *Relación Breve* of 1620, translated by Herbert Eugene Bolton, describes the huge island as if each statement is self-evident. It is the kind of island for which the Marqués del Valle had once yearned—a veritable miniature continent:

> This realm of California is very large and embraces much territory . . . It has the exact form and shape of a casket, being broad at the top and narrow at the point. It is this latter which we commonly call Punta de la California. From there it widens out to Cape Mendocino, which we will describe as being the top and breadth of it . . . If we give sixteen and a half leagues to each degree, according to the reckoning of cosmographers, it is about one thousand leagues long; but if according to the reckoning of mariners, who give twenty-five leagues to each degree, we should say that

its coast and shore is more than fifteen hundred leagues long from northwest to southeast, which is the direction all this realm runs and trends.[8]

So significant a geographical entity as this island-continent called for a respectable body of water to separate it from the mainland. Taking his cue from Gerónimo Marqués, Ascensión upgrades the strait to the status of a "mediterranean sea" of a width of fifty or so leagues:

> The sea between these two realms, which is called the Mediterranean Sea of California, since it is between lands so large and extended, must be about fifty leagues wide. In the middle of it there are many islands, some small and others larger; but I cannot say whether they are inhabited or not.

One of these islands "is the island of Giganta, where lives the queen of the neighboring peoples."

All the other stories are here, of rich pearls, of natives who do not know their value, of abundant silver and gold—which he detects from such "evidence" as yellow pyrites on the beach of what we now call San Diego.

This great boost to the island theory was achieved without benefit of either empirical or rational support. His "case" is largely a bunch of simple, flat, aprioristic assertions such as "two seas surround California," and "California is an island." We are to take his word for it, as though it were an act of faith alone.

When he does embark on a spot of "deductive reasoning" he argues so outrageously, so crazily, from garbled, unfounded or totally invented premises, that we are not a bit surprised Torquemada refrained from publishing his last chapters.

In Ascensión we have a case study of an impressionable simpleton turned crackpot. He had enough imagination to build an illusion out of other people's dreams. Hoist on his own hot air, he simply leaps the chasm between hypothesis and conclusion. He blithely ignores the demands of reason and empiricism for proof to bridge the gap. He unquestioningly accepts unfounded claims as "propositions" and as "evidence." He is enamoured of his own cleverness at deducing such an elegant system. Self-congratulation turns to zeal in advocacy of his own "conceit." He spends his whole life commending and defending it.

There may have been other reasons than the free-floating imagination of a Discalced Carmelite friar for the revival of the island myth. Or at least reasons to encourage him. Such a concept could certainly affect the claim Drake made. Documents made by Cortés in 1537, claiming legal possession of the "island," were in the Archives. Cortés had planted the first colony. Vizcaíno had attempted another more recently. Brass plate or no brass plate, Drake's claim must be invalid. To put this another way, Nova Albion had turned out to be the Island of California, and everybody knew that that belonged to Spain.

So in practical terms the large island concept strengthened Spanish rights to an extensive area as yet unsettled by Spanish colonists. Elizabeth of England had contended that merely naming a few promontories from the ocean was not enough to lay claim to territory. In her view, "prescription without possession is of no validity."[9] This ingenious inflation of the island's size looked like a smart rebuttal by the Spaniards.

Chapter XXV

The California Island Myth Is Accepted in Mexico and Europe

The wonder is that this extraordinary excrescence of the imagination didn't just bloom briefly and die a quick death like an exotic and extravagent flower. Amazingly, it survived until the turn of the next century and, in some quarters, even longer. Little was done in that period to check it out. There must have been a lot of people who wanted to go on believing it for it to have flourished untested for so long. Ironically, it fed the dream-needs of both the Spanish and the "Lutherans."

Once recreated by that fanciful group of Carmelite padres, the island myth became crystallized by uncritical repetition. Ascensión kept on airing it throughout his life. The idea spread quickly, putting down deep roots.

Strong reinforcement came from another company of pearl fishers. In 1611, the King granted Vizcaíno's lapsed concessions to a group headed by Tomás de Cardona. His nephew Nicolás de Cardona, and, later, Juan de Iturbe, led the expeditions.

In 1614, they built three ships at Acapulco. But like the two preceding pearl-fishing companies, they became victims of incredibly bad luck. In 1615, the Dutch freebooter Joris van Spilbergen entered the Pacific and delayed their expedition up the Gulf. Then, on their return to the mainland, Nicolás de Cardona's ship, the *San Francisco*, was seized and plundered by Spilbergen in Zacatula harbor. One of Iturbe's ships was ordered by the Spanish authorities to sail up the coast to warn the galleons.[1]

Again this new "Lutheran" incursion proved the need for a defensive strategy by nipping that strategy in the bud. Fear that the Gulf was the corsair's route was driven ever deeper into the popular consciousness.

Almost ruined by Spilbergen's action, Nicolás de Cardona returned to Spain in 1617 to raise more money for his thwarted enterprise. But like the other pearl-fishing ventures, it was doomed not to succeed. Cardona never made another voyage to the Gulf.

Cardona's contribution to our story is that in 1617 he wrote a report of his 1615 expedition up the Gulf. He may have picked up Ascensión's

and Oñate's views before or after his voyage. In any event, he stated he
had gone up the eastern side of the Gulf to 34 degrees—an impossibility. He continues:

> From this bay it appeared that the mainland joined that of California, but
> after setting sail and crossing to the other side, it was seen that the sea
> divided the land . . . For this reason I imagine that this is the Strait of
> Anian, or at least it proves that California is a large island and not a part
> of the mainland.[2]

Like Ascensión, he reinforced his erroneous conclusion by repetition,
hardening it into absolute conviction as the years passed. We note that
the fictitious strait is now "Anian" all the way along, right from the
Gulf:

> California is an extensive and elongated kingdom the end of which is not
> known, but by geographical conjecture as well as demonstrative reports it
> is shown as an island running from northwest to southeast . . . The early
> and modern authors who have written about this gulf of California . . .
> consider it as enclosed at twenty-eight degrees . . . This seems to be in
> error because that gulf or arm of the sea continues on toward the north
> . . . Thus California is a very large island. Also, this gulf or arm of the sea
> is the strait called Anian.[3]

It is possible Cardona only said what would be popular, perhaps to get
finances for a second chance. But it seems more likely, by the way he
quotes and refers to Ascensión, Vizcaíno, Oñate and Marqués, that as a
newcomer to the region, he unquestioningly accepted what he heard.
He was willing to overrule his own hunch of peninsularity, by "seeing"
what they wanted him to see. Cardona added to California's fabled
reputation by re-echoing that it was "one of the richest lands in the
world, with silver, gold and pearls."[4]

The myth continued to flourish on the New Mexican frontier. It was
passed on by padre to succeeding padre. In 1626, Father Jerónimo de
Zárate Salmerón wrote his history of New Mexico. It carries a full
account of the Oñate expedition. It is all there again—pearls the size of
rosary beads, the gold, the silver, and the scrambled remnants of
monster-and-marvel stories of bald-headed, big-footed, giants and
Amazons:

> They said that they were no farther than five days' journey from there,
> drawing on the ground the sea, and in the middle of it an island, which
> they call Ziñogaba, which is the name of the nation that inhabits it . . .
> They said that the mistress or chieftainess of it was a giantess, and that she
> was called Ciñacacohola, which means chieftainess or mistress. They

pictured her as the height of a man-and-a-half of those of the coast, and like them very corpulent, very broad, and with big feet; and that she was old, and that she had a sister, also a giantess, and there was no man of her kind, and that she did not mingle with anyone of the island. The mystery of her reigning on that island could not be solved, whether it was by inheritance, or tyranny by force of arms. And they said that all on the island were bald, having no hair on the head.[5]

And once more the Indian testimony about a Gulf-strait is reinforced:

[They saw] many Indians, asking all of them about the sea . . . and all answered pointing to the west, northwest, north, northeast, and east, saying that thus the sea curved, and was rather near, for they said that from the other side of the river it was only four days journey, and that that Gulf of California is not closed, but is an arm of the sea which corresponds to [i.e. communicates with] the North Sea and coast of Florida. . . . These Indians . . . indicated that the sea ran behind a very large mountain, on the skirts of which the Buena Esperanza River enters the sea.

These views spread rapidly among religious and secular Spaniards alike. For example, Antonio Vásquez de Espinosa, another Carmelite padre, soon wrote in his *Compendium and Description of the West Indies*: "California is an island, and not continental."[6] And by 1629, Enrico Martinez would comment on the Gulf of California, that its "end has not been seen, although it has been penetrated for a distance of more than 200 leagues."[7]

Ascensión's epiphany did not spread immediately beyond the Spanish sphere. It would take another decade for the fully reactivated Isle-of-California myth to catch fire among European cartographers. But there are clear indications in that decade that some of the same details that triggered the new geography had caught the attention of the "Lutheran corsairs"—the English and the Dutch.

In 1610, for example, a new map was made for Edward Wright's reissue of his treatise *Certaine Errors in Navigation* (Plate 42a). The map for his earlier edition (1599) had shown a closed Gulf of California. The new map by William Kip carries a wide opening at the head of the Gulf. Moreover, the outer coast ends just beyond Cape Mendocino with an abrupt turn to the East, where the name NOVA ALBION appears.

In 1611, Jodocus Hondius experimented with blending the Septentrional Ocean with the Verrazzano Sea from Virginia west (Plate 39). We have noted that he also toyed with connecting that anomaly to his open head of the Gulf of California (*see* page 228).

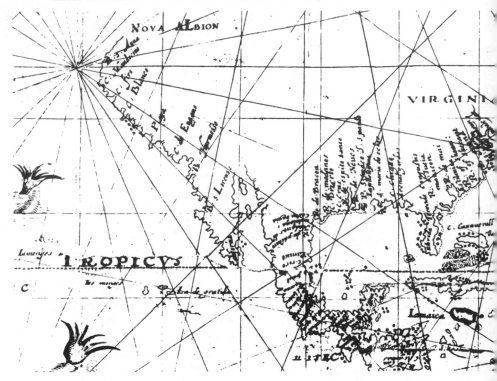

PLATES 42a, b & c.   Precursors of the revived island myth appeared on Dutch and English maps from 1610 to 1614 in the form of experimental inlets on the coasts of California. The inlets at Mendocino reflect Martin d'Aguilar's supposed discovery. An inlet at the head of the Gulf reflects continuing Spanish attempts to probe a Gulf strait. (Discussion on pages 279-83.)

42a. (above): The coast turns east above 40° at "Nova Albion," on a map by William Kip in Edward Wright's *Certaine Errors in Navigation* (1610). There is no northwest "corner" of the continent. Also, a large gap is shown at the head of the Gulf. *Photograph and permission by the Engineering Societies Library, New York.*

42b. (right, above): The coast turns east at 40°—where the name N. Albion appears—and a ghost line questions the northwest "corner" of the continent on this Hessel Gerritsz map of 1612. "Californ" labels the coast north of the Gulf's crotch, prefiguring a large island. *Photograph and permission by the British Library (Maps C. 32. a. 31).*

42c. (right, below): A large inlet breaks the coastline above 40° between a C. Fortunas and a C. del Engano on these four globe gores by Petrus Plancius, Amsterdam, 1614. The coastline resumes, after the gap, on a far-reaching westward course to a C. Mendocino, entrance to the Strait of Anian. *Photograph and permission by the Bibliothèque Nationale (GE. C. 5387).*

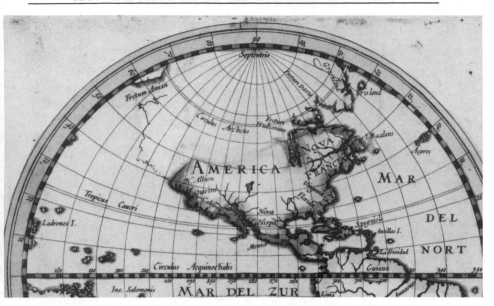

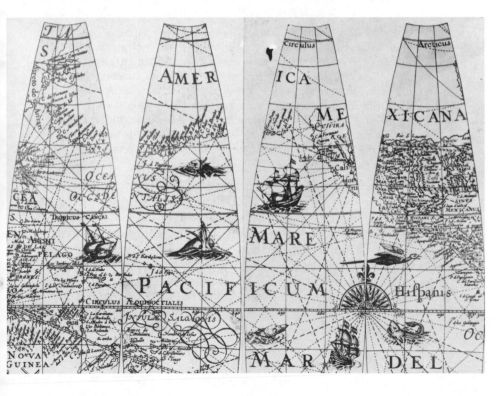

Hessel Gerritsz, geographer of the Dutch East India Company, was another experimenter with the new ingredients. On his map of 1612 (Plate 42b) his west coast, drawn as a bold line, turns abruptly east at Cape Mendocino, where he pens N. Albion. Presumably he had heard about Martin d'Aguilar's "discovery." Beyond the turn, he reduces the northwest "corner" to a ghost line.

Gerritsz discussed the straits in print. He appears to image the North-West Passage and the Strait of California as one strait with the Verrazzano Sea thrown in—rather as though he had been discussing it with Hondius. The following passage appears in his introduction to "Description of the Land of the Samoyeds in Tartary," published in Amsterdam in 1612 (translated here by F. J. Millard):

> The hope of finding out this newly discovered passage or strait above Terra Nova discovered by Mr. Hudson, is strengthened by the testimony of the Virginians and Floridians, who confidently affirm that the north-west of their country is a large sea, saying that they have seen vessels there like those of the English. [8]

He implies that this north-west sea connects with the Mar Vermejo, the Gulf Strait down which the corsairs sailed to rob the galleons:

> We read also in Josephus d'Acosta . . . that the Spaniards believe the English Captain Thomas Candish [sic] to have been well acquainted with this passage. It is also said, that the Spaniards endeavour to keep this road unknown, and that some of them, on returning from the conquest of the Philippines, have come back home along this road. Therefore the King Philip ordered a strong fort to be built on the northern coast of Mar Vermejo, to the west of New Grenada, to prevent our nation [the Dutch] or any of his enemies from depriving him through this avenue, of the riches he possesses in peace near Mar del Zur; this has been related to us as quite true.

The reference to the building of a fort on the Gulf reminds us of the Viceroy's letter of October 28, 1605 (page 264). There, the benefits of the fort included exploration of "the isle of the Californias." The strange reference to those returning from the Philippines is that hint again of Urdaneta finding the "rear entry" of the strait around Mendocino. The reference to Josephus d'Acosta is to the passage quoted and discussed on page 222.

Among other maps with experimental variations are gored maps by Pieter van den Keere, dated 1613, and by Petrus Plancius, dated 1614 (Plate 42c). Each shows a large break in the western coastline where

Cape Mendocino should appear. But the gap occurs between a puzzling C. de Fortuna, and an even more puzzling C. Enganno. Has the long-rumored "entrance" at Cape Engaño from Ulloa's day been shifted here, so many degrees to the north? Even more strange is that after this puzzling interruption the coast continues on to a C. Mendocino and a Strait of Anian.

These precursory experiments prepared the ground for the quick rooting of Ascensión's freak hybrid when it blew that way.

How was Ascensión's Island of California disseminated? The consensus is that it was carried to Holland by Dutch mariners. The rest is conjecture. It has been suggested that Joris van Spilbergen had the opportunity.[9] When he seized Nicolás de Cardona's ship, the *San Francisco*, in Zacatula harbor in 1615, he could have hauled in more than pearls and padres. In view of Cardona's opinions, his maps would have shown an insular California. However, the map showing Spilbergen's voyages, made in Leiden in 1619, depicts California as a peninsula.[10]

Could the Spanish island map have fallen into the possession of Jacob Le Maire? He rounded the Horn into the Pacific in 1615. We only know that the publisher of the Dutch account of Le Maire's expedition used a world map which shows California as an island to decorate the title page (Plate 43). The publisher, Michiel Colijn of Amsterdam, again used this Island-of-California concept in a vignette of the Americas on the title page of Antonio de Herrera's *Descriptio Indiae Occidentalis*. Both these works were published in 1622. To date, no earlier publication of a map showing California as an island has come to light.

If we compare the vignette with Ascensión's description on page 274, we find some affinity in the shape of the island, wide at the top and tapering southward to the point. We are led to wonder if the map the Dutch mariners seized could have been the one, now lost, that accompanied Ascensión's *Relación Breve* of 1620. Supportive of this speculation is a declaration in Diderot's *Encyclopédie* in 1770 that the map was taken by the Dutch "in 1620 on a Spanish vessel."[11]

Publisher Colijn gives no explanation for the use of the captured island map for his vignettes. It is all the more surprising to find in the Herrera Latin edition that a map, carried forward from an earlier edition, still shows California as a peninsula. Perhaps the island map came to Colijn's attention only in the final stages of production.

In the same year, 1622, that the vignettes appeared, there emerged

another publication significant to this story of the island myth of
California. The work was concerned with the British settlement of
what the colonists named Virginia. A book by Edward Waterhouse
called A *Declaration of the state of the Colony and Affaires in Virginia* . . .
had annexed to it "A Treatise . . . by that learned Mathematician Mr.
Henry Briggs of the Northwest Passage to the South sea through the
Continent of Virginia and by Fretum Hudson . . ." In this Treatise,
Henry Briggs again stokes the two theories dear to the hearts of
Englishmen: (1) the Verrazzano theory of the proximity of Pacific and
Atlantic Oceans in the neighborhood of Virginia; (2) the North-West
Passage sought since the days of Robert Thorne:

> Neither is the commodiousnesse of VIRGINIA's situation onely in
> respect of this west ATLANTICKE OCEAN, but also in respect of the
> INDIAN Ocean, which wee commonly call the South Sea, which lyeth
> on the West and North West side of VIRGINIA, on the other side
> of the mountains beyond our Fals, and openeth a free and faire passage,
> not only to CHINA, JAPAN, and the MOLUCCAES; but also to NEW
> SPAINE, PERU, CHILA, and those rich Countries of TERRA AUSTRALIS,
> not as yet fully discovered. For the Sea whereon Master HUDSON did
> winter, which was first discovered by him, and is therefore now called
> FRETUM HUDSON, doth stretch so farre towards the west, that it lieth
> as farre westward as the Cape of Florida . . . This Bay where Hudson did
> winter strechethe it selfe Southward into 49. degrees, and cannot be in
> probability so far distant from the Fals as 200. Leagues . . . Besides that
> Bay, it is not unlikely that the Westerne Sea in some other Creeke or
> River commeth much neerer then that place; For the place where Sir
> THOMAS BUTTON did winter, lying more westerly than Master HUDSON's
> Bay by 190 Leagues in the same Sea, doth extend it selfe very neere as
> farre to the west as the Cape of California . . .[12]

It is at this point in his discussion that Briggs latches onto the new
theory of the Island of California without reservation. His commentary
continues:

> . . . California, which is now found to be an Iland stretching it selfe from
> 22 degrees to 42. and lying almost directly North & South, as may
> appeare in a Map of that Iland which I have seene here in LONDON,
> brought out of HOLLAND; where the Sea upon the Northwest part
> may very probably come much nearer then some do imagine.

Presumably the "map . . . brought out of HOLLAND" was a copy of the
manuscript map used for Colijn's engraved vignette.

Briggs' quotation reveals why the British were attracted to the Cali-

SPIEGHEL

DER

AVSTRALISCHE
NAVIGATIE.

Door Den

𝕌𝕌ijt bermaerden ende cloeck-
moedighen Zee-Heldt/

IACOB LE MAIRE,

President ende Overſte over de twee Schepen, d'Eendracht
ende Hoorn/ uytghevaren den 14. Iunij 1615.

t'AMSTERDAM,

By *Michiel Colijn,* Boeck-bercooper op't Water
by de Oude Brugh/ in't Huys-Boeck.
Anno 1 6 2 2.

PLATE 43.   California as an island appears as a title-page vignette in works published by
Michiel Colijn in Amsterdam in 1622. Perhaps copied from a lost fictional map by
Father Antonio de Ascensión, this is the first extant cartographical expression of the
second flowering of the myth. The works carrying the vignette are Jacob Le Maire's
Spieghel Der Australische Navigatie (shown here), and Antonio de Herrera's *Descriptio
Indiæ Occidentalis.* (Discussion on page 283.) *Photograph and permission by the British
Library (10410 f.28).*

fornia-island myth. Ascensión's chimera had the effect of bringing west and east coasts of North America closer to each other. This narrowing of the continent across the north was implicit in the accounts of Marqués and Escobar. They spoke of native claims that the extension of the strait beyond the nook and delta ran northward, then curved to the northeast and east, heading toward the Bacallaos (page 267). Following suit, Ascensión had his Mediterranean Sea of California run from the crotch of the Gulf to Mendocino where "the coast and land turns to the N.E., and this is the head and end of the mainland of California."[13]

The effect of this was not only to make California into a huge island. It also cut off the great northwest "corner" of the continent, leaving the coast to trend to the northeast and east in a great curve. However, no map by Ascensión survives to verify how he might have represented this, unless the Colijn map was his.

Zárate Salmerón would reinforce this fanciful conception a few years after Briggs:

> The gulf . . . runs behind this mountain northward, according to what all the Indians said, both those of the coast and those of the river, for they declared that it turns to the north, northeast, and east.[14]

A quick comparison with the maps of Gemma Frisius (Plate 33) and the early Mercator and Ortelius will suggest why Briggs was so ready to accept this new geography. Those maps of the middle sixteenth century remind us that the "cornerless" continent and the northeast trending of the coast were longtime components of the insularists' dream. What joy Briggs must have felt to "learn" that "the sea upon the northwest part may very probably come much nearer," and that the Strait of Anian might not be quite the bottleneck that Grenville and others had once feared.

Several maps dated between 1624 and 1626 illustrate this new California-island concept. In 1624, a version engraved by Abraham Goos appeared in *West Indische Speighel*. H. R. Wagner believed Briggs had input into the Goos map; it contains features relevant to Drake's voyage that appear later in the English versions.[15]

In 1625, the Englishman William Grent issued a world map as a broadside showing California as an island (*see* Plate 44). A good deal of descriptive explanation included on the map is taken, apparently, from Briggs' "Treatise." This suggests Briggs' involvement in the map, providing such legends as the following:

> California sometymes supposed to be part of the continent of America is

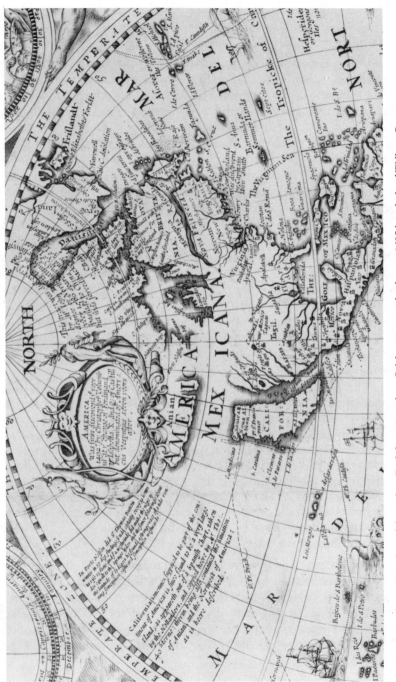

PLATE 44. One of the earliest English maps to show California as an island was a 1625 broadside of William Grent, the North American segment of which is shown here. The legends relate it to Henry Briggs' Treatise of 1622. Features of interest are the unfinished mainland west coast curving toward inlets in Button's and Hudson's Bays, and the names New Albion and P° de Sir Francis Draco on the Island of California. (Discussion on pages 283–89.) *Photograph by Cambridge University Library; permission by the Syndics of Cambridge University Library (Maps AA.1.62.1.).*

since found to be a very large island as appeareth out of a Spanish Chart taken by the Hollanders and coppied heere by Mr. Tho. Sterne . . .

On the Abraham Goos map, the northwest "corner" of the American continent has been eliminated. But on the Grent map Sterne has left a remnant of the "corner," beyond a wide "strait," in a detached landmass to the north, which he has labeled "Anian." The mainland coast, from which the Island of California has now been separated, is made to bend northeast, pointing toward Port Nelson on Button-Hudson Bay.

What Sterne, the mapmaker, is doing, perhaps on Briggs' advice, is melding the new island geography with "findings" of the most recent ventures to the North-West Passage. Briggs was an advisor to Sir Thomas Button, who in 1613 had gone in search of a passage to the "back side of America" in the South Sea. Although Button failed to find the strait, his experience was not regarded as "sufficient assurance of an impossibility."[16] On the contrary, expectations of ultimate success remained strong. This is clearly expressed in the following statement by Thomas Harriott. The behavior of the tides at places named Port Nelson, and "Hubbart's Hope" (after the pilot), in the bay named after Button, gave hope that they would lead to the South Sea beyond:

THREE REASONS TO PROVE THAT THERE IS A PASSAGE FRŌ THE NORTHWEST INTO THE SOUTH SEA

I. The tydes in Port Nelson (wher Sir Tho. Button did winter) were constantly 15 or 18 foote, wch is not found in any Baye Throughout the World but in such seas as lye open att both ends to the Mayne Ocean.

II. Every strong westerne winde did bring into the Harbo^r where he wintered, so much water, that the neap-tydes were equall to the spring-tydes, notwithstanding that the harbo^r was open only to the E.N.E.

III. In coming out of the harbo^r shaping his course directly North, about 60 degrees, he found a strong race of a tyde, setting due East and West, wch in probabilitie could be no other thing, than the tyde coming from the west and returning from the east.

But the truth of the theory remains yet to be proved.

These "hopes" and inferences appear more clearly on the map which accompanies Samuel Purchas's reprint of Briggs' "Treatise" in 1625 (Plate 45). Port Nelson and Hubbart's Hope are depicted as unfinished openings. The "strong race of a tide" is described in a legend at Hubbart's Hope. In another legend "the nearness of the South Sea at Port Nelson" is given as the "cause" of the extraordinary tides experienced there.

The most blatant claim occurs in the descriptive title of the map. It announces that Hudson's Strait and Button's Bay provide "a fair entrance to the nearest and most temperate passage to Japan and China."

So delighted were the British with the Spanish return to the "insularist" configuration that they eagerly swallowed all Ascensión's figments giving rise to it. The Grent-Sterne map and the Purchas map (like Goos's) show California stretching from Cabo San Lucas to Cabo Blanco. The island is wide at the north tapering to a point at the southern end. The dividing strait is now a mediterranean sea, containing an "I. de Gigante."

Wagner sees Briggs' influence in the designation on the "Island" of a "P° de Sʳ Francisco Draco" (the Goos map leaves off the final o). This is placed between "C. Mendocino" and "Punta de los Reyes." Obviously, this placement of Drake's landing is totally speculative. No document surviving then or now could give a precise location of his bay, hence the long debate among Drake enthusiasts throughout the twentieth century.

No doubt Briggs was responsible for some fancy tinkering with facts. "Puerto de San Francisco" would have been the way the name appeared on the "Spanish charte taken by ye Hollanders." That was the name Cermeño gave to the bay where he made landfall in the *San Agustín* in 1595. There off Point Reyes was where the galleon had foundered. Did Briggs, in his eagerness, honestly mistake St. Francis for Sʳ. Francis? Or did he deliberately misread the name to make a case?

But even if the name switch was finagled, Briggs must have felt he had truth on his side. After all, the various accounts of Drake's voyage did put his landfall at between 38 and 44 degrees, and Drake had taken possession of the anchorage and hinterland several years before Cermeño's voyage. It may even have appeared to Briggs that it was Cermeño who had tried to pull the fast one, daring to modify the name to refute British claims. Briggs might have seen himself as simply putting matters to rights again.

The effect of converting Puerto de San Francisco into Puerto de Sr. Francisco Draco was to equate Nova Albion with California. The designation of Nova Albion does not appear on the Goos and Purchas maps. But on the map issued by Grent, Thomas Sterne penned "Nova Albion" across the northern part of *his* Island of California. Others quickly followed suit.

Among these first British renderings of the Island of California we must note John Speed's map of 1626, possibly engraved by Goos. Of very special interest is the fragment of coast seeming to appear out of thin air above the island of California. It is labeled with many names,

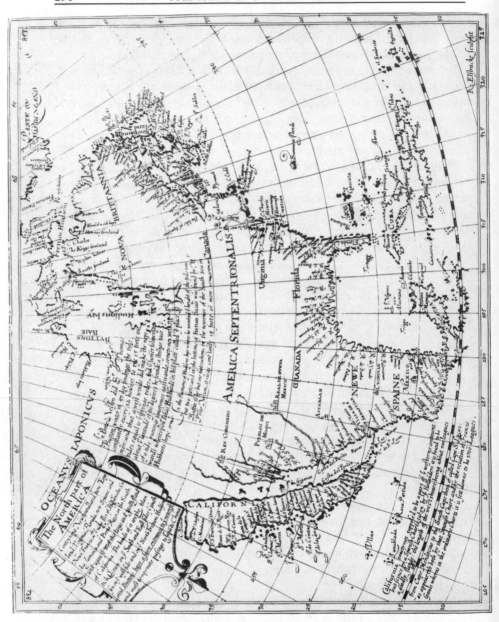

PLATE 45. This California-as-Island map accompanied Samuel Purchas' reprint, in 1625, of Henry Briggs' "Treatise . . . of the Northwest Passage . . . (1622)." The legends promise that Hudson's Strait and Button's Bay provide "a fair entrance" to the South Sea. (Discussion on pages 288 ff.) *Photograph and permission by the British Library* (Purchas His Pilgrimes, *Vol. 3, p. 852).*

ending at the furthest point north with "C. Mendocino." We recognize this strange anomoly as similar to that on the gored maps of Petrus Plancius and Pieter van den Keere, 1613 and 1614 (see Plate 42c). Those maps featured a northwesterly section extending beyond a big interruption in the northwest coastline. This adaptation was a precursory stage in the return of the island myth of California. Speed's map seems to bring together the herald and the heralded.[17]

Not all "Lutheran" geographers fell uncritically for Ascensión's brainchild as blessed by Briggs. In the same year that Purchas reprinted Briggs' Treatise, 1625, Nathanael Carpenter published his Geography Delineated Forth in Two Books . . . Carpenter was open-minded enough to give some weight to reports of California being an island. Discussing the general principles of determining continents and islands and the uncertainties involved, he states:

> Those places which in the first discovery have been taken for the main Continent, or at least for some greater part of Land, have afterward upon more curious examination bin found cloven into many lesser Ilands; As . . . California of late, thought to be a part of the Continent, and so described almost in all our Mapps; yet since by a Spanish Chart taken by the Hollanders, discovered to be an Iland.[18]

Yet Carpenter was a cautious scholar. He warns his reader against too readily accepting the word of mariners, who, being desirous to stimulate hope are often deceived. In this context he cites Hudson's and Button's efforts to find the North-West Passage, as depicted on "a curious Mappe not long since set out by our worthy and learned Professour Mr. Briggs." Carpenter ties Briggs' enthusiasm for the California-as-island map to his old enthusiasm for the North-West Passage:

> To shew the land towards the South-Sea, through which we seek to open this passage, not to be so far off as our ordinary Charts seeme to pretend, may be probably averred, in that California heretofore supposed to be a part of the Westerne Continent, is since by a Spanish Chart taken by the Hollanders, found to be a great Iland.

Therefore, adds this careful geographer:

> These Arguments, I confesse, have swayde my opinion, but not as yet absolutely freed me from doubt.

A little later he grows more wary still:

> That California is an Iland, it may (for ought I know) be well warranted: But the evidence drawne from the Spanish Chart, seemes rather to cherish hope, than perswade consent.

Similar doubts were expressed by the Dutch Geographer Joannes de Laet in his *History of the New World*, issued in Dutch, Latin and French editions between 1625 and 1640. Speaking of California, he notes:

> But it is uncertain up to the present if it is continuous with the continent of North America, or if it is separated from it by some strait.[19]

Oddly, De Laet seems not to be referring to the newest island theory, for he continues:

> One still sees old geographical and hydrographical charts which make California an island.

The adjective "old" could hardly characterize the maps even then being published in Amsterdam and London. Had he seen maps of the Cortés period? Diderot stated so in his *Encyclopédie* in 1770:

> De Laet observes that from the year 1539 there have been Spaniards who have imagined that it was an island; he said in 1633 that he had seen old maps which represented it in that fashion.[20]

De Laet describes that island as being divided from America "by a strait which is rather wide at the beginning, but which narrows as it continues." It does not sound like such maps as that in Alonso de Santa Cruz's *Islario* (Plate 18). If the "Spanish Chart taken by the Hollanders" was Ascensión's concoction, was it passed off as, or taken to be, a chart of much earlier vintage?

De Laet was no pig-headed reactionary unwilling to entertain new possibilities. He sounds like Nathanael Carpenter, cautiously conservative. In the absence of convincing evidence, he will keep an open mind:

> However it may be, these are very extensive regions and but little known in their smallest part, and only near the coast.

De Laet and Carpenter are of that stripe who are ever curious about the world, but skeptical in drawing conclusions. They are eager to go out, but ready to draw back. They are able to tolerate doubts, uncertainties, unanswered questions, when the evidence is not all in. Unlike crackpots, they do not require closure or completeness. They live contingently and existentially. From careful observation they build imaginative theories which they then subject to rigorous experiment and meticulous reasoning. They form a fraternity across time and space, building on one another's work and methodology. In Chapter XXVIII, page 314 for example, we shall find Guillaume de Lisle recognizing his affinity with De Laet, who preceded him by half a century and more.

Few of De Laet's contemporary geographers and cartographers shared his scientific detachment. Large numbers of maps appeared in the following decades depicting California as an island. This full flowering of the myth has been well presented in R. V. Tooley's *California as an Island*, Number 8 of the Map Collectors' Series, and in the beautiful California Book Club production, *California As An Island*, with an introductory essay by John Leighly.[21]

Two maps have been chosen here to represent this extraordinary proliferation. Ogilby's map of 1657 (Plate 46) expresses the yearning for "closure" of the continent between east and west across the north. This is shown in the narrowing of the distance between the Straits of Anian and the Button-Hudson Bay. As in many of the island maps, Ogilby's map labels the northern half of the Isle of California as "Nova Albion," supplementing the designation of the "P. de Sr F. Drake."

PLATE 46.   A yearning for "closure" of the continent across the north is suggested by this representative map made in 1657 by John Ogilby, depicting California as an island, and Nova Albion as part of that island. This map serves as an example of many such maps drawn throughout the seventeenth century. *Photograph and permission by the British Library (152.i.1.Pt.1).*

The second map is Nicolas Sanson's map of 1654. This is shown as No. II of Plate 49, with detail below. It is chosen for the interest to this study of the label "R. de Estrete" close to the northwest opening of the "mediterranean sea." It designates a Rio where no river appears. This odd feature, seen earlier on Joannes Blaeu's world map of 1648, may be the vestige of Ortelius's "Rio de los Estrechos" of his map of 1587 (see Plate 37). The long-sought "river-strait"—first mentioned in Cortés' letter of 1524—has completed its mutation into a "Strait of California" now wide enough to be dubbed a mediterranean sea. The Blaeu-Sanson "R. de Estrete" is like a vermiform appendix—the nonfunctioning remnant of a transitional evolutionary stage.

Sanson's map is also interesting for the different location assigned the Puerto de Francisco Draco. Sanson places it between the Punta de Monte Rey and Pᵗᵒ de Carindo. Carindo is presumably a misreading and miscopying of "Carmelo." The m has been taken as in, and the el joined to make a d.

Was there, perhaps, some Spanish tradition that Drake had trimmed his *Golden Hind* in the Monterey-Carmel area? In 1718 Father Juan Amando Niel writes in his *Apuntamientos* of the port at the mouth of the Rio Carmelo being called "el puerto del Draque."[22] But this is a digression, of more relevance to the debate about Drake's haven than to ours.

Padre Niel is of some interest to our story, however. He is numbered amongst the diehard padres who would support the island myth against an historic challenge which came at the turn of the seventeenth to eighteenth centuries. That challenge is the subject of our next chapter.

Detail of PLATE 49, No. II, Nicolas Sanson's map of 1654, shows "R. de Estrete" and place-ment of "Pto de Francisco Draco" near Monterey. *The Roy V. Boswell Collection for the History of Cartography, California State University, Fullerton.*

Chapter XXVI

KINO CHALLENGES THE
ISLAND FALLACY FROM NEW MEXICO

California went on being represented as an island on innumerable maps throughout the seventeenth century. As a cartographic feature, it commanded wide attention. Yet in that same period the real California receded once more into the shadows. The threats from foreign powers abated. There was no longer any urgency to crack "the northern mystery." Again the region was known only to passing galleons and the occasional pearl fisherman. All this, of course, redounded greatly to the benefit of native tribes.

This is not to say that California was no longer a subject of discussion. Ascensión kept reiterating his set piece. Then in 1628, Felipe IV issued a Royal Order to the Audiencia of Mexico to take testimony from persons who had voyaged to the area. The purpose of these hearings was to determine the feasibility of exploring and settling California.

W. Michael Mathes' collection reveals various views. One witness stated:

> The area from 31 to 40 degrees north latitude, which is to Cape Mendocino, must still be explored to see if there is an outlet to the North Sea. Up to now all those who say they know that there is no outlet are confused . . .[1]

Another witness was supremely confident that "the said gulf comes from the South Sea and runs to the North, and in it, it is certain that the two seas join." Still another opined:

> The Californias are in a bay formed with the mainland of New Spain . . . There are those who say there is another strait in 42 degrees north latitude which can be entered to reach New Mexico . . . All the area is coast that is known to ships that come from the Philippines, and they follow it from one end to the other.

Medieval myths were still embedded in the testimony, the "isle of women" being a vestige of California's Amazons:

> The Bahia de las Palmas is in 24 degrees north latitude and has no fresh water. About two leagues from the mouth of the bay is the Isla de Mujeres, a mountainous island.

These hearings lasted for four years. The debate continued.

In 1636, Alonso Botello y Serrano and Pedro Porter y Casanate drafted a petition to fish the Gulf for pearls. In the tradition established when Santotís got his license, they pledged their best efforts to seek the Strait of Anian. Another public benefit would be to quiet the prevailing controversy about California:

> Some make it an island; others firm land; some join it with Tartary; others with New Spain; some put a Strait of Anian; others do not; many indicate a passage to Spain by the contracosta of Florida, and others place this strait so high that it could not be navigable for ice. The Gulf, say some, runs to the northeast; others to the northwest, and some to the north.[2]

Porter was prevented from immediately carrying out this mission; he served in the Spanish Armada for the next few years. But in 1643, after a quick reconnaissance of the Gulf, he set about building more ships. Like the other pearl fishers, however, he was afflicted with insurmountable misfortunes. Corsairs were present on the coast, and one of his ships was commandeered to warn the galleons. In 1644, someone set fire to the ships still under construction in the shipyards. He made one more unsatisfactory excursion into the Gulf then packed it in, surrendering his vessels to the Crown.

Anyone the least bit superstitious must have felt that California resisted delivering up her secrets, making life miserable every time someone attempted to get close to her.

But California continued to lure adventurers with the promise of great riches. It was said that huge harvests of gold and pearls would reward those daring to brave the hostile gulf. An expedition headed by Francisco de Lucenilla set out in 1668. A Franciscan, Juan Cavallero Carranco, was one of the padres on the trip. In "A Summary Account" he revealed his disgust at the greed of the crew:

> As soon as they saw the California hills, the question rose as to shares in order to see what was to fall to each one's lot, as if the hills were gold, pearl or amber. It was a matter of great unpleasantness . . . not a word was heard regarding the conversion of souls, for everything said was in discussion of riches.[3]

In material and spiritual terms the voyage was a flop. But it gave a new twist to the island myth. Friar Juan made an interesting observation about the Gulf, one that would start to undercut the notion of "the strait so desired by the Crown":

> The more one goes to the north, the closer the land of New Spain reaches toward that of the Californias . . . It could be that farther to the north

the two lands join and their conquest would be more simplified. I believe
this to be the case.[4]

As Mathes notes, "this belief in the peninsularity of California was
unusual" at that period. Another thirty years would elapse before a
person with sufficient perspicacity would come along to make the same
observations and deductions. And still another fifty years would be
required for deracination of the myth.

So let the record now give proper credit to this devout Franciscan for
first sowing the seed of skepticism about the second manifestation of the
island myth. Let us sound a tantara for his straight thinking.

From the Spanish colonial viewpoint, if the mystery of this unknown
region to the northwest was ever to be solved, some hard-headed,
clear-sighted men were needed first to explore, then to settle it. Such
men came in the last couple of decades of the seventeenth century.
Religious support for northward expansion was handed over to the
Society of Jesus. Some members of this order were dedicated, within the
canons of their faith, to a high degree of learning and independence of
thought. Their disciplined modes of observation and study were in
marked contrast to the wild imaginings of the Discalced Carmelites at
the beginning of the seventeenth century.

Overcoming many setbacks, the Jesuits got a foothold on Baja California. In 1697 they founded their first mission at Loreto (see map, page
302), beginning the famous rosary of missions that would run northwards
up the coast. A similar chain of missions was begun on the opposite
mainland. With the advent of these dedicated brethren, and their
permanent establishment on both sides of the Gulf, the stage was set for
the testing of the island myth of California. And what more appropriate
time for this to happen than at the dawn of the eighteenth century
—the Enlightenment in the history of ideas?

When at last the challenge came, it came from the very place where
the revival of the myth had begun—the interior of the mainland
loosely called "New Mexico."

The challenger was the Jesuit Father Eusebio Kino.[5] Well educated in
Germany in mathematics and astronomy, Kino had been sent to Baja in
1681. From there he was sent to the mainland, to Pimeria Alta—
north from Sonora into the present southern Arizona. Among the
missions that he helped to found was the famed San Xavier del Bac,
south of Tucson (see Plate 49, Nos. IV & V, and map, page 302.)

Kino was a man of balanced perception and sound rational faculties.
He cultivated and trusted his own senses and deductive powers. On his

early expeditions to the mainland, Kino began to wonder about California's geography. He came to realize that the myths had impeded a true understanding of the region. Though his job of ministering to the Indians took precedence over his curiosity about the area's geography, he saw that both tasks must ultimately involve clearing the air of superstitious error and deceit. Both could be effected simultaneously:

> If we continue with the promotion and advancement of these new conversions, we shall be able to continue to make correct maps of this North America, the greater part of which has hitherto been unknown, or practically unknown, for some ancients blot the map with so many and such errors and with such unreal grandeurs and feigned riches as a crowned king whom they carry in chairs of gold, of amber, and of corals. With reason Father Mariana rebukes them for deceiving us with these riches which do not exist.[6]

At a time when the insular view of California was widely accepted in Europe, Kino had been taught at Ingolstadt that Baja was a peninsula. (A Jesuit map of 1664, depicting a peninsular California, is extant in Munich.) But on coming to Mexico, he changed to the island view. On the expedition led by Isidro de Atondo y Antillon, Kino wrote to the Duchess of Aveiro such statements as:

> The entire vast Island of California measures, according to modern maps, 1700 leagues lengthwise from the Cape of San Lucas to Mendocino (the two extreme points).[7]

But as his experience of the Gulf increased, he began to raise new questions about the lie of the land—as the Franciscan Juan Cavallero Carranco had before him. Kino was urged on by more than curiosity and love of truth. From his new assignment on the mainland, he wanted to keep close contact with friends from his original assignment—those brethren in Baja still struggling to put down roots. If there really did exist an overland route between the mainland and Baja across the head of the Gulf, Baja could be supplied with material and spiritual support.

This motivation played an important part in Kino's persistent efforts to establish empirically California's true geography. These efforts had profound implications for the island myth.

The account of Kino's growing conviction that the island concept was fallacious is found in the various journals, letters and reports about his many expeditions. His copious writings were discovered in a single manuscript collection called, for short, *Favores Celestiales*, and translated by Herbert Eugene Bolton in 1919. The following quotations show the steps in Kino's change of mind, beginning with his original belief in California's peninsularity, and his conversion to the island view:

> In this belief that California was a peninsula and not an island I came to these West Indies, and when I arrived at Mexico I was assigned by the Father Provincial Bernardo Pardo as missionary and royal cosmographer of California, and, trying to emerge from the doubts which attended these matters, I changed my position; first, because I read the account of the Adelantado of New Mexico, Don Juan de Oñate, who, setting out from the villa of Santa Fe of New Mexico and travelling about one hundred leagues to the westward, came . . . to the sea, and this in latitude thirty-seven degrees. Second, because other accounts by others said the same thing. Third, because many other maps, and the principal modern cosmographers of Germany, Flanders, Italy and France, etc., said the same, and that California was an island, . . . Fourth, because the many currents from north to south which I experienced in the voyages which I made in the Gulf of California were so continuous and at times so strong that it seemed as if the sea communicated with that of the north, and inclined me to the opinion that California was an island.[8]

Having changed once, he would find the switch back to the concept of peninsularity less difficult than would the diehards. He did not, however, immediately believe the evidence of his senses. He gives us this retrospective view of his slow reconversion as he explored the mainland coast:

> When, ten years ago, setting out from Nuestra Senora de los Dolores for the west, . . . I arrived . . . at the coast of the Sea of California, we saw plainly that that arm of the sea kept getting narrower, for in this latitude of thirty-three degrees we already saw on the other side more than twenty-five leagues of California land in a stretch so distinctly that we estimated the distance across or width of that arm of the sea to be no more than fifteen or eighteen or twenty leagues.

> Therefrom arose the desire to ascertain the width higher up; and in the year 1698, at thirty-five latitude, and at one hundred and five leagues by a northwest course from Nuestra Senora de los Dolores, on the very high hill, or ancient volcano, of Santa Clara, I descried most plainly both with a telescope and without a telescope the junction of these lands of New Spain with those of California, the head of this Sea of California, and the land passage which was there in thirty-five degrees latitude. At that time, however, I did not recognize it as such, and I persuaded myself that farther on and more to the west the Sea of California must extend to a higher latitude and communicate with the North Sea or Strait of Anian, and must leave or make California an island.

The Mission Dolores, Kino's headquarters, was near the Río Sonora. The volcanic hill of Santa Clara bears the French label M[ont] de Ste. Claire, 1698, on Plate 49, No. IV, and on the map on page 302.

In February of 1699, however, Kino visited the territory of the Yuma Indians. In the vicinity of the Rio Colorado at its confluence with the Gila this small episode occurred:

> These natives . . . gave us various presents of the unusual sorts which they have there. Among them were some curious and beautiful blue shells, which, so far as I know, are found only on the opposite or western coast of California. Afterward it occurred to me that not very far distant there must be a passage by land to near-by California; and shortly, by Divine Grace, we shall try to find it out and see it with all exactness.

In November of 1699, in the course of ministering to native souls, he took a side trip "to inform ourselves better in regard to the land passage to California." Some leagues north of the Sea of California "we made very careful inquiry in regard to the blue shells of the opposite coast, and to the passage by land to California."

In March of 1700, he received another gift of blue shells, and again reflected on their source. He informed several fathers. In his view the evidence of the shells vindicated those members of the order who "had very strongly urged the exploration of those lands, seas, and rivers of the north and of the northwest." The Rector of the College of Matape replied to Kino:

> God Bless me! And what great news and how rare is that which your Reverence imparts to me . . . to the effect that it is possible to pass overland to California, news truly the greatest, if it is verified, but which, although desired so long, it has never been possible to confirm.

More encouragement came from the Rector to Father Kino in September 1700:

> I thank your Reverence for your most delightful letter, and also for sending of the blue shells; and I shall welcome most heartily the announcement of those discoveries. I am very strongly of the opinion that this land which we are in is mainland and joins that of California. May our Lord grant that there be a road as royal as we think and desire, for thereby the labor as well as the care of California [i.e. Baja] will be lessened.

Perhaps the "Moses Moment" came on October 7, 1700, when Kino was on yet another trip down the Rio Colorado:

> I ascended a hill to the westward, where we thought we should be able to see the Sea of California; but looking and sighting toward the south, the

west, and the southwest, both with a long range telescope and without, we saw more than thirty leagues of level country, without any sea, and the junction of the Rio Colorado with this Rio Gila, and their many groves and plains . . . Returning to our stopping-place we ate, adding some sweetmeats for joy that now, thank the Lord, we had seen the lands pertaining to California, without any sea between and separating those lands from it.

In 1701 he made some precise measurements. On March 22:

At midday I took the altitude of the sun with the astrolabe and found that this gulf of California ended in thirty-one degrees latitude.

He was now ready to assert without equivocation:

With all certainty in various expeditions we have discovered this California Gulf does not come up to thirty-two degrees. Therefore Drake on his return to his country misled all Europe; and almost all the cosmographers and geographers of Italy, Germany, and France, etc., delineated California as an island . . . But now already, thanks to His Divine Majesty, with various expeditions . . . I have discovered with all minute certainty and evidence, with mariner's compass and astrolabe in my hands, that California is not an island but a peninsula, or isthmus, and that in thirty-two degrees of latitude there is a passage by land to California, and that only to about that point comes the head of the Sea of California, the large volumed rivers . . . emptying into the head.

As we have seen, it was not Drake who began the island theory but Cortés. Nor was it Drake who knowingly revived it, but the New Mexico explorers, Oñate, Escobar, and Marqués, with Ascensión's reinforcement and elaboration. Ascensión, the romantic and enthusiast, and Kino, the scientist, seem to square off against each other across the span of a century. The myth reactivated at the beginning of one century is overturned with observational data at the beginning of the next. Manifold maps of conjecture and dream give way to a single map drawn from field experience—the map Kino made in 1701, showing California rejoined to the mainland (see Plate 49, No. IV, and below).

A great cultural phenomenon is being played out in this quiet backwater, almost half a world away from the centers of civilization. Ascensión has taken the last exuberant gallop of the unbridled imagination. The sharp bit of empiricism and rationalism, which Kino applies, now holds him in check. From the hinge of the seventeenth and eighteenth centuries we watch Januslike as one gate closes and another opens on the Age of Reason. Down the vista of the past is the paradise of an Amazon island of pearls and gold, which the dreamers had taken literally. Up the vista of the future is the symbolic paradise of a promising reality—which a companion of Kino dreamed as "very extensive and beautiful plains, one of which was called San Joachin."

PLATE 49, No. IV, Kino's map of 1701, in an English version by Henry Jones, 1721, to show Baja's first mission at Loreto; Mission Dolores, Kino's headquarters in Pimeria; San Xavier del Bac; M. de S. Claire, 1698 sighting of head of Gulf, shown now as closed. *The Roy V. Boswell Collection for the History of Cartography, CSU, Fullerton.*

Chapter XXVII

California's Mystery Continues:
Is It or Isn't It an Island?

Kino's discovery still did not end the Isle-of-California story. The myth had been too deeply entrenched for too long for it to be easily shaken loose. The many exquisite maps produced since Ascensión's reactivation of the myth had seemed to place upon the island view the stamp of scientific authority. It didn't make sense to abandon it on the basis of a handful of blue shells and the say-so of a single eyewitness sighting through a telescope from a low hill. After all, Kino had his own reasons for wishful thinking.

The record of a mind laboring to change itself has come down to us in the testimony of Juan Matheo Manje. Manje accompanied Kino on some expeditions to the head of the Gulf, and kept detailed journals. He had found it difficult to be persuaded by the visual evidence of Baja's peninsularity, sometimes inclining toward Kino's view, sometimes disavowing it:

> In this account, though it may seem tedious, I want to be absolutely sincere without deviating in the least from the truth, which is the fundamental and essential basis of all history . . .
>
> I remained somewhat doubtful because I could not see the head of the Gulf close at hand, and hence I cannot attest in writing to the peninsularity of California with the certitude demanded. Fathers Salvatierra and Kino, however, were so firmly convinced that we had several friendly discussions to ascertain the truth; and, although their arguments did not completely convince me, because we could not fully agree, nonetheless they said that they would not hesitate to state in writing that it was very certain that the two lands joined without there being any intervening sea. Although some doubt still lingers in my mind, recently I have inclined to their opinion. I cannot, however, put it down as something certain, as a chart demands, because the point where we believed the gulf came to the end is thirty-five leagues up the coast; and inasmuch as thirty leagues of this stretch are without any pasture or waterholes—all covered only by sand dunes that blocked the passage of the thirty-three loads we were taking—we could not traverse the remaining area. Further, the Indians maintain that the region is impassable because of the sterility and aridity of the terrain.[1]

Unable to sustain these tentative conclusions without solid proof, Manje reverted to the island view in later years when he wrote his *Luz de Tierra Incógnita*.[2]

The impassable desert mentioned by Manje was the major reason that the controversy could not be resolved once and for all. By March 1701 Kino was aware that though he himself was convinced that a land bridge existed to his "best beloved California," it could not readily be tested, much less conveniently used:

> This California Gulf has at its head to the northward a stretch of sand-dunes so large that it is more than sixty leagues around, and now it became a hindrance to our passing farther by this route . . . Our men and pack-train . . . had been so without water that . . . it was necessary for us to travel until midnight to reach the camp . . . and many of our pack-animals were tired out, while some loads remained on the road.[3]

Kino had discovered that even if Alta California was not islanded by a continuation of the Gulf from Baja, the "sea" of sand would perhaps prove even more hazardous to cross than a mediterranean sea. Travels along the desert's edge under the burning sun with long distances between waterholes had proved perilous. One hundred and sixty years before, Melchior Díaz' men had been stopped by the same insurmountable obstacle (page 148). Here, indeed, might be a Sandy Sea to equal the one described in the *Letter* of Prester John. That barrier had been described as one "nobody can cross, no matter how one tries" unless one let oneself "be carried by griffins, as Alexander did." Kino was too rational a man to set store by such a myth. But his frustration must have been enormous to be thwarted by a natural phenomenon so intractable.

For the rest of his life on the frontier Kino had to reconcile himself to being unable to prove his view conclusively. He failed to persuade many of his brethren even of a high degree of probability that his theory was true. Father Juan Amanda Niel, for example, accompanied Kino on his last visit to the head of the Gulf in 1705–6. But in his *Apuntamientos* of 1718, Niel expressed his doubts by saying that Kino's view was still "in opinion."[4] Padre Luis Velarde, a rector-missionary of Sonora, and his associate, Padre De Campos, questioned the Pimas and Yumas about these matters. The natives informed them, so the padres thought, that a strait did indeed exist. Writing in 1716, after Kino's death, Velarde reverts to seventeenth-century views:

> The Pimas . . . say that the coast of California is in a straight line from west of Caborca, in front of the junction of the Colorado; although,

perhaps, a little way to the south there is a narrow canal or strait in which the two seas merge . . . What makes it more certain that there is a strait is the fact that almost in front of the Yumas the other shore could be distinguished very clearly . . . We cannot find out at what latitude rises the Pimico gulf of California. The only thing that is told is that it bends toward the east and flows out almost in front of Terranova, ending in a large bay . . . [5]

Terranova was the region of the English discoveries on the Atlantic seaboard. Velarde understands the implications of his statement:

I can see very well that what has been said up to here does not coincide with what Father Francisco Eusebio Kino . . . wrote. Perhaps he believed his eyes too much . . . His sight could have been mistaken and used to imagine what does not really exist.

But in resuming the position "as it was before Father Kino's narrative," Velarde rings a change upon the island theme. California is not a single large island:

There is a different island, in my judgement, than that of California . . . One and the other facts are confirmed by a modern Dutch map, making the same strait almost exactly where the Yumas say. It also designates on the opposite shore another island of California running about 35 leagues and ending in another strait of this gulf in the sea of the South.

There had been hints of the lower end of Baja forming a smaller island since Ulloa went searching for a strait up the outside coast. Plates 18 and 19 illustrate this, and Plate 47 gives us a two-island seventeenth century view. Velarde does not rest with two islands, however:

It is hoped that we will . . . discover, once and for all, whether California is an island or a range of islands connected together until they reach the Marianas and, more certainly, Japan.

This thought may be a throwback to the island group called "the Californias" as rendered in Plate 17. Or it could be an atavism of the mythic archipelago of islands of Montalvo's romance.

Velarde's partiality to myth is clearly evinced in the following passage:

[The Pimas] claim to have information about a nation in which the men have only one foot and the women two. I do not affirm this as a fact. Although I do not believe it neither do I believe it to be impossible in philosophy. We already know of many marvels seen in both Americas which if narrated previously would have been taken for the wildest fancy. Such are the stories of the Patagonians, of the Monuculos, of the women who have only one breast, and so on. Let this remain said in faith of those

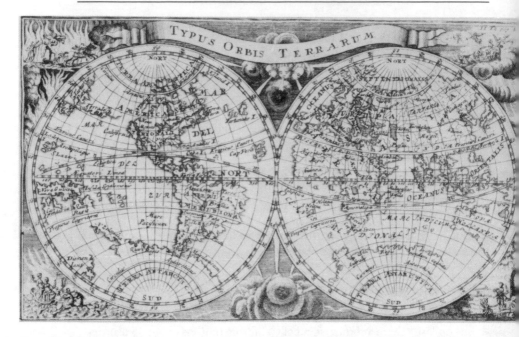

PLATE 47.   California is shown as two islands on a double-hemisphered map of 1738. The two-island theory w
advanced by Father Luís Velarde, S. J., after Father Kino failed to convince him of California's peninsulari
(Discussion on page 305). *Photograph and permission by Stephanie Hoppen and Richard Leech, the Holland Press, Lono
(Cartographica Curiosa, No. 58, a catalogue facsimile. From an atlas by Carolo Ludovico de Launay, Augsburg, 1738*

who assure it. Some of these tales oftentimes come true, although at the
present time it is somewhat difficult to verify this one.

More than a hundred years have passed since Escobar, Marqués and
Ascensión indulged in their imaginative flights, and the realm of
possibility—at least to Velarde's mind—is still inhabited by giants and
Amazons. It is 1716, and California is still a figment of romance. The
minds who are preoccupied with her have still not evolved very far from
the Dark Ages.

Kino's failure to wean many of his colleagues away from recessive
notions meant that for the most part California would remain fast
behind her veil for another half a century and more. She continued to
resemble Montalvo's Amazon island, invulnerable behind cruel barriers
that might now include a Sandy Sea.

Amazingly, resistance to the California-is-not-an-island view was so strong in Kino's own parish, the Sonora-Arizona frontier, that a few decades after Kino's breakthrough, it was as though he had made no impact whatsoever. Thirty-odd years after Kino's death, Father Jacobo Sedelmayr betrayed the continuing confusion between fact and fallacy. In 1744, in a discussion of the management of frontier Indians, Sedelmayr innocently discloses that the peninsula/island controversy remains unresolved:

> As a result of such a development there will follow the oft-desired verification of California, whether it be an island or not, whether it be a continent or not; whether it stands alone or is one of a string of many other islands. This has been a question much disputed among the experts of North America and even among the missionaries. The arguments given on one side and on the other are not convincing, granting that on the one side they carry more force and create more probability, still our knowledge is not certain. But we shall finally be satisfied by the conviction of facts which will be easy to certify by exploring the Colorado River and its outlet to the sea. But whether California be island or continent, it is our prediction that the fertile regions of the rivers we have spoken of will be a fat larder for the sustenance of sterile California . . . The Fathers of California from the twenty-eighth latitude, which is the mission frontier, will in a short time through explorations in that island towards the north come up to the thirty-third parallel, where (added some fraction of a degree) lies the mouth of the river. The missionaries could even advance farther without reaching a point where they would be in need of food and provisions. There would thus follow what has been so often demanded [by the King], the conquest of the whole of California.[6]

In expressing these views, Sedelmayr is faithfully reflecting the viewpoint of his Jesuit superiors in Mexico.

Sedelmayr concedes that the main job of the brethren is to "look for other treasures, namely human souls." But he is optimistic on a more material count as well:

> Should the country become settled, it is very probable that God would reward the royal largess for all disbursement with this additional allurement of mines of gold and silver.

This rehash of the myth reveals once more its remarkable tenacity. It was now more than two hundred years since California was first judged an island. We are halfway into the century that was supposed to mark the ascendancy of reason and induction over the mythic imagination.

Would the dream ever die?

Chapter XXVIII

South Sea Bubbles Don't Burst Easily

As in the New World, so in Europe, the Island-of-California myth refused to be put down. When Kino's deductions began to circulate, they were generally ignored. Despite the fact that some cartographers had featured California as a peninsula throughout the century, the island preference remained strong.

The English enthusiasts could not afford to abandon the island myth. It was inextricably bound up with faith in the North-West Passage. They could hardly admit to a theory that would bring back the dreaded northwest "corner" of the continent of America, and a bottle-neck at the Strait of Anian.

The English geographer, Herman Moll, was one who clung to the island theory. In *A System of Geography or, a New & Accurate Description of the Earth*, published in London in 1701, he includes a chapter titled "The New Kingdom of Mexico, with California, and the other Islands over against it," saying, in part:

> Many *Islands* lye over against the New Kingdom of Mexico, and the nearest are contained in the *Purple Sea*, or Gulph of *California*, particularly *La Isla de Santa Cruz*, i.e. *Holy Cross Island*, and *La Isla de Gigante*, or the *Giants-Isle*, both of small Compass: California, being somewhat more remote, is wash'd on the East by the *Purple Sea*, which separates it from *New Mexico*, as also, on the South, West, and North, by the *Pacifick Sea*. Several Authors have doubted, whether it is a Peninsula, or an Island, and some have taken it for the former; but that Scruple has been since remov'd by the Experience of Navigators. This Island was first discover'd by Ferdinand Cortez, A.D. 1535, and is situated between the 23 and 46th Degr. of Northern Latitude . . . It is apparently the most spacious Island of all Northern *America* and even one of the greatest in the whole World.[1]

Moll's work contains two maps showing California as an island. He is so enamored of islands that he even discusses the old Atlantis theory, and points out that America is also believed by some to be Solomon's Ophir.

By 1709, Moll has grown no wiser. Kino's new deductions have apparently not reached his ears. In his *The Compleat Geographer*, in a section on California, he continues to sound old-fashioned enough to be writing a hundred years earlier. Like certain Spanish writers of the eighteenth century (pages 235 ff.), he also equates the whole island of California with Drake's New Albion:

> California, or New Albion/   Is in the South Sea, on the back of New-Mexico, and it was long dubious whether a Peninsula or an Island, but at last the *Spaniards* sail'd quite round, and made a Map of it, which shows it to extend from 24 to 36 Degrees of North Latitude, lying North West and South-east, being above 500 Leagues in Length,

and so on in Ascensión's vein.

However, more practical Englishmen—buccaneers who had touched at Cape San Lucas—were showing a healthly dubiety toward the California island claims. In *A New Voyage Round the World* (1697), William Dampier suggested that the ambiguity about the "Lake of California (for so the Sea, Channel or Streight, between that and the Continent is called)" was a Spanish ploy:

> I do believe that the Spaniards do not care to have this Lake discovered, for fear lest the European Nations should get knowledge of it, and by that means visit the Mines of New Mexico.[2]

Dampier sailed again to the South Sea, as pilot to Captain Woodes Rogers, in 1708. Rogers displayed similar skepticism in the section "California Described" in *A Cruising Voyage Round the World,* published in 1712:

> It is not yet certainly known whether it be an Island, or joins to the Continent, nor did either our Time or Circumstances allow us to attempt the Discovery. I heard from the *Spaniards*, that some of their Nation had sail'd as far up betwixt *California* and the Main, as Lat. 42 N, where meeting with Shoal Water, and abundance of Islands, they durst not venture any further; So that if this be true, in all Probability it joins to the Continent, a little further to the Northward; for Shoal Water and Islands is a general Sign of being near some main Land; but the *Spaniards* having more Territories in this Part of the World than they know how to manage, they are not curious of further Discoveries. The *Manila* Ships bound to *Acapulco* often make this Coast in the Latitude of 40 North, and I never heard of any that discover'd it farther to the Northward. So old Draughts make it to join to the Land of *Jesso*, but all this being as yet undetermin'd, I shall not take upon me to affirm whether it's an Island, or joins to the Continent. The *Dutch* say, they formerly took a *Spanish* Vessel in those Seas, which had sail'd round *California* and found it to be an Island; but this Account cannot be depended on, and I choose to believe it joins to the Continent.[3]

This account was translated into Spanish by the Jesuit historian Miguel Venegas in 1757, in the final debunking of the myth in his famous *History of California*.

The island-versus-peninsula controversy must have still engaged the London gossips in 1726. Jonathan Swift took an ironic shot at it, locating his Brobdingnag on "a great island or continent (for we know not whether)" off the northwest coast. This was depicted on his fictional map in early editions of *Gulliver's Travels* (*see* Plate 48). The mapmaker

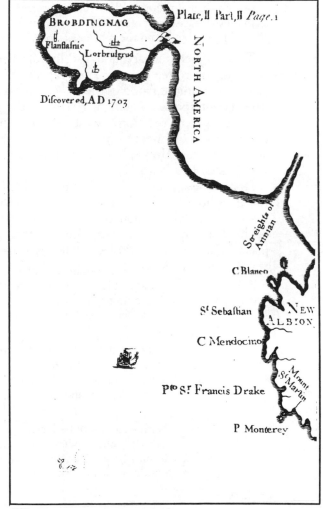

PLATE 48. The insular/peninsular debate was satirized in Jonathan Swift's Brobdingnag, as depicted in this "map" from early editions of *Gulliver's Travels* (1726). *Photograph and permission by the British Library.*

has opted for a jutting peninsula not quite severed from the mainland. Satirizing the fallacious reasoning of imaginative geographers, Swift had his stolid Captain Gulliver indulge in such an exercise:

> The country described. A Proposal for correcting modern Maps.
>
> I now intend to give the reader a short description of the country . . . The whole extent of this prince's dominions reacheth about six thousand miles in length, and from three to five in breadth; whence I cannot but conclude, that our geographers of *Europe* are in a great error, by supposing nothing but sea between *Japan* and *California*: for it was ever my opinion, that there must be a balance of earth to counterpoise the great continent of Tartary; and therefore they ought to correct their maps and charts, by joining this vast tract of land to the northwest part of America, wherein I shall be ready to lend them my assistance.[4]

This represents a marvellous garbling of what must have been current gossip at the coffee houses. The very long, very narrow shape of the prince's dominions parodies the dimensions of the "Isle of California." The "counterpoise" argument resembles the pseudo-reasoning of the enthusiasts about the North-West Passage. Here, too, the "restoration" of the whole northwest corner—which had been removed by Briggs, *et al.*—is advocated by Gulliver, as indeed it was by real live cartographers like Buache (*see* Plate 51).

Perhaps resistance to the breaking of the island dream added fuel to the great hoax of what history calls the South Sea Bubble. This was a stock scam in which thousands of investors lost their money when the bubble burst in 1720. It occasioned Swift to pen his very long satiric poem "The South-Sea Project." Here is a sampling:

> Ye wise philosophers, explain
> What magic makes our money rise,
> When dropt into the Southern main:
> Or do these jugglers cheat our eyes?
> . . . .
>
> Thus the deluded bankrupt raves;
> Puts all upon a desperate bet;
> Then plunges in the Southern waves,
> Dipt over head and ears—in debt.
> . . . .
>
> With eager haste he longs to rove
> In that fantastic scene, and thinks
> It must be some enchanted grove;
> And in he leaps, and down he sinks.
> . . . .

> Each poor subscriber to the sea
> Sinks down at once, and there he lies:
> Directors fall as well as they,
> Their fall is but a trick to rise.
> . . . .
> Thus by directors we are told,
> "Pray, gentlemen, believe your eyes;
> Our ocean's covered o'er with gold,
> Look round, and see how thick it lies,"
> . . . .
> The nation then too late will find,
> Computing all their cost and trouble,
> Directors' promises but wind,
> South Sea at best a mighty bubble.[5]

Enthusiasts would go on ignoring any hint destructive of their island dream until well into the eighteenth century. The cartographers aided and abetted them in the delusion. As R. V. Tooley notes:

> Moll's view was followed by Senex and Overton in England, by De Fer and Chatelain in France, Keulen in Holland, and by the great German firms of Homann and Seutter up to about 1750. Van der Aa 1715–1730 tried to have the best of both worlds, issuing maps of America with California both as an island and as a peninsula so that his patrons could take their choice.[6]

But all the time that the dream-mongers were hanging onto the island myth, a few level-headed thinkers kept the faith. One of these was the great French mapmaker Guillaume de Lisle. Tooley says of him:

> His standard was high, his approach in physical geography scientific, and his examination of original sources careful. He was the first to correct the longitudes of America, and to discard the well established fallacy of California as an island.[7]

In a letter published by a scholarly journal in 1700, De Lisle discusses the question "whether California is an Island or a part of the continent." Unable to make on-site observations himself, he aims to seek clarification from recorded facts alone. His strategy is to review those facts historically as they emerged. He traces Cortés' discovery through Ulloa's dilemma. He comes at last to more recent events giving rise to the theory of a huge island of California:

> When it was found that the sea turned back to the Orient about 43 degrees, there began a belief that this sea went to join the one that had been discovered between California and New Mexico, making an Island

of California. It was the Spanish who began [this belief]; all others believed that the Sea which separates California from New Mexico was a Gulf which terminated in a cul de sac; accordingly they gave it the name of Red or Vermillion Sea, because, said Wytflet, of its resemblance to the Red Sea which separates Arabia from Egypt. But the Dutch, having taken a Marine Chart from the Spanish—as reported by Janssonius in his *Maritime World*—they accepted that California was an island, and since that time they have generally represented it in that way.[8]

Scholar that he is, De Lisle has pinpointed the sole basis for the Isle of California maps. He goes on to expose the flimsiness of this foundation:

It is therefore on the faith of this Spanish Map that they believed and still believe that California is an island: but it is a question of judging the worth of this Map, and of knowing if it was made on good and faithful recollections: and it is of this that I have difficulty persuading myself, because if that thing was sure and constant among the Spanish, their Maps would be uniform on that point.

De Lisle then considers the responsible authority of Joannes de Laet, who wrote during the period the Spanish map was taken (*see* page 292):

And then there is Laet who says that it is an uncertain thing up to now; that one sees, indeed, some old Geographic and Hydrographic Maps which make it [California] an island and which separate it from the Continent by a strait fairly wide at the beginning, but which narrows as it continues; that furthermore in the modern maps it is more often joined to the Continent, that it is not separated from it, and he believes so little that it is an Island, that he enquires into what could have given rise to this error . . .

PLATE 49 (at right).   California's attachment to the continent was reasserted at the beginning of the eighteenth century by Kino. His view is represented by No. IV of this composite in Diderot's *Encyclopédie* (1770). With the exception of Cortés' initiation of the island myth, the different stages of the long insularity/peninsularity debate are assembled in this composite:

I: The peninsular view that held sway to the beginning of the seventeenth century. To this map Buache added an asterisk (to the right of "Veloa" on the 30th parallel) to indicate a place he believed to be flooded at full tide—which then made the southern part into an island. (Discussion on page 319).

II: The island phase prevailing during most of the seventeenth century, represented by Sanson's map. (Discussion on page 294.)

III: Doubt of the island theory expressed by De Lisle. (Discussion on pages 313 ff., 155.)

IV: Kino's return to belief in California's peninsularity. (Discussion on pages 297-302.)

V.   The final phase—confirmation by field experience of the Jesuits of the peninsular nature of California. (Discussion on pages 323-25.)

Photograph by the British Library.

Details of these maps appear in context: I, page 321; II, page 294; III, page 321; IV, page 302 (English version of Kino's map).

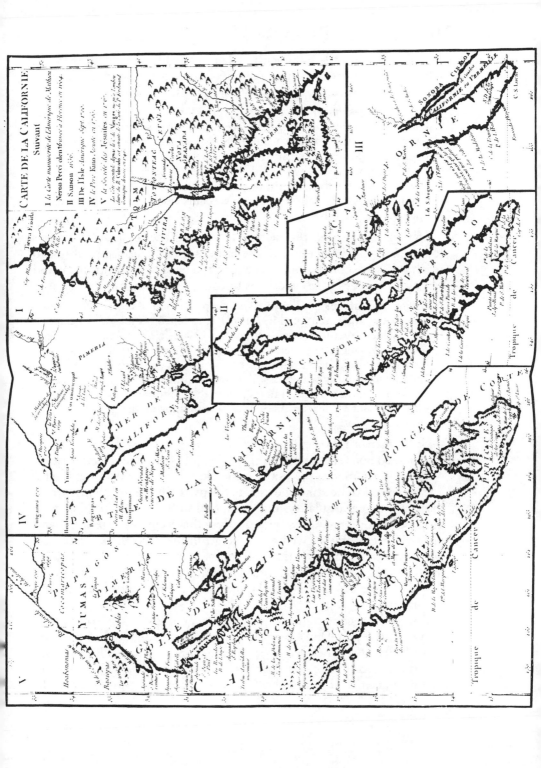

Although De Lisle cannot carry out any field work of his own, he recognizes there are responsible observers already in the area. He relies heavily on the recent testimony of the Jesuits:

At last, the Jesuits who were with . . . the Pimas in 1690 sent word to Europe that at the spot where they were the sea was so narrow that they distinctly saw the coast of California; that they hoped that in going higher up, they would find either that California is joined to the lands of New Spain, which they have ardently wished to learn, but which they haven't been able to establish, or that the sea is so narrow in this place that in a short time in little boats they would be able to pass easily from one shore to the other.

Having reevaluated the facts and weighed the arguments, he has found enough evidence to call the island view in question, but not to reach a positive conclusion. Faced with the need to make his maps and globes, he decides to use methods to convey his open mind:

On my maps and globes I have taken the precaution of representing the coast as cut and interrupted in this place, as much on the side of Cape Mendocino as on the side of the Red Sea. I have left in these two places as though stepping stones [ellipsis marks or a broken line] during an interrupted work, and I have not believed it necessary to make up my mind about a thing which is still so uncertain; therefore I have made California neither an Island nor a part of the Continent, and I will stay with this point of view until I have seen something more positive than I have seen to date.

So his map of 1700 depicts Baja California strictly as it was known by actual, incomplete, exploration (Plate 49, No. III). The eastern (inner) coastline runs only to the nook of the Gulf, where an opening is left.

This device is the same one used in the two earlier mind changes from insularity to peninsularity and back again. It is close to the maps produced in the post-Ulloa period, when the original Cortésian island view was beginning to give way to the peninsula hypothesis. Then, the feature of an unclosed "brazo" had appeared at the crotch on Castillo's map of 1541 (Plate 21). Such unclosed inlets as on the maps of Battista Agnese (Plate 22) and Diogo Homem (Plate 24) helped handle the uncertainty.

During the second transition—from the peninsula back to the island view—in the post-Drake period, cautious cartographers had used the same device of an unclosed inlet (see the Hondius maps, Plates 38 and 39). It is not surprising, then, that the device should be used once more in this transitional period back to the theory of peninsularity. In common with the earlier maps, De Lisle gives the Colorado River a mouth separate from the "brazo." De Lisle also returns to the name given by Alarcón—Río de Bonaguia.

There are other features on De Lisle's map evocative of old controversies. De Lisle has labeled Ulloa's Cabo de Engaño on his map. This was the point of Ulloa's final disappointment in his quest on the outside littoral for a strait. Here De Lisle has left another unfinished opening, trending to the northeast (*see* page 321), with the legend in French:

> Gulf which has not been well discovered but which the Moderns believe very deep.

In one respect, however, Ascensión's fantastic island was indelibly imprinted on the cultural consciousness. As he abandons insularity, De Lisle does not revert to the dimensions of "California" in the post-Ulloa period. On his map of 1722 (Plate 50), the demarcation of his California mimics the boundaries of the huge island, prefiguring the northern limit of Alta California as we know it today.

The De Lisle map of 1700 is included in the composite map of California in Diderot's *Encyclopédie* of 1770. This composite map (Plate 49) shows (1) the early post-Cortés-Ulloa peninsula version; (2) the California-as-an-island view of the seventeenth century; (3) De Lisle's equivocal rendering that could fall either way; (4) Father Kino's map; and (5) a Jesuit map of 1767 depicting the final phase of peninsularity. If the series had included as number one a map showing Cortés' island version, the montage would have been complete, summarizing two centuries of vacillation. But as we have seen, Cortés' initiating impulse was not usually related to the second manifestation. The theory of insularity then tended to be attributed to Drake.

Nevertheless, as has been discussed on page 292, the *Encyclopédie* did acknowledge the existence of the earlier island theory. De Laet was cited as observing that "from the year 1539 there have been Spaniards who have imagined that it was an island," and that he had seen maps supporting this belief.

Despite De Lisle's clear thinking, the island concept still would not lie down. In 1753, Philippe Buache reconsidered the question in his *Considérations Géographiques et Physiques*. His methods are in marked contrast to the scientific mode of enquiry of De Lisle. Buache relies heavily on anecdotal arguments:

> If M. De Lisle the father had known what we know now, he would without doubt have considered with more attention . . . the account of a

Pilot of whom he speaks, and who had assured M. Froger . . . that he had sailed around California.[9]

One of the more suspect of these anecdotes based on hearsay of hearsay is offered by Buache to "resolve" the controversy:

Here is an important fact on this subject of which M. Ellis has given us notice in 1748. "A man," he says, "of great intelligence and very

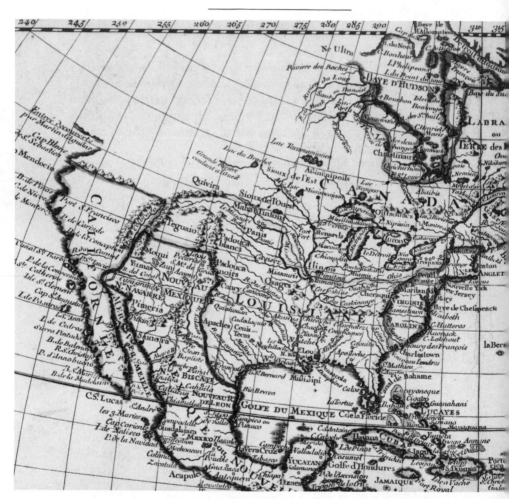

PLATE 50. The island-of-California theory has been totally abandoned in this map by Guillaume de Lisle of 1722. But the huge size of Ascensión's island has been retained in De Lisle's drawing of California's boundaries (Discussion on page 317.) *Photograph and permission by the British Library.*

truthful, having arrived only a few months ago from Portugal (to England), has assured us that . . . he had met an explorer who . . . had been shipwrecked on the northern coast of California, where he had had occasion to observe that this land was at the same time an Island and a Peninsula, the small Isthmus which joined it to the Continent being always submerged at the time of high tides.

This specious compromise reminds us of the way Balthasar de Obregón straddled the issue (page 177). Buache clearly leapt upon this story as a way to have his cake and eat it too:

It [California] could be considered as an Island, at least at certain times, and thus one would not be entirely wrong to speak of it on that basis.

He then proceeds straight to the job of locating the isthmus—without any compunction that he has no data on which to base his conclusion. He simply picks a likely place out of the hat:

But in which spot of California to place this little Isthmus? A large and splendid Spanish manuscript map of all of America which has been made in 1604, and which is at the King's Library . . . represents California with a small Isthmus in 30 degrees latitude . . .

He has the nerve to turn one of De Lisle's suspended judgments to his own ends:

[It is] precisely at this Gulf (next to "Cap D'Enganno") about which Guillaume Delisle said on his Map of 1700, that it had *not yet been well discovered*, and that *the Moderns believed it very deep*. It is therefore in this place that the southern part of California is an Island at the time of high tides, and holds to the Continent at all other times, as it is with the Mount of S. Michel of Normandie, of which the high tides make an Island.

He is "scholarly" enough to know that one must back up one's arguments with illustrations:

To render all this more evident, I give . . . the reduction of a part of the Spanish Map of America of 1604, where one sees the little Isthmus in question.

On this map, at a narrow place on Baja's peninsula, Buache places an asterisk. The footnote to this asterisk reads:

Isthmus covered in high tides. See the *Considerations* &c.

This map may be seen in the composite in Diderot's *Encyclopédie* (Plate 49, No. I), which follows a composite put together by Buache himself to demonstrate the different theories (*see* page 321). This is clear from the statement in his text where he says he presents the Spanish map of 1604 "on the same sheet . . . with the first idea of Guillaume de Lisle, & the Map of 1702 of P. Kino, where are also found the Missions that the Jesuits have just formed."

Buache is no ignoramus. He has marshalled all the counter arguments and evidence in an effort to make his own predilection for the island notion stick. But his map of North America (Plate 51) parades his lack of critical acuity. He had fallen for a hoax published in the *Monthly Miscellany of Memoirs for the Curious* in 1708. That letter, actually written by some wag like Daniel Defoe, purported to be from a Spanish admiral who had negotiated the North-West Passage.[10] Buache gullibly enshrines various such extravagant claims in mythic figments on his map. To the huge incursive Mer de l'Ouest featured by Jean Baptiste Nolin and Pierre Mortier around 1700,[11] Buache adds the Oriental Amazonia of Fousang; the "Grande Eau" of Cabrillo, Urdaneta and the French explorers; and the open inlets associated with Aguilar and Fuca. These hydrographic features connect with lakes and rivers strung out across the continent, expressing the still vital yearning for a northern strait.

But there are bounds even to the fancies and crotchets of romantics. Buache's choice of a map of the pre-island phase to show his isthmus has brought his outline of California a good deal closer to reality.

Can this mean that the ending of the California island myth might be in sight?

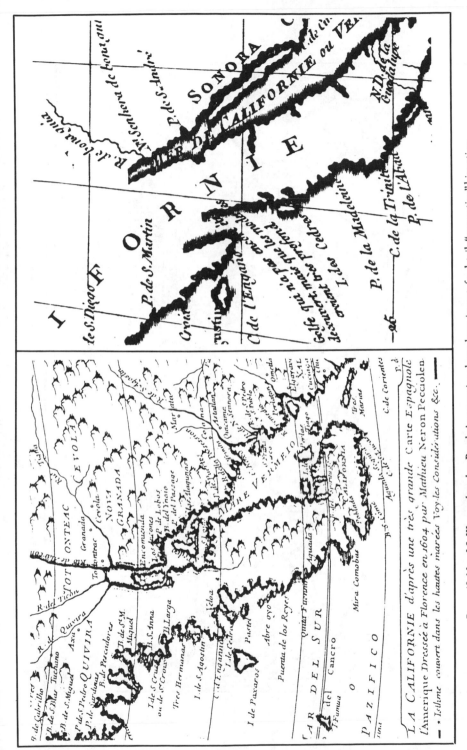

PLATE 49, Nos. I & III, were based on Buache's composite, shown here, in part, for details "supporting" his notion of California as a tidal island: (a) his "isthmus" near Veloa, marked by an asterisk; (b) De Lisle's "Gulf which has not been explored." *The Roy V. Boswell Collection for the History of Cartography*, CSU, Fullerton.

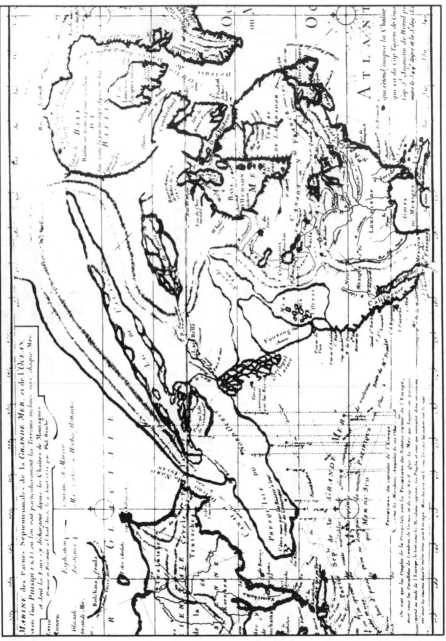

PLATE 51.   California looks reasonably close to reality on this map by Philippe Buache of 1753—except for the huge Mer de l'Ouest (Sea of the West) at the northern boundary. But mythic figments abound, such as "Grande Eau," "Entrée d'Aguilar," "Détroit d'Anian," and even "Fousang." Elements of mythic waterways make Buache useful. Largest is explicit. (Drawings on pages 168, 317, 320.) Photograph and permission by the British Library.

Chapter XXIX

CALIFORNIA IS NOT AN ISLAND, BUT . . .

Many of Kino's closest colleagues in the mainland missions doubted and forgot his views, as we have seen. Fathers Niel, De Campos, and Velarde were among those reverting to pre-Kino thinking. The old ideas clung hardest to life in Mexico. There, according to the historian Miguel Venegas:

> Some did not scruple to treat the discoveries of father Kino as Chimeras, notwithstanding the applause they met with in Europe.[1]

But one group did keep faith with Kino—the brethren he had left behind in the missions of Baja California. It was the hope of keeping closer contact with them that had led to the quest for the land bridge in the first place. These men obviously admired and shared Kino's love of learning, reason, and empiricism. Being of a more experimental persuasion, they planned to put Kino's theory to the test. They appreciated that this might more readily be done from Baja than across the "Sea of Sand."

In 1721, twenty odd years before Father Sedelmayr expressed his retrograde opinions, Father Ugarte had set out to probe the Gulf. His declared intent was to ascertain:

> Whether California was joined to the continent of New Spain as Father Kino affirmed; or whether, on the contrary, it was an island; and that the gulf issued through some unknown passage into the South sea, either on this or the other side of the mouth of the river Colorado, according to the opinion that prevailed in Mexico.[2]

The diehards still believed that such a strait or channel "had been the passage for those vessels which were said formerly to have sailed quite around California," and that "the galleons from the Philippine islands passed through a channel into the gulf of California in their voyage to New Spain." This view, so often implied, is finally articulated.

Ugarte set sail in a large ship built for the purpose. According to the account in Venegas, he proved to his satisfaction that the Gulf was closed:

> Ugarte had a clear and distinct view of the Cape of California joining to the neighboring mountain, and separated from the coast of Pimeria only

by the river . . . The pilot who went on shore in the pinnace at several parts in order to make a complete drawing of it for his chart, was equally convinced that the cape was the extremity of the gulf of California, and that the waters beyond it were those of the river Colorado. By the sounding there appeared no signs of a channel which would have to be large and deep: but four or five fathom was the greatest depth. There is no appearance of a channel as far as eye can reach; which, in a northern direction, everywhere sees the land.

Ugarte corrected the prior interpretation of rapidly rising tides as evidence of a strait. The phenomenon was recognized as the collision of sea and river forces—the tidal bore:

The dangerous and extraordinary tides in those parts, as on both coasts, are a farther proof that the gulf is confined there: for had it any discharge or outlet towards the South sea, its waters would not rise with such rapidity, or to such a height, if they were not contracted at the extremity of their course, and at the end of the streight [i.e. the Gulf] checked by those of the river Colorado.

But Ugarte's ship was too large for the shoals and marshes, and the pinnace too flimsy for the tides and tempests. The expedition decided "it would be rather rashness than courage to proceed." Thus, even after this voyage doubters remained. The crackpots of the island fallacy were as zealous as ever in defense of their pet dream.

Another quarter of a century passed. At last the time grew ripe for fact to triumph. Despite last-minute flarings of the island flame, like that of Sedelmayr in 1744, the powerful old myth seemed ready to be put to rest.

In 1746, another member of the Society of Jesus from Baja California, Fernando Consag, again sailed to the head of the Gulf. This time the group rowed there in canoes. Once more Consag proved that the Baja finger was a peninsula, as his journal indicates in an almost offhand manner. Ironically, and confusingly, he continues to call the waterway a strait, even in the moment of disproof. Yet the notion that the "streight"—the Gulf—was a cul-de-sac appears taken for granted in the assertions highlighted by added italics:

[July] 9th, [1746] . . . From this corner the shore is entirely level, marshy in several parts at spring tides; and in hard weather overflowed. All the way from San Phelipe to the river Colorado there is neither bay nor watering place.

10th, We made little progress this day, a strong N. E. wind blowing from the shore, which was contrary to us: the points in that part running N. E.

and N. N. E. *the streight closing here*. At noon we got ashore with great
difficulty, the water being shallow and a great sea running along this
coast, which is extremely barren . . .

11th, Made but little way, and came to some red marshes, whence we
concluded we were near the mouth of the river Colorado or red river . . .
Under this difficulty we came to an anchor facing an island, which forms
a creek at *the end of the streight* in the form of a bow: the water even here
differs from that of the sea . . .

14th, The smallest canoe . . . brought intelligence, that all the people
and the canoes were safe in the same outlet of the river Colorado . . .

18th, Went up the entrance of the river Colorado . . .

19th, Continued the discovery of the river . . .

25th, *The survey of the gulph*, or sea of California *being carried to its utmost
limit*, we steered . . . to the harbor, from whence we had sailed . . .

. . . Let it be observed, that in this journal we have taken no notice of the
latitude, this being exactly set down in the map of this survey.[3]

Slight as these references are, a single, definite, conclusion emerged
from the findings of this voyage:

It was evident, beyond all possibility of doubt, that California is a
peninsula, joining to the continent of New Spain; and that the extremity
of the gulf, is the river Colorado, which divides the former from the latter.

No doubt the map, more than the journal, of this survey convinced the
last doubting stragglers. The map published in Venegas was Consag's. It
was then incorporated into the montage in Diderot's *Encyclopédie*
(Plate 49, No. V).

On the mainland, in New Mexico, the doubting or ignorant Father
Sedelmayr now readily accepted the results of Consag's survey. Writing
to his rector, José de Echeverria, in 1747, Sedelmayr excuses himself for
his dated ideas by placing the responsibility elsewhere:

Father Fernando has given us the desired information that California is a
peninsula. And although Father Eusebio Francisco Kino saw and constantly
affirmed this, yet because Father Agustin de Campos contradicted it, the
thing remained doubtful, which is now fully settled.[4]

Even then, however, there was not sufficient hard evidence, appar-
ently, to clinch the question for good and all. Twenty years after
Consag's survey, there were still some lingering doubts to be dispelled.
Another Jesuit father, Wenceslaus Linck, probed overland the area
toward the crotch of the Gulf from his mission of San Borja in 1766.
This was the last such effort before the Jesuits were expelled in 1767.

Linck, however, failed to reach the mouth of the Colorado because the pack animals were without shoes. To have continued would have meant ruining their hooves and crippling them. Linck writes:

> We have asked the pagan Indians whom we encountered recently various questions which have been most difficult to get across to them. Asked about the Colorado they gave evidence of knowing quite a bit about the river itself, but they are totally ignorant about the mouth of the stream. They indicate with very expressive gestures that the Pacific Ocean reaches close to the Colorado—or, to put it in other words, the river runs close to the shores of the Pacific, thus forming an isthmus, as the narrow strip of land which lies between the waters of the ocean and the river might well be termed.[5]

Although this upholds the newly established case for peninsulartiy, the "narrow strip of land" between river and ocean seems barely to remove this view from the old ambiguous or fence-straddling theories.

In official circles, however, after Consag's probe, there was no turning back to anything like the pre-Kino misconceptions. Experience and reasoning had triumphed over the dream of ages.

As if to put the final stamp on the empirical view and decide the question for all eternity, Ferdinand VI, in a royal decree of 1747, proclaimed:

"California is not an island."

So when the Preface to the English translation of Venegas's *History of California* was published in 1758, the great topographical mystery was taken as solved. It will be noted, however, that in the summary of the long controversy, as quoted below, no mention is made of Cortés' origination of the island theory. Once more his part has been forgotten; and the origin of California's naming has been lost entirely. The discontinuity in transmitted knowledge is one of the wonders of this early history of California. The quick forgetting of Cabrillo's voyage is a case in point. How irked and grieved we are by the losses, misplacements, withholding, or destruction of vital documents. And, in contrast, how amazed we are by the endurance of myth and dream in the popular or racial memory, now submerging, now resurfacing, as triggered by events.

Here is the summary from the Preface:

> The country of California, taking that denomination in its most extensive sense, has been long discovered; notwithstanding which, it was till lately, but very imperfectly known. Other nations have visited its coasts as well as the Spaniards; but as they only touched upon them, a true and

full description of this vast region could be expected from the Spaniards alone. The first accounts published by them, represented it truly, and as it is, a peninsula; but upon the authority of a Spanish chart, found accidentally by the Dutch, and of the authenticity of which, there never were, or indeed could be, any proofs obtained, an opinion prevailed, that California was an island, and the contrary assertion was treated even by the ablest geographers, as a vulgar error . . . In this indeterminate state, the thing stood till the beginning of the present century, when father Kino published his discovery, founded on his passage by land, from New Mexico into California; by which it appeared that the Vermillion sea was no more than a gulf or bay, though of a large extent, and that California was really a peninsula, as the earlier Spanish writers had described it. Thus we see that old opinions, more especially when they are grounded on matters of fact, are not to be hastily rejected, that inquisitive and even judicious men are capable of being misled.[6]

The resolution of the island controversy did not, however, settle the question of the Straits of Anian and the configuration of the coastline to the north:

But the principal point that has been always had in view, with respect to this country, is its boundary towards the north, which has never yet been ascertained. There has been mention made of a country, and of a strait of Anian, which is supposed to separate it from Asia. Others have affirmed, that California continually stretching to the north west, approached very near to the north east of Tartary, and that the straits of Anian were to be sought on that side. Some again have affirmed, these straits are altogether imaginary.

The British certainly didn't believe the Strait of Anian to be imaginary. They were still looking for the North-West Passage. In 1776, Captain James Cook was instructed to look for it while in the Pacific:

Proceed in as direct a course as you can to the coast of New Albion . . . Proceed northward along the coast as far as the latitude of 65°, or farther . . . and . . . explore such rivers or inlets as may appear to be of a considerable extent and pointing towards Hudsons or Baffins Bays.[7]

Reaching the Oregon coast, Cook surveyed northward to the strait that Bering had died exploring in 1741. Cook found his way blocked by an impenetrable barrier of ice. No ship would pass from ocean to ocean across the north until Roald Amundsen took the Gjöa through between 1903 and 1906.

But in the year Venegas' work was published, Mexican interest was all focussed on the long-disputed and mysterious territory so tantalizingly

glimpsed by Cabrillo, Drake, Vizcaíno and Cermeño. The Preface of
the translation touches on the conflicting rumors and reports that had
cropped up in the records over the two centuries of wary contact,
contradictions that now needed answering:

> In consequence of its being so imperfectly examined, several other
> contradictions, or at least seeming contradictions, have been advanced
> concerning it. There are relations, which make the coasts of California
> intolerable, from the piercing cold. There are again accounts, which say
> these coasts are insupportably hot. Some represent it as a region sterile,
> void of water, and not only unimproved, but unimproveable chiefly from
> this defect. Others speak of it, as fruitful, pleasant, and having very fine
> rivers. Complaints are made of its shores, as difficult and dangerous,
> embarrassed with rocks and shoals, and without so much as tolerable
> ports. In opposition to these, we find it celebrated for a fine beautiful
> country towards the sea, into which several large rivers fall, at the
> entrance of which are many large and fertile islands, and both in them
> and the continent, several safe and very commodious havens. The varia-
> tions are as great, in reference to the worth, as in regard to the face of this
> extensive peninsula; if we rely on some writers, it is a poor barren
> despicable tract, which scarce deserves the protection it has met with. Yet
> as good judges, and who had equal opportunities of being acquainted with
> it, alledge, that it is capable of various kinds of cultivation, that there are
> incontestible marks of its containing rich mines, and that there is a
> profitable pearl fishery upon the coast.

In actual fact the contradictions here mentioned only *seem* mutually
exclusive. As we now know, the apparent contradictions are but
reflections of an extraordinary diversity in climate and topography running all the way from the tip of Lower California to Cabo Blanco or the
present northerly state line at 42°; and from the shores of the Pacific
Ocean to the interior mountain chains and deserts to the east. Some of
this was soon to be discovered by the first band of colonists from Mexico
to be ordered and cajoled into the mysterious region of Alta California.

This Spanish colonization was the direct result of the Jesuits'
reassessment of the area, through their practice of careful observation
and honest thinking. But it was the Franciscans who were charged with
the responsibility of accompanying the overland expedition and estab-
lishing settlements at appropriate havens like San Diego and Monterey.
They set out with Gaspar de Portolá via Baja in 1769. Under the
leadership of Father Junípero Serra they began at once to build their
rosary of missions along the coast.

About the same time that the coastal thrust was under way, the Franciscan missionary Father Francisco Garcés set out from the interior mission of San Xavier del Bac. His aim was to push westward across the arid stretch of land north of the Gulf, which Kino had failed to penetrate. Often disoriented by thirst and heat, he managed to wander across this "Camino del Diablo" until he came in sight of the "Sierra Azul." In these now-called San Jacinto Mountains he glimpsed possible passes that he guessed would give access to the South-Sea coast. And in 1774 he led Juan Bautista de Anza into these mountains, thence into the "Golden Basin" and the newly-founded mission of San Gabriel.

The hazardous ramparts of the "island" fastness had at last been breached.

Yet even then the settlers discovered that in effect California remained an island. Even as they began to build their earthly paradise, they found themselves isolated behind barriers not just of the rocky, stormy, foggy coastline, and the huge desert area to south and west, but of the soon-to-be-discovered mountain ranges to the north, and the huge, snow-capped sierras to the east. It would take another half a century for the scaling of that eastern wall to be attempted, as the great transcontinental westward movement toward California began.

When Jedediah Smith and other fur trappers from the east penetrated the region, quickly followed by such men as Bidwell, Carson, Frémont, and Beale, remnants of the old myth of straits still lingered in the form of fabled waterways supposed to disembogue into the Pacific.

Then, suddenly, in 1849, the Amazon Isle fulfilled her promise. Every California schoolchild knows the story of the discovery of gold, of the immigrants' yearning for the promised land of El Dorado, and of the ordeals they suffered to overcome the awesome obstacles set in their way. For a brief, ecstatic moment it seemed as if the old myth had come true. Then just as speedily it evaporated. In a few short years the gold rush was over.

But this time disappointment was swiftly followed by reconciliation to the pastoral paradise that California promised to become with careful husbanding. The policies of President James K. Polk brought California into the Union, and the great exodus from east to west, to the Promised Land, was on.

In an important respect this realistic paradise remained an "island." California's beauties and bounties are manifestations of an unique ecology. In her book entitled *An Island Called California*, Elna Bakker demonstrates that topography and climate combine to create distinct natural communities clearly distinguishable from the rest of the continent:

> There is ecological validity in thinking of California in insular terms. Not only is it isolated by a combination of topographic and climatic features, it differs from the rest of the continent in a number of significant ways . . . involving . . . both species and the natural communities where they live . . .[8]

Over the last century California's own native variety and abundance have been supplemented by importations from every corner of the world. Almost everything on earth grows somewhere in California, adding greatly to her natural wealth.

Yet even when California entered the mature phase of her development in the last half of the nineteenth century, the old myth continued to crop up in the oddest contexts. In 1860, General E. D. Townsend wrote in his Diary:

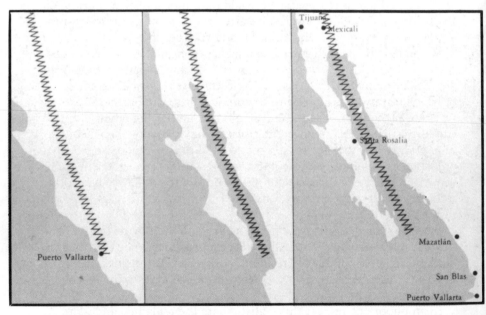

PLATES 52a & b.   California may, one distant day, indeed become an island, as suggested by (above) this illustration of how the Gulf and Baja were created in the geologic past; and (right) the speculative rendering of California on this map of plate tectonics fifty million years hence. (Discussion on pages 332, 151-52.) *Photograph and permission by (a) Lane Book Company, Menlo Park, California (from Robert Iacopi's* Earthquake Country, *1964); and (b) the British Museum (Natural History).*

We had a long, hot and sandy ride . . . our object being to reach Kern
River. It has been a tradition, and is recorded in an old book written by
the Jesuits on this Coast, that the part of California west of the Tulare
Valley, in which we now are, was formerly an Island, and that this Valley
was the bed of a large sheet of water, probably, part of the ocean. There
are evident signs of this being the case, all along our road today.[9]

In this fascinating item, myth and science stand abreast. Empirical
observations of this sort were pieced together to produce a remarkable
geologic history of the state. Geologists have concluded that California
was under the ocean for many millions of years. Then the present
littoral ranges were uplifted—virtually rising like island Venuses out of
the foam.

If there are islands in California's geologic past, there are islands in
her geologic future, too. Studies in plate tectonics suggest that California, in one sense, is already separated from the continent right now,
since separate plates—the continental North American and the Pacific
Plates—converge along the great San Andreas fault. The one plate has
overridden the other, so that the area west of the line drawn from the
crotch of the Gulf of California to San Francisco is riding piggyback
aboard the eastern edge. This dynamic interplay is causing the volcanic
and earthquake activity which keeps California continually stirred up.

These forces perpetuate the northward drift begun several million
years ago. That movement has already detached the east coast of Baja
California from the Mexican mainland. The process is seen to be
continuing in the Salton Trough, from the head of the Gulf through the

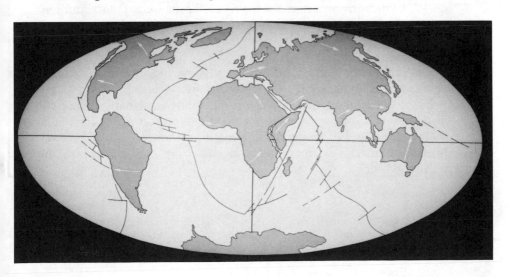

Salton Sea (*see* Plate 52a). It was in this area, north of the Ancón de San Andrés, that the old stories of a Strait of California took root. Such a monumental drift, geologists tell us, will shift all the area west of the San Andreas fault up beyond San Francisco toward Alaska. In many millions of years time, this chunk of land will be severed completely from the continent (*see* Plate 52b).

This speculation also is a form of myth-making. But it is myth-making at its most responsible. The informed imagination has created a possible "explanation" to account for limited observed phenomena. That supposition has now to withstand the deliberate accumulation of quested evidence. If it doesn't stand up, it must be modified, or scrapped to try again. The geologic "island" theory has been continuously tested and corrected throughout this century, and will go on being so. There is no vested psychological interest in the myth-hypothesis per se. The chief rewards of the researchers are the delights of curiosity, suspense, and quest; the enjoyment of the exercise of reason and imagination; and the satisfaction of completion, when evidence clicks into place.

But there are other kinds of mythologizers still among us who may have a bearing on California's future. These are the myth-enthusiasts, lovers of myths for their own sake. Seizing on this awesome geologic theory, they have whipped it up into a sort of new Isle-of-California dream. A nightmare, we might rather say. For it is not an ideal island of gold, pearls, and liberated women that they have in mind, but an apocalypse of annihilation. Enraptured by such fantasies, some predict that California will break off into the ocean at the next great earthquake. Others envision it as collapsing under the weight of the millions crowding across her borders seeking the gold of her sun, her commerce, her groves, her beaches, her thousand golden hills.

For myths are ultimately indestructible. Their spore lies dormant in the subsoil of the culture, awaiting only the proper combination of factors to sprout out again, or mutate into new forms.

But it is not alone in extravagant or fanatic imaginations that the myth survives. As long as there are people to project on California all their dreams and expectations for material well-being and personal liberty, there can be no ending of this story of California as an enchanted isle.

NOTES
BIBLIOGRAPHY
INDEX

FOOTNOTES

INTRODUCTION

[1]*History of the Northwest Coast, Vol. I, 1543–1800,* in *The Works of Hubert Howe Bancroft* as Vol. XXVII (San Francisco: A. L. Bancroft & Co., 1884), p. 4. Abbreviation: Bancroft, Northwest Coast.

[2]"The Northern Mystery," treated in Chapters I to IV of Bancroft, Northwest Coast. Also Chapters I to III of Bancroft's *History of California, Vol. I, 1542–1800,* in *The Works* as Vol. XVIII. Abbreviation: Bancroft, California. Also Chapters I to IV of *History of the North Mexican States and Texas, Vol. I, 1531–1800,* in *The Works* as Vol. XV. Abbreviation: Bancroft, North Mex. & Texas. Wagner's " Some Imaginary California Geography," in the *Proc. of the Amer. Antiq. Soc.,* 36, N.S., Pt. I (April 14, 1926), pp. 83–129. Reprinted separately by the Society (Worcester, Mass: The Davis Press, 1926), pp. 3–49 (refs. are to this pagination). Also Wagner's *Spanish Voyages to the Northwest Coast of America in the Sixteenth Century* (San Francisco: Calif. Hist. Soc., 1929), throughout. Abbreviation: Wagner, Spanish Voyages NW.

[3]*California As An Island, An Illustrated Essay* (San Francisco: Book Club of Calif., 1972), pp. 7–43.

[4] (London: Macmillan 1955; rpt. 1981), p. ix.

[5](Cambridge, Mass.: Harvard Univ. Press, 1936; rpt. New York: Harper, 1960), p. ix.

[6]"Mythistory, or Truth, Myth, History, and Historians," in *Mythistory and Other Essays* (Chicago: The University Press, 1986); rpt. as the 1985 Presidential Address of the American Historical Association in *The American Historical Review,* 91, no. 1 (Feb., 1986), p. 1.

CHAPTER I

[1]P. Hamelius, ed., *Mandeville's Travels, Translated from the French of Jean d'Outremeuse.* Edited from MS. Cotton Titus C. xvi, in the British Museum (London: Kegan Paul, Trench, Trübner & Co., Ltd., and Humphrey Milford, Oxford Univ. Press, for the Early English Text Soc., 1919), I, pp. 119–23.* Abbreviation: Hamelius, Mandeville. D.B. Quinn, et al., *New American World: A Documentary History of North*

*Minor stylistic variations elected.

America to 1612—Volume I, America from Concept to Discovery—Early Exploration of North America (New York: Arno Press and Hector Bye, Inc., 1979), pp. 70–73. Abbreviation: Quinn, N.A. World, I.

[2]Edmond Buron, ed. and trans., *Ymago Mundi de Pierre d'Ailly: Texte Latin et Traduction Française des quatre traités cosmographiques de d'Ailly et des notes marginales de Christophe Colomb* (Paris: Maisonneuve Frères, 1930),I, pp. 164–65, and pp. 242–43. Abbreviation: Buron, D'Ailly.

[3]Hamelius, Mandeville, I, p. 121.

[4]See Samuel Eliot Morison, *The European Discovery of America:* Volume I, *The Northern Voyages–A.D. 500–1600* (New York: Oxford Univ. Press, 1971), pp. 3–26, 81–84, 96–111. Also David Beers Quinn, *England and the Discovery of America: 1481–1620* (New York: Alfred A. Knopf, 1974), pp. 24–25, 57–64. Also Quinn, N. A. World, I, pp. 30–66, 74–82.

[5]Buron, D'Ailly, I, p. 304 Throughout the literature mentioning these dream destinations various spellings occur: Ophir, Ofir, Ofer, Tharshis, Tharsis, Tarsish, Tarsis.

[6]Hamelius, Mandeville, I, pp. 179, 125, and 199. Fragments quoted in next two paragraphs: pp. 122, 200–01, 105, 130.

[7]Hamelius, Mandeville, I, pp. 107–08.

[8]Sir Henry Yule, ed. and trans., *The Book of Ser Marco Polo the Venetian Concerning the Kingdoms and Marvels of the East,* 3rd. ed., revised by Henri Cordier (London & New York: Charles Scribner's Sons, 1902–3; rpt. London: John Murray, 1929), II, pp. 423–24. Abbreviation: Yule, Marco Polo.

[9]John J. Nitti, ed., *Juan Fernandez de Heredia's Aragonese Version of the Libro de Marco Polo* (Madison: Hisp. Seminary of Medieval Studies, 1980), p. 57.

[10]Yule, Marco Polo, II, pp. 263–65. Quinn, N. A. World, I, pp. 69–70.

[11]Yule, Marco Polo, I, Introduction, facing page 108.

[12]Nitti, Aragonese Polo, p. 46.

[13]Henry Raup Wagner, *The Rise of Fernando Cortés—New Series, Number Three of Documents and Narratives Concerning the Discovery and Conquest of Latin America* (Berkeley: Cortés Society, 1944), p. 426. Abbreviation: Wagner, Cortés.

[14]Yule, Marco Polo, II, p. 424, 425, note 6. See Quinn, N. A. World, I, pp. 17–20.

[15](Firenze: Leo S. Olschki, 1937), pp. 51 ff.

[16]"Ponce de Leon's Fountain of Youth: History of a Geographical Myth," *The Hisp. Amer. Hist. Rev.*,21, no. 3 (Aug. 1941), p. 371. See also Pauline Moffitt Watts, "Prophecy and Discovery: On the Spiritual Origins of Christopher Columbus's 'Enterprise of the Indies,' " *The American Hist. Rev.*,90, no. 1 (Feb. 1985), pp. 93–94.

[17]"The Middle Ages in the Conquest of America," *Speculum*, 26, no. 1 (Jan. 1951), p. 131. The full discussion is in Luis Weckmann, *Las Bulas Alejandrinas de 1493 y la Teoría Política del Papado Medieval: Estudio de la Supremacía Papal sobre Islas, 1091–1493* (Mexico: Inst. de Hist., 1949).

[18]Johann Georg Kohl, "Asia and America: An Historical Disquisition Concerning the Ideas which Former Geographers had about the Geographical Relation and Connection of the Old and New World," *Proc. of the Amer. Antiq. Soc.*, N. S. 21 (Oct. 1911), pp. 284–86. Of great help in this section was Daniel J. Boorstin, *The Discoverers* (New York: Random House, 1983; rpt. London: Penguin Books, 1986), pp. 101, 153–54, 200, and 243 especially. Also O. H. K. Spate, *The Spanish Lake: The Pacific Since Magellan*, Vol. I, (Canberra: Aust. Nat. Univ. Press, 1979), Chap. I.

[19]Samuel Eliot Morison, *Admiral of the Ocean Sea: A Life of Christopher Columbus* (Boston: Little, Brown and Company, 1942), I, pp. 138–39. Samuel Eliot Morison, ed. and trans., *Journals and Other Documents on the Life and Voyages of Christopher Columbus* (New York: Heritage Press, 1963), pp. 26–30. Abbreviation: Morison, Journals Columbus.

[20]James A. Williamson, *The Cabot Voyages and Bristol Discovery under Henry VII* (Cambridge: Univ. Press for the Hakluyt Soc., 1962), pp. 204–05. Quinn, N. A. World, I, p. 94.

[21] See Quinn, N. A. World, I, p. 95 (no. 55), p. 101 (no. 64), p. 110 (nos. 77, 78), p. 116 (no. 80), p. 117 (no. 83), pp. 117–118 (no. 84).

[22]Marcel Destombes, *Mappemondes: A. D. 1200–1500*: Catalogue préparé par la Commission des Cartes Anciennes de L'Union Géographique Internationale, I: Monuments Cartographiques Anciens. (Amsterdam: N. Israel, 1964). Discussion in this and next two paragraphs uses this as background, pp. 168–69,

229–35. Another excellent example of a *mappa mundi* with island-encircled *oikoumene* is the woodcut broadside of Hanns Rüst of 1480, the sole existing copy now in the Pierpoint Morgan Library. See illustration in Rodney W. Shirley, *The Mapping of the World: Early Printed World Maps, 1472–1700* (London: Holland Press, 1983) p. 7. This work has been of exceptional value throughout this study.

[23]Shirley, p. xxiii. For comparison with Ptolemy, p. xviii, and p. 10, plate 20.

[24]Shirley, pp. 16–17.

[25]This translation is of the Spanish version, discussed in Henry Vignaud, ed. and trans., *The Letter and Chart of Toscanelli on the Route to the Indies by Way of the West, Sent in 1474 to the Portuguese Fernam Martins, and later on to Christopher Columbus: A Critical Study . . .* (Original edition in French. Paris: Ernest Leroux, Editeur, 1901; Reprint and Translation: London: Sands & Co., 1902), p. 306.

[26] See graphics in Björn Landström, *Columbus: The Story of Don Cristobal Colón, Admiral of the Ocean, and His Four Voyages Westward to the Indies* (New York: Macmillan Company, 1966). Boorstin, pp. 153–54, 225–26.

CHAPTER II

[1]Vsevolod Slessarev, ed. and trans., *Prester John: The Letter and the Legend* (Minneapolis: Univ. of Minn. Press, 1959), p. 72. Abbreviation: Slessarev, Prester John.

[2]Myles Dillon and Nora Chadwick, *The Celtic Realms* (New York: New American Library, 1967), pp. 198–201, and footnotes. Boorstin, *The Discoverers*, pp. 100–04.

[3]Hamelius, Mandeville, I, pp. 201–02.

[4]Buron, D'Ailly, II, pp. 459–63, for this and next quotation from D'Ailly. See also II, 472–73.

[5]For background see Charles Germain Marie Bourel de la Roncière, *La Carte de Christophe Colomb: Texte en Français et en Anglais, avec Cartes.* (Paris: Les Éditions Historiques, Édouard Champion, 1924).

[6]Hamelius, Mandeville, I, p. 179, and next two quotations, I, p. 131, and I, pp. 184–85.

[7]Yule, Marco Polo, II, pp. 139–40.

[8]Sir Henry Yule, ed. and trans., *Cathay and the Way Thither: Vol. II—Odoric of Pordenone*, edition revised by Henri Cordier (London: Hakluyt Society, 1913), pp. 258–59.

[9]Two recent studies: William Blake Tyrrell, *Amazons: A Study in Athenian Mythmaking* (Baltimore and London: Johns Hopkins Univ. Press,

1984), and Abby Wettan Kleinbaum, *The War Against the Amazons* (N. Y: McGraw-Hill, 1983).

[10]Paul Pelliot, *Notes on Marco Polo,* II (Paris: Imprimerie Nationale, Librairie Adrien-Maisonneuve, 1963), p. 711. Yule, Polo, II, pp. 405–06, note 1.

[11]Le Marquis d'Hervey de Saint-Denys, ed. and trans., *Ethnographie des Peuples Étrangers à la Chine: Ouvrage Composé au XIIIᵉ Siècle de Notre Ère par Ma-Touan-Lin* (Genève: H. Georg, Libraire-Éditeur, 1876), I, Appendix, pp. 396–97, and pp. 402–03.

[12]Henriette Mertz, *Pale Ink: Two Ancient Records of Chinese Exploration in America,* 2nd rev. ed. (Chicago: Swallow Press, 1972), discusses this. Saint-Denys discusses nineteenth-century theories, footnotes pp. 375–87, 401–03, and 388–401. See also Charles E. Chapman, *A History of California: The Spanish Period* (N. Y: The Macmillan Co., 1921, 1928), pp. 24–30. Spate, p. 3 and refs.

[13]Robert Silverberg, *The Realm of Prester John* (Garden City, N. Y: Doubleday, 1972), pp. 41–44, discusses Friedrich Zarncke's deductions about interpolations.

[14]Slessarev, Prester John, p. 70; also Silverberg, p. 144.

[15]M. C. Seymour, ed., *The Bodley Version of Mandeville's Travels* (London: Oxford Univ. Press for The Early English Text Soc., 1963), p. 83.

[16]Hamelius, Mandeville, I, pp. 102–03.

[17]Yule, Marco Polo, II, pp. 404–06.

[18]Nitti, Aragonese Polo, p. 55.

[19]Raymond S. Willis, ed., *El Libro de Alexandre: Texts of the Paris and Madrid Manuscripts,* Elliott Monographs No. 32 (Princeton Univ. Press, 1934), pp. 324–29, stanzas 1863 ff.

[20]Francis M. Rogers, *The Travels of the Infante Dom Pedro of Portugal.* (Cambridge, Mass: Harvard Univ. Press, 1961), pp. 143–44. Chapter V yielded valuable information about Iberian publications of the early sixteenth century for this section.

CHAPTER III

[1]"The Middle Ages in the Conquest of America," p. 130.

[2]Buron, D'Ailly, II, pp. 458–59.

[3]Morison, Journals Columbus, pp. 183–86.

[4]*Diario del Primer Viaje de Colon,* revised by Antonio Vilanova, ed. (Barcelona: Ediciones Nauta, S. A., 1965), pp. 115, 117, 120, 122, 123, 148, 151, 154, 155. Consulted: Morison, Journals Columbus, pp. 146, 148, 151, 154,

155. Also *Diario del Descubrimiento,* ed. Manuel Alvar (Madrid: Ediciones del Excmo. Cabildo Insular de Gran Canaria, 1976), I, pp. 213–19, II, pp. 192–209.

[5]Morison, Journals Columbus, p. 249.

[6]Consulted: Francis Augustus MacNutt, ed. and trans., *De Orbe Novo: The Eight Decades of Peter Martyr d'Anghera* (N. Y. & London: G. P. Putnam's Sons, 1912; rpt. N. Y: Burt Franklin, 1970), I, pp. 73–74. Abbreviation: MacNutt, Martyr. Also *Décadas del Nuevo Mundo, por Pedro Mártir de Angleria, primer cronista de Indias,* Spanish trans. of Latin by Agustin Millares Carlo, ed. Edmundo O'Gorman (Mexico: J. Porrúa e Hijos, 1964), I, pp. 116–17. Abbreviation: Mártir, Mexico. Next four quotations: Mártir, Mexico: I, p. 374; I, p. 408; II, p. 631; II, 642. Consulted MacNutt, Martyr: I, p. 390; II, pp. 18, 300–01, 314.

[7]Morison, Journals Columbus, p. 170. Next four quotations: pp. 282, 286, and 287.

[8]Irving A. Leonard, "Conquerors and Amazons in Mexico," *Hisp. Amer. Hist. Rev.,* 24 (1944), pp. 561–79, particularly p. 562.

[9]Irving A. Leonard, *Books of the Brave: Being an account of books and of men in the Spanish conquest and settlement of the sixteenth-century New World* (Cambridge, Mass: Harvard Univ. Press, 1949; rpt. N. Y: Gordian Press, 1964), Chapters IV & V.

[10]Gonzalo Fernández de Oviedo y Valdés, *Historia General y Natural de las Indias* (Sevilla, 1535). In *Biblioteca de Autores Españoles,* Tomo CXVII, ed. Juan Pérez de Tudela Bueso (Madrid: Ediciones Atlas, 1959), Libro VI, Cap. XXXIII, p. 192. Abbreviation: Oviedo, Historia. Edition Abbreviation: B. de A. E. Next ref: B. de A. E., Tomo CXVIII, Libro XXIV, Cap. X, p. 419.

[11]Books of the Brave, p. 57. Leonard cites on p. 346, notes 5 and 6: Juan de San Martin y Alonso de Lebrija, *Relación del descubrimiento y conquista del nuevo reino de Granada, años 1536–1539* (Madrid: Sociedad de Bibliófilos Españoles, 1916), pp. 64–67.

[12]"The Discovery of Guiana . . ." in Richard Hakluyt, *The Principal Navigations, Voyages, Traffiques & Discoveries of the English Nation* (London, 1600; rpt. Glasgow: James MacLehose and Sons; Publishers to the University; and N. Y: The Macmillan Company, 1904), X, p. 367. Abbreviation of edition: Hakluyt, Voyages, MacLehose. Quotations from Hakluyt are modernized in Part I of this work.

[13]Morison, Journals Columbus, pp. 269–70. Next quotation, p. 277.

[14]Buron, D'Ailly, II, pp. 460–61.

[15]Hamelius, Mandeville, I, pp. 203–04.

[16]Slessarev, Prester John, p. 70.

[17]Hamelius, Mandeville, I, p. 103.

CHAPTER IV

[1]C. Edwards Lester, ed. and trans., The Life and Voyages of Americus Vespucius, 4th ed. (New Haven: Horace Mansfield, 1853), p. 154. Abbreviation: Lester. Next three quotations from pp. 197, 214–15, and 201.

[2]Arthur Percival Newton, The Great Age of Discovery (London: Univ. Press Ltd., 1932). Chapters IV and V for background.

[3]Lionel Cecil Jane, ed. and trans., Select Documents Illustrating the Four Voyages of Columbus (London: Hakluyt Society, 1929, 1930; rpt. Nendeln/Liechtenstein: Kraus Reprint Limited, 1967), I, pp. 130–31. See also Morison, Admiral of the Ocean Sea, II, pp. 128–29.

[4]Lester, p. 115, including footnotes, for this and next two quotations.

[5]Lester p. 204.

[6]Background: George E. Nunn, The Geographical Conceptions of Columbus (N. Y: Amer. Geog. Soc., 1924), 3rd problem, pp. 53–90, especially pp. 72–76. Abbreviation: Nunn, Geog. Conceptions. George E. Nunn, Origin of the Strait of Anian Concept (Phila: George H. Beams, 1929), particularly pp. 4–6. Abbreviation: Nunn, Anian. Newton, pp. 108–16.

[7]Nunn, Geog. Conceptions, pp. 72–74. Newton, pp. 114–15.

[8]Morison, Journals Columbus, p. 375.

[9]Morison, Journals Columbus, p. 291 and pp. 282–87 for this and next quotation. Newton, p. 112 and refs.

[10]Newton, pp. 101–02 and refs. MacNutt, Martyr, I, p. 57.

[11]Nunn, Geog. Conceptions, p. 11, including refs. in footnote 14.

[12]Newton, pp. 101–02, 105–06, and p. 110, for fragments and next two quotations from Peter Martyr. MacNutt, Martyr, I. pp. 57–65.

[13]Lester, p. 164. Next three quotations: p. 164, p. 170 (fragment), and p. 153.

[14]Background: Newton, pp. 122, 54–55. Lester pp. 206–07.

[15]Lester, p. 209. Next three quotations: p. 204, p. 196 (fragment), p. 209.

[16]Las Casas on the voyage of Pinzon and Solis, Bk. II, Chap. xxxix, trans. in Clements

R. Markham, ed. and trans, The Letters of Amerigo Vespucci and Other Documents Illustrative of His Career (London: Hakluyt Society, 1894), pp. 113–14.

[17]Roberto Levillier, "New Light on Vespucci's Third Voyage," Imago Mundi, 11 (1954), 37–46, especially p. 44 and footnote 3.

[18]Chapter 92; cited by Levillier.

[19]Edward Luther Stevenson, Terrestrial and Celestial Globes: Their History and Construction (New Haven: Yale Univ. Press for the Hisp. Soc. of Amer., 1921; rpt. New York & London, Johnson Reprint Corp., 1971), p. 109. Abbreviation: Stevenson.

[20]Joseph Fischer, S. J. and Franz von Wieser, S. J., eds. and trans., The Cosmographiae Introductio of Martin Waldseemüller in facsimile (N.Y.: The U.S. Catholic Hist. Soc., 1907) p. 70 for this and next quotation. See Joseph Fischer, S. J., and Franz von Wieser, S. J., The Oldest Map With the Name America of the Year 1507 and the Carta Marina of the Year 1516 by M. Waldseemüller (Innsbruck, 1903; rpt. Amsterdam, 1968).

[21]Nunn, Anian, pp. 4–6.

[22]Wagner, Spanish Voyages NW, pp. 1–3.

[23]Stevenson, pp. 73–85, for information and quotations in this and next paragraph.

[24]Shirley, The Mapping of the World, pp. 24, 26, 32, and p. XXIII, Plate 5 for Juan de la Cosa's map.

[25]Stevenson, pp. 107–10, for this and next quotation.

CHAPTER V

[1]Kathleen Romoli, Balboa of Darien: Discoverer of the Pacific (Garden City: Doubleday and Co., 1953), pp. 100, 378, note 3.

[2]Nunn, Anian, p. 8.

[3]Richard Eden, ed. and trans., The Decades of the Newe Worlde or West India by Pietro Martire d'Anghiera (London: Guilhelmi Powell, 1555; rpt. Ann Arbor, Mich: March of America Facs. Ser., Univ. Microfilms, 1966), Dec. II, Bk. 3, pp. 64–65. Text modernized. Also reprinted in Edward Arber, ed., The First Three English books on America . . . Being chiefly Translations, Compilations, &c., by Richard Eden (Birmingham, 1885). Abbreviation: Arber. Romoli, pp. 100–01.

[4]Angel de Altolaguirre y Duvale, ed., Vasco Nuñez de Balboa (Madrid: Real Academia de la Historia, 1914), Appendix, pp. 16–21. Consulted: Romoli, pp. 146 ff., and Charles L. G.

Anderson, *Life and Letters of Vasco Nuñez de Balboa* (New York: Fleming H. Revell Co., 1941), pp. 115–20.

[5]Oviedo, Historia, B. de A. E., Tomo CXIX, pp. 212–15. Another edition: José Amador de Los Rios, ed. (Asunción del Paraguay: Editorial Guaranía, 1944), Tomo VII, pp. 95–96. Consulted: MacNutt, Martyr, I, pp. 286–97.

[6]MacNutt, Martyr, I, p. 288. Background for the next few paragraphs: Spate, pp. 29–34 and refs.

[7]Altolaguirre, Appendix, p. 58, and Appendix, p. 19, for this and next quotation. Consulted: Romoli, p. 231, and Anderson, p. 119.

[8]MacNutt, Martyr, I, pp. 289–90.

[9]José Miranda, ed., *Sumario de la Natural Historia de las Indias por Gonzalo Fernández de Oviedo y Valdés* (Mexico and Buenos Aires: Fondo de Cultura Economica, 1950), pp. 266–67. Also in B. de A. E., Tomo XXII, p. 513. Consulted: Sterling A. Stoudemire, ed. and trans., *Natural History of the West Indies by Gonzalo Fernández de Oviedo* (Chapel Hill, N. C.: University Press, 1959), pp. 117–18.

[10]Anderson, p, 125.

[11]E. G. R. Taylor, ed., *A Brief Summe of Geographie by Roger Barlow* (London: Hakluyt Society, 1932), Introduction, p. xiv. Abbreviation: Taylor, Barlow. Next quotation: Introduction xvi.

[12]Taylor, Barlow, pp. 10, 137, 80. Consulted: Roger Barlow's manuscript, "Brief Somme of Geographia," British Library, Royal MSS. 18. B. xxviii; the first edition of *Suma de Geographia;* and José Ibáñez Cerdá, ed., *Summa de Geografia* (Bogotá: Biblioteca Banco Popular, 1974).

[13]Taylor, Barlow, p. 11, note 3. This passage was omitted from Barlow's manuscript. In it, Enciso makes the case for the Spanish claim to the ocean containing the isle of Ofir.

[14]Taylor, Barlow, p. 83. Taylor's note 1 points out that Enciso's placement of Ophir with Ciapango and "the ilond doro that is by Java" effectively "brought it within the half-sphere of the king of Spain."

[15]Taylor, Barlow, p. 136, pp. 137–38. Fragments quoted in the next paragraph: pp. 136–37, 137, 66–67, 69.

[16]Taylor, Barlow, page 179, note 2. Enciso, Bogotá, p. 280.

[17]H. J. Wood, "Search for a Western Passage," in Newton, Chap. VII, pp. 161–62. Spate, pp. 37–40, and 208–10.

[18]Lord Stanley of Alderley, ed., James Baynes, trans., *The First Voyage Around the World by Magellan: Translated from the Accounts of Pigafetta and other Contemporary Writers* (London: Hakluyt Society, 1874), pp. 187–197. Abbreviation: Stanley, Magellan. Reprinted in Charles E. Nowell, ed., *Magellan's Voyage Around the World: Three Contemporary Accounts* (Evanston, Ill.: Northwestern Univ. Press, 1962), pp. 279–80.

[19]Stanley, Magellan, pp. 57–66 and 154, for this and quotations to end of chapter. Consulted: James Alexander Robertson, ed., *Magellan's Voyage Around the World* (Cleveland: Arthur H. Clark, 1906), reprinted in Nowell, Magellan.

CHAPTER VI

[1]Ferdinand Flores, "Provinciae sive regiones in India Occidentali . . ." in Henry Raup Wagner, ed. and trans., *The Discovery of New Spain in 1518 by Juan de Grijalva*—New Series, No. Two of Documents and Narratives Concerning The Discovery and Conquest of Latin America (Berkeley: Bancroft Library for the Cortés Soc., 1942; rpt.: New York: Kraus Reprint Co., 1969), Appendix I, p. 60. Abbreviation: Wagner, Grijalva. Next two quotations: Appendix I B, p. 72; p. 191, note 24.

[2]Francisco Lopez de Gómara,*Historia General de las Indias*, in B. de A. E., XXII, p. 185. Abbreviation: Gómara, Historia, B. de A. E.

[3]MacNutt, Martyr, II, pp. 15–18.

[4]Francisco Cervantes de Salazar, *Crónica de la Nueva España*(written about 1560), ed. Francisco Paso y Troncoso (Madrid, 1914), I, pp. 75 ff. Wagner, Grijalva, Appen. VIII, pp, 162–63.

[5]Wagner, Cortés, pp. 25–29.

[6]Joaquín F. Pacheco, Francisco de Cárdenas, Luis Torres de Mendoza and others, eds. *Colección de Documentos Inéditos, Relativos al Descubrimiento, Conquista y Organización de las Antiguas Posesiones Españolas de América y Oceanía . . . de los Archivos . . . de Indias,* (Madrid: Imprenta de Frias y Cía, 1864–1884), Series I [Indias], XII, pp. 225–46, especially Item 26, pp. 242–43. Abbreviation: Colección Indias. Also Wagner, Cortés, p. 30.

[7]Alonzo Zuazo, Letter of November 14, 1521, *Colección de Documentos para la Historia de México*, ed. Joaquín García Icazbalceta (Mexico: J. M. Andrade, 1858–1866), I, p. 365. Abbreviation: García Icazbalceta, Colección. Wagner, Cortés, pp. 419–20.

[8]Bancroft, North Mex. & Texas, p. 1

[9]*Cartas de Relación de Fernando Cortés sobre el Descubrimiento y Conquista de la Nueva España,* in B. de A. E. XXII, p. 90. Abbreviation: Cortés, B. de A.E. Also Hernan Cortés, *Cartas de Relación* (Madrid: Calpe, 1922, rpt. 1932, 1961), II, pp. 49–50. Abbreviation: Cortés, Calpe. Consulted: Francis Augustus MacNutt, ed. and trans., *Letters of Cortés: The Five Letters of Relation from Fernando Cortés to the Emperor Charles V* (New York: George Putnam's Sons, 1908), II, pp. 132–33. Abbreviation: MacNutt, Cortés. Also A. R. Pagden, ed. and trans. *Hernan Cortés: Letters from Mexico* (New York: Grossman, 1971), pp. 267–70. Abbreviation: Pagden, Cortés.

[10]Cortés, B. de A. E., XXII, p.94. Cortés, Calpe, II, pp. 61–62. MacNutt, Cortés, II, pp. 142–44. Pagden, Cortés, pp. 275–77.

[11]Wagner, Spanish Voyages NW, pp. 2–3. Another summary of the contract is in Wagner, Cortés, pp. 423–24.

[12]P. Mariano Cuevas, ed., *Cartas y Otros Documentos de Hernan Cortés novisimamente descubiertos en el Archivo General de Indias de la Ciudad de Sevilla* (Sevilla: Tip. de F. Díaz y comp.ª, 1915), pp. 129–40. This and next two quotations from pp. 130, 131,and 133. Abbreviation: Cuevas, Cortés.

[13]Wagner, Cortés, p. 417. Cédula in Colección Indias, XXIII, pp. 353–68.

[14]Mártir, Mexico, II, pp. 524 and 543. MacNutt, Martyr, II, pp. 176 and 199. Next two quotations: Mártir, Mexico, II, pp. 544–46. MacNutt, II, pp.200–04.

[15]Gómara, Historia, B. de A.E., XXII, Pt. 2, Conquista de México, pp. 395–96.

[16]Cortés, B. de A. E., XXII, p. 102. Cortés, Calpe, II, pp. 84–85. Consulted: MacNutt, Cortés, II, pp.177–78. Pagden, Cortés, pp. 298–300.

[17]Colección Indias, XXVI, pp. 149–59, especially p. 153. Wagner, Cortés, p. 421.

[18]Manuel Orozco y Berra, *Historia de la Dominación Española en México* (México: J. Porrúa e Hijos, 1938), I, pp. 240–41. Wagner, Cortés, p. 421.

[19]Wagner, Cortés, p. 420.

[20]Lesley Byrd Simpson, ed. and trans., *Cortés: The Life of the Conqueror of Mexico by His Secretary: Francisco López de Gómara* (Berkeley: Univ. of Calif., 1964), p. 409. Abbreviation: Simpson, Gómara.

[21]Gómara, Historia, B. de A. E. XXII, p. 221.

[22]*A Natural and Civil History of California . . . translated from the Original Spanish of Miguel Venegas, a Mexican Jesuit, published at Madrid 1758,* translated for James Rivington and James Fletcher (London, 1759; rpt. Ann Arbor, Michigan: March of America Facsimile Series, University Microfilms, 1966), I, pp. 141–42. Abbreviation: Englished Venegas. Gómara, Historia, B. de A. E., XXII, Pt. 2, Conquista de Mexico, p. 428.

[23]Miguel Venegas, S. J., *Noticia de la California y de su Conquista Temporal, y Espiritual, hasta el Tiempo Presente: . . . formada en Mexico Año de 1739* (Madrid, 1757; rpt. México: Editorial Layac, 1943), I, p. 119. Consulted: Englished Venegas, I, pp. 131–32.

CHAPTER VII

[1]Samuel Purchas, ed., *Hakluytus Posthumus, or Purchas His Pilgrimes: contayning a history of the world in sea voyages and lande travells by Englishmen and others* (London, 1625; rpt. Glasgow: James MacLehose and Sons, 1905–7), XVIII, pp. 59–60. Modernized. Abbreviation: Purchas, MacLehose. Leonard, Books of the Brave, p. 51.

[2]García Icazbalceta, Colección, II, p. 451. Also pp. 449 and 457, and "Relación de la Entrada," II, p. 259. Consulted: Leonard, Books of the Brave, p. 52.

[3]Manuel Carrera Stampa, ed., *Memoria de Los Servicios que habia hecho Nuño de Guzmán, desde que fué nombrado Gobernador de Panuco en 1525* (México: José Porrúa e Hijos Sucs., 1955), Appendices, pp. 116–17. Other references to Amazons: pp. 142–43, 157,190.

[4]García Icazbalceta, Colección, I, pp. 484–511, especially p. 496.

[5]Cortés, B. de A. E. XXII, p. 152. Consulted: Pagden, Cortés, pp. 444–45; MacNutt, Cortés, II, p. 350. Wagner, Cortés, p. 427.

[6]Colección Indias, IV, pp. 572–74.

[7]In "Cortés and the First Attempt to Colonize California," *California Hist. Soc. Qtly.*, 53, no. 1 (Spring 1974), pp. 4–16, particularly p. 6. Abbreviation: Miller, Cortés. Cédula of November 5, 1529, confirming contract of October 27, 1529, Colección Indias, XII, pp, 490–95, particularly p. 491. Also W. Michael Mathes, ed. and trans., *The Conquistador in*

California: 1535: The Voyage of Fernando Cortés to Baja California in Chronicles and Documents (Los Angeles: Dawson's Book Shop, 1973), pp. 97–98. Royal Order of November 5, 1529, pp. 109–13. Abbreviation: Mathes, Cortés.

[8]John Ingram Lockhart, ed. and trans., *The Memoirs of the Conquistador Bernal Diaz del Castillo written by himself, Containing a True and Full Account of the Discovery and Conquest of Mexico and New Spain* (London: J. Hatchard and Son, 1844), II, Chap. CC, pp. 349 ff. Abbreviation: Díaz, Lockhart. Consulted: *The True History of the Conquest of New Spain by Bernal Díaz del Castillo, one of its Conquerors: From the only exact copy made of the original manuscript, edited and published in Mexico by Genaro Garcia*, ed. and trans. Alfred Percival Maudslay (London: Hakluyt Society, 1908; rpt. 1916), V, pp. 176 ff. Abbreviation: Díaz, Maudslay. Also *Historia Verdadera de la Conquista de la Nueva España, por Bernal Díaz del Castillo*, ed. Genaro García (México: Oficina tipográfica de la Secretaría de fomento, 1904–1905), Tomo II, Cap. CC ff., pp 411–18, Abbreviation: Díaz, García. Also B. de A. E., XXVI, pp. 290 ff.

[9]Díaz, Lockhart, II, pp. 350–51, for this and quotations to end of chapter. Consulted: Díaz, Maudslay, V, pp. 178–82.

CHAPTER VIII

[1]Díaz, Lockhart, II, pp. 351–52, for this and next two quotations. Consulted: Díaz, Maudslay, V, pp. 182–83.

[2]Pascual de Gayangos y Arce, ed., *Cartas y Relaciones de Hernan Cortés al Emperador Carlos V* (Paris: A Chaix y ca., 1866) p. 532. Abbreviation: Gayangos. Translation from: Miller, Cortés, p. 8.

[3]Díaz, Lockhart, II p. 352. Consulted: Díaz, Maudslay, V, pp. 183–84.

[4]Wagner, Spanish Voyages NW, p. 6, and p. 306, note 30. Also Mathes, Cortés, p. 101, note 1

[5]Miller, Cortés, pp. 9–10. Consulted: Cuevas, Cortés, pp. 171–72. Mathes, Cortés, pp. 117–18.

[6]Miller, Cortés, pp. 11–12. Consulted: Colección Indias, XV, pp. 306–08. Mathes, Cortés, pp. 103–5. Martín Fernández Navarrete et al., eds., *Colección de documentos inéditos para la historia de España.* (Madrid: Viuda de Calero, 1842–1895), IV pp. 190–92. Abbreviation: Navarrete, Colección.

[7]Miller, Cortés, p. 12. Mathes, Cortés, p. 114.

[8]Hakluyt, Voyages, IX, p. 122.

[9]Díaz, Lockhart, II, pp. 352–53. Consulted: Díaz, Maudslay, V, pp. 184–86.

[10]Díaz, Maudslay, V, pp. 186–88, for this and following quotations to end of chapter.

CHAPTER IX

[1]Navarrete, Colección, IV, pp. 201–02.

[2]Colección Indias, XII, pp. 417–29, specifically, p. 419.

[3]"Proceso del Marqués del Valle y Nuño de Guzmán . . . en Madrid, 3 marzo, 1540; 10 junio, 1541," Colección Indias, XV, pp. 300–408, specifically, p. 346.

[4]García Icazbalceta, Colección, II, pp. 296–306, particularly, pp. 302–03.

[5]Wagner, Spanish Voyages NW, p. 368.

[6]Wagner, Spanish Voyages NW, p. 68.

[7]MacNutt, Martyr, I, p. 163. Mártir, Mexico, I, p. 188.

[8]Wagner, Spanish Voyages NW, p. 304, note 1, and pp. 304–5, note 6. Testimony taken from 56 Relaciones de Servicios, published in Francisco A. de Icaza, ed., *Conquistadores y Pobladores de Nueva España; Diccionario Autobiográfico* (Madrid: Impr. de "El Adelantado de Segovia," 1923).

[9]Mathes, Cortés, p. 98.

[10]Mathes, Cortés, p. 98.

[11]Bancroft, Northwest Coast, p. 42.

[12]Henry Raup Wagner, "Francisco de Ulloa Returned," *Calif. Hist. Soc. Qtly.,* 19, no. 3. (Sept. 1940) pp. 240–45, precisely, p. 240. Abbreviation: Wagner, Ulloa Returned.

[13]Wagner, Spanish Voyages NW, p. 307, note 49.

[14]Wagner, Ulloa Returned, p. 241.

[15]Wagner, Ulloa Returned, p. 242.

[16]Díaz, García, II, p. 418.

[17]Díaz, Maudslay, V, pp. 187–88.

[18]Wagner, Spanish Voyages NW, p. 15.

[19]Hakluyt, Voyages, MacLehose, IX, pp. 121–22.

[20]Wagner, Spanish Voyages NW, Appendix III, pp. 418–23, specifically p. 419. Also p. 57 and p. 316, note 40. The other reference to "Isla de Marqués" is in a letter of March 10, 1542, Cartas de Indias (Madrid, 1877), as noted by Wagner.

[21]Hakluyt, Voyages, MacLehose, IX, pp. 125–29.

[22]Navarrete, Colección, IV, pp. 209–17. Also García Icazbalceta, II, Intro. pp. xxviii–xxix. Also trans. in Stephen Clissold, *The Seven Cities of Cibola* (New York: Clarkson N. Potter, 1962), pp. 80–81, note 1. Maurice G. Holmes, *From New Spain by Sea to the Californias, 1519–1668* (Glendale, Calif: Arthur H. Clark, 1963), p. 80 and note 12. Abbreviation: Holmes.

[23]Hakluyt, Voyages, MacLehose, IX, p. 148.

[24]Shirley, The Mapping of the World, pp. 64–65.

[25]D. Antonio Blázquez, ed., *Islario General de Todas Las Islas del Mundo por Alonso de Santa Cruz* (Madrid: Real Sociedad Geográfica, 1918), Volume I (Text), p. 542. Background: Juan de Mata Carriazo, ed., *Alonso de Santa Cruz: Crónica de los Reyes Católicos* (Sevilla: Escuela de Estudios Hispano-Americanos, 1951).

CHAPTER X

[1]Díaz, García, pp. 417–18.

[2]Wagner, Spanish Voyages NW, p. 293; p. 309, note 90; p. 310, note 110. Alvaro del Portillo y Díez de Sollano, *Descubrimientos y Exploraciones en las Costas de California*—Publicaciones de la Escuela de Estudios Hispano-Americanos de Sevilla, XX, Serie 2.a. Monografías. Núm. 7 (Madrid: Blass, S. A. Tipográfica, 1947), pp. 116–17. Abbreviation: Portillo, Descubrimientos. Preciado's account is trans. in Hakluyt, Voyages, MacLehose, IX, pp. 207–78.

[3]Wagner, Spanish Voyages NW, Ladrillero testimony trans. pp. 66–91, particularly, p. 69, commentary pp. 63–65. Amando Zugarte Cortesão, "An Unknown Portuguese Cartographer . . ." in *The Geo. Rev.*, 29, no 2 (April 1939) pp. 205–25.

[4]Wagner, Spanish Voyages NW, pp. 80 and 84.

[5]Wagner, Ulloa Returned, p. 242.

[6]"The Discovery of California," (July 1922), pp. 36–56, particularly, p. 37.

[7]"El Bautizo de la California," *Estudios Geográficos*, No. 7, Mayo, 1942, p. 386. Mentioned in Portillo, Descubrimientos, pp. 111 to 112, notes 4 and 12.

[8](London: John Murray, 1849), I. p. 209. Revised edition (Boston and New York: Houghton Mifflin, 1863), I, pp. 244–45.

[9]"The Queen of California," in '*His Level Best' and Other Stories* (Boston: Roberts Brothers, 1872), pp. 234–78, particularly, p. 234. (Rpt. San Francisco: The Colt Press, 1945).

First published in *Proc. of the Amer. Antiq. Soc.*, April 1862; *Historical Magazine*, 6, p. 313; *Atlantic Monthly*, 13, p. 265.

[10]Background re publications: Henry Thomas, *Spanish and Portugese Romances of Chivalry* (Cambridge: Univ. Press, 1920; rpt. New York: Kraus Reprint Co., 1969), especially pp. 65 ff. Also Leonard, Books of the Brave, Chapters VIII and IX.

[11] *El Ramo que de los cuatro libros de Amadís de Gaula sale: Llamado Las Sergas del Muy Esforzado Caballero Esplandian, Hijo del Excelente Rey Amadís de Gaula,* in B. de A. E., XL, pp. 539 ff. Abbreviation: Las Sergas.

[12]Slessarev, Prester John, p. 70.

[13]Buchan Telfer, trans., *The Bondage and Travels of Johann Schiltberger . . .* (London: Hakluyt Society, 1879), pp. 37–38.

[14]Hamelius, Mandeville, I, pp. 103–104.

[15]Slessarev, Prester John, p. 68, and p. 73.

[16]Hamelius, Mandeville, I, pp. 178-79. Yule, Polo, II, pp. 412–18.

[17]Morison, Journals Columbus, p. 340, and p. 342, note 8.

[18]Fray Toribio de Benavente ó Motolinia, *Historia de los Indios de Nueva España,* García Icazbalceta, Colección, I, p. 185.

[19]Consulted for background in this section: George Davidson, "The Origin and the Meaning of the Name California," *Trans. and Proc. of the Geog. Soc. of the Pacific,* Ser. II, 4, Pt. 1 (1910) pp. 1–50. Ruth Putnam, with Herbert Ingram Priestly, "California: The Name," *Univ. of Calif. Pubs. in History,* 4, no. 4 (1917), pp. 293–365.

[20]Bruce Chatwin, *In Patagonia* (New York: Summit Books, 1977), pp. 95–96.

[21]Díaz, Maudslay, II, p. 37.

[22]Thomas, Spanish and Portuguese Romances, p. 67. Leonard, Books of the Brave, pp. 41, 90.

[23]Leonard, Books of the Brave, pp. 95–99.

[24]Bancroft, California, pp. 66–67.

[25]Putnam, pp. 347–48.

[26]History of California, pp. 67–68.

[27]*Spanish and Indian Place Names of California: Their Meaning and Their Romance* (San Francisco: A. M. Robertson, 1914), pp. 13–18. Also "The name of our beloved California: Was it given in derision?" in *Grizzly Bear Mag.* (Los Angeles), 18, Nos. 6 and 8 (April 1916).

[28]"Of the generation of metals and their mines with the maner of finding the same: Written in the Italian tongue by Vannuccius Biringuczius

in his book called *Pyrotechnia*," ed. and trans. Richard Eden (London, 1555), reprinted in Arber, Eden, pp. 362 and 357.

[29]pp. 33–34.

[30]p. 241.

[31]pp. 357–58, Appendix A.

[32]Gerard J. Brault, ed. and trans., *The Song of Roland: An Analytical Edition*, II, Oxford Text and English Translation (London & University Park: Penn. State Univ. Press, 1978), pp. 176–77.

[33]pp. 63–64.

[34]For references, see Lynn Townsend White, Jr., "Changes in the Popular Concept of 'California'," *Calif. Hist. Soc. Qtly,*, 19, no. 3 (Sept. 1940), pp. 219–24, specifically, p. 220, and notes 4 to 7, p. 223. Herbert D. Austin, "New Light on the Name California," *Pubs. of the Hist. Soc. of So. Calif.*, 12, no. 3 (1923), pp. 29–31. A. E. Sokol, "California: A Possible Derivation of the Name," *Calif. Hist. Soc. Qtly.*, 28, no. 1 (March 1949), pp. 23–30.

[35]"Sources of the Name 'California,'" in *Arizona and the West: A Qtly Jnl. of Hist.*, 3, no. 3 (Autumn 1961) pp. 233–44.

CHAPTER XI

[1]Díaz, Maudslay, V, pp. 187–88.

[2]Lawrence C. Wroth, *The Voyages of Giovanni da Verrazzano: 1524–1528* (New Haven and London: Yale Univ. Press for the Pierpont Morgan Library, 1970), trans. Susan Tarrow, p. 136, note 8.

[3]Raleigh Ashlin Skelton, *Explorers' Maps: Chapters in the Cartographic Record of Geographical Discovery* (London: Routledge & Paul, 1958), p. 87.

[4]MacNutt, Cortés, II, pp. 207–09. Pagden, Cortés, pp. 326–28. Cortés, B. de A. E., XXII, pp. 112–13, for this and next quotation.

[5]MacNutt, Cortés, II, p. 354. Cortés, B. de A. E. XXII, p. 152. Pagden, Cortés, p. 447. Wagner, Spanish Voyages NW, p. 291, note 11. Gayangos, p. 492.

[6]Skelton, Explorers' Maps, p. 87.

[7]García Icazbalceta, Colección, II, p. 303.

[8]"The Voyage of Francisco de Ulloa," trans. Irene A. White, Wagner, Spanish Voyages NW, pp. 11–50, precisely, p. 20. Next quotation, p. 25.

[9]See Wagner, Ulloa Returned. Wagner, Spanish Voyages NW, pp. 13–14.

[10]Hakluyt, Voyages, MacLehose, IV, pp. 207

ff., particularly pp. 212, 214, 215, and 219, from which this and the next four quotations are taken.

[11]Antonio de Herrera y Tordesillas, *Historia General de los hechos de los Castellanos en las Islas y Tierra Firme del Mar Océano* (Madrid, 1601–1615; rpt. Madrid: Oficina Real de Nicolás Rodriguez Franco, 1726). Abbreviation: Herrera, Historia Castellanos.

[12]Hakluyt, Voyages, MacLehose, IV, p. 225.

[13]Wagner, Spanish Voyages NW, p. 20.

[14]*Ibid.*, p. 307, note 49.

[15]Cornelius Wytfliet, *Histoire Universelle des Indes Occidentales, Divisée en deux livres*, faicte en Latin par Monsieur Wytfliet (Paris: A Douay, Chez François Fabri, 1607) Livre II, pp. 122–23. French translation of: *Descriptionis Ptolemaicae Augmentum Sive Occidentis Notitia Brevi . . .* (Lovanii, 1597), pp. 167–175.

[16]Father Luis Sales, *Observations on California, 1772–1790*, ed. and trans. Charles N. Rudkin, Early California Travel Series, No. 37 (Los Angeles: Glen Dawson, 1956), p. 8.

CHAPTER XII

[1]Hakluyt, Voyages, MacLehose, IX, pp. 115–16. Cortés complains of Mendoza's predation in a "Memorial" of 1539 in Navarrete, Colección, IV, pp. 201–09. General background for this section: A. Grove Day, *Coronado's Quest: The Discovery of the Southwestern States* (Berkeley and Los Angeles: Univ. of Calif. Press, 1964).

[2]Colección Indias, III, pp. 325–29. Consulted: Madeleine Turrell Rodack, ed. and trans., *Adolph F. Bandelier's 'The Discovery of New Mexico by the Franciscan Monk, Friar Marcos de Niza in 1539'* (Tucson, Arizona: Univ. of Ariz. Press, 1981), p. 71. George P. Hammond and Agapito Rey, eds. and trans., *Narratives of the Coronado Expedition 1540–1542* (Albuquerque: The Univ. of N. M. Press, 1940), p. 60. Abbreviation Hammond-Rey, Coronado. Percy M. Baldwin, "Fray Marcos de Niza's *Relación*," *New Mexico Historical Review*, 1 (April 1926), 193–223, particularly, p. 200.

[3]Consulted: Hammond-Rey, Coronado, p. 71, and others above.

[4]Hakluyt, Voyages, MacLehose, IX, pp. 281, 312, and 316.

[5]George Parker Winship, ed. and trans., *The Journey of Coronado 1540–1542 . . . as told by himself and his followers* (New York: Allerton Book Co., 1922; rpt. Ann Arbor, Mich.: Univ.

Microfilms, Inc., 1966), p. 27. Abbreviation: Winship, Coronado. Next three quotations: pp. 28, 58–59.

[6]Hammond-Rey, Coronado, p. 249.

[7]Mariano Cuevas, ed., Historia de los Descubrimientos Antiguos y Modernos de la Nueva España, Escrita por el Conquistador Baltasar de Obregón Año de 1584 (México: La Sria. de Education Publica, 1924), p. 225. Abbreviation: Obregón, Cuevas. Consulted: George P. Hammond and Agapito Rey, eds. and trans., Obregon's History of 16th Century Explorations in Western America: Entitled Chronicle, Commentary, or Relation of the Ancient and Modern Discoveries in New Spain and New Mexico, 1584 (Los Angeles: Wetzel Pub. Co., 1928), pp. 251–52. Abbreviation: Obregón, Hammond-Rey.

[8]Hammond-Rey, Coronado, p. 282.

[9]Obregón, Hammond-Rey, p. 23.

[10]Winship, Coronado, p. 59.

[11]Wagner, Some Imag. Geog., pp. 24–25. Next quotation: p. 14.

[12]Wagner, Spanish Voyages NW, p. 1. Also E. G. R. Taylor, Tudor Geography: 1485–1583 (London: Methuen & Co., 1930), p. 11. Abbreviation: Taylor, Tudor Geog.

[13]Hakluyt, Voyages, MacLehose, IX, p. 214.

CHAPTER XIII

[1]Hakluyt, Voyages, MacLehose, IX, pp. 225–27. Next two quotations: pp. 227, 227–28.

[2]Hakluyt, Voyages, MacLehose, IX, p. 234.

[3]Wagner, Spanish Voyages NW, p. 45.

[4]Gómara, Historia, B. de A.E., XXII, p. 428. Simpson, Gómara, p. 403: "Ulloa ... sailed north to the parallel of San Andrés, at a point he named Cape Disappointment."

[5]Bancroft, Northwest Coast, p. 46.

[6]Wagner, Spanish Voyages NW, pp. 54–57.

[7]Hakluyt, Voyages, MacLehose, IX, p. 116.

[8]Colección de Documentos Inéditos Relativos al Descubrimiento, Conquista y Organización de las Antiguas Posesiones Españolas de Ultramar, Series II (Madrid: Real Academia de la Historia, 1886–1888), II, pp. 1–29, especially 2–3, and 9. Abbreviation: Colección Ultramar. See also Mendoza's letter of October 6, 1541, quoted in translation in Wagner, Spanish Voyages NW, p. 56.

[9]Gómara, Historia, B. de A. E., XXII, p. 165.

[10]Wagner, Spanish Voyages NW, p. 69.

[11]Justin Winsor, The Kohl Collection (Now in the Library of Congress) of Maps Relating to America. A Reprint of Bibliographical Contribution Number 19 of the Library of Harvard Univ. With Index by Philip Lee Phillips. (Washington: Library of Cong., G.P.O., 1904), p. 126, nos. 278 and 279. Next several quotations are from Kohl's notes accompanying his sketch map, consulted in the Library of Congress.

[12]Wagner, Spanish Voyages NW, pp. 343–44.

[13]Ref. in Holmes: Ms Justicia 290, fols. 47 ff., A.G.I. The "Probanza" of Cabrillo's merits and services, substantiated by witnesses, including Vargas, is summarized by Holmes on pp. 110–12.

[14]Ibid., and Wagner, Spanish Voyages NW, p. 336, note 113. "Informacion"—evidence of Lazaro de Cárdenas and Francisco de Vargas, Archives of Sevilla, 1–4–34/3, No. 2, R. 4, 22–24 verso.

[15]Bancroft, Northwest Coast, pp. 7–8.

[16]Herrera, Historia Castellanos, IV, Decade VII, Book V, Chapter iiii; in 1601 ed., p. 114. Trans. of this account is in Wagner, Spanish Voyages NW, Appendix IV, pp. 426–30, specifically p. 427. Also pp. 72–74 and 59–60.

[17]Winship, Coronado, p. 242. Hammond-Rey, Coronado, p. 183.

[18]"The Voyage of Juan Rodriguez Cabrillo," Wagner, Spanish Voyages NW, pp. 72–93, particularly p. 88. Consulted: Colección Indias, XIV, pp. 165–91, particularly, p. 177 and pp. 188–9.

[19]Wagner, Spanish Voyages NW, p. 92.

[20]Colección Ultramar, II, Doc. 17, pp. 132–34. Cabrillo ref. Colección Indias, XIV, p. 165. Holmes, p. 132; pp. 192–193. Wagner, Spanish Voyages NW, p. 106.

[21]Wagner, Spanish Voyages NW, p. 80. Quotations to end of chapter, pp. 86–92, specifically, pp. 87–88, 89, 90, 92, 85, 86, 86, 90.

CHAPTER XIV

[1]Díaz, García, II, p. 418. Díaz, B. de A.E., XXVI, p. 292.

[2]Herrera, Historia Castellanos, Decade VIII, Bk. VI, Chapter xiiii; 1601–1615 ed., IV, p. 178; 1726 ed., VIII/IX, p. 139.

[3]Wagner, Spanish Voyages NW, p. 106, and p. 349, notes 54–56. Consulted: "Expedicion de Legazpi," Document 17: "Derrotero . . . hecho por Fr. Andrés de Urdaneta," in Colección Ultramar, II, p. 119 ff. particularly pp. 132–34 for this and next quotation. Also Wagner's discussion "Urdaneta and the Return

Route from the Phillippine Islands," in *The Pac. Hist. Rev.*, 13, No. 3 (Sept. 1944), pp. 313–16, especially p. 315.

[4]Wagner, Spanish Voyages NW, p. 106.

[5]Henry Raup Wagner, *Apocryphal Voyages to the Northwest Coast of America* (Worcester: Amer. Antiq. Soc., 1931). Also W. Michael Mathes, "Apocryphal Tales of the Island of California and Strait of Anian," *Calif. Hist.*, 62, No. 1 (Spring 1983), pp. 52–59. Abbreviation: Mathes, Apocryphal Tales.

[6]Bancroft, Northwest Coast, p. 111.

[7]Bancroft, Northwest Coast, pp. 587–96 and notes.

[8]Donald Jackson and Mary Lee Spence, eds., *The Expedition of John Charles Frémont* (Urbana, Chicago: Univ. of Ill. Press, 1970) pp. 669 and 30.

[9]Wagner, Spanish Voyages NW, p. 375, note 3. Also H. R. Wagner, "Pearl Fishing Enterprises in the Gulf of California," *The Hisp. Amer. Hist. Rev.*, 10, no. 2 (May 1930).

[10]Obregón, Cuevas, pp. 197, 225, and 197.

[11]Obregón, Hammond-Rey, p. 254. Obregón, Cuevas, pp. 226–27.

[12]Obregón, Hammond-Rey, p. 125. Obregón, Cuevas, p. 115.

[13]Wagner, California Voyages 1539–1541, p. 9; Spanish Voyages NW, p. 304, note 1; pp. 304–05, note 6

[14]Obregón, Hammond-Rey, p. 254. Obregón, Cuevas, pp. 226–27, for this and next quotation.

[15]Obregón, Hammond-Rey, pp. 251–52. Obregón, Cuevas, p. 225.

[16]Obregón, Cuevas, p. 225, for this and next quotation.

[17]Bancroft, Northwest Coast, p. 42. Next quotation, p.102.

[18]Wagner, Some Imag. Geog., p. 22.

[19]Wagner, Spanish Voyages NW, p. 388, for this quotation and the next.

CHAPTER XV

[1]E.G.R. Taylor's *Tudor Geography*, and Introduction to *A Brief Summe of Geographie* were of special value in preparing this section. Also A. L. Rowse, *The Expansion of Elizabethan England*; F.T. McCann, *English Discovery of America*.

[2]Lansdowne MS 100, no. 7.

[3]"The Booke Made by the Right Worshipfull Master Robert Thorne . . ." in Richard Hakluyt, ed., *Divers Voyages* . . . (London, Thomas Woodcocke, 1582). Rpt. in *Divers Voyages Touching the Discovery of America and the Islands Adja-*

cent: *Collected and Published by Richard Hakluyt*, ed. John Winter Jones (London: The Hakluyt Society, 1850), pp. 33–54, particularly p. 48. Abbreviation: Hakluyt, Divers Voy. The original spelling is retained throughout this section to convey the flavor of Tudor England

[4]"A Note of Sebastian Gabotes Voyage . . .," in Hakluyt, Divers Voy., pp. 23–26, particularly, p. 25. Also "A discourse on western planting, written in the year 1584, by Richard Hakluyt," in *Documentary History of the State of Maine, II*, ed. Charles Deane (Cambridge: Maine Hist. Soc., John Wilson & Son, 1877), p.110. Abbreviation: Hakluyt, Western Planting.

[5]Hakluyt, Divers Voy., p. 50.

[6]Hakluyt, Western Planting, pp. 113–14, nos. 10 & 11.

[7]Edward Arber's Preface, Arber, Eden, pp. xiii to xv, for this quotation and those in next paragraph.

[8]Hakluyt, Divers Voy., p. 33; and pp. 49 and 51 for next two quotations.

[9]"A Declaration of the Indies and Landes discovered . . . and to be discovered . . . ," Hakluyt, Divers Voy., pp.27–32, particularly, p. 31, for this and next three quotations.

[10]Taylor, Tudor Geog., pp. 50–52.

[11]Taylor, Barlow, p. 182. Taylor, Tudor Geog., Doc. 4b, p. 247.

[12]Taylor, Barlow, quoted in Appen. III: "The parentage of Roger Barlow," p. 189.

[13]Letter of Jehan Scheyfve, June 24, 1550. Imperial Archives, Vienna, E. 17. *Calendar of Letters, Despatches and State Papers Relating to the Negotiations Between England and Spain*, Preserved in the Archives at Vienna, Brussels, Simancas and Elsewhere, X, Edward VI 1550–1552, ed. Royall Tyler (London: His Majesty's Stationery Office by Hereford Times, Ltd., 1914), pp. 111–17, especially pp. 115–16. See also Taylor, Barlow, Introduction p. liv.

[14]*Ibid.*, pp. 213–19, especially p. 217. Letter of January, 1551, Imperial Archives, Vienna, E. 19.

CHAPTER XVI

[1]Arber, Eden, pp. 55, 7, 8, 51, 54, 59.

[2]Arber, Eden, pp. 335–38, 340.

[3]Gwyn A. Williams, *The Welsh in their History* (London & Canberra: Croom Helm, 1982), Chapter I, pp. 13–30 (including footnotes) for most of the information in this paragraph.

[4]Williams, p. 23, and Boorstin, The Discoverers, pp. 204–17

[5]Hakluyt, Voyages, MacLehose, VII, pp. 149–50: and p. 152.

[6]See Taylor, Tudor Geog., Chapters V and VI, for general background. Also Gwyn A. Williams, *Madoc: The Making of a Myth* (London: Eyre Methuen, 1979), especially Chap. 3. Richard Deacon, *John Dee: Scientist, Geographer, Astrologer, and Secret Agent to Elizabeth I* (London: Muller, 1968).

[7]Colin Steele, *English Interpreters of the Iberian New World from Purchas to Stevens: A Bibliographical Study 1603–1726* (Oxford: Dolphin Book Co., 1975), pp. 142–43.

[8]Subtitle: *Annexed to the Paradoxical Cumpas in Playne: Now first published: 24 yeres, after the Invention thereof* (London: John Daye, 1577). Abbreviation: Gen. & Rare Mem.

[9]Gen. & Rare Mem., p. 62.

[10]Verso of map shows Elizabeth's claim deriving from such British explorers as Welsh Prince Madoc, St. Brandon, and King Arthur, as well as from Sebastian Cabot and Robert Thorne, Sr. British Library Cotton MS, Augustus I.i.1.

[11]Robert Ellis Jones, trans., "A Literal Translation of the Welsh Manuscript No. LXI of Jesus College, Oxford," in Acton Griscom, *The Historia Regum Britanniae of Geoffrey of Monmouth . . .* (London: Longmans, Green and Co., 1929), pp. 221–22, and 248–49.

[12]Gen. & Rare Mem., p. 38.

[13]Dee's Preface to Henry Billingsly's *English Translation of Euclid* (London, 1570), quoted in Taylor, Tudor Geog. p. 105.

[14]George Best's "A True Discourse . . . " is in Richard Collinson, ed., *The Three Voyages of Martin Frobisher in Search of a Passage to Cathaia and India by the North-West, A. D. 1576–8* (London: Hakluyt Society, 1867). Abbreviation: Collinson, Frobisher. Hakluyt, Western Planting. Hakluyt, Voyages, MacLehose, IX, pp. 244–50. Rowse, Expansion Eliz. Eng., pp. 206 ff. McCann, Ch.VIII.

[15]Rowse, Expansion, Eliz. Eng., pp. 191–92. *Calendar of State Papers, Col. East Indies, 1513–1616*, 94. Also D. B. Quinn, *The Voyages and Colonising Enterprises of Sir Humphrey Gilbert* (London: Hakluyt Society, 1940), I, 6–11.

[16]"George Gascoigne Esquire, To The Reader," pp. iii–iiii.

[17]Gen. & Rare Mem., p. 2. Taylor, Tudor Geog., p. 99. Taylor's list of contemporary works and documents includes this item and description: "Dee, John. Reipublicae Britannicae Syn-

opsis, in English. 1565. A Tract on British expansion overseas written at the request of Edward Dyer. It belongs to the period of first advocacy of the search for a north-west passage, and its corollary of planting in N. America."

[18]*The Great Volume of Famous and Rich Discoveries*, fourth part of Dee's magnum opus, British Library, Cotton MS Vitellius C. VII. Entry dated: "1577, May 15."

[19]Hakluyt, Voyages, MacLehose, VII, pp. 160–61 for this and next three quotations.

[20]Collinson, Frobisher, p. 36.

CHAPTER XVII

[1]Taylor, Tudor Geog., Documents, pp. 276–77. Consulted: British Library, Cotton MS Vitellius C. VII, f. 177 r., 180 r. For derivation of term and concept: Yule, Marco Polo, II, p. 266, Note 4.

[2]Included in Collinson, Frobisher, pp.8–12. Consulted: British Library Lansdowne MS 100, no. 4. Background: A. L. Rowse, *Sir Richard Grenville of the 'Revenge'* (London, Boston, New York: Houghton Mifflin, 1937; rpt. London: Jonathan Cape, 1963), pp. 102–05. Abbreviation: Rowse, Grenville.

[3]Collinson, Frobisher, p.9.

[4]Taylor, Tudor Geog., p. 101. Rowse, Grenville, p. 102. British Library Lansdowne MS 100, No. 4.

[5]*Calendar of State Papers, Domestic Series*, of the Reigns of Edward VI, Mary, Elizabeth, 1547–1580, Preserved in the State Paper Department of Her Majesty's Public Record Office, ed. Robert Lemon (London: Longman, Brown, Green, Longmans & Roberts, 1856), p. 475, no. 63. Rowse, Grenville, pp. 88–100. Taylor, Tudor Geog., pp. 101–02.

[6]In Collinson, Frobisher, pp. 4–8.

[7]Collinson, Frobisher, p. 12. Next quotation, p. 7.

[8]Abraham Darcie, trans., *The True and Royall History of the Famous Empresse Elizabeth* (London, 1625), p. 429. This is a translation of the French translation of William Camden, *Annales Rerum Anglicarum, et Hibernicarum, regnante Elizabetha . . .* (London, 1615). Abbreviation: Camden, Darcie. In Henry Raup Wagner, *Sir Francis Drake's Voyage Around the World* (San Francisco: John Howell, 1926), p. 323. Abbreviation: Wagner, Drake.

[9]Collinson, Frobisher, pp. 11–12 to end of next quotation.

[10]Taylor, Tudor Geog., p. 83. Arber, Eden,

trans. of Vannuccio Biringuccio's *Pyrotechnia*, pp. 355–69, particularly, p. 363. Eden's "Epistle to the Reader," p. 7.

[11]Collinson, Frobisher, p. 4.

[12]Lord Amherst of Hackney and Basil Thomson, eds., *The Discovery of the Solomon Islands by Alvaro de Mendaña 1568*, (London: Hakluyt Society, 1901), I, p. 83.

[13]*Ibid.*, Introduction, I, pp. lix–lxvii.

[14]Hakluyt, Voyages, MacLehose, IX, pp. 378–97, particularly, p. 392.

[15]Taylor, Tudor Geog., Document 14, p. 278. Consulted: British Library, Cotton MS Vitellius C. VII.

[16]Purchas, MacLehose, I, pp. 93, 108, 112, 114.

[17]Hakluyt, Divers Voy., p. 31.

[18]Taylor, Tudor Geog., Document 13 (iv), p. 277.

[19]E. G. R. Taylor, "Master John Dee, Drake and the Straits of Anian," *The Mariner's Mirror* (Cambridge Univ. Press), 15 (April 1929), pp. 125–29.

[20]British Library, Cotton MS Vitellius C. VII. Translation of Maximilianus in Stanley, Magellan.

[21]"Out of John Dee's book, entitled, *Famous and rich discoveries:* written in the year 1577," in *Johannis, Confratis & Monachi Glastoniensis, Chronica sive Historia de Rebus Glastoniensibus*, ed. Thomas Hearnius (Oxonii: E Theatro Sheldoniano, 1726), pp. 552–56, for this and the next quotation.

[22]Cited above in reference 21.

[23]E. G. R. Taylor, "More Light on Drake," and "John Winter's Report," *The Mariner's Mirror*, 16 (1930) pp. 134–46, and pp. 147–51, particularly p. 138 and p. 150. Of course, the "Magellan" that each could have had on board might have been "A Briefe declaration of the viage or navigation made about the Worlde. Gathered out of a large booke written hereof by Master Antoni Pigafetta . . . one of the compagnie of that vyage in the which Ferdinando Magalianes, a Portugale, was generall captayne of the navie," in Richard Eden, ed. and trans., finished by Richarde Willes, *The History of Travayle in the West and East Indies*. . . (London, 1577), pp. 431v.–448. British Library, 304.d.10. Winter Ms. is in Lansdowne MS 100, No. 2.

[24]Dee, Hearnius, pp. 552–56, for this and next quotation.

[25]British Library, Lansdowne MS 122, No.

4, f. 22 and f. 26. Cotton MSS—Otho E, VIII.

[26]Zelia Nuttall, ed. and trans., *New Light on Drake: A Collection of Documents Relating to His Voyage of Circumnavigation, 1577–1580* (London: Hakluyt Society, 1914), p. 162. Abbreviation: Nuttall, New Light.

[27]Nuttall, New Light, pp. 171–72; also 178. Another trans., Wagner, Drake, p. 365.

CHAPTER XVIII

[1]Hakluyt, Voyages, MacLehose, IX, pp. 381–82.

[2]Rowse, Grenville, pp. 96–100, particularly p. 97. Letter of May 17, 1574, to the Grand Commander of Castile, B.M. Cotton, Galba, C.v., original draft. *Calendar of Letters and State Papers Relating to English Affairs*, Preserved Principally in the Archives of Simancas, II, Elizabeth 1568–1579, ed. Martin A. S. Hume (London: Her Majesty's Stationery Office, by Eyre and Spottiswoode, 1894), No. 398, pp. 480–82, especially p. 481.

[3]Wagner, Spanish Voyages NW, pp. 63–64, and p. 318, notes 4 and 5.

[4]Holmes, pp. 148–61. Ms. Justicia 1041, A.G.I. cited.

[5]Wagner, Spanish Voyages NW, "Declaration of Juan Fernández de Ladrillero," pp. 66–71, for this and next quotation.

[6]Rowse, Expansion, p. 181. Drake hinted at this himself. Nuttall, New Light, p. 172.

[7]Rowse, Grenville, pp. 106–09.

[8]Nuttall, New Light, pp. 5–12, particularly, p.9 for this quotation, and p. 10 for next three quotations.

CHAPTER XIX

[1]In addition to the many works on Drake's Circumnavigation, two recent works afforded many insights: (1) Norman J. W. Thrower, ed., *Sir Francis Drake and the Famous Voyage, 1577–1580* (Berkeley, Los Angeles: Univ. of Calif. Press, 1984), especially the essays by John H. Parry, Helen Wallis, Norman J. W. Thrower, and Benjamin P. Draper. Abbreviation: Thrower, Drake. (2) Helen Wallis, ed., *Sir Francis Drake: An Exhibition to Commemorate Francis Drake's Voyage Around the World: 1577–1580* (London: British Library, 1977).

[2]Camden, Darcie, pp. 418–19. Wagner, Drake, p. 318. Another trans. in Purchas, MacLehose, XVI, pp. 114–15.

[3]Rowse, Grenville, p. 89.

[4]E. G. R. Taylor, "The Missing Draft Project of Drake's Voyage of 1577–80," in *The Geog. Jnl.*, 75 (Jan.–June 1930), pp. 44–47.

[5]*The World Encompassed By Sir Francis Drake . . . Carefully collected out of the notes of Master Francis Fletcher, Preacher . . .* (London: Nicholas Bourne, 1628; rpt. Ann Arbor: Univ. Microfilms, 1966), pp. 43–45.

[6]*The Observations of Sir Richard Hawkins, Knight, in his Voyage into the South Sea, Anno Domini 1593* (London, 1622). Wagner, Drake, pp. 90–91. Also Purchas, MacLehose, XVII, p. 128. Also Clements R. Markham, ed., *The Hawkins Voyages* (London: Hakluyt Society, 1878).

[7]Rowse, Grenville, p. 112.

[8]Wagner, Drake, p. 277. For support of this claim, see Bob Ward, "Lost Harbour Found! The Truth about Drake and the Pacific," *The Map Collector*, Winter 1988, pp. 2–8.

[9]World Encompassed Facsimile, pp. 60–61.

[10]Wagner, Drake, p. 349. Nuttall, New Light, p. 317.

[11]Wagner, Drake, pp. 393, 395, and 133, for this and next two quotations. Nuttall, New Light, pp. 75, 85, and 234.

[12]Wagner, Drake, pp. 148–49 and 494, notes 53 and 57. Wagner, Some Imag. Geog., pp. 25–26. Wagner, Spanish Voyages NW, p. 389.

[13]Mathes, Apocryphal Tales, p. 53, and p. 59, note 3. Jerónimo de Zárate Salmerón's account is in *Documentos para servir a la Historia de Nuevo México, 1538–1778* (Madrid: Ediciones José Porrúa Turanzas, 1962), pp. 114–204, especially pp. 197–98. Abbreviation: Doc. Nuevo Mex. Also in *Documentos para la Historia de México*, Ser. III (México: Vicente García Torres, 1856), Tomo I, pte. 1. Consulted: Charles F. Lummis' translation in *The Land of Sunshine*, 10 and 12 (Nov. 1899, and Feb. 1900).

[14]*Relaciones by Zárate Salmerón: An Account of things seen and learned by Father Jerónimo de Zárate Salmerón from the Year 1538 to Year 1626*, trans. Alicia Ronstadt Milich (Albuquerque, N. M: Horn & Wallace Pubs., 1966), pp. 96–97. Abbreviation: Zárate Salmerón, Milich. Wagner, Drake, pp. 148–49.

[15]*The Natural and Moral History of the Indies, by Father Joseph de Acosta, Reprinted from the English Translated Edition of Edward Grimston, 1604*, ed. Clements R. Markham (London: Hakluyt Society, 1880), I (Books 1-4), Chapter XII, p. 141, quotation modernized.

Consulted: José de Acosta, *Historia Natural y Moral de las Indias* (Sevilla, Juan de Leon, 1590); rpt. ed. Barbara G. Beddall (Valencia: Hispaniae Scientia, 1977), Cap. 12, p. 153.

[16]Helen Wallis, "The Cartography of Drake's Voyage," in Thrower, Drake, pp. 121–63, provided background. On the Verrazzano Sea concept re Virginia, Helen Wallis, ed., *Raleigh & Roanoke: The First English Colony in America, 1584–1590: The British Library Exhibit . . .* (Raleigh: N. C. Dept. of Cultural Resources, 1985).

[17]Bancroft, Northwest Coast, p. 66. Hakluyt, Voyages, MacLehose, VIII, p. 444.

[18]Hakluyt, Western Planting, pp. 113–14, no. 10.

[19]Wagner, Drake, p. 383.

[20]Herbert Eugene Bolton, ed. and trans., *Kino's Historical Memoir of Pimería Alta: A Contemporary Account of the Beginnings of California, Sonora, and Arizona, by Father Eusebio Francisco Kino, S. J. . . . 1683–1711* (Cleveland: Arthur H. Clark Co., 1919; rpt. Berkeley, Calif: Univ. of Calif., 1948), I, p. 329. Also II, p. 244 and p. 260. Abbreviation: Bolton, Kino.

CHAPTER XX

[1]Bolton, Kino, I, p. 329, for this and next quotation. Also II, p. 244.

[2]Nuttall, New Light, pp. 100–07, especially p. 100 and p. 107.

[3] Wagner, Drake, p. 330. "Old" and "New" California, and "Upper" and "Lower" California — the southern peninsula section "divided" from the northern mainland section — did not come into steady use until Dominicans took over the missions of Baja from the Franciscans in 1773. This ecclesiastical demarcation then became the international frontier under Article V of the Treaty of Guadalupe Hidalgo in 1848.

[4]"The Famous Voyage of Sir Francis Drake into the South Sea . . ." six unnumbered folio leaves between p. 643 and p. 644 in Hakluyt's Voyages of 1589. Hakluyt, Voyages, MacLehose, IX, p. 321. Wagner, Drake, p. 274.

[5]Wagner, Drake, p. 277.

[6]World Encompassed Facsimile, p. 64 and pp. 79–80. Next quotation, pp. 81–82.

[7]Lady Fuller Eliott-Drake, *The Family and Heirs of Sir Francis Drake* (London: Smith, Elder & Co., 1911), II, Appendix 1, Spanish text, p. 348; trans., pp. 356–57. Another version: Nuttall, New Light, p. 31.

[8]Eliott-Drake, II, Appendix 2, Spanish text, p. 371; trans. pp. 392–93. Another version, Nuttall, New Light, p. 50.

[9]"Famous Voyage," Wagner, Drake, pp. 276–77. Hakluyt, Voyages, MacLehose, IX, p. 325.

[10]World Encompassed Facsimile, p. 80.

[11]"Famous Voyage," Wagner, Drake, p. 277. Hakluyt, Voyages, MacLehose, IX, p. 326.

[12]Wagner, Drake, p. 277. Hakluyt, Voyages, MacLehose, IX, p. 325.

[13]Historia General del Mundo del tiempo del Señor Rey Don Felipe el Prudente (Valladolid, 1606) II, Bk. 9, Chap. 13. Trans. in H. R. Wagner, Drake, pp. 333–34.

[14]". . . Other news and observations by Reverend Father Luis Velarde of the Company of Jesus, rector and minister of the Pimeria," which Captain Juan Mateo Manje included in Luz De Tierra Incógnita, II. See Harry J. Karns and associates, trans., Unknown Arizona and Sonora, 1693–1721: Francisco Fernandez del Castillo version of Luz de Tierra Incognita by Captain Juan Mateo Manje—An English Translation of Part II (Tucson: Arizona Silhouettes, 1954), Chapter IX, p. 232. Abbreviation: Manje, Luz. Consulted: Juan Mateo Manje, Luz de tierra incógnita en la America Septentrional y diario de las exploraciones en Sonora (Mexico: Talleres Gráficos de la nación, 1926). Consulted: Ernest J. Burrus, S. J., "Velarde's Description of Pimeria Alta," in Kino and Manje, Explorers of Sonora and Arizona: Their Vision of the Future—A Study of Their Expeditions and Plans With An Appendix of Thirty Documents (Rome and St. Louis: Jesuit Hist. Inst. & St. Louis Univ., 1971), Appendix XIV, pp. 622–75, particularly, p. 636. Abbreviation: Burrus, Manje.

[15]Kino and the Cartography of Northwestern New Spain (Tucson: Ariz. Pioneers' Hist. Soc., 1965), p. 39. Abbreviation: Burrus, Kino.

[16]Origen de los Indias de el Nuevo Mundo e Indias Occidentales (Madrid, 1729), Libro Quarto, ff. xii, p. 289.

[17]Hakluyt, Voyages, MacLehose, IX, p. 122. Quotations to end of chapter are from pp. 127, 129, 148, 212, and 318–19.

CHAPTER XXI

[1]Letter of October 16, 1580, B.M. MSS. 28, 420. Calendar of Letters and State Papers Relating to English Affairs Preserved Principally in the Archives of Simancas, III, Elizabeth 1580–1586,

ed. Martin A. S. Hume (London: Her Majesty's Stationery Office, by Eyre and Spottiswoode, 1896), No. 44, pp.54–56, for this and next two quotations.

[2]See Helen Wallis, "The Cartography of Drake's Voyage," in Thrower, Drake, pp. 136–37. MS in Latin, Lib. of Cong., Kraus Collection; H. P. Kraus, Sir Francis Drake: A Pictorial Biography (Amsterdam, 1970).

[3]The California Coast: A Bilingual Edition of Documents from the Sutro Collection, translated and edited in 1891 by George Butler Griffin; re-edited and emended by Donald C. Cutter (Norman: Univ. of Okla. Press, 1969), pp. 10–11. Abbreviation: Sutro, Cutter. Consulted: George Butler Griffin, ed. and trans., Documents from the Sutro Collection—Pubs. of the Hist. Soc. of So. Calif. (Los Angeles: Franklin Pntg. Co., 1891). Abbreviation: Sutro, Griffin.

[4]Sutro, Cutter, pp. 20–23, for this and next quotation.

[5]Antonio de Espejo, "Account of the Journey to the Province and Settlements of New Mexico, 1583," Herbert Eugene Bolton, Spanish Exploration in the Southwest: 1542–1706 (N. Y: Charles Scribner's Sons, 1908; rpt. New York: Barnes & Noble, 1946, 1952), pp. 168–92, particularly, p. 187. Abbreviation: Bolton, Span. Explor. SW.

[6]Obregón, Hammond-Rey, p. 253.

[7]Bancroft, Northwest Coast, p. 63. "Testimonio dado en Mexico sobre el descubrimiento . . . ," Colección Indias, XV, pp. 80–151, particularly, for Vargas, pp. 133–34.

[8]Sutro, Cutter, Spanish, p.22. Wagner, Spanish Voyages NW, p. 153.

[9]Obregón, Hammond-Rey, p. 253; Obregón, Cuevas, p. 226.

[10]Hakluyt, Voyages, MacLehose, IV, pp. 335–37, for this and next quotation.

[11]Wagner, Spanish Voyages NW, pp. 139–53, particularly p. 143, and for next quotation, p. 149.

[12]Henry Raup Wagner, trans., "The Voyage of Sebastian Rodriguez Cermeño," Calif. Hist. Soc. Qtly., 3, no. 1 (April 1924), pp. 11–17 for this and the next three quotations.

[13]Sutro, Cutter, pp. 36–39.

[14]Background from: W. Michael Mathes, ed., Californiana II, Documentos para la Historia de la Explotación Comercial de California: 1611–1679 (Madrid: Ediciones José Porrúa Turanzas, 1970), I, Introduction, pp. xxxix–xlix. Abbre-

viation: Mathes, Californiana II, Doc. Explotación Com. I. Also Mathes, *The Pearl Hunters in the Gulf of California 1668* (Los Angeles: Dawson's Book Shop, 1966), Introduction, pp. 9–19. Abbreviation: Mathes, Pearl Hunters.

[15]Hakluyt, Voyages, MacLehose, VII, p. 423. Also Thomas Rundall, ed., *Narratives of Voyages Towards the North-West in Search of a Passage to Cathay and India: 1496–1631* (London: Hakluyt Society, 1849), pp. 50–51. Abbreviation: Thomas Rundall, Voyages NW.

CHAPTER XXII

[1]W. Michael Mathes, *Vizcaíno and Spanish Expansion in the Pacific Ocean: 1580–1630* (San Francisco: Calif. Hist. Soc., 1968) provided background. Abbreviation: Mathes, Vizcaíno.

[2]"Autos Hechos por Sebastian Vizcaíno . . . 1593–1596," Mathes, *Californiana I: Documentos para la Historia de la Demarcación Comercial de California: 1583–1632* (Madrid: José Porrúa Turanzas, 1965), I, pp. 179–260, particularly, p. 186. Abbreviation: Mathes, Californiana I: Doc. Demarcación Com. I.

[3]"Asiento que Tomo el Virrey . . . con Sebastian Vizcaíno," Mathes, Californiana I: Doc. Demarcación Com., I, No. 15, pp. 96–116, particularly pp. 98 and 99.

[4]Day, Coronado's Quest, pp. 325–26, note 4. Irving Berdine Richman, *California under Spain and Mexico, 1535–1847* (Boston and N. Y: Houghton Mifflin, 1911), p. 364. See a similar statement in Wagner, Pearl Fishing Enterprises, p. 219.

[5]Sutro, Cutter, pp. 74–77.

[6]Sutro, Cutter, pp. 74–75, note 3. Sutro, Griffin, p. 47, note 4.

[7]Sutro, Cutter, pp. 94–95, and 90–91, and 109, for next two quotations.

[8]Wagner, Spanish Voyages NW, p. 278. A letter, from the Viceroy to the King, of Aug. 4, 1607.

[9]Portillo, Descubrimientos, Apendice II, pp. 301–07, particularly p. 306. Francisco Carrasco y Guiasola, ed., *Documentos Referentes al Reconocimiento de las Costas de las Californias desde el Cabo San Lucas al de Mendocino*, Anuario de la Dirección de Hidrografía (Madrid, 1882), Parte V, pp. 447–48. Consultado: Trans. in Wagner, Spanish Voyages NW, pp. 376–77, Note 27, for this and next quotation.

[10]Wagner, Spanish Voyages NW, pp. 176 and 376, notes 24 and 25.

[11]Bolton, Span. Explor. SW, pp. 52–103, particularly pp. 75 and 91–97, for this and next eight quotations.

[12]Bolton, Span. Explor. SW, pp. 101–02, particularly note 2. Portillo, Descubrimientos, Apendice IV, p. 351. "Relación que dío el Contra Maestre de la fragata Los Tres Reyes," at end of "Derrotero desde Acapulco al Cabo Mendocino."

[13]Juan de Torquemada, *Monarquía Indiana* (Seville, 1615; rpt. Mexico: Editorial Porrúa, S. A., 1969), I (Lib. V, Cap. LV), p. 719. Consulted: Englished Venegas, II, pp. 292–93

[14]Wagner, Spanish Voyages NW, p. 389, and context. Wagner, Some Imag. Geog., p. 4, pp. 22–23 and following. These two works provided background for this section, together with Bancroft's and Leighly's cited works.

[15]Mathes, Californiana I, Doc. Demarcación Com., II, No. 80, pp. 715–20, particularly, p. 719. Mathes, Vizcaíno, p. 114, note 19.

CHAPTER XXIII

[1]Bancroft, Northwest Coast, I, pp. 62–63. Mathes, Vizcaíno, p. 162.

[2]Zárate Salmerón, Milich, p. 96.

[3]Colección Indias, XV, pp. 138–41. Bancroft, Northwest Coast, I, p. 63.

[4]George P. Hammond and Agapito Rey, eds. and trans., *Don Juan de Oñate: Colonizer of New Mexico, 1595–1628* (Albuquerque: Univ. of N. M. Press, 1953), II, p. 602. Abbreviation: Oñate, Hammond-Rey. Next three quotations and fragments are from: II, pp. 620, 621, 921.

[5]"Father Escobar's Relation of the Oñate Expedition to California," ed. and trans. Herbert Eugene Bolton, *Cath. Hist. Rev.*, 5, no. 1 (April 1919), pp. 23–41, specifically, pp. 36–37. Abbreviation: Escobar, Bolton. Consulted: Oñate, Hammond-Rey, II, pp. 1023–27.

[6]Escobar, Bolton, pp. 30–38, for this and next seven quotations.

[7]Oñate, Hammond-Rey, II, pp. 1009–10, for this and next two quotations.

[8]Wagner, Spanish Voyages NW. p. 409, note 212. Wagner deduces that Zárate Salmerón "evidently had in his possession" Marqués' account when he wrote his Relaciones.

[9]Wagner, Spanish Voyages NW, p. 266. Quo-

tations to end of chapter are from pp. 266–67, pp. 408, 409, notes 212, 216.

CHAPTER XXIV

[1] Wagner, Spanish Voyages NW: "Bibliographical Note on the Accounts of Father Antonio," p. 378.

[2] California As An Island, p. 25.

[3] Wagner, Apocryphal Voyages, pp. 8–13. Mathes, Vizcaíno, pp. 51–52, 118–19. Mathes, Apocryphal Tales, pp. 54–55.

[4] García Icazbalceta, Colección, II, p. 303.

[5] Wagner's translation in Spanish Voyages NW, pp. 180–272, particularly pp. 180–81 and 190, for this and next four quotations. Mathes, Apocryphal Tales, pp. 54–55, and p. 59, note 16.

[6] Wagner, Spanish Voyages NW, pp. 244–55.

[7] Wagner, Spanish Voyages NW, pp. 265–67 for this and next four quotations.

[8] Bolton's translation in Span. Explor. SW, pp. 104–34, particularly pp. 109–12 for this and next two quotations. Consulted: Colección Indias, VIII, pp. 539–74.

[9] Camden, Darcie, p. 429. Wagner, Drake, p. 323.

CHAPTER XXV

[1] W. Michael Mathes, ed. and trans., *Geographic and Hydrographic Descriptions of Many Northern and Southern Lands and Seas in the Indies, Specifically of the Discovery of the Kingdom of California (1632). By Nicolás de Cardona* (Los Angeles: Dawson's Book Shop, 1974), Introduction, pp. 11–19. Abbreviation: Mathes, Cardona. Mathes, Californiana II. Doc. Explotación Com. I. Intro. pp. xliii–xliv. Relevant documents in Part II.

[2] Mathes, Cardona, pp. 95–106, particularly p. 104. Colección Indias, IX, pp. 30–42, particularly p. 39.

[3] Mathes, Cardona, pp. 95–98.

[4] Mathes, Cardona, p. 97 and p. 106.

[5] Bolton's translation in Span. Explor. SW, pp. 268–80, particularly pp. 272–76 for this and next quotation. Consulted: Zárate Salmerón, Milich, pp. 68–72.

[6] Trans. Charles Upson Clarke (Washington: Smithsonian Misc. Coll., 1942), p. 220. Quoted in Leighly, p. 27. Leighly's essay provided background for this section.

[7] Portillo, Descubrimientos, Apendice IX, pp. 447–48. Quoted in Leighly, p. 31

[8] Fred John Millard, ed. and trans., *The Arctic North-East and West Passage — Detectio Freti Hudsoni, or Hessel Gerritsz's Collection of Tracts . . . new English trans.* (of Dutch and Latin editions of 1612, 1613), (Amsterdam: Frederik Muller & Co., 1878), pp. 7–8, for this and next quotation.

[9] "Cartographical Note," Wagner, Spanish Voyages NW, pp. 384–91. Wagner, Some Imag. Geog., pp. 28–29. Also Henry Raup Wagner, *The Cartography of the Northwest Coast of America to the Year 1800*, (Berkeley, Calif: Univ. of Calif. Press, 1937). I, pp. 114–15. Also used Bancroft, Leighly, and Portillo.

[10] Shirley, Mapping of the World, Plate 233, p. 327.

[11] Denis Diderot and Jean Le Rond d'Alembert, *Encyclopédie*, (Paris, 1751–1772), Volumes VII and VIII, Supplement, Tome 2, "Californie" entry p. 133.

[12] Published London: 1622, pp. 45–50, particularly p. 48. Rpt., rev., Purchas, MacLehose, XIV, pp. 422–26.

[13] Bolton, Span. Explor. SW, p. 121. Similar statements, Wagner, Spanish Voyages NW, pp. 255, 267.

[14] Bolton, Span. Explor. SW, p. 278.

[15] Wagner, Spanish Voyages NW, pp. 387–88. Map is reproduced as Plate VII. Wagner, Some Imag. Geog. pp. 29–34.

[16] Thomas Rundall, ed., Voyages NW, pp. 84, 90, 91, for this and next quotation.

[17] Shirley, The Mapping of the World, p. 341, Plate 241.

[18] (Oxford: For the University, 1625; 2nd ed., 1635), Book II, Chapter VII, p. 115. Next three quotations from Book II, Chapter VII, pp. 130–31. See also J. N. L. Baker, "Nathanael Carpenter and English Geography in the Seventeenth Century," *The Geog. Jl.*, 71, no. 3 (March 1928), pp. 261–71, particularly, p. 268.

[19] (Leyden, 1625; 2nd. ed., 1630, in Dutch; rev. 1633, in Latin). Trans. from French version: *L'Histoire du Nouveau Monde ou Description des Indes Occidentales . . .* (A Leyde: pour l'Université, 1640), Book 16, Chapter XI, p. 207, for this and all following quotations from De Laet.

[20] Encyclopédie, "Californie," p. 133.

[21]*California as an Island, a Geographical Misconception: Illustrated by 100 examples from 1625–1770* (London: The Map Collectors' Circle, 1964).

[22]Doc. Nuevo Mex., p. 244.

CHAPTER XXVI

[1]W. Michael Mathes, trans. and ed., *Spanish Approaches to the Island of California, 1628–1632* (San Francisco: Book Club of Calif., 1975). This and the next three quotations are from pp. 8, 25, 45, and 7. Introduction provided background.

[2]Colección Indias, IX, pp. 19–29, particularly p. 27. Consulted: trans. Bancroft, Northwest Coast, p. 107, note 12.

[3]Trans. Holmes, pp. 226–61, particularly p. 234. Consulted: Mathes, Pearl Hunters, pp. 40–41.

[4]Mathes, Pearl Hunters, pp. 39–40, note 38; p. 57, note 70. Holmes p. 243.

[5]General background: Burrus, Manje, First Part. Bolton, Kino. Bolton, Span. Explor. SW, Introduction. Burrus, Kino.

[6]Bolton, Span. Explor. SW, p. 457.

[7]Ernest J. Burrus, S. J., ed. and trans., *Kino Writes to The Duchess: Letters of Eusebio Francisco Kino, S. J., to the Duchess of Aveiro* (Rome: Jesuit Hist. Inst., and St. Louis: St. Louis Univ., 1965), Letter XXIII, p. 167.

[8]Bolton, Kino, I, pp. 333–34. Quotations to end of chapter: pp. 229, 195–96; 208–09; 231; 231–32; 241; 249; 284; 330, 334–35; 345.

CHAPTER XXVII

[1]Burrus, Manje, p. 273. Second part of quotation, p. 270. See main refs. at note 14 of Chap. XX.

[2]Burrus, Manje, p. 477, note 32. Cf. p. 504, note 44. Also p. 107.

[3]Bolton, Kino, I, p. 284

[4]Doc. Nuevo Mexico, pp. 244–48.

[5]Manje, Luz, pp. 227–31, for this and next five quotations. Consulted: Burrus, Manje, Appendix XIV, pp. 630–38.

[6]Peter Masten Dunne, ed. and trans., *Jacobo Sedelmayr, Missionary, Frontiersman, Explorer in Arizona and Sonora: Four Original Manuscript Narratives, 1744–1751* (Tucson: Ariz. Pion. Hist. Soc., 1955), pp. 35–37, and p. 51, note 67. Abbreviation: Sedelmayr, Dunne.

CHAPTER XXVIII

[1]Part II, Section VII, Chapter VI, p. 177.

Background: Tooley, California as an Island, Introduction, p. 4. Next quotation: Part II, Chapter XI, pp. 280–81.

[2](Rpt. New York: Dover Publications, 1968), p. 189.

[3](London: A. Bell, 1712), pp. 312–13. Englished Venegas, II, Appendix IV, pp. 353–54.

[4]*Gulliver's Travels by Jonathan Swift, DD. The Text of the First Edition*, Part II: A Voyage to Brobdingnag, ed. Harold Williams (London: First Edition Club, 1926), facsimile of map opp. p. 107; text, pp. 146–47.

[5]"The South-Sea Project. 1721," *The Works of the Rev. Jonathan Swift, D.D., Dean of St. Patrick's Dublin, Arranged by Thomas Sheridan*, corrected and revised by John Nichols (London: J. Johnson and others, 1808), XVI, pp. 235–42. History of poem: "The Bubble," 1720, *The Poems of Jonathan Swift*, ed. Harold Williams (Oxford: Clarendon Press, 1937), I, pp. 248–59.

[6]Tooley, California as an Island, Introduction, p.4.

[7]*French Mapping of the Americas* (London: Map Collectors' Circle, 1967), Fourth Volume, Series number: 33, Introduction, p. 5.

[8]"Seconde Lettre de M. De Lisle à M. Cassini pour justifier quelques endroits de Ses Globes et de Ses Cartes," *Le Journal des Sçavans pour L'Année MDCC* (Paris: Chez Jean Cusson, 1700), 20, Monday, May 24, pp. 208–14. Reprinted as "Lettre de M. de Lisle touchant la California," in *Recueil de Voyages au Nord* (Amsterdam, 1715), III, pp. 268–77. Background, Wagner, Cartography NW, I, pp. 140–42; Leighly, pp. 37–38, etc. This ref. serves this and the next four quotations.

[9]*Considérations Géographiques et Physiques sur les Nouvelles Découvertes au Nord de la Grande Mer, Appellée Vulgairement la Mer du Sud* (Paris: L'Academie Royale des Sciences, 1753), pp. 68–73. This and remaining quotations to end of chapter are from pp 71–72.

[10]Sarah Tyacke, "Maps and Myths" in Gillian Hill, *Cartographical Curiosities* (London: The British Library, 1978), p. 29.

[11]Shirley, The Mapping of the World, Plates 417 and 426, pp. 600 and 612.

CHAPTER XXIX

[1]Englished Venegas, II, p. 42.

[2]Englished Venegas, II, p. 42. On p. 71, Venegas regrets having to work without Ugarte's papers, which "could not be found." Next four quotations are from: pp. 24, 68, 60–61.

[3]Englished Venegas, II, Appendix III, pp. 308–53, particularly, pp. 344–49. The next quotation is from pp. 201–02, where Venegas cites "a curious extract of this journal" to be seen in the new "Theatro Americano." The map is between pp. 12 and 13, in I.

[4]Sedelmayr, Dunne, p. 51, note 67.

[5]Ernest J. Burrus, S. J., ed. and trans., *Wenceslaus Linck's Diary of his 1766 Expedition to Northern Baja California* (Los Angeles: Dawson's Book Store, 1966), p. 80.

[6]Englished Venegas, Preface, pp. A2 to A4, for this and following quotations.

[7]Thrower, Drake, essay by Thrower, "The Aftermath: A Summary of British Discovery in the Pacific between Drake and Cook," pp. 164–72. John C. Beaglehole, ed., *The Journals of Captain James Cook on his Voyages of Discovery. . . 1776–1780* (Cambridge: Hakluyt Society, 1967). p. ccxxi.

[8]Elna S. Bakker, *An Island Called California: An Ecological Introduction to its Natural Communities* (Berkeley: Univ. of Calif. Press, 1971), preface, p. xi.

[9]Malcolm Edwards, ed., *The California Diary of General E. D. Townsend* (Los Angeles: Ward Ritchie Press, 1970), p. 130.

Bibliography

Acosta, José de. *See* Beddall, Barbara G. *José de Acosta: Historia. Also* Markham, Clements R., ed. *The Natural and Moral History.*

Ailly, Pierre d'. *See* Buron, Edmond, ed. *Ymago Mundi.*

Aiton, Arthur Scott. *Antonio de Mendoza: First Viceroy of New Spain.* Durham, N.C: Duke Univ. Press, 1927.

Alarcón, Hernando. *See* Hakluyt, Richard. *The Principal Navigations*, IX, containing "The Voyage and Discovery of Fernando Alarchon."

Altolaguirre y Duvale, Angel de, ed. *Vasco Nuñez de Balboa: Estudio Histórico.* Madrid: Real Academia de la Historia; Imprenta del Patronato de Huérfanos de Intendencia é Intervención Militares, 1914.

Alvar, Manuel, ed. *Diario del Descubrimiento.* 2 vols. Madrid: Ediciones del Excmo. Cabildo Insular de Gran Canaria, 1976.

Amherst, William Amhurst Tyssen-Amherst, and Basil Thomson, eds. and trans. *The Discovery of the Solomon Islands by Alvaro de Mendaña 1568.* 2 vols. London: The Hakluyt Society, 1901.

Anderson, Charles L.G. *Life and Letters of Vasco Nuñez de Balboa.* New York: Fleming H. Revell Co., 1941.

Arber, Edward, ed. *The First Three English Books on America [? 1511]–1555 A.D. Being chiefly Translations, Compilations, &c., by Richard Eden, From the Writings, Maps, &c., of PIETRO MARTIRE, of Anghiera (1455–1526), SEBASTIAN MUNSTER, the Cosmographer (1489–1552), SEBASTIAN CABOT, of Bristol (1474–1557), With Extracts, &c., from the Works of other Spanish, Italian, and German Writers of the Time.* Birmingham, 1885.

Ascensión, Father Antonio de la. *See* Wagner, Henry Raup, ed. and trans. *Spanish Voyages*, containing "Father Ascensión's Account." *Also see* Bolton, Herbert Eugene, ed. and trans. *Spanish Explorations*, containing "A Brief Relation." *Also* Pacheco, Joaquín F., et al., eds. *Colección de Documentos, Indias*, VIII.

Austin, Herbert D. "New Light on the Name California." *Publications of the Historical Society of Southern California*, 12, No. 3 (1923), 29–31.

Baker, J.N.L. "Nathanael Carpenter and English Geography in the Seventeenth Century." *The Geographical Jnl.*, 71, No. 3 (March, 1928).

Bakker, Elna S. *An Island Called California: An Ecological Introduction to its Natural Communities.* Berkeley: Univ. of Calif. Press, 1971.

Balboa, Vasco Nunēz de. *See* Altolaguirre y Duval, Angel de, ed. *Also* Anderson, Charles L. G.; and Romoli, Kathleen.

Baldwin, Percy M. "Fray Marcos de Niza's *Relación.*" *New Mex. Hist. Rev.,* 1 (April, 1926), 193–223.

Bancroft, Hubert Howe. *History of California, I, 1542–1800. The Works of Hubert Howe Bancroft,* XVIII. San Francisco: A. L. Bancroft & Co., 1884.

Bancroft, Hubert Howe. *History of the North Mexican States and Texas, I, 1531–1800. The Works of Hubert Howe Bancroft,* XV. San Francisco: A. L. Bancroft & Co., 1884.

Bancroft, Hubert Howe. *History of the Northwest Coast, I, 1543–1800. The Works of Hubert Howe Bancroft,* XXVII. San Francisco: A. L. Bancroft & Co., 1884.

Bandelier, Adolph F. *See* Rodack, Madeleine Turrell, ed. and trans. *Adolph F. Bandelier's 'The Discovery of New Mexico'.*

Barlow, Roger. "Brief Somme of Geographia." British Library, Royal MSS. 18. B. xxviii. *See also* Taylor, E. G. R., ed. *A Brief Summe of Geographie.*

Beaglehole, John C., ed. *The Journals of Captain James Cook on his Voyages of Discovery: The Voyage of the "Resolution" and "Discovery," 1776–1780.* Cambridge: The Hakluyt Society, 1967.

Beddall, Barbara G., ed. *José de Acosta: Historia Natural y Moral de las Indias (Sevilla, Juan de Leon, 1590).* Valencia: Hispaniae Scientia, 1977.

Best, George. *A True Discourse of the late Voyage of Discovery, for finding a passage to Cathaya.* London: H. Bynneman, 1578; rpt. in Collinson, Richard, ed. *The Three Voyages of Martin Frobisher . . .* London, 1867.

Biringuccio, Vannuccio. *Pyrotechnia.* 1540. *See* Arber, Edward, ed. *The First Three English Books on America.*

Blázquez y Delgado Aguilar, Antonio, ed. *Islario General de Todas Las Islas del Mundo por Alonso de Santa Cruz.* 2 vols. Madrid: Real Sociedad Geográfica, 1918.

Bolton, Herbert Eugene, ed. and trans. "Father Escobar's Relation of the Oñate Expedition to California." *Cath. Hist. Rev.,* 5, No. 1 (April, 1919), 23–41.

Bolton, Herbert Eugene, ed. and trans. *Kino's Historical Memoir of Pimería Alta: A Contemporary Account of the Beginnings of California, Sonora, and Arizona, by Father Eusebio Francisco Kino, S. J., 1683–1711.* 2 vols. Cleveland: Arthur H. Clark Co., 1919; rpt., 1 vol., Berkeley: Univ. of Calif. Press, 1948.

Bolton, Herbert Eugene. *Spanish Exploration in the Southwest: 1542–1706*. New York: Charles Scribner's Sons, 1908; rpt. New York: Barnes & Noble, 1946, 1952.

Boorstin, Daniel J. *The Discoverers*. New York: Random House, 1983; rpt. London: Penguin Books, 1986.

Brault, Gerard J., ed. and trans. *The Song of Roland: An Analytical Edition*. 2 vols. *Volume II, Oxford Text and English Translation*. London and University Park: The Penn. State Univ. Press, 1978.

Briggs, Henry. "A Treatise of the Northwest Passage to the South Sea through the Continent of Virginia and by Fretum Hudson." *See* Edward Waterhouse, *A Declaration of the state of the Colony and Affaires in Virginia*; rpt. Purchas, Samuel, ed. *His Pilgrimes*, XIV.

Buache, Philippe. *Considérations Géographiques et Physiques sur les Nouvelles Découvertes au Nord de la Grande Mer, Appellée Vulgairement la Mer du Sud*. Paris: L'Académie Royale des Sciences, 1753.

Buron, Edmond, ed. and trans. *Ymago Mundi de Pierre d'Ailly: Texte Latin et Traduction Française des quatre traités cosmographiques de d'Ailly et des notes marginales de Christophe Colomb*. 3 vols. Paris: Maisonneuve Frères, 1930–31.

Burrus, Ernest J. *Kino and Manje, Explorers of Sonora and Arizona: Their Vision of the Future—A Study of Their Expeditions and Plans With An Appendix of Thirty Documents*. Rome and St. Louis: Jesuit Hist. Inst. & St. Louis Univ., 1971.

Burrus, Ernest J. *Kino and the Cartography of Northwestern New Spain*. Tucson: Ariz. Pioneers' Hist. Soc., 1965.

Burrus, Ernest J., ed. *Kino Escribe a la Duquesa: Correspondencia del P. Eusebio Francisco Kino con la Duquesa de Aveiro*. Madrid: José Porrúa Turanzas, 1964.

Burrus, Ernest J., ed. and trans. *Kino Writes to the Duchess: Letters of Eusebio Francisco Kino, S. J., to the Duchess of Aveiro*. Rome and St. Louis: Jesuit Hist. Inst., and St. Louis Univ., 1965.

Burrus, Ernest J., ed. and trans. *Wenceslaus Linck's Diary of his 1766 Expedition to Northern Baja California*. Los Angeles: Dawson's Book Store, 1966.

Cabrillo, Juan Rodriguez. *See* Wagner, Henry Raup. *Spanish Voyages*, containing "The Voyage of Juan Rodriguez Cabrillo." *Also* Pacheco, Joaquín F. ed. *Colección de Documentos Inéditos*, Indias, XIV.

Calendar of Letters and State Papers Relating to English Affairs, Preserved Principally in the Archives of Simancas, II, Elizabeth 1568–1579, and III, Elizabeth 1580–1586. Ed. Martin A. S. Hume. London: Her Majesty's Stationery Office, by Eyre and Spottiswoode, 1894 and 1896.

Calendar of Letters, Despatches and State Papers Relating to the Negotiations Between England and Spain, Preserved in the Archives at Vienna, Brussels, Simancas and Elsewhere, X, Edward VI 1550–1552. Ed. Royall Tyler. London: His Majesty's Stationery Office by Hereford Times, Ltd., 1914.

Calendar of State Papers, Domestic Series, of the Reigns of Edward VI, Mary, Elizabeth, 1547–1580, Preserved in the State Paper Department of Her Majesty's Public Record Office. Ed. Robert Lemon. London: Longman, Brown, Green, Longmans & Roberts, 1856.

Camden, William. *See* Darcie, Abraham, trans. of *Annales Rerum Anglicarum, et Hibernicarum, regnante Elizabetha, ad Annum Salutis MDLXXXIX.* London, 1615.

Cardona, Nicolás de. *See* Mathes, W. Michael, ed, and trans. *Geographic and Hydrographic Descriptions. Also see* Mathes, W. Michael, ed. *Californiana II, Explotación Comercial,* I. *Also* Pacheco, Joaquín F., et al., eds. *Colección de Documentos,* Indias IX.

Carpenter, Nathanael. *Geographie Delineated Forth in Two Bookes.* Oxford: John Lichfield and Wm. Turner, Printers to the famous University for Henry Cripps, 1625; 2d, corrected ed., 1635.

Carrasco y Guiasola, Francisco, ed. *Documentos referentes al reconocimiento de las costas de las Californias desde el cabo de San Lucas al de Mendocino.* Anuario de la Dirección de Hidrografía. Madrid, 1882.

Carrera Stampa, Manuel, ed. *Memoria de los Servicios que habia hecho Nuño de Guzmán, desde que fué nombrado Gobernador de Panuco en 1525.* México: José Porrúa e Hijos Sucs., 1955.

Carriazo, Juan de Mata, ed. *Alonso de Santa Cruz: Crónica de Los Reyes Católicos.* Sevilla: Escuela de Estudios Hispano-Americanos, 1951.

Castañeda, Pedro de. *See* Winship, George Parker, ed. and trans. *The Journey of Coronado;* Hammond, George P., and Agapito Rey, eds. and trans. *Narratives of the Coronado Expedition.*

Cavallero Carranco, Father Juan, and Francisco de Lucenilla. *See* Holmes, Maurice G. *From New Spain by Sea. Also* Mathes, W. Michael. *The Pearl Hunters in the Gulf.*

Cermeño, Sebastian Rodriguez. *See* Wagner, Henry Raup. "The Voyage of Sebastian Rodriguez Cermeño." *Spanish Voyages,* 154–167.

Cervantes de Salazar, Francisco. *Crónica de la Nueva España,* I. ed. Francisco Paso y Troncoso. Madrid: Hispanic Society of America, 1914.

Chapman, Charles E. *A History of California: The Spanish Period.* New York: Macmillan, 1921, 1928.

Chatwin, Bruce. *In Patagonia.* New York: Summit Books, 1977.

Clarke, Charles Upson, trans. *Compendium and Description of the West Indies, by Antonio Vasquez de Espinosa*. Washington: Smithsonian Misc. Coll., 1942.

Clissold, Stephen. *The Seven Cities of Cibola*. New York: Clarkson N. Potter, Inc., 1962.

Colección de Documentos Inéditos . . . de Indias. See Pacheco, Joaquín F., et al., eds.

Colección de Documentos Inéditos . . . de Ultramar. See Pacheco, Joaquín F., et al., eds.

Colección de Documentos Inéditos para la Historia de España. See Navarrete, Martín Fernández de, et al., eds.

Colección de Documentos para la Historia de México. See García Icazbalceta, Joaquín, ed.

Collinson, Richard, ed. *The Three Voyages of Martin Frobisher in Search of A Passage to Cathaia and India by the North-West, A. D. 1576–8*. London: The Hakluyt Society, 1867.

Columbus, Christopher. See Morison, Samuel Eliot, ed. and trans. *Journals and Other Documents*. Also Jane, Lionel Cecil, ed. and trans. *Select Documents*; Vilanova, Antonio, ed. *Diario*; Alvar, Manuel, ed. *Diario*.

Consag, Father Fernando. See Venegas, Miguel. *A Natural and Civil History*, II, Appendix III.

Coronado, Francisco Vásquez de. See Hakluyt, Richard, ed. *The Principal Navigations*, IX, containing "The Relation of Francis Vasquez de Coronado." Also Hammond, George P., and Agapito Rey, eds. and trans. *Narratives of the Coronado Expedition*; Winship, George Parker, ed. and trans. *The Journey of Coronado*.

Cortés, Fernando. *Cartas de Relación de Fernando Cortés sobre el Descubrimiento y Conquista de la Nueva España* in *Biblioteca de Autores Españoles desde la formación del lenguaje hasta nuestros dias*, XXII, *Historiadores Primitivos de Indias I*. Ed. Enrique de Vedia. Madrid. Imprenta de los Sucesores de Hernando, 1918. Rpt. 1946.

Cortés, Hernan. *Cartas de Relación de la Conquista de México*. Madrid: Calpe, 1922. 2nd ed. 2 vols. Madrid: Espasa-Calpe S.A., 1932, 1961.

Cortés, Hernan (also Fernando). See MacNutt, Francis Augustus, ed. and trans. *Letters of Cortés*. Also Pagden, A. R., ed. and trans. *Hernan Cortés: Letters*; Mathes, W. Michael, ed. and trans. *The Conquistador in California*; Cuevas, P. Mariano, ed. *Cartas . . . de Cortés*; Gayangos y Arce, Pascual de, ed. *Cartas . . . de Cortés*; Wagner, H. R. *The Rise of Fernando Cortés*. Miller, Robert Ryal.

Crockett, Grace Lilian, trans. *Mange's Luz de Tierra Incognita: A Translation of the Original Manuscript, together with an Historical Introduction.* M.A. Thesis, Univ. of Calif., Berkeley, 1918.

Cuevas, P. Mariano, ed. *Cartas y Otros Documentos de Hernan Cortés, novisimamente descubiertos en el Archivo General de Indias de la Ciudad de Sevilla.* Sevilla: Tip. de F. Díaz y comp^a., 1915.

Cuevas, P. Mariano, ed. *Historia de los Descubrimientos Antiguos y Modernos de la Nueva España, Escrita por el Conquistador Baltasar de Obregón Año de 1584.* Mexico: La Sria. de Education Publica, 1924.

Cutter, Donald C. "Sources of the Name 'California.'" *Arizona and the West: A Qtly. Jnl. of Hist.*, 3, No. 3 (Autumn, 1961), 233–244.

Cutter, Donald C., ed. and trans. *The California Coast: A Bilingual Edition of Documents from the Sutro Collection, translated and edited in 1891 by George Butler Griffin: Re-edited and Emended.* Norman: Univ. of Okla. Press, 1969.

D'Ailly, Pierre. *See* Buron, Edmond. *Ymago Mundi.*

Dampier, William. *A New Voyage Round the World.* London: James Knapton, 1697; rpt. New York: Dover Publications, 1968.

Darcie, Abraham, trans. *The True and Royall History of the Famous Empresse Elizabeth, Queene of England, France and Ireland &c.* London: Printed for Benjamin Fisher, 1625. *See* Camden, William.

Davidson, George. "The Origin and the Meaning of the Name California." *Trans. and Proc. of the Geog. Soc. of the Pacific*, Ser. II, 4, Pt. 1 (1910), pp. 1–50.

Day, Arthur Grove. *Coronado's Quest: The Discovery of the Southwestern States.* Berkeley and Los Angeles: Univ. of Calif. Press, 1964.

Deacon, Richard. *John Dee: Scientist, Geographer, Astrologer, and Secret Agent to Elizabeth I.* London: Muller, 1968.

Deane, Charles, ed. *Documentary History of the State of Maine. II. Containing A Discourse on Western Planting, Written in the Year 1584, by Richard Hakluyt.* Cambridge: Published by the Maine Hist. Soc., Press of John Wilson and Son, 1877.

Dee, John. *General and Rare Memorials, Pertayning to the Perfect Arte of Navigation, Annexed to the Paradoxical Cumpas in Playne: Now first published 24 yeres, after the Invention thereof.* London: John Daye, 1577.

Dee, John. *The Great Volume of Famous and Rich Discoveries.* British Library, Cotton MS Vitellius C. VII.

Dee, John. *See* Hearnius, Thomas. *Johannis . . .*

De Laet. *See* Laet, Joannes de.

De Lisle *or* De L'Isle. *See* Lisle, Guillaume de.

Destombes, Marcel. *Mappemondes: A. D. 1200–1500:* Catalogue préparé par la Commission des Cartes Anciennes de L'Union Géographique Internationale. I: Monuments Cartographiques Anciens. Amsterdam: N. Israel, 1964.

Díaz del Castillo, Bernal. *Historia Verdadera de la Conquista de la Nueva España.* Madrid 1632; rpt. 3 vols. México: Pedro Robredo, 1939. *Also* México: Editorial Porrúa, S.A., 1960.

Díaz del Castillo, Bernal. *See* García, Genaro, ed. *Historia Verdadera;* Maudslay, Alfred Percival, ed. and trans. *The True History;* Lockhart, John Ingram, ed. and trans. *The Memoirs.*

Diderot, Denis, and Jean le Rond d'Alembert. *Encyclopédie.* Paris, 1751–1772. "Californie," VII & VIII, Supplement, Tome 2, 133.

Dillon, Myles, and Nora Chadwick. *The Celtic Realms.* New York: New American Library, 1967.

Documentos para la Historia de la Demarcación Comercial de California: 1583–1632 — *See* Mathes, W. Michael, ed. *Californiana I.*

Documentos para la Historia de la Explotación Comercial de California: 1611–1679 — *See* Mathes, W. Michael, ed. *Californiana II.*

Documentos para la Historia de México. 4 series. 21 vols in 19. México: Imprenta de Vicente García Torres and others, 1853–1857.

Documentos para servir a la Historia del Nuevo México, 1538–1778. Madrid: Ediciones José Porrúa Turanzas, 1962.

Documentos referentes al reconocimiento de las costas de las Californias . . . See Carrasco Y Guiasola, Francisco, ed.

Drake, Sir Francis. *See: The World Encompassed. Also* "The Famous Voyage" in Hakluyt, Richard, ed. *The Principall Navigations, 1589; The Principal Navigations,* IX; Wagner, Henry Raup. *Sir Francis Drake's Voyage.*

Dunne, Peter Masten, ed. and trans. *Jacobo Sedelmayr, Missionary, Frontiersman, Explorer in Arizona and Sonora: Four Original Manuscript Narratives, 1744–1751.* Tucson: Ariz. Pioneers' Hist. Soc., 1955.

Eden, Richard, ed. and trans. *The Decades of the Newe Worlde or West India . . . by Peter Martyr of Angleria.* London: Guilhelmi Powell, 1555; rpt. Ann Arbor, Michigan: March of America Facs. Ser., Univ. Microfilms, 1966.

Eden, Richard, ed. and trans., finished by Richarde Willes. *The History of Travayle in the West and East Indies.* London, 1577.

Eden, Richard. *See* Arber, Edward, ed. *The First Three English Books on America.*

Edwards, Malcolm, ed. *The California Diary of General E. D. Townsend.* Los Angeles: The Ward Ritchie Press, 1970.

Enciso, Martín Fernández de. *Suma de Geographia.* Sevilla: Jacobo Cromberger, 1518; rpt. *Summa de Geografia.* Bogotá: Biblioteca Banco Popular, 1974. *See also* Taylor, E. G. R., ed. *A Brief Summe of Geographie.*

Escobar, Father Francisco de. *See* Bolton, Herbert Eugene, trans. "Father Escobar's Relation." *Also* Hammond, George P., and Agapito Rey, eds. and trans. *Don Juan de Oñate.*

Espejo, Antonio de. *See* Bolton, Herbert Eugene. *Spanish Explorations. Also* Hakluyt, Richard, ed. *The Principal Navigations,* IX.

Fernández del Castillo, Francisco, ed. *Luz de Tierra Incognita en la America Septentrional y Diario de las Exploraciones en Sonora por el Capitan Juan Matheo Mange.* Publicaciones del Archivo General de la Nación. X. México: Talleres Gráficos de la Nación, 1926.

Fernández de Navarrete. *See* Navarrete.

Fischer, Joseph, S. J., and Franz von Wieser, S. J., eds. and trans. *The Cosmographiae Introductio of Martin Waldseemüller in facsimile.* New York: The U. S. Catholic Hist. Soc., 1907.

Fischer, Joseph, S. J., and Franz von Wieser, S. J. *The Oldest Map with the Name America of the Year 1507 and the Carta Marina of the Year 1516 by M. Waldseemüller.* Innsbruck, 1903; rpt. Amsterdam, 1968.

Fuller Eliott-Drake, Lady. *The Family and Heirs of Sir Francis Drake.* 2 vols. London: Smith, Elder & Co, 1911.

García, Genaro, ed. *Historia Verdadera de la Conquista de la Nueva España por Bernal Díaz del Castillo.* 2 vols. México: Oficina tipográfica de la Secretaría de fomento, 1904–1905.

García, Gregorio. *Origen de los Indias de el Nuevo Mundo e Indias Occidentales.* Madrid: F. Martinex Abad., 1729.

García Icazbalceta, Joaquín, ed. *Colección de Documentos para la Historia de México:* 2 vols. México: J. M. Andrade, 1858–1866.

Gayangos y Arce, Pascual de, ed. *Cartas y Relaciones de Hernan Cortés al Emperador Carlos V.* Paris: A Chaix y ca., 1866.

Gerritsz, Hessel. *See* Millard, Fred. John, ed. and trans. *The Arctic North-East and West Passage.*

Gilbert, Sir Humphrey. *A Discourse of a Discoverie for a New Passage to Cataia.* London, 1576; rpt. Hakluyt, Richard, ed. *The Principal Navigations,* VII.

Gómara, Francisco López de. *Historia General de las Indias.* Zaragosa, 1522; rpt. in *Biblioteca de Autores Españoles desde la formación del lenguaje hasta nuestros dias,* XXII, *Historiadores Primitivos de Indias I.* Ed. Enrique de Vedia. Madrid: Imprenta de los Sucesores de Hernando, 1918, 1946. Another edition: 2 vols. Mexico City: Pedro Robredo, 1943.

Gómara, Francisco Lopez de. *See also* Simpson, Lesley Byrd, ed. and trans. *Cortés: The Life.*

Grenville, Richard. "A Discourse concerning a Straighte to be discovered toward the Northweste, with a Confutacion of their errour that think the discoverye ther of to be moste convenientlye attempted to the Northe of the Baccalaos." British Library, Lansdowne MS 100, No. 4; printed in Collinson, Richard, ed. *The Three Voyages of Martin Frobisher.*

Griffin, George Butler, ed. and trans. *Documents from the Sutro Collection.* Pub. of the Hist. Soc. of So. Calif. Los Angeles: Franklin Printing Co., 1891.

Griscom, Acton. *The Historia Regum Britanniae of Geoffrey of Monmouth. Together with a Literal Translation of the Welsh Manuscript No. LXI of Jesus College Oxford by Robert Ellis Jones.* London: Longman's, Green and Co., 1929.

Gualle (or Gali), Francisco de. *See* Hakluyt, Richard, ed. *The Principal Navigations,* IX.

Guzmán, Nuño Beltran de. *See* Carrera Stampa, Manuel, ed. *Memoria de los Servicios que habia hecho Nuño de Gusman. Also* García Icazbalceta, Joaquín, ed. *Colección,* II; Purchas, Samuel, ed., *His Pilgrimes,* XVIII.

Hakluyt, Richard. "A particular discourse concerning the greate necessitie and manifolde comodyties that are like to growe to this Realme of Englande by the Westerne discoveries lately attempted, written in the yere 1584 . . . at the requeste and direction of . . . Mr. Walter Rayhly, nowe Knight." 1585 copy, MS, Harkness Coll., New York Public Library; printed in Deane, Charles, ed. *Documentary History of the State of Maine,* II, as "A Discourse on Western Planting."

Hakluyt, Richard. *Divers voyages touching the discoverie of America and the Ilands adjacent unto the same, made first of all by our Englishmen and afterwards by the Frenchmen and Britons.* London: Thomas Woodcocke, 1582; rpt. Jones, John Winter, ed. *Divers Voyages . . . by Richard Hakluyt.* London: The Hakluyt Society, 1850.

Hakluyt, Richard, ed. *The Principall Navigations Voiages and Discoveries of the English Nation . . .* London, 1589.

Hakluyt, Richard, ed. *The Principal Navigations, Voyages, Traffiques and Discoveries of the English Nation.* 3 vols. London, 1598–1600; rpt. 12 vols. Glasgow: James MacLehose and Sons, 1903–1905.

Hale, Edward Everett. "The Queen of California." 'His Level Best' and Other Stories. Boston: Roberts Brothers, 1872; rpt. The Queen of California. San Francisco: The Colt Press, 1945.

Hamelius, P., ed. Mandeville's Travels, Translated from the French of Jean d'Outremeuse. Edited from MS. Cotton Titus C. xvi, in the British Museum. 2 vols. London: Kegan Paul, Trench, Trübner & Co., Ltd., and Humphrey Milford, Oxford Univ. Press—For the Early English Text Society, 1919.

Hammond, George P., and Agapito Rey, eds. and trans. Don Juan de Oñate: Colonizer of New Mexico, 1595–1628. 2 vols. Coronado Cuarto Centennial Publications, 1540–1940. Albuquerque: Univ. of N. M. Press, 1953.

Hammond, George P., and Agapito Rey, eds. and trans. Narratives of the Coronado Expedition 1540–1542. Albuquerque: Univ. of N. M. Press, 1940.

Hammond, George P., and Agapito Rey, eds. and trans. Obregón's History of 16th Century Explorations in Western America: Entitled Chronicle, Commentary, or Relation of the Ancient and Modern Discoveries in New Spain and New Mexico, 1584. Los Angeles, California: Wetzel Publishing Co., 1928.

Hawkins, Sir Richard. The Observations of Sir Richard Hawkins, Knight, in his Voyage into the South Sea. London, 1622; rpt. in Purchas, Samuel, ed. His Pilgrimes XVII; rpt. Markham, Clements R., ed. The Hawkins Voyages. London: The Hakluyt Society, 1878.

Hearnius, Thomas. Johannis, Confratis & Monachi Glastoniensis, Chronica sive Historia de Rebus Glastoniensibus. Oxonii: E Theatro Sheldoniano, 1726.

Herrera y Tordesillas, Antonio de. Historia General de los hechos de los Castellanos en las Islas y Tierra Firme del Mar Océano. 4 vols, Madrid: Imprenta Real, 1601–1615. Another edition: 9 vols. Madrid: Oficina Real de Nicolás Rodriguez Franco, 1726. Another edition: 17 vols. Madrid: Real Academia de la Historia, 1936–1957.

Herrera y Tordesillas, Antonio de. Historia General del Mundo del tiempo del Señor Rey Don Felipe II el Prudente. 3 vols. Valladolid, 1606 (I and II), 1612 (III).

Hill, Gillian. Cartographical Curiosities. London: The British Library, 1978.

Holmes, Maurice G. From New Spain by Sea to the Californias, 1519–1668. Glendale, Calif: Arthur H. Clark, 1963.

Icaza, Francisco A. de, ed. Conquistadores y Pobladores de Nueva España; Diccionario Autobiográfico. 2 vols. Madrid: Impr. de "El Adelantado de Segovia," 1923.

Jackson, Donald, and Mary Lee Spence, eds. The Expedition of John Charles Frémont. Urbana, Chicago: Univ. of Ill. Press, 1970.

Jane, Lionel Cecil, ed. and trans. *Select Documents Illustrating the Four Voyages of Columbus.* 2 vols. London: The Hakluyt Society, 1929; rpt. Nendeln/ Liechtenstein: Kraus Reprint Co., 1967.

Jones, John Winter, ed. *Divers Voyages Touching the Discovery of America and the Islands Adjacent: Collected and Published by Richard Hakluyt.* London: The Hakluyt Society, 1850.

Karns, Harry J., and associates, trans. *Unknown Arizona and Sonora, 1693– 1721: Francisco Fernandez del Castillo version of 'Luz De Tierra Incognita' by Captain Juan Mateo Manje—An English Translation of Part II.* Tucson: Arizona Silhouettes, 1954.

Kino, Francisco Eusebio. *Favores Celestiales y Relacion Diaria de la Entrada al Norueste.* México: Archivo General de la Nación, 1913–1922. *See also* Bolton, Herbert Eugene, ed. and trans. *Kino's Historical Memoir.*

Kino, Francisco Eusebio. *See* Burrus, Ernest J., ed. *Kino Escribe a la Duquesa;* trans. *Kino Writes to the Duchess. Also* Burrus. *Kino and Manje;* and *Kino . . . Cartography.*

Kleinbaum, Abby Wettan. *The War Against the Amazons.* New York: McGraw-Hill, 1983.

Kohl, Johann Georg. "Asia and America: An Historical Disquisition Concerning the Ideas which Former Geographers had about the Geographical Relation and Connection of the Old and New World." *Proc. of the Amer. Antiq. Soc.,* N.S. 21 (Oct., 1911).

Kraus, H. P. *Sir Francis Drake: A Pictorial Biography.* Amsterdam: 1970.

Ladrillero, Juan Fernández de. *See* Wagner, Henry Raup. *Spanish Voyages,* containing "Declaration of Juan Fernandez de Ladrillero."

Laet, Joannes de. *L'Histoire du Nouveau Monde ou Description des Indes Occidentales.* Leyden: Chez Bonaventure & Abraham Elseviers, Imprimeurs ordinaires de l'Université, 1640.

Landström, Björn. *Columbus: The Story of Don Cristobal Colón, Admiral of the Ocean, and His Four Voyages Westward to the Indies.* New York: Macmillan, 1966.

La Roncière, Charles Germain Marie Bourel de. *La Carte de Christophe Colomb: Texte en Français et en Anglais, avec Cartes.* Paris: Les Éditions Historiques, Édouard Champion, 1924.

Leighly, John Barger. *California As An Island, An Illustrated Essay, 1622–1785.* San Francisco: Book Club of Calif., 1972.

Leonard, Irving A. *Books of the Brave: Being an Account of Books and of Men in the Spanish Conquest and Settlement of the Sixteenth-Century New World.* Cambridge, Mass: Harvard Univ. Press, 1949; rpt. New York: The Gordian Press, 1964.

Leonard, Irving A. "Conquerors and Amazons in Mexico." *Hispanic Amer. Hist. Rev.*, 24, No. 4. (Nov., 1944), 561–579.

Lester, C. Edwards. *The Life and Voyages of Americus Vespucius*, 4th ed. New Haven: Horace Mansfield, 1853.

Levillier, Roberto. "New Light on Vespucci's Third Voyage." *Imago Mundi*, 11 (1954), 37–46.

Linck, Wenceslaus. *See* Burrus, Ernest J., ed. and trans. *Wenceslaus Linck's Diary.*

Lisle, Guillaume de. "Seconde Lettre de M. De Lisle a M. Cassino pour justifier quelques endroits de Ses Globes et de Ses Cartes." *Le Journal des Sçavans pour L'Année MDCC*. Paris: Chez Jean Cusson, 1700. 20 (Monday, May 24, 1700).

Lockhart, John Ingram, ed. and trans. *The Memoirs of the Conquistador Bernal Diaz del Castillo written by himself, Containing a True and Full Account of the Discovery and Conquest of Mexico and New Spain.* 2 vols. London: J. Hatchard and Son, 1844.

Lovejoy, Arthur O. *The Great Chain of Being.* New York: Harper, 1960.

Lummis, Charles F., trans. "Zarate Salmeron's Relaciones." *Land of Sunshine*, 10 and 12 (Nov. 1899, Feb. 1900).

MacNutt, Francis Augustus, ed. and trans. *De Orbe Novo: The Eight Decades of Peter Martyr D'Anghera.* 2 vols. New York and London: G.P. Putnam's Sons, 1912; rpt. New York: Burt Franklin, 1970.

MacNutt, Francis Augustus, ed. and trans. *Letters of Cortes: The Five Letters of Relation from Fernando Cortes to the Emperor Charles V.* 2 vols. New York and London: G. P. Putnam's Sons, 1908.

Magellan, Ferdinand. *See* Stanley of Alderley, Lord, ed., and James Baynes, trans. *The First Voyage. Also* Nowell, Charles E., ed. *Magellan's Voyage.*

Mandeville, Sir John. *See* Hamelius, P., ed. *Mandeville's Travels*; Seymour, M. C., ed. *The Bodley Version.*

Manje, Juan Mateo. *Luz de tierra incógnita en la America Septentrional y diario de las exploraciones en Sonora.* Mexico: Talleres Gráficos de la nación, 1926. *See also* Karns, Harry J., trans. *Unknown Arizona and Sonora*; Burrus, Ernest J., ed. and trans. *Kino and Manje*; Crockett, Grace Lilian, trans. *Mange's Luz.*

Markham, Clements R., ed. *The Hawkins Voyages.* London: The Hakluyt Society, 1878.

Markham, Clements R., ed. and trans. *The Letters of Amerigo Vespucci and Other Documents Illustrative of His Career.* London: The Hakluyt Society, 1894.

Markham, Clements R., ed. *The Natural and Moral History of the Indies, by Father Joseph de Acosta, Reprinted from the English Translated Edition of Edward Grimston, 1604*. 2 vols. London: The Hakluyt Society, 1880.

Marqués, Gerónimo. *See* Wagner, Henry Raup, trans. "Father Antonio de la Ascención's Account." *Spanish Voyages.*

Martyr, Peter. *See* Peter Martyr.

Mathes, W. Michael. "Apocryphal Tales of the Island of California and Strait of Anian." *California History*, 62, No. 1 (Spring, 1983), 52–59.

Mathes, W. Michael, ed. *Californiana I. Documentos para la Historia de la Demarcación Comercial de California: 1583–1632.* 2 vols. Madrid: José Porrúa Turanzas, 1965.

Mathes, W. Michael, ed. *Californiana II. Documentos para la Historia de la Explotación Comercial de California: 1611–1679.* 2 vols. Madrid: Ediciones José Porrúa Turanzas, 1970.

Mathes, W. Michael, ed. and trans. *Geographic and Hydrographic Descriptions of Many Northern and Southern Lands and Seas in the Indies, Specifically of the Discovery of the Kingdom of California (1632). By Nicolás de Cardona.* Los Angeles, Calif: Dawson's Book Shop, 1974.

Mathes, W. Michael. *Spanish Approaches to the Island of California, 1628–1632.* San Francisco: Book Club of Calif., 1975.

Mathes, W. Michael, ed. and trans. *The Conquistador in California: 1535: The Voyage of Fernando Cortés to Baja California in Chronicles and Documents.* Los Angeles, Calif: Dawson's Book Shop, 1973.

Mathes, W. Michael, ed. and trans. *The Pearl Hunters in the Gulf of California 1668, Summary Report of the Voyage made to the Californias by Captain Francisco de Lucenilla: Written by Father Juan Cavallero Carranco.* Los Angeles, Calif: Dawson's Book Shop, 1966.

Mathes, W. Michael. *Vizcaíno and Spanish Expansion in the Pacific Ocean: 1580–1630.* San Francisco: Calif. Hist. Soc., 1968.

Ma-Touan-Lin. *See* Saint-Denys, Le Marquis d'Hervey de, ed. and trans. *Ethnographie des Peuples Étrangers.*

Maudslay, Alfred Percival, ed. and trans. *The True History of the Conquest of New Spain by Bernal Diaz del Castillo, one of its Conquerors: From the only exact copy made of the original manuscript, edited and published in Mexico by Genaro Garcia.* 5 vols. London: The Hakluyt Society, 1908; rpt. 1916.

Maximilianus Transylvanus. Letter of 1522. *See* Stanley of Alderley, Lord, ed. *The First Voyage*; Nowell, Charles E., ed. *Magellan's Voyage.*

McCann, Franklin T. *English Discovery of America to 1585.* New York, 1952.

McNeill, William H. "Mythistory, or Truth, Myth, History, and Historians." *Mythistory and Other Essays*. Chicago: The University of Chicago Press, 1986; rpt. as the 1985 Presidential Address in *The American Historical Review*, 91, No. 1 (Feb., 1986), 1–10.

Mertz, Henriette. *Pale Ink: Two Ancient Records of Chinese Exploration in America*. 2nd rev. ed. Chicago: Swallow Press, 1972.

Milich, Alicia Ronstadt, trans. *Relaciones by Zárate Salmerón: An Account of things seen and learned by Father Jerónimo de Zárate Salmerón from the Year 1538 to Year 1626*. Albuquerque, N. M: Horn & Wallace Pub., 1966.

Millard, Fred. John, ed. and trans. *The Arctic North-East and West Passage— Detectio Freti Hudsoni, or Hessel Gerritsz's Collection of Tracts*. New English translation of Dutch, Latin eds., 1612, 1613. Amsterdam: Frederik Muller & Co., 1878.

Miller, Robert Ryal. "Cortés and the First Attempt to Colonize California." *Calif. Hist. Soc. Qtly*, 53, No. 1 (Spring, 1974), 5–16.

Miranda, José, ed. *Sumario de la Natural Historia de las Indias por Gonzalo Fernández de Oviedo Y Valdés*. México and Buenos Aires: Fondo de Cultura Economica, 1950.

Moll, Herman. *A System of Geography or a New & Accurate Description of the World*. London: Printed for Timothy Childe, 1701.

Moll, Herman. *The Compleat Geographer or the Chorography and Topography of all the known Parts of the Earth*. London: Printed for Awnsham and John Churchill, 1709.

Montalvo, Garcí Ordóñez de. *See* Ordónez de Montalvo, Garcí.

Morison, Samuel Eliot. *Admiral of the Ocean Sea: A Life of Christopher Columbus*. 2 vols. Boston: Little, Brown & Co., 1942.

Morison, Samuel Eliot, ed. and trans. *Journals and Other Documents on the Life and Voyages of Christopher Columbus*. New York: Heritage Press, 1963.

Morison, Samuel Eliot. *The European Discovery of America: Volume I, The Northern Voyages—A.D. 500–1600*. New York: Oxford Univ. Press, 1971.

Navarrete, Martín Fernández de, et al., eds. *Colección de Documentos Inéditos para la Historia de España*. 113 vols. Madrid: Viuda de Calero, 1842–1895.

Newton, Arthur Percival. *The Great Age of Discovery*. London: University Press Ltd., 1932.

Nichols, John, ed. *The Works of the Rev. Jonathan Swift, D. D., Dean of St. Patrick's Dublin, Arranged by Thomas Sheridan*. 19 vols. London: J. Johnson and others, 1808.

Niel, Father Juan Amando. *See: Documentos para la Historia de México*, Series 3, I. "Apuntamientos." *Also in: Documentos . . . de Nuevo Mexico*. 205–304.

Nitti, John J., ed. *Juan Fernandez de Heredia's Aragonese Version of the Libro de Marco Polo*. Madison: Hispanic Seminary of Medieval Studies, 1980.

Niza, Father Marcos de. *See* Hakluyt, Richard, ed. *The Principal Navigations*, IX, containing "The Voyage of frier Marco de Nica." *Also* Rodack, Madeleine Turrell, ed. *Adolph F. Bandelier*. *Also* Hammond, George P., and Agapito Rey, eds. and trans. *Narratives of the Coronado Expedition*.

Nowell, Charles E., ed. *Magellan's Voyage Around the World: Three Contemporary Accounts*. Evanston, Ill.: Northwestern Univ. Press, 1962.

Nunn, George E. *Origin of the Strait of Anian Concept*. Philadelphia: George H. Beams, 1929.

Nunn, George E. *The Geographical Conceptions of Columbus: A Critical Consideration of Four Problems*. New York: Amer. Geog. Soc., 1924.

Nuttall, Zelia, ed. and trans. *New Light on Drake: A Collection of Documents Relating to His Voyage of Circumnavigation, 1577–1580*. London: The Hakluyt Society, 1914.

Obregón, Baltasar de. *See* Cuevas, P. Mariano, ed. *Historia de los Descubrimientos*; Hammond, George P., and Agapito Rey, eds. and trans. *Obregón's History*.

Odoric of Pordenone. *See* Yule, Sir Henry, ed. and trans. *Cathay and the Way Thither*.

O'Gorman, Edmundo, ed., Águstin Millares Carlo, trans. *Décadas del Nuevo Mundo, por Pedro Mártir de Angleria, Primer Cronista de Indias*. 2 vols. México: J. Porrúa e Hijos, 1964.

Olschki, Leonardo. "Ponce de Leon's Fountain of Youth: History of a Geographical Myth." *The Hispanic Amer. Hist. Rev.*, 21, No. 3 (Aug., 1941), 361–385.

Olschki, Leonardo. *Storia Letteraria delle Scoperte Geografiche*. Firenze: Leo S. Olschki, 1937.

Ordóñez de Montalvo, Garcí. *El Ramo que de los cuatro libros de Amadís de Gaula sale: Llamado Las Sergas del Muy Esforzado Caballero Esplandian, Hijo del Excelente Rey Amadís de Gaula*. Sargossa, 1508; rpt. in *Biblioteca de Autores Españoles, desde la formación del lenguaje hasta nuestros dias*. XL. Libros de Caballerias. Ed. Pascual de Gayangos. Madrid, 1857, 1950.

Orozco y Berra, Manuel. *Historia de la Dominación Española en México*. 4 vols. México, 1880; rpt. México: Antigua Librería Robredo, de J. Porrúa e Hijos, 1938.

Oviedo y Valdés, Gonzalo Fernández de. *Historia General y Natural de las Indias, Islas y Tierra-Firme del Mar Océano.* Sevilla, 1535; rpt. in *Biblioteca de Autores Españoles desde la formación del lenguaje hasta nuestros dias.* CXVII to CXXI. Ed. Juan Pérez de Tudela Bueso. Madrid: Real Academia Española, 1959. Another edition: José Amador de los Rios, ed. Asunción del Paraguay: Editorial Guaranía, 1944.

Oviedo y Valdés, Gonzalo Fernández de. *See* Miranda, José, ed. *Sumario de la Natural Historia de las Indias. See also* Stoudemire, Sterling A., trans. *Natural History of the West Indies.*

Oxenham, John. *See* Nuttall, Zelia, ed. and trans. *New Light on Drake.*

Pacheco, Joaquín F., Francisco de Cárdenas, and Luis Torres de Mendoza, and others, eds. *Colección de Documentos Inéditos relativos al Descubrimiento, Conquista y Organización de las Antiguas Posesiones Españolas de América y Oceanía del Real Archivo de Indias.* 42 vols. Title variations. Madrid: Imprenta de Frias y Cía, 1864–1884.

————.*Colección de Documentos Inéditos relativos al Descubrimiento, Conquista y Organización de las Antiguas Posesiones Españolas de Ultramar.* Segunda Serie. 25 vols. Madrid: Real Academia de la Historia, 1885–1932.

Pagden, A. R., ed. and trans. *Hernan Cortés: Letters from Mexico.* New York: Grossman, 1971.

Pelliot, Paul. *Notes on Marco Polo: Volume II*—Ouvrage Posthume. Paris: Imprimerie Nationale, Librairie Adrien-Maisonneuve, 1963.

Pereyra, Carlos. "El Bautizo de la California." *Estudios Geográficos*, Núm. 7 (Mayo, 1942) 385–404.

Peter Martyr. *De Orbe Novo.* Alcalá, 1530.

Peter Martyr. (Mártir). *See* O'Gorman, Edmundo, ed. Águstin Millares Carlo, trans. (Span.) *Décadas del Nuevo Mundo;* MacNutt, Francis Augustus, ed. and trans. (Eng.) *De Orbe Novo;* Arber, Edward, ed., Richard Eden. *The First Three English Books on America;* Eden, Richard, ed. and trans. *The Decades.*

Pigafetta, Antonio. *See* Stanley of Alderley, Lord, ed., James Baynes, trans. *Also* Nowell, Charles E., ed. *Also* Robertson, James Alexander, ed.

Polo, Marco. *See* Yule, Sir Henry, ed. and trans. *The Book. Also* Nitti, John J., ed. *Also* Pelliot, Paul.

Porter y Casanate, Pedro. *See* Pacheco, Joaquín F. et al., eds. *Colección de Documentos*, Indias IX.

Portillo y Díez de Sollano, Alvaro del. *Descubrimientos y Exploraciones en las Costas de California.* Publicaciones de la Escuela de Estudios Hispano-Americanos de Sevilla, XX, Serie 2a, Monografías, Núm. 7. Madrid: Blass, S. A. Tipográfica, 1947.

Preciado, Francisco. *See* Hakluyt, Richard, ed. *The Principal Navigations*, IX. "Voyage of Ulloa."

Prester John. *See* Slessarev, Vsevolod, ed. and trans. *Prester John: The Letter.*

Purchas, Samuel, ed. *Hakluytus Posthumus, or Purchas His Pilgrimes: contayning a history of the world in sea voyages and lande travells by Englishmen and others.* 4 vols. London, 1625, 1 vol. 1626; rpt. 20 vols. Glasgow: James MacLehose and Sons, 1905–7.

Putnam, Ruth, with Herbert Ingram Priestly. "California: The Name." *Univ. of Calif. Pub. in History*, 4, No. 4 (1917), 293–365.

Quinn, David Beers. *England and the Discovery of America: 1481–1620.* New York: Alfred A. Knopf, 1974.

Quinn, David Beers, ed. *The Voyages and Colonising Enterprises of Sir Humphrey Gilbert.* 2 vols. London: The Hakluyt Society, 1940.

Quinn, David B., Alison M. Quinn, and Susan Hillier, eds. *New American World: A Documentary History of North America to 1612.* 5 vols. Vol. I: *America from Concept to Discovery—Early Exploration of North America.* New York: Arno Press and Hector Bye, Inc., 1979.

Ramusio, Giovanni Battista. *Terzo Volume delle Navigationi et Viaggi nel quale si contengono le Navigationi al Mondo Nuovo.* Venice, 1556.

Richman, Irving Berdine. *California under Spain and Mexico, 1535–1847.* Boston and New York: Houghton Mifflin, 1911.

Robertson, James Alexander, ed. *Magellan's Voyage Around the World.* Cleveland: Arthur H. Clark, 1906.

Rodack, Madeleine Turrell, ed. and trans. *Adolph F. Bandelier's 'The Discovery of New Mexico by the Franciscan Monk, Friar Marcos de Niza in 1539'.* Tucson: Univ. of Ariz. Press, 1981.

Rogers, Francis M. *The Travels of the Infante Dom Pedro of Portugal.* Cambridge, Mass: Harvard Univ. Press, 1961.

Rogers, Captain Woodes. *A Cruising Voyage Round the World . . . Begun in 1708 and finished in 1711.* London: Printed for A. Bell, 1712. Span. trans. in Venegas, Miguel. *Noticia de la California.*

Romoli, Kathleen. *Balboa of Darien: Discoverer of the Pacific.* Garden City, New York: Doubleday, 1953.

Rowse, A. L. *Sir Richard Grenville of the 'Revenge'.* London, Boston, New York: Houghton Mifflin, 1937; rpt. London: Jonathan Cape, 1963.

Rowse, A. L. *The Expansion of Elizabethan England.* London: Macmillan and Company Ltd., 1955; rpt. 1981.

Rundall, Thomas, ed. *Narratives of Voyages Towards the North-West in Search of a Passage to Cathay and India: 1496–1631.* London: The Hakluyt Society, 1849.

Saint-Denys, Le Marquis d'Hervey de, ed. and trans. *Ethnographie des Peuples Étrangers à la Chine: Ouvrage Composé au XIIIe Siecle de Notre Ère par Ma-Touan-Lin.* 2 vols. Genève: H. Georg, Libraire-Éditeur, 1876–83.

Sales, Father Luis. *Observations on California, 1772–1790.* Ed. and trans. Charles N. Rudkin. Early California Travel Series, 37. Los Angeles: Glen Dawson's Bookstore, 1956.

Sánchez, Nellie Van de Grift. *Spanish and Indian Place Names of California: Their Meaning and Their Romance.* San Francisco: A.M. Robertson, 1914.

Sánchez, Nellie Van de Grift. "The name of our beloved California: Was it given in derision?" *Grizzly Bear Magazine* (Los Angeles), 18, Nos. 6 and 8 (April, 1916).

Santa Cruz, Alonso de. *See* Blázquez, D. Antonio, ed. *Islario General.*

Sedelmayr, Jacobo. *See* Dunne, Peter Masten, ed. and trans.

Seymour, M. C., ed. *The Bodley Version of Mandeville's Travels.* London: Oxford Univ. Press—For the Early English Text Society, 1963.

Shirley, Rodney W. *The Mapping of the World: Early Printed World Maps— 1472–1700.* London: The Holland Press, 1983.

Silverberg, Robert. *The Realm of Prester John.* Garden City, N. Y: Doubleday, 1972.

Simpson, Lesley Byrd, ed. and trans. *Cortés: The Life of the Conqueror of Mexico by his Secretary: Francisco López de Gómara.* Berkeley: Univ. of Calif. Press, 1964.

Skelton, Raleigh Ashlin. *Explorers' Maps: Chapters in the Cartographic Record of Geographical Discovery.* London: Routledge & Paul, 1958.

Slessarev, Vsevolod, ed. and trans. *Prester John: The Letter and the Legend.* Minneapolis: The Univ. of Minnesota Press, 1959.

Sokol, A. E. "California: A Possible Derivation of the Name." *Calif. Hist. Soc. Qtly.,* 28, No. 1 (March, 1949), 23–30.

Spate, O. H. K. *The Spanish Lake.* Canberra: Australian National Univ. Press, 1979.

Stanley of Alderley, Lord, ed., James Baynes, trans. *The First Voyage Around the World by Magellan: Translated from the Accounts of Pigafetta and Other Contemporary Writers.* London: The Hakluyt Society, 1874.

Steele, Colin. *English Interpreters of the Iberian New World from Purchas to Stevens: A Bibliographical Study 1603–1726.* Oxford: The Dolphin Book Co., 1975.

Stevenson, Edward Luther. *Terrestrial and Celestial Globes: Their History and Construction, Including a Consideration of Their Value as Aids in the Study of Geography and Astronomy.* 2 vols. New Haven: Yale Univ. Press—For the Hispanic Society of America, 1921; rpt. New York & London: Johnson Reprint Corp., 1971.

Stoudemire, Sterling A., ed. and trans. *Natural History of the West Indies by Gonzalo Fernández de Oviedo.* Studies in the Romance Languages and Literatures, Number 32. Chapel Hill, N. C: University Press, 1959.

Swift, Jonathan. *See* Nichols, John, ed. *Also* Williams, Harold, ed.

Taylor, E. G. R., ed. *A Brief Summe of Geographie by Roger Barlow.* London: The Hakluyt Society, 1932.

Taylor, E. G. R. "Master John Dee, Drake and the Straits of Anian." *The Mariner's Mirror,* 15 (April, 1929), 125–129.

Taylor, E. G. R. "More Light on Drake," and "John Winter's Report." *The Mariner's Mirror,* 16 (1930) 134–151.

Taylor, E. G. R. "The Missing Draft Project of Drake's Voyage of 1577–80." *The Geographical Journal,* 75 (Jan.–June, 1930), 44–47.

Taylor, E. G. R. *Tudor Geography: 1485–1583.* London: Methuen & Co., 1930; rpt. New York: Octagon Books, 1968.

The World Encompassed. By Sir Francis Drake, Being his next voyage to that to Nombre de Dios formerly imprinted; Carefully collected out of the notes of Master Francis Fletcher Preacher in this imployment, and divers others his followers in the same. London: Nicholas Bourne, 1628. Facsimile rpt. Ann Arbor, Mich: University Microfilms, Inc., 1966.

Thomas, Henry. *Spanish and Portuguese Romances of Chivalry.* Cambridge: University Press, 1920; rpt. New York: Kraus Reprint Co., 1969.

Thorne, Robert. Letter. British Library Lansdowne MS 122, No. 4. Printed in Hakluyt, Richard, ed. *Divers Voyages;* rpt. Jones, John Winter, ed. *Divers Voyages . . . by Richard Hakluyt.*

Thrower, Norman J. W., ed. *Sir Francis Drake and the Famous Voyage, 1577–1580: Essays Commemorating the Quadricentennial of Drake's Circumnavigation.* Berkeley, Los Angeles: Univ. of Calif. Press, 1984.

Ticknor, George. *History of Spanish Literature.* London: John Murray, 1849; rev. ed. 3 vols. Boston and New York: Houghton Mifflin, 1863.

Tooley, R. V. *California as an Island, a Geographical Misconception: Illustrated by 100 examples from 1625 to 1770.* Map Collectors' Series, No. 8. London: The Map Collectors' Circle, 1964.

Tooley, R. V. *French Mapping of the Americas.* Map Collectors' Series, No. 33. London: The Map Collectors' Circle, 1967.

Torquemada, Juan de, O.F.M. *Los veynte i un Libros Rituales y Monarchia Yndiana, con el origen y guerras de los Yndias Occidentales.* Known as *Monarquía Indiana.* Sevilla: 1615; rpt. 3 vols. México: Editorial Porrúa, S. A., 1969.

Toscanelli, Paolo del Pozzo. *See* Vignaud, Henri, ed. and trans. *The Letter and Chart of Toscanelli.*

Tyrrell, William Blake. *Amazons: A Study in Athenian Mythmaking.* Baltimore and London: The Johns Hopkins Univ. Press, 1984.

Ugarte, Father. *See* Venegas, Miguel. *A Natural and Civil History,* II.

Ulloa, Francisco de. *See* Wagner, Henry Raup. *Spanish Voyages,* containing "The Voyage of Francisco de Ulloa."

Unamuno, Pedro de. *See* Wagner, Henry Raup. *Spanish Voyages.*

Urdaneta, Fr. Andrés de. *See* Pacheco, Joaquín F., *et al., Colección de Documentos Inéditos — Ultramar,* II.

Velarde, Father Luis. *See* Manje, Juan Mateo. *Luz de Tierra Incognita;* Karns, Harry J., trans. *Unknown Arizona;* Burrus, Ernest J., ed. and trans. *Kino and Manje;* Crockett, Grace Lilian, trans. *Mange's Luz*

Venegas, Miguel. An anonymous English trans. *A Natural and Civil History of California: Containing An Accurate Description of that Country . . . The Customs of the Inhabitants . . . Translated from the original Spanish of Miguel Venegas, A Mexican Jesuit, published at Madrid 1758.* London: James Rivington and James Fletcher, 1759: rpt. 2 vols. Ann Arbor, Mich: March of America Facsimile Ser., University Microfilms, 1966.

Venegas, Miguel, S. J. *Noticia de la California y de su Conquista Temporal y Espiritual hasta el Tiempo Presente, formada en Mexico año de 1739.* Madrid, 1757; rpt. 3 vols. México: Editorial Layac, 1943.

Verrazzano, Giovanni da. Annotations to Cèllere Codex. The Pierpont Morgan Library Ms. MA 776. *See* Wroth, Lawrence C. *The Voyages of Giovanni da Verrazzano.*

Vespucci, Amerigo. *See* Lester, C. Edwards; Fischer, Joseph, S. J., and Franz von Wieser, S. J., eds. and trans. *The Cosmographiae Introductio.*

Vignaud, Henry, ed. and trans. *The Letter and Chart of Toscanelli on the Route to the Indies by Way of the West, Sent in 1474 to the Portuguese Fernam Martins, and later on to Christopher Columbus: A Critical Study.* Original French ed: Paris: Ernest Leroux, Editeur, 1901; Eng. trans: London: Sands & Co., 1902.

Vilanova, Antonio, ed. *Diario del Primer Viaje de Colon.* Barcelona: Ediciones Nauta, S. A., 1965.

Vizcaíno, Sebastian. "Diary of Sebastian Vizcaíno." *See* Bolton, Herbert Eugene. *Spanish Explorations.*

Wagner, Henry Raup. "Apocryphal Voyages to the Northwest Coast of America." *Proceedings of the American Antiquarian Society,* N.S. 41 (April 1931). Separate rpt. Worcester: The American Antiquarian Society, 1931.

Wagner, Henry Raup. "Francisco de Ulloa Returned." *Calif. Hist. Soc. Qtly.,* 19, No. 3 (Sept., 1940), 240–244.

Wagner, Henry Raup. "Pearl Fishing Enterprises in the Gulf of California." *The Hispanic Amer. Hist. Rev.,* 10, No. 2 (May, 1930).

Wagner, Henry Raup. *Sir Francis Drake's Voyage Around the World.* San Francisco: John Howell, 1926.

Wagner, Henry Raup. "Some Imaginary California Geography." *Proc. of the Amer. Antiq. Soc.,* N.S. 36, Pt. 1 (April 14, 1926), 83–129. Rpt. Worcester, Mass: For the Society by the Davis Press, 1926.

Wagner, Henry Raup. *Spanish Voyages to the Northwest Coast of America in the Sixteenth Century.* San Francisco: Cal. Hist. Soc., 1929.

Wagner, Henry Raup. *The Cartography of the Northwest Coast of America to the Year 1800.* 2 vols. Berkeley: Univ. of Calif. Press, 1937.

Wagner, Henry Raup. "The Discovery of California." *Calif. Hist. Soc. Qtly.,* 1, No. 1 (July, 1922), 36–56.

Wagner, Henry Raup, ed. and trans. *The Discovery of New Spain in 1518 by Juan de Grijalva.* Documents and Narratives Concerning the Discovery and Conquest of Latin America. N.S. No. 2. Berkeley, Calif: Bancroft Library— For the Cortés Society, 1942; rpt. New York: Kraus Reprint Co., 1969.

Wagner, Henry Raup. *The Rise of Fernando Cortés.* Documents and Narratives Concerning the Discovery and Conquest of Latin America, N. S. No. 3. Berkeley, Calif: Bancroft Library—For the Cortés Society, 1944; rpt. New York: Kraus Reprint Co., 1969.

Wagner, Henry Raup. "The Voyage to California of Sebastian Rodriguez Cermeño." *Calif. Hist. Soc. Qtly.,* 3, No. 1 (April, 1924).

Wagner, Henry Raup. "Urdaneta and the Return Route from the Philippine Islands." *The Pacific Hist. Rev.,* 13, No. 3 (September, 1944), 313–316.

Waldseemüller, Martin. *See* Fischer, Joseph, S. J., and Franz von Wieser, S. J. Facsimile of *Cosmographiae Introductio* . . . . St. Dié, 1507.

Wallis, Helen, ed. *Raleigh & Roanoke: The First English Colony in America, 1584–1590*. The British Library Exhibit Hosted by the North Carolina Museum of History, 1985. Raleigh: America's Four Hundredth Anniversary Committee, North Carolina Department of Cultural Resources, 1985.

Wallis, Helen, ed. *Sir Francis Drake: An Exhibition to Commemorate Francis Drake's Voyage around the World: 1577–1580*. London: The British Library, 1977.

Waterhouse, Edward. *A Declaration of the stuic of the Colony and Affaires in Virginia . . . Together with . . . A Treatise Annexed, Written by that Learned Mathematician Mr. Henry Briggs, of the Northwest Passage to the South Sea through the Continent of Virginia and by Fretum Hudson.* London: Published by Authorities, imprinted by G. Eld, for Robert Mylbourne, 1622.

Watts, Pauline Moffitt. "Prophecy and Discovery: On the Spiritual Origins of Christopher Columbus's 'Enterprise of the Indies.'" *The American Hist. Rev.*, 90, No. 1 (Feb., 1985), 73–102.

Weckmann, Luis. *Las Bulas Alejandrinas de 1493 y la Teoría Política del Papado Medieval: Estudio de la Supremacía Papal Sobre Islas, 1091–1493*. México: Instituto de Historia, 1949.

Weckmann, Luis. "The Middle Ages in the Conquest of America." *Speculum*, 26, No. 1 (Jan. 1951), 130–141.

White, Lynn Townsend, Jr. "Changes in the Popular Concept of 'California.'" *Calif. Hist. Soc. Qtly.*, 19, No. 3 (Sept., 1940), 219–224.

Williams, Gwyn A. *Madoc: The Making of a Myth*. London: Eyre Methuen, 1979.

Williams, Gwyn A. *The Welsh in Their History*. London & Canberra: Croom Helm, 1982.

Williams, Harold, ed. *Gulliver's Travels by Jonathan Swift, DD. The Text of the First Edition*. London: The First Edition Club, 1926.

Williams, Harold, ed. *The Poems of Jonathan Swift*. 3 vols. Oxford: At the Clarendon Press, 1937.

Williamson, James A. *The Cabot Voyages and Bristol Discovery under Henry VII*. With the Cartography of the Voyage by R. A. Skelton. Cambridge: The University Press—For the Hakluyt Society, 1962.

Willis, Raymond S., ed. *El Libro de Alexandre: Texts of the Paris and Madrid Manuscripts*. Elliott Monographs No. 32. Princeton: University Press, 1934.

Winship, George Parker, ed. and trans. *The Journey of Coronado 1540–1542: From the City of Mexico to the Grand Cañon of the Colorado and the Buffalo Plains of Texas, Kansas and Nebraska: As told by himself and his followers.* New York: Allerton Book Co., 1922; rpt. Ann Arbor, Mich: University Microfilms, Inc., 1966.

Winsor, Justin. *The Kohl Collection (Now in the Library of Congress) of Maps Relating to America.* A Reprint of Bibliographical Contribution Number 19 of the Library of Harvard University. With Index by Philip Lee Phillips. Washington: Library of Congress, Government Printing Office, 1904.

Wright, Edward. *Certaine Errors in Navigation.* London: 3 Editions—1599, 1610, 1657.

Wroth, Lawrence C. *The Voyages of Giovanni da Verrazzano: 1524–1528.* New Haven and London: Yale Univ. Press for the Pierpont Morgan Library, 1970.

Wytfliet, Cornelius. *Histoire Universelle des Indes Occidentales.* Paris: A Douay, Chez François Fabri, 1607.

Yule, Sir Henry, ed. and trans. *Cathay and the Way Thither: Vol. 11—Odoric of Pordenone.* Ed. rev. by Henri Cordier. London: The Hakluyt Society, 1913.

Yule, Sir Henry, ed. and trans. *The Book of Ser Marco Polo the Venetian Concerning the Kingdoms and Marvels of the East.* 2 vols. 3rd. ed. rev. by Henry Cordier. London and New York: Charles Scribner's Sons, 1902–3; rpt. London: John Murray, 1929.

Zárate Salmerón, Father Jerónimo. *See* Milich, Alicia Ronstadt, trans. *Relaciones by Zárate Salmerón. See also Documentos para servir a la Historia del Nuevo Mexico.* 114–204. Also Lummis, Charles F., trans.

Zugarte Cortesão, Amando. "An Unknown Portuguese Cartographer." *The Geographical Review,* 29, No. 2 (April, 1939), 205–225.

INDEX

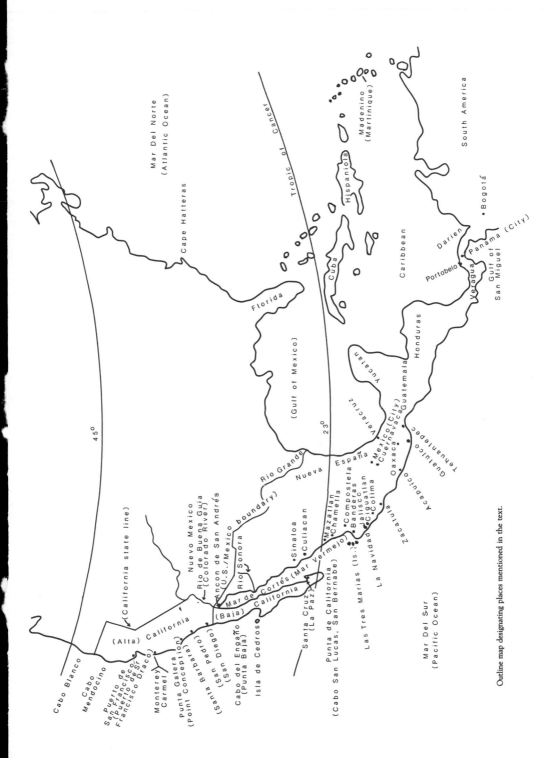

Outline map designating places mentioned in the text.